Library of
Davidson College

MARING HUNTERS AND TRADERS

STUDIES IN MELANESIAN ANTHROPOLOGY

General Editors

Gilbert H. Herdt
Fitz John Porter Poole
Donald F. Tuzin

1. Michael Young, *Magicians of Manumanua: Living Myth in Kalauna*
2. Gilbert H. Herdt, ed., *Ritualized Homosexuality in Melanesia*
3. Bruce M. Knauft, *Good Company and Violence: Sorcery and Social Action in a Lowland New Guinea Society*
4. Kenneth E. Read, *Return to the High Valley: Coming Full Circle*
5. James F. Weiner, *The Heart of the Pearl Shell: The Mythological Dimension of Foi Society*
6. Marilyn Strathern, *The Gender of the Gift: Problems with Women and Problems with Society in Melanesia*
7. James G. Carrier and Achsah H. Carrier, *Wage, Trade, and Exchange in Melanesia: A Manus Society in the Modern State*
8. Christopher Healey, *Maring Hunters and Traders: Production and Exchange in the Papua New Guinea Highlands*

MARING HUNTERS AND TRADERS

Production and Exchange in the Papua New Guinea Highlands

Christopher Healey

University of California Press
Berkeley and Los Angeles, California

University of California Press
Oxford, England

Copyright © 1990 by
The Regents of the University of California

Library of Congress Cataloging-in-Publication Data

Healey, Christopher J.
  Maring hunters and traders: production and exchange in the Papua
New Guinea highlands / Christopher Healey.
    p.   cm.
  Includes bibliographical references.
  ISBN 0–520–06840–8 (alk. paper)
  1. Maring (New Guinea people)—Commerce. 2. Maring (New Guinea
people)—Hunting. 3. Exchange—Papua New Guinea. 4. Human ecology—
Papua New Guinea. I. Title.
DU740.42.H42 1990
306.3'0899912—dc20   89-20649
                                                                    CIP

Printed in the United States of America

1 2 3 4 5 6 7 8 9

The paper used in this publication meets the minimum requirements of American
National Standard for Information Sciences—Permanence of Paper for Printed Library
Materials, ANSI Z39.48–1984 ∞

In memory of Ralph Bulmer, scholar, teacher, and friend

Contents

Preface	xiii
A Note on Conventions	xxi
Introduction	1
Trade as an Analytic Category	5
A Model of Trade	7
1. The Kundagai: Environment and Society	13
The Physical Environment	15
Vegetation and Ecological Zones	18
Effects of Human Activity on the Environment	24
Population Density	26
Kundagai Social Organization	28
Population and Settlement Patterns	34
Marriage Patterns	36
Social Status	40
The Spirit World	44
A History of Settlement	47
Territoriality and Redistribution of Land Rights	49
2. The Uses and Significance of Plumes	60
Birds Used in Decorations	60
Storage and Life of Plumes	65

Decorations	68
The Social Significance of Plume Use	71

3. Hunting and Its Regulation — 86
- Hunting Methods and Productivity — 86
- Hunting Restrictions — 100
- Intensity and Effects of Hunting — 116

4. Valuables and Prestations — 127
- Trade and Prestation — 127
- Valuables — 131
- Prestations — 148
- Prestations in Relation to Marriage Patterns — 163

5. The Structure of Trade — 170
- Trade Transactions — 170
- Directions of Trade — 172
- Bird Plumes — 175
- Marsupial Furs — 183
- Minor Animal Products — 184
- Local Live Animals — 184
- Other Minor Local Products — 186
- Salt — 186
- Pigs — 187
- Shells — 190
- Cutting Tools — 196
- Pigments — 197
- Other Minor Goods of European Manufacture — 199
- Money — 200
- Summary of the Flow of Goods in Trade Through Tsuwenkai — 203
- Maintenance of the Trade System — 209
- Conclusion — 232

6. The Development of Trade — 234
- Overview of Change — 234
- Intensification of Trade — 247
- The Peripheralization of the Kundagai — 257
- Conclusion — 268

Contents

7. Exchange Rates ... 271
   Exchangeability of Items ... 275
   Exchange Rates, Past and Present ... 278
   Conclusion ... 310

8. Utilitarianism, Sociability, and the Organization of Trade ... 314
   Overt Reasons for Trade ... 316
   Occasions for Trade and the Conduct of Transactions ... 322
   Trade and Sociability ... 327
   Conclusion ... 350

Appendixes
   1. Marriage Patterns ... 357
   2. Birds Used in Decorations ... 360
   3. Valuables and Trade Goods ... 365
   4. Trade Regions ... 368

Notes ... 371

Bibliography ... 381

Index ... 393

List of Tables, Figures, Maps, Illustrations

Tables

1. Maring Population Densities	27
2. Tsuwenkai Population	35
3. Reasons for Kundagai Marriages	39
4. Maring Hierarchy of Decorative Value of Plumes	64
5. Means of Acquisition of Plumes of Local and Nonlocal Species in Kundagai Collections	65
6. Holdings of Plumes in Four Jimi Settlements	81
7. Productivity of Kundagai Hunting	97
8. Hunting Productivity in Four Highland Societies	99
9. Restricted Game	101
10. Personal Hunting Territories in Tsuwenkai, 1974	109
11. Ratio of Hunters to Hunting Land in Maring Territories	117
12. Index of Annual Predation Rates on Birds, Pre- and Post-1956	124
13. Hierarchy of Valuables	134
14. Acquisition of Animal Remains in Valuables Census, 1973–1974	135
15. Ownership of Shells in Valuables Collections, by Age Group, 1973–1974	136
16. Means of Acquisition of Shells in Valuables Collections, by Age Group, 1973–1974	137
17. Pig Ownership, September 1974	144

18. Pig Kills, Tsuwenkai, Nov. 1973–Nov. 1974	146
19. Annual Pig Kills in Ten Maring Populations	147
20. Composition of Bridewealth	154
21. Composition of Death Payments	156
22. Kundagai Salt Pork Prestations to Allies, 1952 and 1960 Combined	159
23. Distribution of Kundagai Marriages to 1974 Patterning Mandatory Prestations	166
24. Patterns of Trade in Major Plumes	177
25. Patterns of Trade in Pigs	188
26. Contribution of Imports and Local Breeding to Exports of Pigs	191
27. Patterns of Trade in Shells	192
28. Patterns of Trade in Axes and Bushknives	198
29. Patterns of Trade in Money	204
30. Importance of Local Production and Trade in Acquisition of Locally Obtainable Goods	220
31. Importance of Different Means of Acquisition and Disposal for Classes of Goods	224
32. Rates of Accumulation or Loss in Trade Flow of Plumes	229
33. Disposal of Kundagai Pigs Obtained by Trade to 1974	231
34. Importance of Plume Imports in Funding Exports from Tsuwenkai	244
35. Incidence of Trade by Item and Period	246
36. Rates of Trade by Age Group, to 1974	248
37. Weighted Annual Trading Velocities	254
38. Exchangeability of Items	277
39. Monetary Value of Trade Goods, 1965–1985, in Kina	282
40. Hierarchies of Exchange Value, 1940 and Post-1970	284
41. Frequency of Exchange, by Item	285
42. Changes in Frequency of Exchangeability of Selected Goods for Pigs	294
43. Proportion of Transactions Using Trader's Own Stocks, to 1974	317
44. Occasions for Trade to 1974	324
45. Directions in Initiative in Proposing Trade	328
46. Delayed and Immediate Exchange	329
47. Relationship of Traders by Direction and Period	332
48. Kundagai Trade with Relatives	338

Figures

1. The Kundagai Clans and Their Locations	31
2. Simple Trade Web	211
3. Exchangeability of Trade Goods, 1965–1974, 1979–1985	279
4. Changing Cash Values of Pigs, 1965–1985	293

Maps

1. Jimi Valley	14
2. Tsuwenkai Vegetation and Settlement	16
3. Tsuwenkai Geographic Features and Territories	50
4. Trade Regions	167

Illustrations

Long-tailed Buzzard; *Henicopernis longicauda*; rukump.	62
Papuan Lory (black phase); *Charmosyna papou*; goli.	66
Vulturine Parrot; *Psittrichas fulgidus*; kopel.	69
Common Paradise Kingfisher; *Tanysiptera galatea*; joli.	72
Black Sicklebill; *Epimachus fastosus*; kalanc gi yondoi.	75
Princess Stephanie's Astrapia; *Astrapia stephaniae*; kombam.	77
Superb Bird of Paradise; *Lophorina superba*; yenandiok.	79
Lesser Bird of Paradise; *Paradisaea minor*; yambai.	82
King of Saxony Bird of Paradise; *Pteridophora alberti*; balpan.	84

Preface

The Maring are well known in anthropological literature, principally from Roy A. Rappaport's seminal *Pigs for the Ancestors* (1968). Until recently much of the considerable research among the Maring has taken an ecological approach, concentrating on subsistence agriculture and adaptation to the environment. Although I maintain this ecological orientation, I turn my attention to the exploitation of nonsubsistence, nondomesticated resources. In particular, I focus on the extraction of forest products, especially the hunting of birds killed for their decorative plumes, and on the organization of trade. Forest products have long been the only resource locally available to the Maring which are in high demand elsewhere in the highlands. It is through the production of plumes and other forest goods and their exchange that the Maring are able to provision themselves with other items that are important in prestations of social reproduction but are not locally available. Notable among these latter goods are marine shells and steel tools, which were still widely used in prestations into the late 1970s, along with cash and pigs. Although the latter are, of course, locally bred, significant numbers are also acquired in trade. Geographic patterns of trade and the nature of goods passed in transactions have, however, changed considerably over the last six decades. Many of these changes predated direct contact with the colonial authority. Others have come more recently as the state and the cash economy have increased their institutional penetration of the Maring region. A major objective of this book is to document and analyze the changing nature of trade.

I argue that in the heyday of Maring trade from the period immediately preceding contact until the late 1970s, it was the passage of forest products that gave a dominating structure to the pattern of trading networks. This was a consequence of a combination of ecological and cultural factors. First, the significant deforestation of much of the central highlands means that many valuable plume-bearing birds—notably birds of paradise, parrots, and hawks—and other forest products, are to be found mainly in the more heavily forested regions of the highland fringes. Here, human settlement is generally sparser, affording hunters easier access to the bounty of the forests. In passing, it should be noted that this ecological situation is significantly influenced by past and continuing human action—the clearing of forest for gardens and, more recently, for timber and to make way for smallholder cash crops and larger-scale plantations and the like. As a consequence, game is increasingly confined to relict stands of mountain forest where it becomes ever more vulnerable to further disturbance of habitat and pressure from hunting.

Second, one finds a high cultural value assigned to bird plumes, marsupial pelts, cassowaries, and other forest products in a number of central-highlands cultures, notably the Simbu, Kuma, and Melpa. Here, such goods are important as items of decoration on ceremonial occasions and also for use in prestations. This high demand for forest products, coupled with a lack of their local availability—at least in sufficient quantities—sets up conditions for the emergence of networks of supply connecting more peripheral areas of the highlands to centers of consumption. The organization of Maring trade must be understood by looking at trade in its regional rather than more narrow or local context.

These broad ecological and cultural parameters are obvious dominating forces on the structure of trade networks. Nonetheless, a fuller understanding of trade also requires a detailed analysis of the ecological and sociocultural organization of trade at the local level. Typically, the Melanesian trader is only hazily aware of the shape, extent, and organization of the "systems" of networks within which he is located. His perspective is more parochial and ethnocentric, even egocentric. Yet ultimately, the regional systems we analyze are built up of the uncoordinated activities of individual producers, transactors, and consumers.

The objectives of this book are to provide an examination of the local exploitation of forest products—as a particular form of production—and of patterns of exchange and consumption. I examine the articulation of such exploitation, distribution, and consumption with wider regional, economic, ecological, and historical processes. I do this by way of a quantitative and diachronic analysis of production and trade over a roughly sixty-year timeframe, tracing the relation of production and trade to other forms of exchange in Maring society.

Beyond all else the book is intended as an ethnography of a hitherto neglected aspect of production and exchange in Melanesia, taking as my focus the organization of hunting and trade among one community of the Maring speakers on the northern fringe of the Papua New Guinea highlands. This work, however, is also an attempt to combine some of the approaches of ecological and economic anthropology. In regard to the latter my sympathies lie with the substantivists in opposition to the formalists. Yet, as will become clear in the following pages, I consider that despite the substantivists' professed respect for the cultural order, wherein "economy" is treated as a category of culture rather than behavior or action, too often the substantivist economic anthropologist smuggles in materialist and utilitarian notions that fail to apprehend the fuller cultural significance of "economy." Substantivists and formalists alike tend to represent trade as a mundane, utilitarian, and practical activity. The general trend of my analysis is to outline the material conditions of production and exchange, moving on in later chapters to examine the embeddedness of trade in the wider social and cultural order to indicate—in an admittedly partial and preliminary way—something of the meaningful and experiential dimensions of trade to those involved.

This work is an outgrowth of a more limited study of the exploitation of birds of paradise which I took up soon after joining the Department of Anthropology and Sociology, University of Papua New Guinea (UPNG) in 1970. That project had been established in 1969 by Ralph Bulmer, then Professor of Anthropology at UPNG, and Max Downes, then Chief of the Wildlife Division of the PNG Department of Agriculture, Stock, and Fisheries. The aim was to help in framing a policy for the conservation of the birds that would be consistent with the objectives of wildlife management and the economic and cultural interests of rural people in continued hunting and trade of bird plumes.

My initiation into the mysteries of fieldwork came in 1971 with a very brief visit to the Kyaka Enga of the Baiyer Valley to collect material on trade in bird plumes, and two trips to the Jimi Valley in 1972 (totaling three months) in a survey of hunting of birds of paradise and trade in plumes, taking in settlements of Maring, Narak, and Kandawo speakers. This gentle introduction to fieldwork was of immense benefit; it helped in coping with the usual traumas of being thrown into a new and confusing social world, gave me experience of the practical problems entailed in establishing a fieldwork base, and allowed me to gain a preliminary familiarity with research techniques. Perhaps most importantly, my 1972 visits to the Jimi gave me the opportunity to survey the ethnography, geography, and ornithology of a large area of the valley and to choose a field site best suited for my more-embracing study of hunting and trade.

In November 1973 I returned to the Kundagai Maring settlement of Tsuwenkai for twelve months' fieldwork. The central focus of my research was again on the exploitation of birds of paradise, but the study was broadened to locate hunting of birds and trade in plumes in the wider contexts of the production and exchange of valuables. This study formed part of a three-pronged research program by the Papua New Guinea Wildlife Division for the conservation of birds of paradise. This program consisted of the collection of basic data on bird biology and ecology by officers of the Wildlife Division, an examination of legal aspects of regulating hunting and trade in plumes, and the collection of ethnographic data on the use and significance of birds of paradise to rural people. As a postgraduate student at UPNG, I undertook the last task on behalf of the Wildlife Division. I wish to acknowledge my gratitude for the official support of my project by the Department of Agriculture, Stock, and Fisheries. (Subsequently the Wildlife Division was moved to a series of departments.)

This book is based on my Ph.D. dissertation submitted in 1977 to UPNG. In the intervening years I have had the opportunity to reflect on the earlier work and to return to the field for short periods in late 1978 and again in 1985. I have substantially rewritten the text for this book, although my analysis remains essentially the same. The work of revision mainly took the form of condensing the material, excising several chapters (which have been published separately), refining certain arguments, and incorporating data on change from my later field trips. The "ethnographic present" relates to the early 1970s, on the eve of Independence from Australian administration.

The book is not simply an ethnography of a "traditional past" but includes certain recent transformations. Nonetheless, even into the 1980s change in Tsuwenkai has been slight. The greatest changes have stemmed from the political encapsulation of the village into the nation-state, with some attendant modification of internal village politics (see Maclean 1984*b* for a detailed and perceptive account). These new alignments, however, have not engendered any major alterations in the organization of production and exchange which forms the major orientation of this book. This situation may not last long. The very heart of Tsuwenkai is under threat—its soil and rocks and forests—and with it the social and cultural fabric. Mineral exploration has revealed potentially very valuable deposits of gold and other minerals in Tsuwenkai and nearby areas.

Faced with the possibility of large-scale mining development, many Kundagai are filled with alarm for the future of their children in a radically altered social and physical environment. Whatever the outcome, I can only hope that those Kundagai who may read this account will find it an acceptable view of their world as perceived by a foreigner—one mindful of the great honor done him by the generosity of their hospitality and companionship.

I began my studies at UPNG under the late Ralph Bulmer, and to him I owe my greatest intellectual debt, for guiding my entree into the field and for helping define my research problem. He commented generously and profusely on drafts of my dissertation and otherwise gave me the benefit of his wide scholarship in all matters of Melanesian ethnography and ornithology. I am also indebted to Andrew Strathern, who acted as supervisor in my studies and offered much-needed encouragement and advice in the field, and who steered the preparation of the dissertation on which this book is based to a successful conclusion.

Many others have contributed to the writing of this book. In particular I wish to thank Roy Rappaport for his comments and suggestions, Bill Clarke for ethnographic discussions and botanical information in the field, and an anonymous reader for the Press who made numerous valuable suggestions that have improved the final text. To Fitz Poole, an editor of this series, I owe thanks for his patience and counsel while the manuscript was under consideration with the Press. I have gained many ethnographic and analytic insights from discussions with Neil Maclean who has worked among the Tugumenga Maring. More generally, I have benefited enormously from the stimulus of friends and former colleagues at the University of Adelaide, especially Tom Ernst, Bruce Kapferer, Deane Fergie, and Neil Maclean, and from Jane Goodale who spent a year and a half in Darwin.

Three months' fieldwork in 1972 was supported by the University of Papua New Guinea. My 1973–1974 fieldwork was partly funded by grants from the New York Zoological Society, the Myer Foundation, and the then PNG Department of Natural Resources. In late 1978 I returned to the field for one month, while a grant from the Wenner–Gren Foundation for Anthropological Research enabled me to conduct a further two months' fieldwork in May–July 1985. I thank all these institutions for their support, and the national government and the Western Highlands Provincial government for permission to undertake research. It is also a pleasure to acknowledge the help offered by my parents and parents-in-law.

For hospitality and logistical support in the field I am grateful to Rev. Peter and Mrs. June Etterley, Rev. Brian Bailey, and the staff of Saint John's Church, Koinambe, and the staff of Tabibuga and Simbai government stations. Mr. (now Rev.) Alban Berobero helped me settle in at Tsuwenkai. Thanks are also due to Sue Plavins for typing the manuscript and the support of the Northern Territory University in preparing the manuscript for publication.

It is a convention at this point to acknowledge one's debt to the companion who has shared the burdens and pleasures of fieldwork, and who has put up with one in the process of distilling order out of the chaos of fieldnotes; but I have been asked to forgo such gratuitous gestures. As for my two daughters, they unwittingly delayed the writing of this book by exercising their right to attention, but in the process they helped keep me human. The resulting manuscript is perhaps better than it might have been otherwise.

Finally, I must acknowledge my debt to the Kundagai. My wife and I first came to Tsuwenkai unbidden and unexpected for a brief visit in 1972. We were invited back, yet the continuing warmth and generosity of our hosts surpassed our expectations. The memory we shall cherish but can hardly repay. To everyone in Tsuwenkai I must offer thanks for their hospitality, companionship, and friendship, no less than for their willingness to impart information to an often obtuse student. In particular, I acknowledge my gratitude to the late Kar and Planc who helped me understand the past, to Councillor Menek for his wise advice and support, and to Philip Amang for his help around the homestead and in the collection of data. Matthew Deimang Kuk cheerfully left his home up-river in Kwiop to join me as an assistant and give me the benefit of his talents as an interpreter. Bernard Kwie was a fount of information, advice, and support during my most recent fieldwork. And last, I must record my profound gratitude to Lucien Yekwai for the special gifts of his knowledge, wit, and friendship.

Ralph Bulmer's untimely death in 1988 was a great loss to his many friends in Papua New Guinea and elsewhere, and to Melanesian studies. This book owes immeasurably to his inspiration, example, and guidance, and is dedicated to his memory.

A Note on Conventions

There is no standard orthography to represent Maring speech, and each ethnographer has tended to develop his or her own system. This variability partly reflects dialect differences: Maring put some importance on sometimes minor variations in pronunciation and vocabulary in different dialects. The orthography I have chosen is only broadly phonetic; I have tried to render Maring words readable rather than indicate precisely how they sound. Letters used have the same values as in Tok Pisin (Neo-Melanesian Pidgin), with the exception that the letter *c* indicates the *ch* sound in English "church." The letters *ng* sound as in "sing" and *ngg* as in "finger." The greatest liberty I have taken is with the use of the schwa, the short, unrounded vowel as in the first vowel of the British pronunciation of "banana," for which no romanized symbol suffices. In some words I have simply omitted this vowel, as in *ambra* ("woman") where it occurs between *b* and *r*; in others I have rendered it with a vowel that most closely approximates its sound in context, as in both vowels of the personal name *Menek,* or the last vowel of *yimunt* ("tree fern").

Tok Pisin words and phrases are indicated by the letters TP in parentheses.

Bird and other animal names present some problem. There are few standardized English vernacular names, and many are cumbersome (e.g., Yellow-billed Mountain Lory). Scientific names may be more acceptable to specialists but are even less comprehensible to the general reader (e.g., the parrot just mentioned is known to ornithologists as *Neopsittacus muschenbroekii*). Although I feel that precise identifications are important, I mostly refer to birds (and some other animals) by English vernaculars, the more cumbersome ones sometimes shortened. Precise identifications are listed in appendix 2.

The Maring have known three currencies: Australian pounds (to 1965) and dollars, and national Kina (K) since Independence in 1975. All monetary values are expressed in Kina (though most valuations occurred before 1975), with no adjustment for revaluations, at the rate of 10 shillings to $A1 to K1. There are 100 Toea to the Kina. The Kina was at parity with the Australian dollar, though revaluations now place it at about $A1.50. To avoid confusion with the marine shell known in Tok Pisin by the same name (and after which the currency is named), the shell (also known as pearlshell) is referred to with a lower case "k," the currency with a capital "K."

Introduction

The island of New Guinea nudges the equator at its western extremity. Yet between the steamy coastal plains the land is compressed and heaped up into a series of high ranges and temperate valleys. On the northern and southern fringes of the highlands in particular, the topography is heavily dissected. Here it is possible for the traveler to move within a day's march through several resource zones spanning many hundreds, even thousands, of meters from major valley floors to the mountain peaks. Such close-packed environmental differences are paralleled by cultural diversity.

Despite their sometimes forbidding habitats, no New Guinea societies were ever truly isolated. Exchanges of goods and people across cultural boundaries assumed great importance in many areas. This natural and cultural diversity encouraged considerable traffic in material objects, and studies have clearly shown that trade is most highly developed between communities of differing ecological or cultural regions with specialized natural or manufactured resources. It is such locally specialized products that provide the bulk of goods traded across regional divisions (Gewertz 1983; Harding 1967; Hughes 1977; Keil 1974; Schwartz 1963; Tueting 1935). This book is concerned with the social, cultural, and ecological dimensions of the production of valuables and trade among the Maring people on the northern fringe of the central highlands of Papua New Guinea.

Trade is but one aspect of regional and intergroup relations and must be understood in the context of other kinds of dealings, such as marriage, warfare, ceremonial exchange, and their political-economic dimensions. But trade is also bound up with humankind's interaction with the environment—the economics and ecology of production or exploitation, by which the supply of trade goods is affected, as well as the distribution and consumption of goods whereby continued demand is generated.

Although there are numerous studies of intergroup relations throughout the New Guinea region, systematic attention to trade has concentrated on the lowlands and islands. Numerous ethnographies of the highlands make passing reference to trade. The only substantial treatments are by Hughes (1973; 1977) for a large area of the highlands and foothills, and Keil (1974) for the Benabena region of the Eastern Highlands. Other briefer descriptions and analyses of note include those provided by Rappaport (1968) for the Maring, Strathern (1971) for the Melpa, Heider (1970) for the Dani, Kelly (1977) for the Etoro, Reay (1959) for the Kuma, and Godelier (1977; 1986) for the Baruya.

Highland trade can be characterized by a constellation of features: traditionally a virtual absence of any form of organization approaching markets (but cf. Keil 1977) and a general lack of communal or cooperative activities beyond expeditions of men traveling for companionship and protection; the short distances individual traders travel; the passage of goods in small consignments, generally in one-for-one exchanges; the overwhelming concentration of trade in the hands of men; and the general restriction of goods to valuables or luxuries other than food. Even within these limits on goods, the range of items is quite astonishing, though highly variable from one region to another. In aboriginal times trade goods included stone axes, a variety of marine shells, salts, live animals (notably pigs and cassowaries, but also dogs, fowls, and marsupials), plumes of numerous species of birds, furs and skins of several marsupials, animal-tooth and vegetable-bead necklaces, cosmetic tree oil and pandanus oil, tobacco, pigments, medicinal and magical earths, weapons, drums, string bags, kilts, bark capes, bone daggers, fiber belts and armbands, besides other handicrafts. Luxury foods were seldom distributed in trade, and staple foods never. With the exception of pigs, the great bulk of high-value goods were produced exclusively by men and were generally for the use of men in ceremonial gifts, decorations, or ritual observances.

Introduction 3

The organization of trade and the range of items traded is, perhaps, more varied in lowland and island New Guinea. The most obvious contrast with the highlands are the great maritime trading systems of the north coast (Barlow 1985; Hogbin 1951; Lipset 1985; Tiesler 1969), Admiralties (Schwartz 1963), Vitiaz Strait (Harding 1967), Massim (Belshaw 1955; MacIntyre and Young 1982; Malinowski 1922; Seligman 1910), south coast of Papua (Dutton 1982; Malinowski 1915), and the Fly-Torres Strait region (Landtman 1927). Some of these systems, notably the Vitiaz Strait, involve specialist middlemen traders. Trade importantly depends on cooperation between groups of individuals, not least because of the technical requirements of sailing. Besides a great variety of valuables similar to those traded in the highlands, numerous luxury and everyday items of manufacture were traditionally traded in lowland and island New Guinea. Importantly, luxury and staple foods were, and still are, commonly traded.

Where trade systems were dominated by high volumes and frequent consignments of staple foods, rather than other goods, markets were significant institutions, and the bulk of transactions were conducted by women. The lower and middle Sepik and the Tolai area of New Britain are examples of such female-dominated, subsistence-food-oriented traditional markets (Barlow 1985; Epstein 1968; Gewertz 1983; Salisbury 1970).

Although trade has been a neglected field of study in the highlands, a great deal of attention has been focused on systems of the distribution of great volumes of valuables—primarily pigs and shells—in ceremonial exchange (e.g., Bulmer 1960; Feil 1984; 1987; Josephides 1985; Lederman 1986; Meggitt 1974; Sillitoe 1979; Strathern 1971). In some regions ceremonial exchange may indeed have developed at the expense of trade, or by the transformation of trading relations (cf. Healey 1978*a*), but I suspect that highland trade has attracted so little attention not because it is of limited material significance, but because in comparison to ceremonial exchange it appears so utterly mundane. And whereas the analysis of the exchange of valuables continues to concentrate on its more dramatic and ceremonialized forms (e.g. Lederman 1986), the study of production has concentrated on subsistence foods rather than valuables. The pig, of course, is a paramount valuable that has figured prominently in analyses of production, if only because it is largely nurtured on garden produce. There are, nonetheless, massive amounts of other objects variously known as valuables, wealth objects, and prestige goods which require considerable labor to produce, are consumed in very different ways from subsistence items, and which are redistributed in prestations and trade.

This work examines the interconnection between the ecology of the production of valuables through the exploitation of nonsubsistence goods and the social and cultural organization of production and exchange. An important focus is the dynamic operation of production and trade through time. Although synchronic studies illuminate the functions of trade (or other activities) in effecting the distribution of specialized goods between ecologically and culturally distinct provinces, they do not allow us to test for the temporal stability or otherwise of trade systems. Equilibrium in functional models, ecological and anthropological, does not imply constancy but a dynamic balance of forces (Kormondy 1969; Rappaport 1979). Simply because a system has been identified does not presuppose that it is in equilibrium. The capacity of a trade system to achieve a degree of permanence and stability through the balance of supply and consumption depends not only on the proportions of different goods in circulation but also on the ecology of initial production. Where trade goods are derived from plants or animals, the ability of those producing or extracting the goods to maintain supply becomes theoretically infinite; the raw materials are self-perpetuating. The demand of populations desiring these goods sets a base level or rate at or above which these goods must be supplied, whereas the capacity of the animals or plants to reproduce sets an upper limit on supply. If the producers or exploiters attempt to inject more of these goods into the trade system than natural regeneration can replace, then the system must at best be interrrupted and at worst be destroyed with the extinction of the resources if substitutes cannot be found.

Products of animal and vegetable origin, such as bird plumes, marsupial pelts, bows and arrows, tree oil, and net bags, are still highly desired and traded in many parts of the highlands. It is therefore still possible to study the ecological bases of production—to discover the mechanisms whereby demand can be met and balanced within the limitations of supply set by the capacities of the raw materials to reproduce themselves. It is also possible to explore the social and cultural forces that, in conjunction with ecological factors, give a trade system its distinctive geographic shape, modes of operation, and historical dynamics.

TRADE AS AN ANALYTIC CATEGORY

At this point some indication of what I mean by *trade* is essential. There are two prevailing uses of the term in anthropology: it is applied loosely and generally to refer to any passage of goods by a variety of means, and it is applied in a more limited sense as a category distinct from ceremonial or gift exchange or prestation. Indeed, some ethnographies and undergraduate texts even set trade apart from exchange— referring to "trade and exchange"—which is at once an unfortunate imprecision, for what is really meant is "ceremonial exchange," and an absurdity, for trade is obviously one form of exchange.

Theoretical and ethnographic understandings of ceremonial exchange, gift exchange, or prestation have achieved a degree of elaboration and sophistication. Trade, barter, or commodity exchange have fared less well. In some ethnographies trade is implicitly everything that gift exchange is not. Those works that deal with trade explicitly commonly characterize it as being "more economic," "commercial," or less sociable than gift exchange; an activity engaged in by calculating, self-interested individuals out of crudely utilitarian and materialistic motives of private gain (see e.g., Tueting 1935; Podolefsky 1984). Trade thus hovers on the boundary between hostility and friendship and can be made a positive force of social (as distinct from regional) integration by inflecting the practice of trading in the direction of gift exchange through such acts of sociability as entering into formal partnerships with others, honoring trade partners with gifts or favored terms of trade, and the like (e.g., Sahlins 1972). This view may adequately characterize the practice of trade in some areas, but it may obscure as much as it reveals. Certainly, as the present ethnography will show, the presumption that trade is essentially grounded in utilitarian and materialistic forces is unacceptable as a generalization.

Anthropologists have long distinguished between ceremonial exchange and trade, following native practice. The most notable example for Melanesia is the Trobriand distinction between *kula* and *gimwali* (Malinowski 1922), but there are many similar instances. Sahlins (1972: 185 ff.) has developed a general framework for the discussion of exchange of material goods in his scheme of reciprocities. He identifies certain factors—kinship distance, rank, relative wealth or need, the types of goods transferred—which among others influence the nature of reciprocity. His discussion of the continuum of forms from generalized through balanced to negative reciprocity points to the difficulties of separating one form of exchange from another for definitional purposes. This conclusion is important in that it derives from a consideration of the interplay of social forces acting on the parties to an exchange, rather than from a comparison of the observable character of different forms of exchange.

Some ethnographers, however, have attempted to distinguish trade from other forms of exchange on the basis of the outward or observable form of exchange, rather than on the basis of the relationship of the actors. Such definitions may consist of a list of characteristics demarcating trade from prestation (e.g., van Baal 1975; Hughes 1977). Such definitions are inadequate because they refer to the actual conduct of the transaction by which goods are exchanged—the nature of the objects, the relationships of those involved, the relative amounts of ceremonialism, publicity, corporation, magic, or politics involved during the exchange. In societies where economic activities, ceremony, politics, and so forth are not sharply demarcated but are infused in many institutions and situations, this kind of definitional view of trade and prestation necessarily overlaps. Using this approach it is not always easy to classify a material transaction observed in the field. An unceremonial, private, delayed exchange of dissimilar goods of equal value between affines combines descriptive attributes of both trade and gift. Although what is normally understood as trade, barter, or commodity exchange falls within the categories of balanced or negative reciprocity in Sahlins's scheme, his approach to the question of definitions offers no clear way out of the problem. But it does provide a useful theoretical model for a consideration of the structural and economic implications of different substantive forms of exchange. Nonetheless, I argue that if we are to gain a proper understanding of production, distribution, and consumption of goods in sociological terms, a distinction between fundamental forms or modes of exchange must be made. In nonmarket exchange (cf. Polanyi 1968) there are two such modes, which I term trade and prestation. I use the latter term in a general sense, derived from Mauss (1954), to include a diversity of reciprocal gifts transacted by individuals or collectivities on specific formal occasions, such as moments in an individual's life cycle, as well as informal occasions when gifts are not normatively prescribed. For the moment, I take refuge in a particular ethnographic understanding—that of the Maring

Introduction 7

who are the subject of this book. The Maring term *munggoi rigima* (literally "valuables exchange"), which I translate as trade, refers to transactions explicitly concerned with the acquisition and distribution of goods whereas *munggoi awom* (literally "valuables give"), or prestations, refers to transactions explicitly concerned with the establishment, continuation, or discharge of social relations, rights, and obligations. Trade is thus overtly concerned with relations between material objects mediated by social relations, and prestations, with relations between people mediated by material goods. (The Maring concepts are examined more fully in chap. 4.) This distinction is fundamental to what follows, though it would be naive to expect it to be recognized explicitly in all precapitalist societies. Boldly stated, it has clear applicability to different forms of exchange elsewhere but is hardly profound. The rest of this book, however, amounts, among other things, to an elaboration and explication of the nature and significance of this distinction. In the final chapter I arrive at some important modifications of this definition of trade which soften the rigidity of the present position.

A MODEL OF TRADE

A striking feature of central-highlands societies is the richness of their ceremonial decorations (see Strathern and Strathern 1971). The most impressive element is often a headdress of bird of paradise plumes, parrot skins, and eagle, hornbill, and other feathers. Plumes are not only highly prized as items of visual splendor but are wealth objects redistributed in bridewealth and other prestations. It is in a relatively limited area of the central highlands—the Simbu and eastern Wahgi Valleys—that plume use is most highly developed in terms of the quantities and varieties desired. Because of extensive deforestation, many densely settled communities lack access to what forest remains in narrow belts above the level of agriculture (about 2,200 meters). Since the majority of bird species most highly valued for their plumes live either in high-altitude forest or in lower altitudes on the northern and southern highland fringes, the central highlanders are unable to satisfy their own requirement for plumes from their own forests and must obtain the bulk of feathers from communities on the fringes with easy access to wild birds. In the latter areas population densities are generally lower and extensive forests support a rich and diverse fauna, including birds of paradise, parrots and hawks, marsupials, and other forest products.[1]

These conditions set the parameters for an analysis of trade that takes as its focus the provision of one class of goods: forest products, most especially bird plumes. Simply stated the model is a center–periphery one consisting of a trading network of plumes and their exchange goods made up of concentric rings arranged around a core of communities I call ultimate consumers of plumes. Feathers, mammal skins, live cassowaries, and other such products of the forest are traded toward this central area where they remain until worn out or destroyed. They may be redistributed in trade or prestation but not exported beyond the center. At the extremities of the model are located numerous primary suppliers of plumes and skins who obtain all of their stocks for local use and trade by hunting. Intervening areas are occupied by intermediate suppliers who receive plumes in trade from the periphery and augment the volume sent on to ultimate consumers by adding more feathers by local hunting. Such communities may also be intermediate consumers to a greater or lesser degree and are therefore critical for the volume of plumes delivered to the central consumption area.

This scheme clearly involves two "systems" of exchange that are only partially connected. One involves the socially and culturally mediated passage of dissimilar goods in opposing flows—the organization of trade. The relative kinds, quantities, and values of different categories of goods and the demand for them may vary through time and from one sector of the trade sphere to another, so engendering a degree of internal tension that may be necessary for the continued functioning and survival of trade as a means of supply. The second system involves the ecological relationship between human communities and the wild populations of birds and other resources on which they prey to sustain their position in the trade network.

The overall structure of trade is articulated in terms of patterns of distribution of plumes. Their supply is thus critical, and ultimately the number of plumes available for trade—and so the volume of exchange goods in passage—rests on the recruitment rate in wild-bird populations. To maintain trade humans must not reduce bird populations below certain critical levels by destruction of habitat or by predation rates that exceed recruitment rates. This scheme does not necessarily imply homeostasis in the system of exploitation and trade, but it does require that the birds are not eradicated without compensatory shifts to new supply areas. This means that in particular locations birds may be subjected to extreme under- or overexploitation provided that the volume of plumes delivered to ultimate consumers remains much the same. The model does not therefore involve any necessary stable or dynamic equilibrium between human activity and bird populations, either overall or in particular locations. It is possible, then, for some suppliers to pass out of the trade network entirely by destroying their resource base, since there are no negative feedback loops connecting goods received in exchange for plumes (from consumers) with the subsystem of plume production that rests on the breeding biology of birds.

From this concentric structure of networks it follows that the products of a multiplicity of primary suppliers become fed into progressively fewer or more densely packed channels. Loss rates of plumes from damage and age may vary in different parts of the network, but all things being equal this funneling effect results in the delivery of massive quantities of plumes to the center, even though the contribution of individual supply communities might be quite small.

The dynamics of this scheme can be elaborated considerably.[2] For the moment, the point to stress is that the model provides a focus for the detailed analysis of specific ethnographic data on trade. From an initial concentration on the production of one class of valuables for use in trade, one can expand the analysis to encompass the wider social, cultural, and ecological context within which that production occurs.

Elsewhere I have documented the trade in bird plumes in the New Guinea region and shown that the pattern of distribution in the interior—roughly encompassing the Papua New Guinea highlands—conforms broadly to the geographic structure of the model sketched above (Healey 1980). The purpose of the present work is to examine the organization of production and exchange at the level of the local community. In that respect it differs from most other studies of trade that take a regional perspective. I seek to show how local production and exchange are articulated in sociocultural and ecological dimensions with wider regional forces.

This book, then, explores, through the example of the Kundagai Maring, how goods enter, move in, and leave the larger sphere. In the absence of markets or centralized organization, trade networks of the kind dealt with here are always managed at the local level, and ultimately by individuals who may be quite unaware of their economic and ecological role in the region as a whole. What sustains production and trade at the local level cannot, therefore, be accounted for by reference to the larger structure. That structure is the consequence of the interconnections of local producers and transactors, not the determinant of their activities.

A further caution must be added. The scheme just outlined treats plumes as the products of ecologically specialized peripheral regions. For consumers to signal effectively a demand for plumes they must offer in exchange goods that are desired by plume suppliers. In general, the exchange items are also specialized products unavailable locally to plume suppliers for ecological or cultural reasons. The goods in demand may vary from one area to another. Further, there is no necessity that ultimate plume consumers be primary suppliers of other goods. One may imagine several patterns of trade in a variety of goods superimposed on a landscape so that their boundaries overlap. Thus, the model is not one of a trade system as such, but of one category of goods passed in trade. Indeed, to speak of systems is to suggest that there are boundaries of a reasonably determinate nature. Empirically it may be possible to demarcate the patterns of distribution of material goods, but the degree of noncongruence in these geographic patterns, added to the variable sociological means of distribution, make it impossible to define trade systems. There are no isolated, impervious trade systems in operation in Melanesia, if anywhere. It is clear, nonetheless, that there are areas where there is a concentration of most exchanges within certain geographic and sociological limits, and I shall refer to them as trade regions.

This book deals with the operation of a segment of one such region, which is indeterminate in extent but centered on the major highland valleys. Hughes (1977) has ably described the ecological structure of the region on the eve of the colonial era. The segment in question consists of a number of communities on the rugged northern fringe of the highlands, whose place in the wider trade region is assured by virtue of their privileged place as one of the major supply areas of various forest products in trade directed toward ultimate plume consumers. The particular focus is on the Kundagai of Tsuwenkai, a group of some three hundred Maring speakers.

Much of what follows amounts to the construction of a more elaborate model of trade in terms of ethnographic and ethnohistorical evidence. The picture just outlined is one couched largely in ecological and functional terms. It is important, however, to avoid allowing such formulations to dominate the process of producing an ethnography—both in the field situation and, more importantly, in the final presentation and analysis of data.³ It is well, then, to state the general perspectives adopted. The model is essentially one of equilibrium. This study, however, does not assume homeostasis as a necessary tendency of the complex of transactions examined. I am concerned to discover the capacity for trade to be sustained, but this does not involve any presumption of steady states. Besides, even to discover an equilibrium is not to show that it is systematically achieved.

Second, although production and exchange occur in particular ecological contexts, I accept that all activity is crucially shaped by cultural factors. Ecological conditions, therefore, cannot be determinants of individual or collective repetitive action, nor of features of culture. Finally—and flowing from this attention to the cultural order—the analysis rejects formalism in the explanation of exchange, most especially its common appearance in ideas of material utility.

The following two chapters set the context for an examination of hunting and trade. Chapter 1 outlines critical features of the Kundagai physical environment and aspects of social organization. Such data are obviously necessary for a fuller understanding of the social and cultural organization of production and exchange. Chapter 1 also outlines Maring concepts of spirits and their place in the natural world within which hunting occurs. Finally, I provide a discussion of the historical dimensions of settlement of the Kundagai village of Tsuwenkai and of transfers of rights to land, events that clearly have contributed to the contemporary social and geographic patterns of exploitation of the environment.

In chapter 2 I seek to show the cultural significance of bird plumes among the Maring as objects of decoration. The uses of plumes and other forest products are a significant but not sole impetus to local production. An important point that emerges from this chapter, moreover, is that many kinds of feathers retained for decorations are not available locally but must be obtained from elsewhere. Just how this is organized is the focus of later chapters.

Ecologically focused studies of production in agricultural societies have, understandably, concentrated on subsistence foodstuffs. Little systematic attention has been paid to either the production of nonsubsistence valuables, on the one hand, or to the exploitation of non-domesticated resources, on the other hand. Marks's (1976) study of big-game hunting among the central-African Bisa is a rare exception.

Chapter 3 takes up these issues and provides an examination of the ecology of hunting of birds for their valuable plumes and the social and cultural organization and regulation of hunting.

The remainder of the book is concerned with the ecology and sociocultural organization of aspects of the distribution and consumption of material objects. In particular, I seek to show how levels of production and exchange of one class of goods—forest products—relates to the total flow of goods by a variety of means. This involves specifying the kinds of goods, material and otherwise, that are transferred parallel to or in opposition to forest products, their patterns of ownership, and the kinds of transactions in which they are passed. Chapter 4 introduces this analysis, presenting data on valuables, their ownership, and their redistribution in prestations. An important aspect of this chapter is the analysis of gross levels and directions of passage of goods in prestations.

The following chapters are devoted to the analysis of trade. Chapter 5 provides an ecologically oriented description of trading patterns over time and an analysis of mechanisms for the maintenance of a more or less constant passage of goods in the absence of any regulatory institutions. Chapter 6 provides an overview of the historical dimensions of trade, pointing to the importance of European penetration of the central highlands for the consolidation of changing trade patterns in the northern fringe of the highlands and the significance of plume trade in the contemporary cash economy. In chapter 7, I develop an analysis of exchange value and suggest the mechanisms by which rates of exchange of some trade goods remain stable while others have changed.

The concluding chapter shifts the focus from the relationship between objects passed against one another, which characterizes the preceding chapters, and concentrates on the social relationships between the traders themselves. Through a discussion of the manner in which trade may be employed as a communicative means expressive and constitutive of social relationships, I argue that prevailing utilitarian understandings of trade require some reappraisal.

The general objectives of this study are twofold. Substantively, this work provides an added dimension to the ethnography of the Maring and of hunting and trade in the highlands in general. Theoretically, the book is an attempt to develop a more thorough understanding of the articulation of production and exchange, combining the insights of ecological and economic anthropology.

1
The Kundagai

Environment and Society

The Western Bismarck and Schrader Mountains form the last bastion of the central highlands before the land falls away to the humid lowlands of the Ramu floodplain. Several cultural groups inhabit these northern fringes: the Maring, Narak, and Kandawo whose affinities are close to Wahgi Valley central highlanders, and the Kopon, Kalam, and Gainj comprising a language family only distantly related to the main highlands stock (see map 1).

Like their fellow highlanders the Maring are swidden agriculturalists and pig-raisers. The staple diet is provided by sweet potato and taro, but a great variety of other crops is grown. Some have always been present, others have been introduced from their neighbors over the last hundred years or more. The list includes yams, cassava, bananas, sugar cane, pitpit, corn, and cucurbits, besides numerous leafy greens and tree crops, notably the fruit pandanus and breadfruit. In addition to pigs, which are seldom eaten outside of irregular ritual and ceremonial occasions, the Maring keep a few fowls, dogs, and cassowaries. Many local groups enjoy a higher intake of meat than one might otherwise suppose, however, for game is plentiful in some areas. Nonetheless, exploitation of wild resources is not solely geared toward satisfying gustatory desires, for the forests abound in a great variety of birds and mammals whose feathers and pelts are eagerly sought by those less favorably endowed.

The Kundagai are one such community who engage in considerable

Map 1. Jimi Valley

hunting to supply trade goods. They are one of more than twenty Maring local populations and occupy a large territory stretching between the Jimi and Simbai Rivers. They live in three settlements: Bokapai and Tsuwenkai in the Jimi Valley, and Kinimbong in the Simbai. I am concerned mainly with the people of Tsuwenkai (map 2), and unless stated otherwise I mean the name Kundagai to refer to that section of the population living there.

This chapter describes the environmental and ethnographic context for the subsequent account of hunting and trade. I begin with attention to aspects of the natural environment, with some general notes on the impact of human occupation. There follows an account of critical aspects of Kundagai social organization. I conclude with a summary of settlement history with particular attention to land tenure.

THE PHYSICAL ENVIRONMENT

The government rest house of Tsuwenkai lies at about 5°25' S, 144°38' E, at an altitude of 1,680 meters. The settlement is in the headwaters of the Pint River, a tributary of the Jimi. The Jimi Valley comprises the Tabibuga District of the Western Highlands Province and is administered from Tabibuga on the Tsau–Jimi Divide. Until the early 1970s, when a road suitable for four-wheel drive vehicles was completed from Tabibuga to Banz in the Wahgi Valley, the only means of contact within and beyond the Jimi was by walking tracks or light aircraft. By the mid-1980s the Kundagai and others had invested around twenty years' of manual labor into building a road connecting settlements on the north bank of the Jimi to Tabibuga. Although the Jimi River was bridged in 1978, the road was still not passable in 1985 to traffic beyond a few kilometers from the bridgehead. Long, well-graded, but unconnected sections of road were continually reclaimed by secondary growth or swept away in landslides. The labor involved in roadbuilding and maintenance was compounded by repeated rerouting of extensive sections of the road.

The north wall of the Jimi Valley is formed by a western extension of the Bismarck Range. The valley is separated from the densely populated Wahgi Valley to the south by the Sepik–Wahgi Divide that rises to over 3,700 meters in places. These two ranges converge in jagged, cloud-piled ridges on the central massif of Mount Wilhelm. On clear days this highest peak in Papua New Guinea is visible from Tsuwenkai some 60 kilometers to the southeast, rendered a mere hummock by the

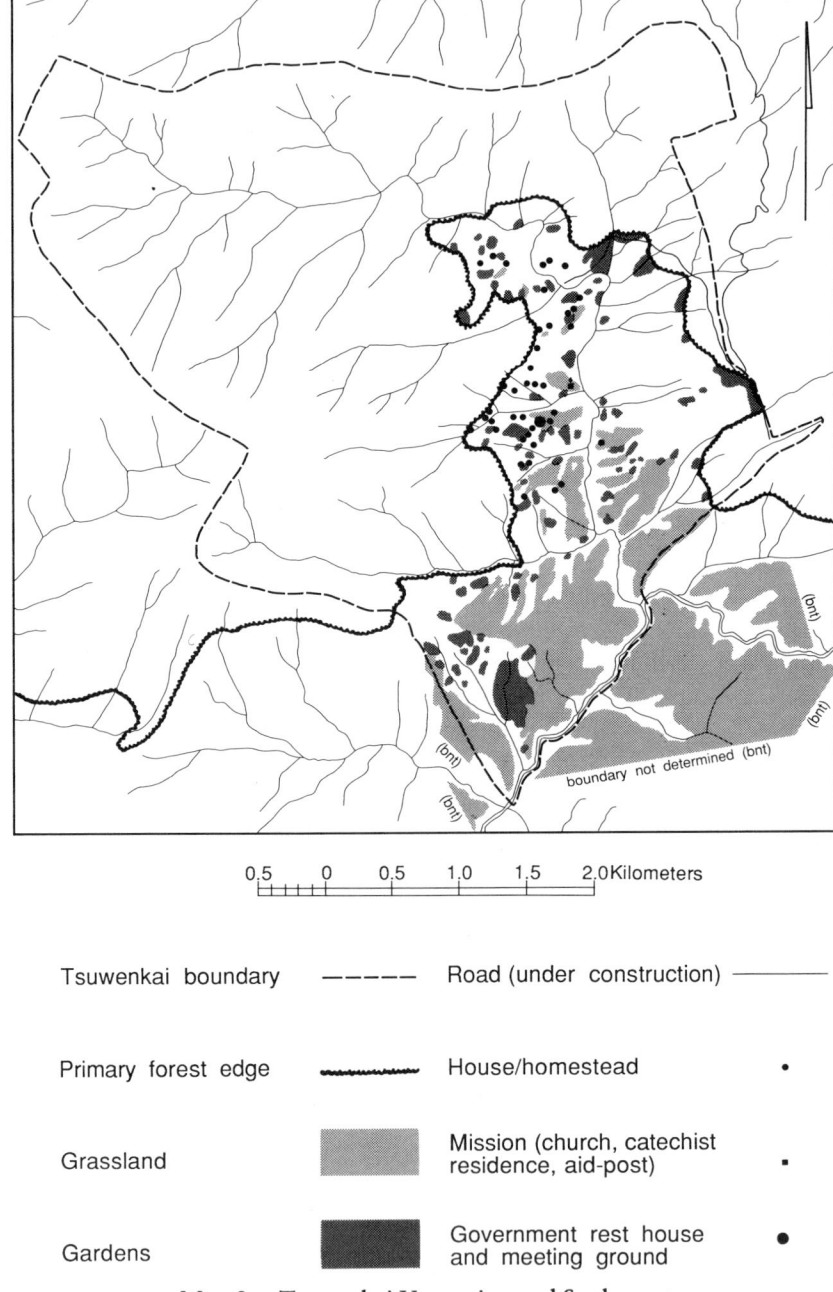

Map 2. Tsuwenkai Vegetation and Settlement

The Kundagai: Environment and Society

closer, more dramatic ranges. The Jimi is a turbulent, rock-strewn river that rises on the snow-fed slopes of Mount Wilhelm and plunges down its narrow, cliff-hung bed on its way to the Sepik River to the northwest. To the north of the Bismarck Range the Simbai River flows eastward and then north to join the Ramu River.

I made no detailed records of climate during fieldwork other than noting temperatures for 204 days over 12 months in 1973–1974. Clarke (1971: 39–50) and Rappaport (1968: 32–33) give details of rainfall at Gunts, Tsembaga, and Simbai Patrol Post in the Simbai, and at Tabibuga in the Jimi. On comparative grounds the annual rainfall at Tsuwenkai is probably between 3,000 and 4,000 millimeters.

During the wetter season, about November to April, rain falls almost every afternoon, and mountain peaks are often obscured by cloud for much of the day. In the late afternoon heavy banks of cloud well up in the Simbai to spill over into the Jimi, and the evening is often enlivened by the ominous roll of distant thunder and the flicker of lightning from the Ramu lowlands. The dank and miserable reputation those regions enjoyed among my Kundagai friends seemed well deserved.

In the drier season, May to October, the sky is often cloudless and no rain may fall for periods of up to a week. Occasionally the dry season does not become properly established, or is shorter than usual, and so hampers garden preparations as gardeners wait for fine weather. Under these circumstances a gardener may be unable to clear as much land as desired or to achieve an adequate burn of trash. Such times create anxiety over food shortages, although the Kundagai mainly suffer hunger for favored crops rather than any serious absolute shortage of food. Heavy afternoon rains sometimes cause minor flooding of streams, small landslides beside tracks, some sheet erosion in gardens with sparse vegetation cover, and damage to sugar crops flattened in the downpour. Although excessive rain periodically causes problems, the Jimi does not appear to be significantly affected by drought, although many smaller streams dry up toward the end of the drier season.

Daily maximum temperatures varied during fieldwork from 16.5° C in June to 29° C in October, averaging 22.8° C. Minima were usually reached around six A.M. and ranged from 11° C to 18° C (both records in November), averaging 14.9° C. I do not know if frosts ever occur; certainly the Jimi was not affected by the devastating frosts in higher altitudes of the Western and Southern Highlands Provinces of 1972, which occurred while I was in the upper Jimi.

As elsewhere on the highland fringes the landscape is dramatic. The Jimi River flows along the northern part of the valley so that a cross-section of the valley is a lop-sided V shape, with a steep north wall and more gentle southern slopes. Especially on the north side the numerous watercourses are deeply incised, producing a rugged topography. Tsuwenkai itself is situated on the flanks of a range on the west of the Kant River, extending southward from the Bismarck crest. The Kant Valley is narrow, with short, steep lateral spurs and intervening streams. The Kant joins the Pint River south of Tsuwenkai. Aside from some tiny marshy patches by the river, there is no flat land in the Kant Valley and only a few gently sloping areas along the upper course of the Pint. Tsuwenkai territory ranges in altitude from about 1,200 meters to at least 2,800 meters in the short space of about six kilometers.

North of Tsuwenkai a low pass, Gendupa, allows fairly easy access across the Bismarcks to the Simbai Valley. A similar pass at Gachambo at the headwaters of the Kant connects with the Mieng drainage system. Another pass north of the Mieng gives access to Kumbruf in the Simbai.

The loose shales and clays of the Tsuwenkai region are prone to landslides, especially after the shallow soils are waterlogged with rain. Small slides are common on embankments beside tracks and gardens. Larger slides of one or more hectares in extent occur in both grasslands and primary forest.

VEGETATION AND ECOLOGICAL ZONES

The Tsuwenkai region totals about 25 square kilometers, excluding 1 to 1.5 square kilometers of high-altitude forest claimed by the Simbai Valley Tuguma (see below).

On the basis of vegetation and fauna, Tsuwenkai can be viewed as a montane region. The Kundagai of Tsuwenkai are probably the only Maring group to be confined exclusively to the montane zone, although they do have some access to lower areas at Kinimbong in the Simbai. The Tsuwenkai region can be divided into three ecological zones with characteristic vegetation types.

Montane Zone

This zone consists of primary montane forest[1] and extends down from the mountain peaks of over 2,800 meters to the forest edge at about 1,700–1,850 meters. The Maring call such forest *kamungga, apng geni,* or *apng geni mai.* The last two terms refer to virgin forest. *Kamungga* is often used as a synonym for montane forest but may also refer to secondary growth. The connotations are generally wider than a vegetation type, including high altitudes, a cold and wet climate, and a characteristic fauna. The term, then, refers not only to a vegetation type but to a particular ecological zone.

Clarke (1971: 207 ff.) and Rappaport (1968: 271 ff.) give details of the floristic composition of montane forest. Characteristic of this zone are groves of tall Pandanus palms and huge *cenda* trees (unident.). Above about 2,400 meters are stands of *kamai, Nothofagus* Beech.[2]

The Kundagai say that in the recent past montane forest extended over most of the Tsuwenkai area right down to the Kant River. Much of this in the lower altitudes was apparently oak forest of *Castanopsis* and *Lithocarpus* species. There are small stands of remnant oaks in the Kant Valley.

Montane forest has a more or less continuous canopy about 30 meters or more above the ground. Two, sometimes one, substages are generally present. The ground level is usually fairly clear, though where a dominant tree has fallen or trailing bamboo becomes established the undergrowth can be quite dense. Most trees are heavily laden with moss, especially above about 2,200 meters where trees become somewhat stunted.

The montane zone covers about sixteen square kilometers or 64 percent of the Tsuwenkai area.

ZONE OF HUMAN HABITATION

In Tsuwenkai most of the land below the montane zone falls into this category. This region presents a patchwork pattern of secondary forest in various stages of development, gardens, homesteads, and groves of planted trees. Tracts of anthropogenic grassland are interspersed within this area. The zone owes its origins almost entirely to the presence of humans, having developed where man has cut or burnt the original forest. Because of the diversity of vegetation it is convenient to distinguish several subzones.

Secondary Forest and Woodland. While recounting the oral history of Tsuwenkai, informants often made reference to former vegetation cover. From their remarks it appears that secondary forest transforms into forest classed by the Maring as *apng geni mai* after forty to seventy years. [In the lower and wetter Ndwimba Basin of the Simbai regeneration is quicker (Clarke 1971: 61).]

The speed of development of secondary forest and woodland varies from one site to another but, on average, growth reaches a height of about nine meters in ten to fifteen years. The Kundagai attribute such variations to differences in soil fertility and the floristic composition of the fallow growth—no doubt interrelated factors. Moisture content of the soil probably also influences regeneration. Thus, relatively open-spaced communities dominated by the trees *Trema orientalis, Dodonaea viscosa,* and *Alphitonia incana,* shading a scrubby understory, tend to form woodlands on drier sites. In wetter areas secondary forest is denser, supporting a greater variety of plants. Various *Piper* and *Ficus* species, and tree ferns, *Cyathea,* are common on such sites, as well as succulents such as wild ginger, *Alpinia* spp.

Bush Fallow. Lower growth is generally composed of dense stands of saplings pushing their way through a tangled layer of shrubs and bushes. On damp sites beds of pitpit (*Miscanthus* cane-grass) are common.

The distributions of secondary forest and woodlands and bush fallow are not differentiated on map 2 but comprise all areas not shown under primary forest, gardens, and grassland.

Homesteads and Plantations. These are areas dominated by vegetation actively induced by human activity. In contrast to gardens they tend to be semipermanent. There are around forty separate homestead or single-house sites scattered along the west flanks of the Kant Valley. Frequently a leveled space must be excavated into a hillside to provide room for a house. Settlement patterns are discussed below; here it need only be said that the Kundagai do not generally form any strong attachments to a particular homestead site, other than of convenience or sentiment. Once a house is beyond repair after two or more years' occupancy, the householder may rebuild nearby or more than a kilometer away. Moves are motivated by various factors: a desire to be close to new gardens, to friends or relatives, or to escape from unpleasant neighbors or sickness and witchcraft associated with a particular location.

Tobacco and bananas are often planted among the hearths and refuse of old house sites, and the yard may be planted extensively with casuarina trees. Once these reach a suitable height, coffee seedlings are often planted in their shade. In this way old homesteads are transformed into relatively permanently altered areas. Sites that are totally abandoned generally revert to secondary forest, or occasionally to a disclimax of grass.

Groves of bananas, sugar, and green-leaved vegetables are usually planted within a homestead yard, along with shrubs and trees of an ornamental, utilitarian, or magical nature, such as casuarinas, tankets, crotons, bamboos, and various succulents and aromatic herbs.

Most coffee groves are established close to homesteads, in old kitchen gardens. Coffee requires a good shade cover, and casuarinas are favored for this purpose because they grow rapidly, yield superior timber for firewood, building, and fencing, and enrich the soil.

Groves of various other tree crops, especially the *marita* Pandanus, *Pandanus conoideus,* are scattered about in secondary growth or in homestead gardens. Few other propagated tree crops are grown in Tsuwenkai as they fare poorly at this altitude.

Included in this subzone are the *raku*[3] or ceremonial pig-killing groves and ossuaries. There are at least fifteen of these scattered throughout the zone of human habitation. *Raku* are generally small, less than about 0.2 hectares, although some are on the edge of primary forest or within secondary forest. Many *raku* are composed of remnant patches of montane forest, others are of secondary growth that has sprung up in the shade of casuarinas, *Araucaria* pines, and other trees planted by early Kundagai immigrants to Tsuwenkai. *Raku* are associated with particular clans, and the bones of the dead clansmen were formerly secreted in the ground or in tree hollows and epiphytic plants. Under government and mission influence the dead are now buried in graves, usually outside *raku*. The spirits of the dead are believed to linger about *raku* and, although one may gather firewood and creepers or resin from *Araucaria* pines from a *raku,* one should not cause undue disturbance lest the spirits visit sickness on the living.

The distribution of homesteads and isolated houses is shown in map 2. I have no estimate of the total area involved, nor of the area of groves of coffee or casuarinas and *raku*. These latter areas have not been distinguished on the map but are included within the type of vegetation surrounding them.

Secondary forest, bush fallow, homesteads, planted groves, and *raku* together cover about 6.3 square kilometers or 25.2 percent of the Tsuwenkai area. Spontaneous fallow growth constitutes the larger part of this area.

Gardens. The Maring practice swidden or slash-and-burn agriculture (see Clarke 1971; Manner 1977; Rappaport 1968; 1971, for details of agricultural practices and energetics). Each householder clears two or more gardens a year. Yields can be sustained from a little over one year to two years after planting depending on the crops planted. Sugar, bananas, and pitpit, *Saccharum edule,* can be harvested for the greatest length of time. The Kundagai generally plant their gardens only once and, although they are weeded periodically, much secondary growth has already sprung up among the crops by the time they are abandoned.

Map 2 shows gardens ranging in age from those just cleared in the dry season of 1974 to gardens about two years old. The total area under cultivation (excluding smaller homestead gardens that are not shown on the map) is less than 0.5 square kilometers. This constitutes no more than 2 percent of the total Tsuwenkai area or 8.3 percent of the area currently under a fallow of secondary forest, woodland, and bush.[4] There is a concentration of gardens on the southern slopes of Komongwai. This area is particularly favored because of the fertility of the soil, in consequence of which crops and fallow develop more rapidly than elsewhere, permitting more intensive cultivation under shorter fallow periods.

Gardens are cut at altitudes ranging from the Kant River (about 1,200 meters at lowest) to the edge of montane forest at about 1,850 meters. In the Simbai Valley, gardens are mainly cut between 900 meters and 1,520 meters, mostly below the lower limit of Tsuwenkai gardens. Rappaport (1968: 52) states that Tsembaga fallow periods are shorter in lower altitudes and, overall, average around fifteen to twenty-five years.

Tsuwenkai gardens do not appear to conform to this pattern, having shorter fallow periods despite higher altitude. Of a sample of twenty-nine gardens in preparation during 1973–1974, one was being cut in primary forest at about 1,720 meters. The remainder were in secondary forest. All these sites had been gardened at least once previously,[5] while one was being planted for the fourth time. According to the Kundagai, fallow periods vary in relation to soil fertility and floristic composition of regrowth, not altitude, although these factors are partially dependent on altitude. The type of crops to be grown also occasions some variation: sweet potato is considered to grow adequately on poorer soils or on land left fallow for shorter periods. The average fallow period for the twenty-eight gardens is fifteen to sixteen years (range six to twenty-two years, mode twelve years, eight cases). A sample of a further twenty-six newly prepared gardens in 1978 yielded the same average and modal figures (range ten to twenty-six years). In 1985 a sample of thirty-two new gardens indicated a slight lengthening of fallow cycles. Three gardens were being prepared in primary forest; the average fallow period for the remaining twenty-nine gardens was eighteen to nineteen years (range nine to thirty-five years with a bimodal distribution of ten to eleven years, six cases, and sixteen to seventeen years, five cases). This shorter fallow cycle than Simbai regimes may reflect a slightly higher recovery rate of soil fertility. The Kundagai themselves consider Tsuwenkai to be sufficiently fertile, though they compare it unfavorably with lower altitudes in Kinimbong, Koinambe, and Bokapai. Informants were adamant that fallow periods were not limited by a shortage of garden land,[6] and the tendency toward longer fallow cycles and clearing of virgin land in 1985 is indicative of abundant land resources rather than falling productivity.

GRASSLAND

The most extensive grasslands in the Tsuwenkai region are close to its southern boundary. Oral traditions indicate that the larger tracts of grassland from Korapa southward have remained relatively stable in area for about two hundred years, although there may have been some expansion of grassland on Komongwai. Aside from oral traditions the antiquity of these grasslands is further suggested by the component species. *Themeda,* which grows on older grasslands with poorer soils (Henty 1969: 1), is probably the dominant species in most grassland associations. Kunai grass, *Imperata cylindrica,* dominates in some widely scattered areas. Grassland covers about 2 to 2.5 square kilometers, or about 9 percent of the total Tsuwenkai area. The largest single area of grassland, on Komongwai, is just over one square kilometer in area.

There is one further vegetational and ecological zone in the middle and lower reaches of the Jimi. This is characterized by primary lower-montane rainforest, termed *wora* by the Maring to distinguish it as an ecological zone from the *kamungga.* There is no such forest in Tsuwenkai territory, although it is present in Kundagai lands in Bokapai and Kinimbong. The term *wora,* however, is sometimes applied to advanced secondary forest near the Kant River to distinguish it from primary high-altitude forest.

EFFECTS OF HUMAN ACTIVITY ON THE ENVIRONMENT

As already noted, the zone of human habitation owes its characteristics largely to the activities of man, having developed on sites cleared for gardens. Humans continue, however, to have an influence on the vegetation long after regrowth has reclaimed their gardens. Primary and secondary forest is exploited for a wide range of vegetation used for technological, ritual, or magical purposes. During the productive life of gardens, the Maring practice selective weeding, generally removing weeds and shrubs but sparing tree seedlings (Rappaport 1968). The result of such selectivity almost certainly produces forest somewhat different in composition and conformation from what it might have been if allowed to develop without interference. Foraging domestic pigs also cause some damage to the forest ground cover, uprooting saplings and shrubs up to altitudes of about 2,000 meters on ridges closest to the settlement. Such interference need not be detrimental to the ecosystem. The succession of secondary growth to climax forest is apparently not prevented, though it may be retarded.

The area of secondary growth and gardens is largely the product of about the last seventy years of continuous occupation (see below). There is evidence, however, to suggest that most if not all the stable grasslands in the Pint Basin are disclimax communities growing on former forested land gardened by earlier inhabitants of the region.

Several Kundagai recognized that stable grassland can develop on sites of former human occupation and attributed the extensive grasslands of the Pint Basin to human activity. The role of fire is also recognized in maintaining grassland, and with this in mind the Jimi Local Government Council has drawn up a by-law forbidding the burning of grassland. The Kundagai actively attempt to reclaim grassland for agricultural use by planting casuarinas. The success of this program was evident in the marked reduction in areas of grassland within the settlement between 1978 and 1985.

Pigs are probably also instrumental in maintaining grassland communities. Except on rare occasions feral pigs are unknown in Tsuwenkai. The effects of pigs on the environment are therefore ultimately a consequence of human occupation. By uprooting tussocks in grassland, pigs may also destroy seedlings of other plants colonizing some areas. Pigs can churn up large areas without killing the grasses themselves.

Factors contributing to the maintenance and reclamation of grassland probably balance one another, for the total area of grassland in the Pint Basin as a whole does not appear to have changed much in the decade 1959–1969 (Healey 1973: 17).

It is not clear, however, whether the amount of Tsuwenkai forest has decreased over recent years. The population appears to be increasing (see below), and one might therefore expect that more gardens are now being cut. It seems likely, nonetheless, that the amount of Kundagai land under cultivation has actually decreased over the last two decades. In the 1940s the Maring as a whole were reduced by about 25 percent in a severe dysentery epidemic (Buchbinder 1973). Then in 1955 or 1956 the Kundagai suffered another epidemic, probably of influenza, which informants say took a heavy toll of life. Before this epidemic they were more numerous than at present. My genealogical data are insufficiently detailed to test this statement statistically, but they do suggest a higher death rate of young and middle-aged adults for the time of sickness than for other periods. It is quite likely, therefore, that informants' statements are accurate and that the Kundagai do not require as much garden land now as in the past.

Although there has been continuous settlement of Tsuwenkai for the last seventy years, the population fluctuated greatly until about 1955–1956. The largest population up to that date was probably in about 1930–1935 or 1940 when the figure may have approximated the present level. In the mid-1950s a major movement from Kinimbong to Tsuwenkai occurred. Since then the population has remained fairly constant or grown somewhat. In the years preceding the last Kundagai *konj kaiko* or pig-killing festival in 1960, however, many more gardens than usual were cleared to support the growing pig herd and to provision feasts associated with the ritual cycle. These years probably saw the most extensive clearing of primary and secondary forest for gardens, a conclusion supported by the large amounts of advanced secondary forest in the upper Kant Valley and on the east bank of the Kant, which are said to have been last gardened prior to the *kaiko*. It seems likely, therefore, that for the present, the area of climax forest is actually increasing slightly as older secondary growth completes its stages of succession.

This situation may not continue for long, as population growth appears to be accelerating, partly because of easier access to medical facilities in Tsuwenkai—an Aid Post was established in 1974—and at the Koinambe Hospital. Undoubtedly the area under cultivation will have to be expanded in the future. However, since there appears to be more secondary growth than the present demands for garden sites require, it will be some time before the Kundagai find it necessary to clear more primary forest or shorten the fallow cycle in existing secondary growth to accommodate more gardens.

Increases in coffee plantings may accelerate population pressure on the land. Coffee is the only cash crop grown in Tsuwenkai and was introduced in the late 1960s. Extensive plantings did not occur until the 1970s, and now most men have at least one small plot of a few score trees.

I cannot estimate the total area of coffee plantations, although it is probably only a very small proportion of the zone of human habitation. Rising coffee prices, however, stimulated greater plantings in the late 1970s. Since coffee is a semipermanent crop, further planting means that increasing amounts of land are being lost to the subsistence economy. This expansion coupled with a growing population will necessitate the cutting of new gardens in the pool of secondary forest in excess of present requirements for fallow land.

POPULATION DENSITY

The overall population density is about 12 persons per square kilometer. The economic density—the ratio of people to areas of garden and fallow land—is 48.25 persons per square kilometer. This figure would be lower if areas of potentially arable primary montane forest were considered in addition to currently and formerly cultivated land.

The overall population density in Bokapai land is about twenty-one persons per square kilometer, and in Kinimbong about nineteen to thirty-one per square kilometer. The lower figure relates only to Kundagai inhabitants, the higher includes about sixty Aikupa clansmen living in association with the Kinimbong Kundagai. I do not have data on the area of arable land in these locales to estimate economic densities, though these are possibly higher than in Tsuwenkai. Overall density throughout Kundagai territory, comprising some fifty-nine square kilometers, is about seventeen persons per square kilometer.

Table 1 compares the population densities of several Maring communities.

The Funggai–Korama of the Simbai Valley have the lowest known overall population density of any Maring group. The Tsuwenkai Kundagai have the next lowest figure, whereas their economic density is just above the mean for all fifteen populations listed. It is notable that the

The Kundagai: Environment and Society

TABLE 1. MARING POPULATION DENSITIES

Population[a]	Number	Territory size (km^2)	Overall pop. density/ km^2	Area arable[b] land(km^2)	Economic density /km^2
Tsuwenkai Kundagai	304	25.0	12.0	6.3	48.3
Bokapai Kundagai	605	28.8	21.0		
Kinimbong Kundagai[c]	90	4.8	19.0		
All Kundagai	999	58.6	17.0		
Tsembaga[d]	203	8.5	23.9	3.3	61.5
Tuguma	255	7.8	32.7	5.8	44.0
Kanump-Kauwil	342	10.6	32.3	6.1	56.1
Kandambent-Namikai	324	11.6	27.9	6.7	48.4
Tsenggamp-Mirimbikai	160	8.2	19.5	2.6	61.5
Bomagai-Anggoiang[e]	130	9.0	14.4	8.1	16.0
Funggai-Korama[f]	155	16.9	9.2	11.5	13.5
Ipai-Makap	200	11.6	17.3	3.2	61.8
Kauwatyi[g]	850	28.5	30.0	23.0	36.9
Manamban[h]	622	28.0	22.0		
Tugumenga[h]	800	25.0	32.0		
Ambrakwi[h]	270	14.5	18.6		
Total	5,310	227.2		73.4	
Mean	354	16.2	22.1	8.1	44.8

[a] See app. 4 for locations. Data source: own material and Buchbinder (1973) unless otherwise noted below.
[b] Includes only land currently under cultivation and fallow.
[c] Excludes allied Aikupa clan, territory size unknown.
[d] From Rappaport's (1968) data the equivalents are: population 204; territory size 8.3 km^2; overall density 24.6/km^2; area arable land 3.5 km^2; economic density 58.3/km^2.
[e] From Clarke's (1971) data the equivalents are: population 154; economic density 32.7/km^2; from which the area of arable land can be computed as 4.7 km^2.
[f] Lowman-Vayda (1971) gives population densities as 9.3 and 28.7/km^2.
[g] From Lowman-Vayda (1971). Areas are computed from recorded densities.
[h] Own data on territory areas; population figures from VPR (1973). Official census for Tugumenga includes Iremban clan cluster. Tugumenga population used here is my own estimate based on official census.

Kauwatyi, who are said to be pressing on the resources of their land (Vayda 1971), have a relatively low economic density, whereas the Tsembaga, whose territory could support a 50-percent increase in population (Rappaport 1968: 94) exhibit one of the highest economic densities in Maring land.

All Maring densities are considerably lower than those recorded in more densely settled regions of the central highlands (Brown and Podolefsky 1976). This fact alone is not enough to support any claims that Maring densities are well within the carrying capacity of the land

and that demographic pressure on resources is unlikely to lead to environmental degradation. The presence of anthropogenic grassland is evidence of such degradation in limited areas. Nonetheless, given extensive reserves of primary and secondary forest, in the Tsuwenkai region at least, it is safe to argue that the territory could support a considerably larger population under present technological and social means of exploitation. Practical and theoretical difficulties associated with the concept of carrying capacity render any attempt to specify population limits superfluous.

KUNDAGAI SOCIAL ORGANIZATION

The Maring number about 8,000 persons, some 5,000 of whom live in the Jimi Valley, the remainder in the Simbai. Like so many labels for ethnic groups in New Guinea the name Maring has no currency among those it identifies. It derives from the term *Malng* by which the Kalam refer to their eastern neighbors. The Maring call their own language Menga or Mengace (Menga speech) but rarely use this label or attach any significance to the social category it denotes. A few young educated men are aware that they are branded "Maring" by anthropologists and administrators. There are, in fact, minor dialectal, cultural, and social-structural differences between groups of Menga-speaking local populations. These differences, in conjunction with similarities to other ethnic groups, make it difficult to conceptualize the Maring as forming a distinctive unit except in terms of sharing such features as a common language, styles of dress, architecture, agriculture, and so on. In certain contexts, nonetheless, people we call Maring do distinguish themselves, from all others, as Menga. The anthropologist finds such ethnic labels useful, but to avoid confusion I will use the established name, Maring, with the caution that no single group can be taken as representative of the whole.

The Maring feel no corporate identity beyond speaking the same language and sharing certain other cultural traits, while the lack of such mutuality is no bar to interaction with members of neighboring Narak, Kalam, Gainj, and other ethnic groups. Ethnic boundaries and defining characteristics have no absolute relevance but are only recognized in particular contexts, and prior to pacification Maring local populations fought one another as vigorously as they did their non-Maring neighbors.

The Maring language is classified as belonging to the Jimi subfamily of the Central Family of the East New Guinea Highlands Stock (Wurm 1964). Linguistically and in other cultural features the Maring are most closely linked with the Narak to the east. Although these two groups also share some linguistic and cultural traits with others of the central highlands to the south, their location and cultural differences nonetheless mark them off as being a highland fringe population.

The Maring population is unevenly distributed, becoming less dense in the lower altitudes of the Simbai and Jimi Valleys. This trend is continued among the neighbors of the Maring in the Jimi, with the Narak and Kandawo populations to the east becoming larger and more densely distributed and the Kalam populations to the west smaller and sparser. The distribution of the Maring and their neighbors is shown in map 1.

The Maring are organized into more than twenty named territorial and political units. Some of these groups in the more thinly settled areas of the Simbai and Jimi are composed of a single clan. Most, however, consist of two or more clans. Ryan (1959) has termed such groups among the Mendi of the southern highlands as *clan clusters,* and various authors on the Maring have adopted this terminology. A clan cluster is a nonexogamous association of clans, ideally acting as a single unit in warfare and ceremonies, although alliances have existed between clan clusters for the purposes of warfare.

The present study was conducted among the Kundagai clan cluster, the westernmost and largest Maring clan cluster.[7] The population is sometimes referred to as Kundagai–Aikupa. The Aikupa are a semi-autonomous clan closely allied to the Kundagai. Some claim that the Aikupa once formed a clan within the Kundagai cluster but established a separate identity following a fight with other Kundagai. Shortly thereafter the Kundagai and Aikupa reestablished friendly relations, intermarriage resumed, and intermingling of garden land occurred. The two groups together fought as major enemies of the Tsembaga clan cluster immediately to the east in the Simbai, and they participated together in *konj kaiko* pig-killing festivals that mark the end of each round of warfare and associated taboos (see Rappaport 1968 for a detailed account of *konj kaiko*). Some informants now consider that the Aikupa are fully reestablished as a clan within the Kundagai although the balance of opinion seems to be against this view.

The Kundagai are atypical of Maring clan clusters in living in more than one distinct settlement. Bokapai and Tsuwenkai are about one hour's walk distant, Tsuwenkai and Kinimbong about two to three hours' walk apart on either side of the Bismarck crest. The only other similarly divided population is the Yomban, with two settlements in the Jimi, Togban, and Matsomp. Other large Maring populations such as the Kauwatyi and Tugumenga have large, sprawling settlement areas, but in neither case would it be meaningful to divide the settlements into distinct units, separated by distances of more than a few minutes' walk apart.

Maring social organization has been analyzed by others (e.g., LiPuma 1980; 1983; 1988; Lowman 1980; Lowman-Vayda 1971; Maclean 1984*b*; 1985; Rappaport 1968; 1969; Vayda and Cook 1964). Here I discuss only those aspects of social organization most relevant to the present study.

In all the Kundagai number about 1,000; 605 in Bokapai (VPR 1973), 304 in Tsuwenkai (my own census), and about 90 in Kinimbong (my own estimate). Perhaps a further 60 inhabitants of Kinimbong comprise the Aikupa clan. The Kundagai clan cluster is composed of eleven clans (fig. 1). Clans range widely in size from a single adult member of the Yimya–Gomkai clan to over 50 adult males (besides women and children) in the dispersed Wendekai clan.

Members of two subclans of Kolomp (1) live in Tsuwenkai, though most are in Bokapai. One small subclan and part of another of the Wendekai clan live in Bokapai, and this is the only clan with members in all three settlements. All Aikupa clansmen live in Kinimbong. No clans are confined in residence to Tsuwenkai, although most members of Wendekai and Atikai live there.

The Kundagai clans do not all claim common descent but are linked on the basis of residence within a common territory. Informants claim that the original or core clans of the Kundagai lived at Kinimbong and dispersed from there to Bokapai and Tsuwenkai. The population was later swelled by immigrants, who by virtue of common residence became included in the Kundagai clan cluster. These immigrant clans moved to Bokapai after brief residence in Kinimbong. The original Kundagai clans are said to have been Kolomp, Wendekai, Amankai, and Atikai. Kolomp subsequently split into two clans (which I have distinguished by the figures "1" and "2" in parentheses). Similarly, Baikai (1) split off from Atikai and settled in Bokapai, while Baikai (2) split off from Wendekai, also to reside in Bokapai. Whereas the fission of the two Kolomp clans is complete and intermarriage is permitted, the fission of the two Baikai clans is incomplete, and neither may intermarry with its parent clan.

Clan	Bokapai	Tsuwenkai	Kinimbong
Aiwaka	XXXXX		
Baikai (1)	XXXXX		
Baikai (2)	XXXXX		
Cembokai	XXXXX		
Yimya-Gomkai	XXXXX		
Kolomp (1)	XXX	XX	
Kolomp (2)	XXXXX		
Wendekai	X	XXX	X
Amankai		XX	XXX
Atikai		XXXX	X
Kwibukai			XXXXX

[a] The crosses indicate approximate proportions, but not sizes of clans based in the settlements.

Figure 1. The Kundagai Clans and Their Locations[a]

The only case of the incorporation of a non-Kundagai clan which is of relevance here concerns the formerly autonomous Kwibukai clan of Kinimbong. Following serious depopulation, Kwibukai clansmen joined the neighboring Kundagai and Tsembaga clan clusters. Their former territory near the Simbai River was incorporated into the Kundagai and Aikupa territories, while an isolated strip of land at Yongga in the Kant Valley was divided between the Kundagai and Tsembaga, the latter gaining the higher-altitude land. Two male descendants of a Kwibukai man who lived in Tsuwenkai have been incorporated into Atikai Kwibukaipe subclan.

The Kundagai recognize a division of their population into two major sections, which I call clan subclusters (cf. Vayda and Cook 1964: 800). A well-defined boundary between Bokapai and Tsuwenkai marks these subclusters as territorial units. Tsuwenkai and Kinimbong constitute one subcluster because the inhabitants of both settlements share the same clan affiliations and rights to land. Kinimbong is also the recent homeland of most residents in Tsuwenkai. Although some Bokapai residents also have equally strong kinship ties and rights to land in Tsuwenkai [notably Baikai (1) and (2) and Kolomp (1) clans], all Bokapai residents are not linked in the same manner. This division into two subclusters is not a function of distance, for Bokapai and Tsuwenkai are closer than Tsuwenkai and Kinimbong. The two subclusters possess separate dance grounds where they hold ceremonies from which members of the other subcluster may be excluded as fellow protagonists. Each subcluster held separate *konj kaiko* ceremonies. In the last *kaiko* of 1960, each group held three separate ceremonies, by coalitions of clans, synchronized to culminate on the same day.

In the past the subclusters also had separate enemies. The major enemies of Tsuwenkai–Kinimbong were the Tsembaga, those of Bokapai being the Ambrakwi. Each subcluster rendered military aid to the other, but in the role of ally, *nokomai,* not as fellow major belligerent, *cenang yu.*

Maring clans are localized, exogamous, ideologically agnatic descent groups. As in many other highland societies, however, there is a fairly high degree of residential mobility among married males, and a rather weak emphasis on agnation. It is not uncommon for a man to live uxorilocally, and if his affines feel he is likely to remain with them they may consider his children to be members of their own clan rather than that of their father, who retains membership in his natal clan. Such persons deriving their affiliations through maternal links and residence share equal rights with fellow clansmen related agnatically (Healey 1979; cf. LiPuma 1988).

There is in Tsuwenkai and Kinimbong a cluster of clans assumed by their members to be cognatically related. It is unnamed and consists of Wendekai, Amankai, and Atikai clans. These are the only Kundagai clans that are said to share a common, but unnamed, ancestor. Informants assume—but hasten to point out that this is merely speculation—that this ancestor had three sons. The descendants of the first son forming Wendekai clan, of the middle son forming Amankai, and of the youngest son forming Atikai. The names of the clans are offered as circumstantial evidence for this supposed origin: Wendekai meaning "first clan," Amankai "middle clan," and Atikai "last clan." As such, the members of the clans assume common agnatic relationships. Although the three groups ideally form an exogamous unit, localized with respect to male and unmarried female members, each group owns its own separate burial and sacrificial groves (*raku*) and is the largest unit within which agnatic ties are invoked when members aid each other in bride and death payments. When members of other units also give this aid, it is usually expressed in terms of cognatic rather than agnatic ties. As such, these groups conform analytically and, in the opinion of their members, also conform to the characteristics of other named clans. Although agnatic relationships are assumed to pertain between these clans, they can be termed a *cognatic cluster* insofar as agnation is not the only or even principal means of relationship.[8] Although no agnatic ties can be demonstrated between members of different clans, other cognatic and affinal ties can be demonstrated by some individuals who apply appropriate kinship terms in preference to presumed agnatic relationships.[9]

These three clans also maintain corporate rights to land in the Simbai and Kant Valleys. Members of Atikai clan claim to hold sole rights to some of this land, though their claim is not recognized by all members of the cluster.

This cognatic cluster contains two further subclusters: Atikai–Baikai (1) and Wendekai–Baikai (2). As noted above, the two Baikai clans of Bokapai split off from their parent clans of Atikai and Wendekai. Although the fission is not complete, it seems reasonable to distinguish the Baikai groups as clans for the same reasons given above for distinguishing Wendekai, Amankai, and Atikai as clans. Members of the Baikai clans are residentially segregated from Atikai and Wendekai and own land neither currently nor formerly belonging to their parent clans. Informants state, however, that members of both Baikai clans have the right to garden on the land of the Wendekai–Amankai–Atikai cognatic cluster in Tsuwenkai and Kinimbong. No Baikai (2) clansmen have done so, although a few Baikai (1) men have made small gardens in Tsuwenkai over the last ten or fifteen years. Although Baikai (1) has retained close ties with Atikai, and bridewealth received by one clan is shared with members of the other, Baikai (2) and Wendekai seem to be much less closely linked. Fission is therefore possibly more advanced in the case of Wendekai and Baikai (2). Although some members of Baikai (1) and Atikai can demonstrate real agnatic links, I am unclear if the same holds for Baikai (2) and Wendekai. My ignorance itself is suggestive that such links are largely unknown.

Informants state that the rule of antigamy between the clans of the cognatic cluster is now becoming relaxed. This relaxation has been greatest between the Wendekai and Atikai and the Wendekai and Amankai clans, and least relaxed between Atikai and Amankai clans, which are sometimes spoken of as *gwi gwi* (brothers) in contrast to Atikai and Wendekai, which are *birua* (TP: affines; literally "enemies"). The cognatic cluster is thus recognized by its members as being in a state of fission into intermarrying clans, while a secondary cognatic cluster of Amankai–Atikai persists.

LiPuma (1988: 111) notes that Wendekai, Amankai, and Atikai are "the most characteristic subclan names." This observation, together with the ideal of antigamy within the Wendekai–Amankai–Atikai cognatic cluster and its subclusters, suggests a stage in a complex process of the transformation of subclans into clans, and of clan fission. Ethnohistorical testimony is insufficient to specify the processes involved, being more an expression of effect than of cause or underlying structural and ideological principles. LiPuma (1988: 140 ff.) addresses the issue of the growth and decline of agnatic units in some detail, in terms of a model of the sharing and exchange of culturally defined substance (maternal blood and paternal "grease") within and across clan lines. Although his model is persuasive, its evidential basis is unclear. The model runs into operational difficulties when he attempts to link the process of fusion and fission to the capacity of agnatic groups autonomously to meet demands of exchange of wealth of goods for women. This is so because his exposition does not adequately link the discussion of exchange to the contingent and practical, as contrasted with ideological, structures of production for exchange. A central concern of my own analysis is to interweave the influence of both cultural, material, and contingent factors in the articulation of production with exchange.

POPULATION AND SETTLEMENT PATTERNS

During fieldwork the population of Tsuwenkai fluctuated between 286 in early 1974 and 273 later in the year. Table 2 gives further details of the population as it was in the last few months of fieldwork.

The greatest source of population changes during 1973–1974 was births (thirteen males, two females) and the movements of young men on work contracts (seven returned, seventeen departed). Other sources of change included deaths (three women), the departure of widows and their children for their natal settlements, and the temporary move of one family to Kinimbong to escape the molestation of witches (in all, four adults and eleven children).

The sex ratio (including absentees) is 115 males per 100 females. Forty-one percent of the population is aged under fifteen years. These ratios are within the range of ratios reported from the Simbai Maring (Buchbinder 1973: 64). The Tsuwenkai population triangle is thus similar to those of the Simbai and suggests that the Kundagai population experiences a rather slow growth rate (despite the disproportionately high birth rate in 1973–1974).

Houses are dispersed for about 2.5 kilometers along the flanks of the

TABLE 2. TSUWENKAI POPULATION[a]

A.	RESIDENTS, 1973-1974	
	1. Males:	
	Married, widowers	47
	Unmarried over 15 years	11
	Subtotal:	
	Aged over 15 years	58
	Under 15 years	74
	Total males:	132
	2. Females:	
	Married, widows of Tsuwenkai clans	22
	Married, widows of non-Tsuwenkai clans	50
	Subtotal:	
	Married, widows	72
	Unmarried over 15 years	17
	Subtotal:	
	Aged over 15 years	89
	Under 15 years	52
	Total females:	141
	3. Total resident population:	273
B.	ABSENTEES	
	Adult males (on coastal plantations etc.):	31
C.	TOTAL TSUWENKAI-BASED POPULATION:	304

[a] Estimated ages, based on appearance, stated birth times in relation to dated historical events, or deduced from a consideration of birth order and postpartum taboo (approx. 3 years) in relation to estimated birth dates of siblings and parents.

Kant–Mieng divide. They are mostly grouped into small homesteads comprising one to four houses within a fenced yard to prevent the entry of pigs. A small kitchen garden sometimes abuts onto the yard. Residential segregation of the sexes is general but by no means as prevalent as in some parts of the highlands. Male children over the age of about seven or eight years spend increasing amounts of time in their father's or other older male kinsmen's houses. Some men build separate shelters for their pigs at a distance from homesteads, but generally a man's pigs spend the night in a fenced-off partition in the house of one of his female dependents. Fenced lanes from the women's houses allow the pigs access to foraging land beyond the homestead yard. Co-wives and their children of a polygynist invariably live in separate houses.

All but a few men's houses are of the traditional construction. Typically such houses are low, roughly rectangular or oval in plan, with a turtle-backed roof of pandanus fronds.

Homesteads are mostly situated on the crests or upper flanks of lateral ridges running toward the Kant River and are between about 1,500 and 1,820 meters altitude. Most homesteads are close to the forest edge. Areas between homesteads are under cultivation or fallow, with a few patches of grassland and disturbed primary forest (see map 2).

Except for Kolomp (1) householders there is little pattern in house sites on the basis of clan affiliations. The few Kolomp clansmen have built south of Renmapai Creek. With them live one Wendekai householder and an aged Kalam man living sororilocally. There is a tendency for Atikai homesteads to be sited further upstream along the Kant Valley than Wendekai homesteads, but it is not possible to draw a clear dividing line between the residences of these clans. Amankai homesteads are scattered from Tsuwenkai ridge to Randenak, the northern extremity of Tsuwenkai settlement.

This mixed pattern is in accord with the ideal of agnation and corporate territory of the Wendekai–Amankai–Atikai cognatic cluster. This pattern contrasts with that described for other Maring settlements (Clarke 1971; Healey 1973; Maclean 1984*b*) where householders of each clan tend to build close to one another.

MARRIAGE PATTERNS

There is an explicit as well as statistical preference for marriage within the clan cluster (cf. Rappaport 1969: 121; LiPuma 1988). Over time there has been some change in marriage patterns (app. 1). Since around the time of contact with the government in 1956 there has been a trend toward greater intermarriage within the Kundagai–Aikupa population. Marriage with the Simbai Kalam and Maring, and with Maring settlements upstream in the Jimi, has always been prevalent. Since the mid-1950s, however, intermarriages with lower-Simbai (Maring) populations have decreased at the expense of relations with upper-Simbai (Kalam) groups. Marriage ties to Up-Jimi settlements, notably neighboring Kompiai, have increased considerably since that date.

Ideally, the Maring do not marry major enemies, *cenang yu* (literally "axe men"). Besides their major enemies, the Tsembaga and Ambrakwi, the Kundagai also fought other clan clusters as allies of kinsmen of yet other populations. Men of one local group might therefore find themselves on opposing sides, but only in the role of allies of the respective major enemies, never as major belligerents themselves.

Over the last fifty or so years of hostilities several intermarriages between the Tsuwenkai Kundagai and the Ambrakwi, and the Bokapai Kundagai and the Tsembaga, have occurred. These marriages do not transgress the rule of avoiding intermarriage between major enemies since the Tsuwenkai Kundagai fought the Ambrakwi only as allies of Bokapai kin, who in turn fought the Tsembaga as allies of Tsuwenkai men.

Major enemies observe taboos on eating the produce of each other's territories and on sharing the same fires. Failure to observe these taboos invites sickness or even death sent by angry ancestral spirits, and women married to *cenang yu* are considered vulnerable to such attacks, as are men who merely visit enemy communities. Maring ideas of the supernatural and taboos thus serve to isolate enemy populations, inhibiting intermarriage and a variety of other contacts resulting from the marriage bond. Nonetheless, the exchange of women is a recognized principle in the formal establishment of friendly relations between formerly hostile groups. To establish peace, each enemy group sends to the other as many women as men were killed by them in warfare.

Rappaport (1969: 128) notes that in 1963 the Tsembaga were already considering the exchange of women with the Kundagai to establish peace. Despite a marriage between a Kundagai girl and a Tsembaga in 1974—a union opposed by the bride's kin—the exchange of women to formally establish peaceful relations between the two populations remained unresolved in 1985.

Maring marriage patterns differ markedly from those of some other highland groups, such as the Mae Enga, who told Meggitt (1964: 218), "We marry the people we fight." The avoidance of such marriages may correlate with a less marked antagonism between the sexes and a milder concern with the polluting capacities of women, as Meggitt (1964) has suggested.

By contrast, men state that the ideal marriage is either contracted within the clan cluster or with allies. The latter are called *nokomai*, literally "road" or "track," but this was also explained to mean "the way or road of the ancestors, along which flow women, pigs, and other valuables." The principal *nokomai* groups of the Tsuwenkai and Kinimbong Kundagai are the Kundagai of Bokapai, the Kauwatyi and, to a lesser extent, the Cenda, Manamban, Tuguma, and Kanump–Kauwil. These, and to a lesser extent some other Maring and Kalam groups, were those from whom military aid was sought. Such assistance was reciprocal. Aid in war was negotiated individually between kinsmen. The number of allies who might be recruited depended mainly upon the extent of intermarriage and the distance between groups. Thus the Tsuwenkai and Kinimbong Kundagai received most aid in war from the Bokapai Kundagai and the Kauwatyi, among whom they had the greatest number of affines and cognates, and whose settlements are among the closest to Tsuwenkai and Kinimbong. Some 94.2 percent of existing marriages contracted outside the Kundagai subcluster settled in Tsuwenkai and Kinimbong are with allies, 2.3 percent are with enemies (including the Ambrakwi in this category), and 3.4 percent—all contracted since the suppression of warfare—are with populations beyond the limits of Kundagai alliance in warfare.

Rappaport (1969) and LiPuma (1988) have discussed Maring marriage arrangements in detail. Here it need only be noted that the ideal form of marriage is one arranged by the agnates of a girl or young man. In this way they are able to establish affinal links in the most economically and politically advantageous location. In practice, many young people form romantic attachments leading to marriages that may not meet with their agnates' approval. Marriages are often unstable until the birth of children.

I determined the reasons for marriage in a nonrandom sample of thirty-six cases (table 3) (see also Lowman-Vayda 1971 for a list of reasons men give for offering women to specific clans).

There are other means of acquiring a wife not revealed in the table. Kundagai claim that the sororate, wherein a man is permitted to marry a clan sister of his deceased wife, is occasionally practiced.[10] Marriage by capture has occurred at odd times in the past, when women of enemy populations found trespassing were given in marriage to allies. Rappaport (1969) has identified the sole prescriptive marriage rule among the Maring, whereby the daughter of a woman's son is given in marriage to her paternal grandmother's natal subclan. Several marriages recorded in Kundagai genealogies conform to this pattern but were not included in the sample on which the table is based. Kundagai genealogical material indicates, however, that the rule is not often adhered to, as Rappaport (1969) also notes for the Tsembaga, and it seems inappropriate to refer to the pattern as a "prescriptive rule."

TABLE 3. REASONS FOR KUNDAGAI MARRIAGES

Reason	No. of cases	%	Comments
1. Stealing the bride	11	30.5	Comparable to Tsembaga rate (Rappaport 1969). So termed when union made without consent of woman's agnates. Usually her initiative.
2. Sister exchange	10	27.8	Real or classificatory Z. More than twice the rate reported by LiPuma (1988: 167) for the Kauwatyi.
3. Widow inheritance	1	2.8	W of deceased real B. Classificatory clan brothers may also inherit a widow.
4. Blood debts	2	5.6	Compensation for murder, accidental killing.
5. Reward payment	1	2.8	In settlement of dispute arising from failure of woman's agnates to pay assassination fee of shells to the H who killed a witch on their behalf. Woman given in lieu of payment.
6. Land payment	7	10.4	Five to Bokapai in return for land grants. Two to Cenda as part of larger payment for land.
7. Bestowal	3	8.3	One by B as sign of hospitality to refugees sheltered in Tsuwenkai. One by B in appreciation for man's service as woman's guardian; woman given to S of guardian. One by F to a Tsuwenkai man to keep her nearby for support in F's old age.
8. Rearing the Bride	1	2.8	Rappaport (1969) notes that the Kalam sometimes send a young girl to her prospective groom's parents some years before she is married. This woman as a child had been cared for by her MZS at Kumbruf. He asked for the right, in view of his care, to bestow her on his FBS of Gondomben. Prof. Bulmer (personal communication) has not encountered this practice in the Kaironk. This case could be included under item 7.

To conclude this section I would note that discussion of formal patterns and rules of marriage reveals little about the choices underlying particular marriages, or the structured embeddedness of marriage within a system of social reproduction (see also LiPuma 1988). Within the constraints on marriage imposed by cultural understandings of incest, clan exogamy, and nonmarriageable kin, there remains a wide field of choice of particular marriage partners. Whether a particular marriage can be classified as sister exchange, widow inheritance, blood debt, and so on is, in at least some cases, a post hoc rationalization for a marriage that may have begun as an instance of "stealing the bride." More generally, reasons given by Maring or anthropologists for marriage, as a set of typologies, may be somewhat epiphenomenal to the exercise of strategic choices by those involved in contracting marriages. Factors influencing men's decisions on their own or their clansmen's choice of spouse include the control potential affines exercise over valued economic and political resources.

SOCIAL STATUS

Contrary to the usual stereotype of highlands societies the Maring do not place an emphasis on the manipulation of wealth and prestations in public ceremonies as an attribute of a big-man, *yu-yondoi* (literally "man large"). The Maring big-man achieves his status by virtue of his maturity, vigor, temperament, relationship to powerful clansmen, and ability to communicate with his fellows or the spirits (see also Lowman-Vayda 1971; and Rappaport 1968: 28 ff.).

The Kundagai recognize three categories of big-man.[11] These are:

1. *Bamp kunda yu,* Fight Magic Man
2. *Tep yu,* Big-man
3. *Mengr yu,* Leading Warrior.

Other positions of some influence are *rawa yu* (Ancestor Spirit Man or Medium) and *kunkace yu* (Spirit Woman Man or Shaman). Such men, who form important channels of communication between the living and certain spirits, are not big-men unless they also fall into one of the above three categories. Some Maring also recognize the *aram ku yu* or Fight Medicine Man, but the functions of this specialist among the Kundagai seem to be performed by the *bamp kunda yu* without the two roles being distinguished (cf. Lowman-Vayda 1971: 341).

The *bamp kunda yu* is responsible for the protection of warriors and the enhancing of their strength. It is also he who sorcerizes the enemy and performs magic in connection with *konj kaiko* ceremonies. There are five *bamp kunda yu* in Tsuwenkai. An aging specialist chooses a successor and coaches him in the esoteric knowledge that is the sole preserve of the *bamp kunda yu.* Nowadays younger men often refuse to accept such an invitation because of the limited relevance of status received and the numerous and onerous dietary taboos. In the very revelation of secrets to his successor, the specialist dissipates his vitality and hastens his own rapid decline and death.

Tep yus, literally "Talk Men," are persuasive talkers. They achieve their big-man status by their oratorical skill and their ability to influence public opinion and mobilize group activities through example and exhortation. They should also be men of vigor and commanding appearance and strong fighters. *Tep yu* are instrumental in initiating warfare and preparations for *konj kaiko*. There are two surviving *tep yu* in Tsuwenkai.

Because *bamp kunda yu* and *tep yu* are instrumental in protecting warriors, sorcerizing the enemy, and persuading their fellows to engage in hostilities, they are also invariably *mengr yu*. The term literally means "Shell Man" and is derived from the custom of the enemy of offering a reward of shells for their assassination. *Bamp kunda yu* and *tep yu* are singled out for killing because it is thought that with their removal the *yu aure* ("man nothing" or ordinary men), lacking magical and moral support, will be killed easily. Other men, however, may also achieve *mengr yu* status by demonstrating their strength, courage, and endurance on the fight ground. Such men, valued as warriors, may become *mengr yu* even if the enemy is not known to have offered a bribe for their assassination. Informants named five *mengr yu* who were not also *bamp kunda yu* or *tep yu*.

The duties of Kundagai *bamp kunda yu* are now confined to the performance of magic to enhance the strength and beauty of dancers at ceremonies. With the cessation of warfare *bamp kunda yu* and *mengr yu* have no influence over others, other than the persuasive talents they may possess. By contrast, *tep yu* are still important in the molding of public opinion, arbitrating disputes, and initiating communal activities.

The Maring do not have a well-developed hierarchy of status, nor do they compete with one another for status, unlike the pattern that has become familiar in the central-highlands literature (e.g., Strathern 1971). The big-man is therefore not constrained continually to negotiate and legitimize his status through performance or demonstration of his ability. Thus it was that the aged Planc, in his eighties when I last saw him in 1978, and largely confined to his house yard, was still spoken of respectfully as a current *tep yu*.

A lazy man, with few or poor gardens and no pigs, may be called *rukunemp yu,* "rubbish man," but no one would identify any in Tsuwenkai. Such men are also liable to be considered witches, and reluctance to name any *rukunemp yu* may have stemmed from a desire to avoid giving offence to any witches.

Following government contact new positions of political office were created. *Bosbois* were appointed by early patrols in 1956, but the higher posts of *tultul* and *luluai* were not assigned until 1960. Those appointed *bosboi* were generally younger men who were not big-men. *Tultuls* and *luluais* were generally big-men, mainly of the *tep yu* category. Government appointees had little influence unless they were already *tep yu*. The former *luluai* for Tsuwenkai was a rising *tep yu* (and is now the leading *tep yu*). On the establishment of the Jimi Local Government Council in 1966 he was elected councillor (*kaunsil*) but passed this office to his brother's son in 1967, who has retained the office ever since.

Traditional big-men have no power to demand obedience. Kaunsils often claim such power, arguing that they are the local elected representatives of the government administrative officer (*kiap*), who demonstrably has power to command obedience. Although the present Tsuwenkai kaunsil does not enjoy total obedience to his directives, he possesses a greater measure of coercive power than the traditional big-man. This does not appear to be because people fear the anger of the kiap should the kaunsil be disobeyed[12] so much as because of the man's personal qualities, well suited to his position as a political entrepreneur in a new field of extra-village relations. The kaunsil has appointed as his deputies three Committee members (*komitis*). Neither the kaunsil nor komitis are regarded as big-men. Informants state that such offices in themselves do not confer big-man status. Although Council officebearers are seen as acting on the community's behalf, they have not usurped the position of the *tep yu* in intracommunity affairs. In such matters, any man, regardless of status, may express his opinion, and decision making is reached by consensus, not by the fiat of big-man, kaunsil, or komiti. Only in matters concerning the government and other outside organizations or individuals does the kaunsil wield any coercive power. Thus, for instance, although the kaunsil may order people to work on the government road, he cannot order them to work in his coffee gardens,[13] however much he may welcome such aid.

There are two categories of people considered to be deviant in some respects. These are "madmen" and witches. Clarke (1973) has discussed the occurrence of temporary madness among the Maring. Several Tsuwenkai men and one woman were said to suffer bouts of temporary madness. The "madman," *yu plim*, is not regarded as responsible for his actions. His condition is caused by a *menjawai* forest demon plugging a man's ears with its fingers, making him deaf (*plim*). Deafness is synonymous with madness. Once the condition has passed, within a few days at the most, the "madman" is accepted back into normal social interaction and is in no way discriminated against.

One man is considered to be permanently *plim* because of his odd behavior. He became thus while serving a jail sentence shortly after contact. His "madness" manifests itself in an almost constant good humor. He is reputedly incapable of conducting a serious conversation—a reputation I found to be exaggerated—and is regarded as a man of infinite wit. Because he is believed to be simple-minded, he is not entrusted with valuable possessions. Periodically he indulges in the typically wild behavior of the *yu plim*.

One other adult male and at least five youths and boys are sometimes referred to as *plim,* not because they act in an unrestrained or crazy way but because of apparent partial or complete deafness. Some of the boys show mild to severe ataxia and slight squint. It is probable that the younger males are suffering from varying degrees of cretinism, known to be endemic to the Jimi, and possibly due to the replacement of native salts by uniodized trade salt (Buchbinder 1973; Paine 1971; Pharoah 1971). The younger males are occasionally teased or admonished when orders or questions put to them go unheeded. The adult male is treated with some caution, but this is because he is believed to be a witch.

The Kundagai are preoccupied with witches, *kwimp*, which they consider to be more numerous than in the past. They attribute this increase to the modern practice of burying the dead instead of exposing them on platforms until the flesh has rotted away. A dead person's kin would guard the platform at night if the death was attributed to witchcraft and shoot animal or human intruders, considered to be witches come to feed on the corpse. Traps set around the platform accounted for other witch-visitors. Fear of imprisonment now also inhibits the slaying of a witch in its human form, although animals believed to be disguised witches are still killed. Obviously, the believed increase in the incidence of witches is to be explained in other terms, but this is best attempted elsewhere.

Witches are said to be motivated to attack their victims from anger over some real or imagined slight, such as failure to share food or bridewealth.

Witchcraft is a delicate subject among the Kundagai. Only one male (the partially deaf man mentioned above) and an aged widow appear to be identified as witches by most Kundagai. Both suspects have publicly admitted to practicing witchcraft, as have several others. Only my closest friends and associates were prepared to name other suspects—a further ten. Doubtless many Kundagai would not agree to all these identifications but might add other names. Most suspects are older women and are considered to be responsible for generally nonlethal attacks. The man and the widow mentioned above are the most feared of all Tsuwenkai witches and are avoided by most Kundagai if this can be done without giving offence, which might invite a witchcraft attack.

THE SPIRIT WORLD[14]

Maring spirits, *rawa*, fall into two main categories—shades of the dead and autochthonous spirits. Crosscutting these categories is a further distinction between spirits of the lower altitudes and those of higher altitudes.

The only class of spirits believed to inhabit the full range of Kundagai territory is the *rawa menjawai* or *mandawai*. This is a wild and dangerous forest demon living mainly in the primary forest. It is hostile to man, sending him mad or shooting invisible objects into his body which cause sickness, if disturbed by the intrusion of men into its haunts.

Inhabiting the high-altitude primary forest, *kamungga* are a host of spirits known as *rawa meki*, "spirits red." The Tsembaga, Funggai, and Kauwatyi Maring consider them to be the spirits of those killed in war (Rappaport 1968; Lowman-Vayda 1971). Most Kundagai denied that the *rawa meki* are of human origin, claiming they have always existed. An elderly shaman stated, however, that the spirits of those killed in warfare went to join the *rawa meki*, though there has always been a nucleus of these spirits of nonhuman origin.

Two further spirits, each consisting of a single member, live in the *kamungga*. These are the Kunkace Ambra (Smoke Woman) or Piakai Ambra (Above Woman), and Ambenggi.

Lowman-Vayda (1971) states that the Kunkace Ambra first entered the Maring pantheon of spirits in about the early 1940s, when she possessed several men in the Simbai and Jimi. The arrival of the Kunkace Ambra among the Kundagai may have been somewhat earlier, as I was told of one man who was possessed by the spirit early this century.

The Kundagai generally refer to this spirit by the alternative name,

Piakai Ambra, a reference to her abode in high places (*piak* meaning "above"). She periodically possesses men, making them temporarily mad. After their period of initiation is over such men become *kunkace yu*, shamans, who under the influence of bespelled cigarettes are able to communicate with the Piakai Ambra. She acts as an intermediary between the living and spirits of the dead, revealing to the shaman, for instance, those spirits responsible for sickness and to whom sacrifices must be made.[15]

Contrary to the Tsembaga view (Rappaport 1968), the Piakai Ambra of the Kundagai is associated with various animals, including marsupials and eels. The association of spirits with animals will be further discussed in chapter 3.

Ambenggi is a spirit of the *kamungga*, specific only to the Kundagai. He is described as a huge wild boar, although he is occasionally seen in the guise of a skinny old man. He roams the forest from Kinimbong to Bokapai, sleeping sometimes in a lair under a rock by the Minjeki Creek near Tsuwenkai. In deference to him the Kundagai observe a taboo on the eating of feral pigs. This causes the Tsuwenkai Kundagai little inconvenience, as feral pigs rarely enter their domain, but they are found near the Simbai River at Kinimbong, and near the Jimi River below Bokapai. It seems that the Kundagai have never been very scrupulous in their observance of this taboo, and nowadays many people, especially the young and Christians, ignore it. However, Mount Konjmoi (meaning "pig taboo"), near Ambenggi's lair in the Minjeki Valley, is still strongly associated with the spirit, and even domestic pigs should not be killed or cooked too close to the forest edge there.

Ambenggi is regarded as being an essentially benevolent spirit who aids the Kundagai in warfare. Occasionally, however, when hungry for meat, he sends sickness on the living, who must sacrifice wild mammals to induce him to withdraw the sickness.

Spirits of the lower altitudes, *wora*, are collectively termed *rawa mai*. *Mai* is used to indicate animals of female gender, but in other contexts the term implies maturity or productivity. This terminology is consistent with the Maring conception of *rawa mai* as being concerned with fertility.

Two types of *rawa mai*, called *koipa* and *manggiang*, live in association, close to settlements in large trees and rock holes. *Koipa* were never human, but informants are divided on the origins of *manggiang*, some saying that they have always existed, others that they are the spirits of the dead. These spirits may be referred to collectively as *koipa-manggiang*. The Tsembaga view this category as comprising a single spirit of nonhuman origin (Rappaport 1968: 38). Like the Piakai Ambra, the *koipa-manggiang* ensure the health and fertility of people, pigs, and crops.

Also living in the lower altitudes are the *rawa tukump* ("spirit mold or rot"). These are spirits of the dead and are viewed by the Kundagai as malevolent beings; they enter the bodies of the living to cause sickness that may lead to death unless they are magically expelled. A second type of *rawa tukump*, called *rawa tukump rakai* or *rawa awua* ("spirit other"), also inhabit the lower altitudes. These are spirits of the dead of enemy clan clusters, even more dangerous than *rawa tukump*.

Although some class spirits of the dead as either *rawa meki* or *rawa tukump*, most informants assert that these spirits are known simply as *rawa*. Male spirits of the same or first ascending generations reside in the high-altitude forest, while spirits of all-female kin and male kin of the second and beyond ascending generations live in valley bottom forests. Thus, say the Kundagai, there is a continual movement of ancestral male spirits from the high to low altitudes as the spirits of the dead of subsequent generations join the *rawa meki* in the high forest. Spirits of the dead live at greater distance from the living than do other types of spirit. The Piakai Ambra, *rawa meki*, and *rawa koipa-manggiang* act as intermediaries between the spirits of the dead and the living. If an ancestral spirit hungers after pork or wishes to punish the living who neglect to honor it with sacrifices or otherwise offend, it requests the *rawa meki* or *koipa-manggiang* to send sickness. *Koipa-manggiang* also act as intermediaries between the *rawa tukump* and the living and, although the *rawa tukump* are directly able to affect the living, the *koipa-manggiang* may request them to desist in their attacks. [The Tsembaga believe that the reverse situation pertains (Rappaport 1968).]

One of the reasons that spirits, particularly the *rawa meki*, may visit sickness or even death upon the living is that men disturb them by clearing their virgin forest retreat or by making too much noise. This belief acts as a constraint on the clearing of primary forest by the Kundagai, although people add that the low productivity of gardens cleared from primary forest does not justify the additional time and effort involved in felling large trees. Spirits can be requested to vacate tracts of forest if these need to be cleared. As already noted, however, the Kundagai have ample fallow land for their present requirements and are therefore under little pressure to clear primary forest.

The belief that spirits are associated with various categories of wild animals may influence hunting intensity to some extent, as will be discussed in chapter 3. Arboreal marsupials and rodents and birds, notably plume-bearing species and large ground birds, are described as the "pigs" of the *rawa meki,* Ambenggi, and the Piakai Ambra. Larger game mammals and birds, and plume-bearing birds of lower altitudes, are the "pigs" of the *rawa mai,* whereas eels are the "pigs" of the Piakai Ambra and the *koipa-manggiang* spirits. All wild creatures, but especially feral pigs and cassowaries, are the "pigs" of the *menjawai* demon. All classes of spirits are angered if a hunter kills many larger animals and may punish him or his family with sickness.

To summarize, I have discussed at some length various aspects of Kundagai social organization and other ethnographic data of relevance to subsequent chapters. I have noted that some finer details of the ethnography of the Kundagai differ somewhat from data of other anthropologists working elsewhere among the Maring. Variations in some details of Maring ethnography might be explained by reference to the apparently varied origins of different groups, the influence of an ecologically diverse habitat, and by the inevitable differences in behavior and beliefs that might be expected in a large population of people who do not seek any corporate identity in terms of language, beliefs, or practices.

A HISTORY OF SETTLEMENT

Tsuwenkai has been occupied permanently for a relatively short time, yet oral traditions indicate sporadic settlement of some antiquity. Insofar as this history has a bearing on territorial divisions and rights to resources, a brief summary of the history of settlement will be given here. An expanded account is given elsewhere (Healey 1985c).

The earliest known inhabitants of the Tsuwenkai area were of the Kolomp clan and are thought to have come originally from Kinimbong. On genealogical and biogeographic evidence this settlement probably occurred as much as two hundred years ago. Kolomp residence was apparently brief and came to a sudden end when a devastating mystical sickness sent by the Pig Spirit, Ambenggi, descended on the Kolomp. Survivors of the sickness fled to the Simbai and several Maring and Narak settlements in the Jimi. Some clansmen settled between Bokapai and Kandambiamp and subsequently constituted the separate Kolomp (2) clan. Those who took refuge in Bokapai formed the nucleus of the

Kolomp (1) clan, while another contingent became incorporated into the Cenda clan cluster of Koinambe as the still-surviving Kolomp clan. Some of the former Tsuwenkai Kolomp land became part of the Cenda territory.

Since the first Kolomp settlement, emigrants from Simbai Maring, and Kalam clans established several short-lived settlements in the Kant Valley before moving on to Bokapai, Koinambe, and Wum. Since the late 1890s or early 1900s a small contingent of Kolomp (1) clansmen have maintained a permanent settlement in the lower Kant Valley.

Around 1870 an Atikai man left Kinimbong after a bitter argument there and settled briefly on Tsuwenkai ridge, to which he was granted primary use rights by the Kolomp (1) occupants. The Atikai man later moved to Bokapai where his descendants form the Baikai (1) clan.

During the first Kundagai–Tsembaga war in about 1915–1920, several Kinimbong Kundagai moved to Tsuwenkai to escape Tsembaga raiding parties. Shortly after this war the Kinimbong Kundagai had a brief but bloody fight with their Aikupa allies, when a group of Aikupa clansmen, bribed by the Tsembaga, attempted to assassinate a leading Kundagai big-man. Immediately after this fight the Bokapai Kundagai advised their Kinimbong compatriots to relocate in Tsuwenkai to escape possible further attacks from the Aikupa, Tsembaga, and their allies. This movement of the early 1920s constituted the first major settlement of Tsuwenkai. The new settlers found that much of the area had reverted to climax forest after the emigration of most of the Kolomp and other, short-term residents.

In the 1940s war again broke out between the Kundagai and Tsembaga. By this time the rift between the Kundagai and Aikupa had been repaired, and exchanges of women and the intermingling of garden land consolidated the alliance.

Following the *konj kaiko* in about 1950–1952 after this latest war with the Tsembaga, many Kundagai returned to Kinimbong, where they were subjected to renewed attacks by Tsembaga raiding parties seeking to balance the score of deaths suffered in the 1940s war. In the mid-1950s hostilities escalated to major warfare, which culminated in the rout of the Tsembaga.

At about this time the Kundagai experienced their first contact with Europeans. In 1954 or 1955 Bokapai was visited by a government patrol, and in late 1955 or early 1956 the Kinimbong Kundagai saw Mr. Jim McKinnon, who prospected for gold in the Kumbruf area of the Simbai.

The Kundagai: Environment and Society

In 1956, while the Tsembaga were still in exile, an epidemic, possibly of influenza, broke out in Kinimbong. The sickness was attributed to the sorcery of the Tsembaga and their allies, sent in retribution for the fatalities they had suffered in the war. To escape its effects many Kundagai left Kinimbong and joined those who had remained in Tsuwenkai. Most members of the Aikupa and Amankai clans remained in Kinimbong, as did a few Wendekai and Atikai. The majority of those who came to Tsuwenkai at this time have remained until the present, although a few maintain houses in Kinimbong, which they visit occasionally to tend gardens and tree crops. Shortly after the outbreak of the sickness, Kinimbong and Tsuwenkai were visited for the first time by a government patrol.

On moving to Tsuwenkai the Kundagai began preparations for a *konj kaiko* following the Tsembaga war. The Kundagai *kaiko* culminated on Christmas Day in 1960, suggesting the ready acceptance of mission influence in the Jimi. An Anglican mission station had been established at Koinambe only that year, although Solomon Island Brothers had set up a temporary base in Bokapai two years before.

TERRITORIALITY AND REDISTRIBUTION OF LAND RIGHTS

The present boundaries of Tsuwenkai territory (map 3) encompass an area appreciably larger than the earliest known territory held by the Wendekai–Amankai–Atikai cognatic cluster and the original Kolomp settlers. Wendekai, Amankai, and Atikai clans jointly owned the land stretching from the Simbai River at Kinimbong over the Bismarck crest to the Kant River. In the Kant Valley this territory was bounded in the west by the Gacambo saddle and in the east by Tembi Creek. All land southward from here west of the Kant belonged to the Kolomp, whose territory also included Yongga. On the departure of the Kolomp the autonomous Kwibukai clan from near Kinimbong gained ownership of Yongga, though by what means is forgotten. When the Kwibukai clan ceased to exist as an independent population, the upper part of Yongga was incorporated into Tsembaga territory when some Kwibukai joined that clan cluster. The rest became Kundagai land, and the two adult male descendants of Kwibukai clan now resident in Tsuwenkai are today "fathers of the land" of the lower part of Yongga.

The Maring term translated as "fathers of the land" is *ren kump ni yoko* (literally, "land belly father its"). "Title holder" is an inappropri-

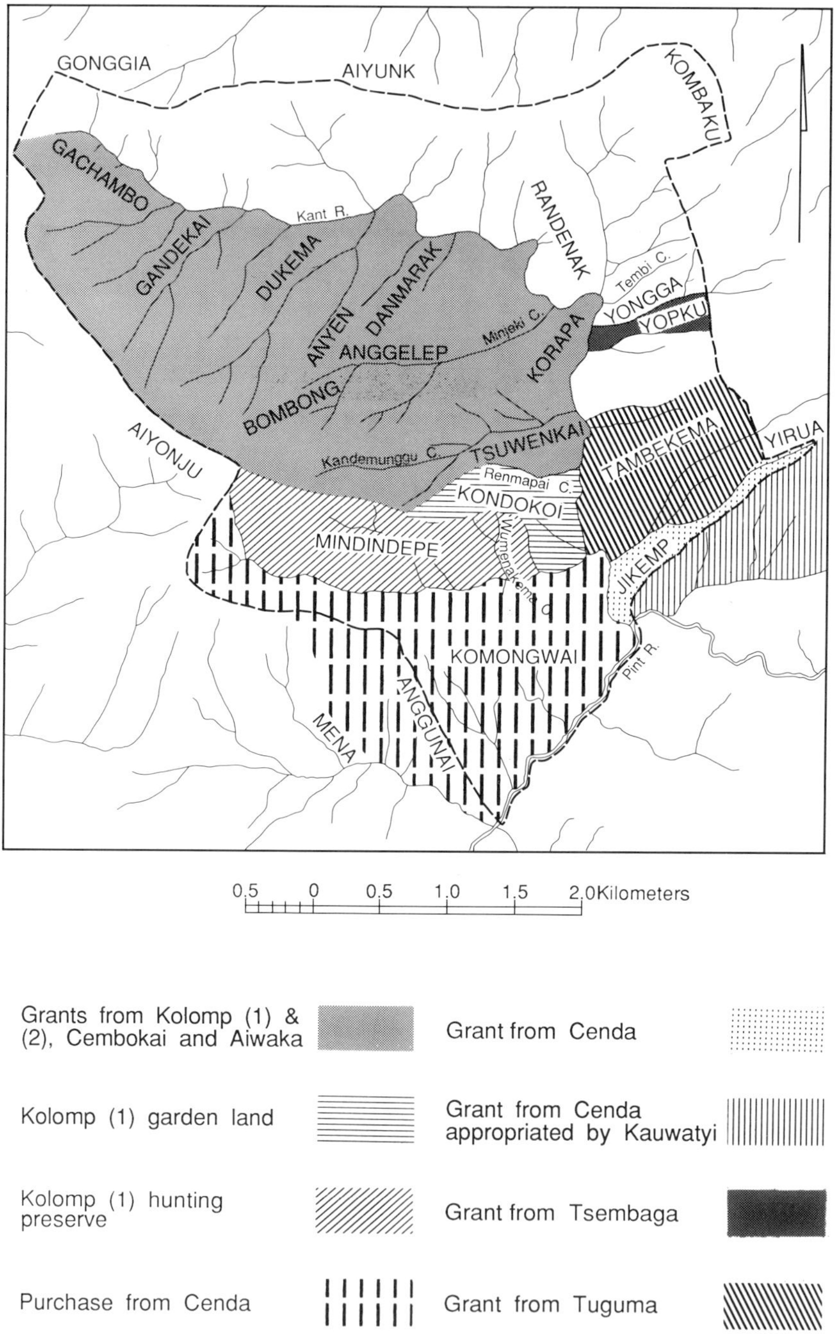

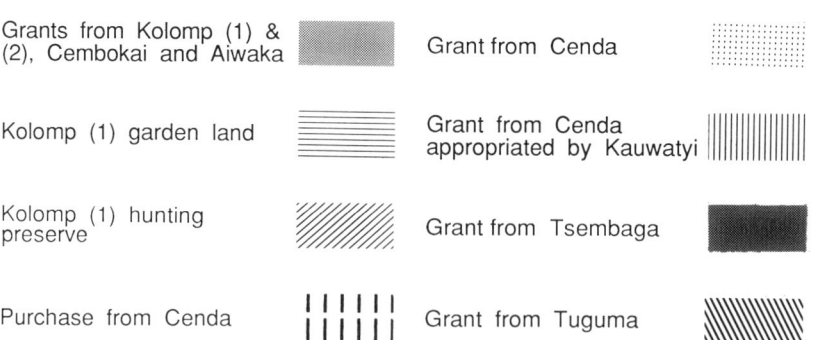

Map 3. Tsuwenkai Geographic Features and Territories

ate translation, as this implies a sense of absolute ownership. "Fathers of the land" are ultimate custodians of rights to the land. Often, however, they do not retain exclusive, or even primary, usufruct rights, for they may make grants of land to others. The underlying principle of land grants is that it is primary use rights to land which are generally transferred, not absolute custodianship. "Fathers of the land" may thus cede primary usufruct rights, retaining only residual rights. Recipients of primary rights may themselves extend use rights to other individuals or groups, or even make subsidiary grants to third parties. Individual and corporate rights to land thus operate at several levels, being residual or active, older and more general and diffuse, recent or in relation to more clearly defined sites or particular kinds of resources. In certain circumstances, "fathers of the land" may relinquish even residual rights to land which thereby are transferred to new custodians.

The Kundagai recognize several principles by which land rights may be transferred to other groups or individuals. Rights may be given in perpetuity or temporarily for purposes of occupancy or gardening. Rappaport (1968) and LiPuma (1988) have discussed both types of grants. I am concerned here with grants in perpetuity, especially of more extensive tracts of land. These grants are usually made in connection with marriages, but groups can also obtain de jure rights in exchange for a prestation of valuables, or de facto rights that in time come to be regarded as de jure by the occupation of *ren wabera,* "deserted land."

Affinal transfers of land take two forms. The simplest is where rights of land are granted by wife receivers to wife givers, that is, where there is a counterflow of land against women. In the second type wife givers are also land-right givers. The rationale behind this is that the land is given by a woman's agnates to ensure that she has sufficient gardening land in her new home.

I learned of three such cases involving large tracts of land (see Healey 1985c for a detailed treatment). In two of these, wife and land receivers gave valuables in return for the land to their affines in addition to bridewealth. The third case is more complex, as the same tract of land, or parts of it, were subject to a number of grants but involved differing donors and recipients. The land between Renmapai Creek in the south and the Kant River to the east and north was formerly Kolomp territory. In the mid-1800s all this area was given to Wendekai Kolompepe and Atikai Kolompepe subclans to support their Kolomp wives. The recipient groups extended use rights to all members of the

Wendekai–Amankai–Atikai cognatic cluster. After the fission of the Kolomp, some Kundagai say that the Kolomp (2) clan granted rights over the same area to Cembokai and Aiwaka clans of Bokapai, though the circumstances are unknown to my informants. Kolomp (1) made a further grant of part of the land—Tsuwenkai ridge—to Atikai Kolompepe subclan as part of ongoing affinal transactions, by now consolidated by sister exchanges. After the 1920s fight with the Aikupa, Bokapai clansmen invited the Kinimbong Kundagai to settle in the Kant Valley, and Kolomp (1), Cembokai, and Aiwaka clans jointly granted rights to the whole tract. In return Wendekai and Atikai clans gave women in marriage to the three donor groups. These marriages are viewed as being payment for the land, in consequence of which Tsuwenkai men say the donors cannot dispossess them: they have acquired primary use rights. Nonetheless, if one asks who are the "fathers of the land," informants generally reply Kolomp (2) or Cembokai and Aiwaka for the land north of Kandemunggu Creek, and Kolomp (1) for Tsuwenkai ridge. The Bokapai-based clans retain residual rights to the land although they ceded usufruct rights to Wendekai, Amankai, and Atikai; the Bokapai clans own the land but have no superior right to use it.

The granting of land does not necessarily deprive grantors of active usufruct rights, provided these are periodically activated by productive activity and the sacrifice of pigs in *raku*. The Kundagai regard the sacrifice of pigs as an essential expression of occupancy and usufruct rights. Success in gardening and hunting is bound up with the maintenance of proper relations with the ancestral spirits that inhabit the land, and clan spirits abandon any land once sacrifices cease there. Kolomp (1) is the only Bokapai-based clan that maintains active *raku* in Tsuwenkai and which therefore retains usufruct rights in the area.

This principle of pig sacrifice is also given importance by the Kundagai when discussing two other major grants of land that subsequently became subject to dispute. In the early 1900s the Tsembaga granted in perpetuity the lower part of Yopku to support Tsembaga women married to the Kundagai. (The two groups were still on friendly terms.) The recipients (two men of Atikai clan) were assisted by fellow clansmen and cognates of Wendekai and Amankai in making a prestation of valuables in return for the land. The Tsembaga ceased sacrifices at Yopku and, in view of this and the exchange of valuables, the Kundagai argue that all rights in the land have passed to the Atikai descendants of the original recipients, who are now the "fathers of the land" of Yopku. Other Tsuwenkai residents wishing to garden the area should first seek permission of these men.

In similar vein, an adjoining tract of land was given by the Tuguma to two Tsuwenkai men: a matrilateral parallel cousin of Atikai clan and an affine of Amankai. Both men joined a party of Tuguma resident at Tambekema in the Kant Valley. The Atikai man gave valuables in return for the grant, and when the Tuguma returned to the Simbai they ceased use of the land and sacrifices of pigs there. The senior descendants of the original recipients are again the "fathers of the land" and have extended usufruct rights to all coresidents.

More recently, the Tsembaga and Tuguma have pressed claims to be recognized as "fathers of the land" previously granted to the Kundagai and to regain exclusive primary usufruct rights. The Kundagai justified their own superior claims to all rights to the land by recounting the history of the grants and stressing that they periodically sacrificed pigs at Yopku and Tambekema, whereas the Tsembaga and Tuguma had long since ceased to do so.

Aside from grants, Kundagai territory has also increased through the purchase of land from other groups in recent times. These transfers are complicated by the de facto rights the Kundagai held in these areas by virtue of their occupation of what they considered was deserted land.

Before their defeat and rout at the hands of the Kauwatyi in 1955 the Cenda territory included large tracts of land in the Pint and Kant Valleys. The Kundagai helped both the Cenda and Kauwatyi and supported many Cenda in refuge after their defeat. In appreciation the Cenda transferred to the Kundagai the tract of land shown on map 3, most of which became part of Tsuwenkai territory. Much of this area was formerly part of the territory of the original Kolomp settlers of Tsuwenkai but was incorporated into the Cenda territory when some Kolomp joined that clan cluster. Most of this land had long been neglected by the Cenda, and the Kundagai, considering it *ren wabera*, deserted land, had gardened on it. Some Kauwatyi had also gardened on Komongwai and, at the time of the grant, were extending their cultivations there. The Kundagai saw this as an attempt by the Kauwatyi to establish de facto rights to this land. The grant from the Cenda was timely, as it gave the Kundagai primary rights to the land and legitimacy to demand the removal of the Kauwatyi. The Kundagai were not entirely successful in pressing their demands, although the Kauwatyi withdrew their gardens on Komongwai to the lower slopes above the Pint River, where they continue to garden. The Kauwatyi, however, also quickly occupied most of the wedge of land stretching from the Kant River to Mount Yirua. The Kundagai did not press their rights here, and they now consider that the Kauwatyi have become "fathers of the land" south of Jikemp ridge by virtue of long and continued occupation and sacrifice of pigs. Significantly, LiPuma's ethnography of the Kauwatyi indicates a heightened concern for access to land compared with other Maring local groups. This may be attributable to a comparatively high population density and local perception of pressure on land (see also Lowman 1980).

In about 1959 or 1960 the Cenda demanded payment for the land. The Tsuwenkai Kundagai made a payment only for the land on the west of the Kant. Several women were given in marriage, as well as shell valuables, steel tools, and bird plumes. Bridewealth was received for the women. The Bokapai Kundagai made a similar payment. The Kundagai now claim to be "fathers of the land" and therefore to be free to make use of it for cash-earning ventures, such as coffee plantings. Since the Kundagai do not consider themselves "fathers" of the Jikemp grant, they say it would be unwise to use the land for *bisnis* (TP: "cash-earning activities").

The Kundagai of Kinimbong and Tsuwenkai seem never to have appropriated land vacated by defeated enemies. The Bokapai Kundagai have expanded their territory in this way on at least one occasion. About the turn of the last century the Went–Kai clan lived in the Mieng Valley near Bokapai. Their land extended into the high-altitude forest at Aiyonju. Following a dispute the Went–Kai were routed by the Kundagai and fled to Rinyimp where they still live with the Kolomp–Kambek. Somewhat later two Wendekai men of Tsuwenkai gave a pig to their Went–Kai mother's brother for sacrifice in his sickness. In appreciation they were granted permanent usufruct rights to Aiyonju. The Kundagai had already gained de facto rights there, by gardening in the lower slopes and harvesting forest products in the high forest. The Went–Kai still consider themselves, nonetheless, to be "fathers" of Aiyonju land and have forbidden the Kundagai to make *bisnis* from the land by hunting valuable birds for trade—an injunction that has so far been ignored.

The grants of usufruct rights discussed here differ from those treated by Rappaport (1968) and LiPuma (1988) in that they involve large tracts of land of marginal use to their original owners because of the distance from settlements. Generalizing from these few cases, I suggest it is easier to obtain both exclusive usufruct rights to and custodianship of land obtained from other clan clusters. This is perhaps partly a function of distance—other populations are less able systematically to exploit the land because of its distance from their homes, and they are therefore less likely to press their claims as "fathers of the land," either implicitly by the sacrifice of pigs there or explicitly through statements of ownership. The Tsuwenkai Kundagai have acquired land in exchange for valuables or women or both from the Tsembaga, Tuguma, Cenda, and Bokapai Kundagai. Only the Bokapai Kundagai are still acknowledged as "fathers of the land," although all Tsuwenkai informants agree that no Bokapai clans, with the exception of Baikai (1), have any right to garden or harvest valuable forest products on this land. The transfer of ultimate custodianship thus may also be a function of ideas of in-group and out-group. It is not possible, however, to draw any firm conclusions concerning such transfers, in view of the vagueness of Kundagai notions regarding them. The situation is further complicated by recent claims by the Tuguma, Tsembaga, and Went-Kai to continuing rights and custodianship.

The Kundagai assert that all residents of Tsuwenkai are free to clear gardens in any part of the whole territory. Although the area south of Renmapai Creek is Kolomp (1) land and the area to the north is held jointly by the Wendekai–Amankai–Atikai cognatic cluster, individual sites are held by particular males. Initial ownership of garden plots is achieved by clearing the primary forest. Such sites generally are inherited patrilineally, but grants in perpetuity to other cognates or affines are commonly made. By these means individuals gain primary gardening rights to specific sites located in landholdings of other clans. To plot the garden sites of individuals does not reveal any clear pattern of clan territorial holdings. Garden sites of Wendekai, Amankai, and Atikai men are more or less evenly distributed throughout the whole area of agricultural land from Anggunai to Danmarak. Most Kolomp (1) gardens, however, have been cut south of Renmapai Creek within Kolomp (1) territory and the land purchased from the Cenda. Although specific garden sites are spoken of as being owned by individuals, these men in fact own usufruct rights, while the "father of the land" is the corporate group within whose territory the site is located.

During his first patrols to Tsuwenkai, kiap Griffin, who established the government station at Tabibuga, recorded boundaries for Tsuwenkai territory, an exercise no doubt prompted by armed clashes between several Jimi groups over territorial disputes. Griffin evidently relied largely on Tsuwenkai informants to determine the boundary, for the line he declared as the official boundary corresponds to Kundagai notions (see map 3) with exceptions at only two points. Griffin declared that the northern boundary of Tsuwenkai should follow the Bismarck crest. The Kundagai, however, assert that there is no territorial division between Mounts Aiyunk and Kombaku but that Tsuwenkai and Kinimbong lands constitute a single territory within which members of either settlement are free to garden or harvest forest products, because members of both settlements comprise a single clan subcluster. Members of the Wendekai–Amankai–Atikai cognatic cluster have equal usufruct rights to the whole estate of lands occupied by them in Tsuwenkai and Kinimbong. Other Kundagai clans that do not share rights of usufruct to this land are not entitled to garden on it or extract valuable forest products without permission. Few Kinimbong Kundagai avail themselves of their right to garden or harvest in Tsuwenkai because Kinimbong is more fertile. Many Tsuwenkai members of Wendekai, Amankai, and Atikai clans occasionally garden in the lower altitudes in Kinimbong, and most maintain groves of breadfruit and *Gnetum* trees (TP: *tulip*) and marita pandanus there, as these fare badly in Tsuwenkai's colder climate. Baikai (1) technically shares this right, though it is unclear if Baikai (2) does also. The issue has not arisen and informants are reluctant to express an opinion. No other clans based in Bokapai or Tsuwenkai have this right except on invitation. There is ample lower-altitude land in Bokapai where special crops may be grown or game hunted.

The second section of the boundary established by Griffin which is not recognized by the Kundagai lies on the east side of the Kant Valley. Griffin ruled that the boundary should follow the Bismarck crest from above Jikemp to Mount Kombaku. Some Kundagai also state this to be the present boundary. Most declare that the site of the new road has been the eastern boundary of Kundagai land since the Tuguma and Tsembaga land grants. The Tuguma and Tsembaga's claim to repossess the land below this level, mentioned earlier, occurred sometime before I entered the field, and there had been some discussion of the issue in informal *kot* (TP: "courts," but here referring to discussion of disputes) at Tsembaga. The Kundagai say these claims were inspired by the expectation that the road being cut in the Kant Valley might open up the forests to commercial exploitation. No further *kot* were held during my major period of fieldwork. By 1978, the matter had been referred to a committee of the Jimi Local Government Council, but no decision was reached, and by 1985 the claims seem to have been in abeyance.

With the grant of Komongwai and Anggunai from the Cenda and its subsequent purchase, the southern boundary of Tsuwenkai was extended so that Bokapai and Tsuwenkai land met in the zone of human habitation. Formerly the two territories met only in montane forest. Residents of either territory, as members of different clan subclusters, do not have the right to extend their gardens across the Anggunai border. Baikai (1) may garden north of Anggunai because of their association with Atikai. Informants suppose that Baikai (2), associated with Wendekai, might also do this, but none could recall any case where they had gardened in this region.

Tsuwenkai Kundagai claim that they do not garden in Bokapai territory but complain about encroachments on their land at Anggunai by Bokapai men. The incursions of the Kauwatyi on the lower slopes of Komongwai do not prompt serious complaints, probably because their activities are at a distance from Tsuwenkai settlement and gardens, whereas sites cleared by Bokapai Kundagai abut onto Tsuwenkai gardens, thus reducing the amount of land in easily accessible regions available for new Tsuwenkai cultivations. Tsuwenkai complaints about encroachments by Bokapai men have gone no further than occasional grumblings and fistfights.

The Kundagai tolerated the Kauwatyi annexation of much of the Cenda grant on the east of the Kant Valley because this area was far from the settlement and therefore unsuited to more intensive cultivation. It is probable that they also did not wish to antagonize a powerful ally who had already revealed expansionist designs by occupying Cenda land adjoining Kauwatyi borders elsewhere. Since this annexation, however, the Kauwatyi have attempted to include more of this former Cenda land within their territory, a move that the Kundagai have successfully resisted with the aid of government personnel.

Although most Kundagai are fairly clear about the location of territorial boundaries, it would be incorrect to suggest that they are concerned about the occasional transgression of gardening rights that these boundaries demarcate. They believe that they have ample land, and although they evidently do not wish to relinquish ownership of large tracts of land, such as are claimed by the Tsembaga and Tuguma, they are tolerant of their Kauwatyi and Bokapai neighbors making gardens inside their territory.

This chapter has reviewed the ecological, social, cultural, and historical context within which the exploitation of forest products and the exchange of goods is located. In the last few pages I have shown that the population of the Tsuwenkai region has fluctuated considerably and that continuous Kundagai occupancy is relatively recent. There is, however, circumstantial evidence of human occupation of the Tsuwenkai area extending back at least two hundred years (Healey 1985c). Oral historical material indicates that there was a succession of small, sporadic settlements until around the turn of the century. Tsuwenkai has been occupied continuously since then, although the population remained small but fluctuating for two or three decades. The area thus remained an essentially pioneer zone until recently. In this period much of the land was owned by clans in Bokapai or Kinimbong and exploited primarily as a hunting preserve and only to a very limited extent as garden land by a few resident households. As the region was periodically subjected to more intensive exploitation by larger concentrations of people seeking refuge from hostilities elsewhere, so grants of extensive tracts of land were made to occupants. Although the parameters of past population numbers and the kind and intensity of exploitation cannot be drawn with any accuracy, this historical material points to an important conclusion. There are no grounds for assuming that the ecological relations of humans to the environment in the Tsuwenkai region have achieved a dynamic equilibrium. Most particularly for the present study, one cannot posit any long-term homeostatic relationship between human exploitation of the environment and its direct and indirect effects on bird populations. As it happens, however, the period of continuous occupation, with a population approximating and sometimes exceeding present levels, roughly coincides with the period for which I was able to gather case material from individuals on their hunting and trading histories. The period from the mid-1920s saw a consolidation of a regime of extensive shifting horticulture in Tsuwenkai and an expansion of the zone of human habitation. The effects of human presence on habitat and bird numbers by clearing, hunting and, less directly, by the ravages of pigs, are mainly the consequence of the last few decades. This is a relatively short time in the ecology of both humans and birds. Although the forests had long been exploited for game, in all probability the impact of hunting on bird populations was considerably less than it has been in the last fifty or sixty years. The analysis of the impact of habitat restriction and of hunting by the Kundagai, as revealed by present horticultural practices and case histories of hunting, thus covers the greater part of the period of most intensive, continuous human occupation of the area. Before presenting an analysis of the ecology of hunting focused on the exploitation of birds of paradise for their plumes, it is necessary to outline the significance of plumes within Maring culture, a matter to which I turn in the next chapter.

2
The Uses and Significance of Plumes

Forest products are the only resource locally available to the Kundagai which are in high demand elsewhere in the central-highlands trading region. The most important of these items are bird plumes, but marsupial skins and live cassowaries are also traded. Kundagai trade is therefore closely connected to the production of plumes through hunting. However, only a limited range of different kinds of birds can be harvested in the Tsuwenkai forests; many are acquired from elsewhere. The Kundagai are therefore both suppliers and consumers of plumes. Production of decorative feathers through hunting is geared to meet local demand as well as to provide objects to trade. To set the context for subsequent examinations of the organization of production and trade, in this chapter I outline the patterns of plume ownership, the uses to which they are put, and the varied significance of such uses.

BIRDS USED IN DECORATIONS

The Kundagai preserve the feathers of at least fifty-three species of birds for use in decorations. Only a few of this number are regarded as of any great decorative value, whereas the feathers of almost any bird may be tucked into the hair at a jaunty angle to signal, for instance, a casual hunting success.

During the early months of my major period of fieldwork I made a census of valuables collections kept by Tsuwenkai men and youths. I saw collections belonging to fifty-five residents, who claimed that they showed me all their stored goods. Two youths and three old men said they had no valuables at the time, while another man declined to show me his collection but described its contents. A few stores I examined included goods belonging to absent relatives. Some men store their valuables in several bundles lodged in separate houses for safekeeping. I cannot therefore be certain that I saw the full contents of all collections.

In appendix 2 I list the bird species represented in the census of valuables and which parts of the plumage or skins are used in decorations. I also give information on the habitat, local status, and Maring and English vernacular names of each species. It is from this stock of plumes that most decorations are drawn for festive occasions. Many feathers destined for trade are also lodged temporarily in these collections.

The remains of at least 491 birds of 53 species were revealed in the census of valuables. Although I did not make a follow-up census, data on trade and hunting during fieldwork indicate that plume holdings changed considerably over time as men acquired feathers to use in a series of ceremonies and disposed of others in trade, gifts, or loans, both within and beyond Tsuwenkai.

The most numerous plumes in collections were of the long-tailed blue and white Common Paradise Kingfisher (*Tanysiptera galatea*) or *joli* in Maring: remains of at least sixty-eight birds were held by a total of sixteen men. The most widely represented species, appearing in thirty-three collections, was the White Cockatoo (*Cacatua galerita*), Maring *akaka*. The next most commonly held species (in twenty-five collections) was the Yellow or Lesser Bird of Paradise (*Paradisaea minor*), Maring *yambai*. This is one of the more familiar forms of paradise birds to westerners, with long filamentous golden flank plumes, although most Kundagai specimens were old and faded.

To rank the importance or desirability of species by the number of birds represented or the number of men retaining them does not reflect the value the Maring place on different species as items of decorations. Nor is the decorative value necessarily reflected in the value of plumes expressed in terms of money or other exchange items. For instance, the striking red and black feathers of the Vulturine Parrot (*Psittrichas fulgidus*), Maring *kopel,* have among the highest exchange values of plumes but are considered only minor decorations by the Maring. Although there is no firmly expressed hierarchy of the relative importance

Long-tailed Buzzard, *Henicopernis longicauda*, Maring *rukump*

of different birds as decorations, I have attempted in table 4 to construct such a scheme. I base this partly on informants' identifications of the most important species and those considered most appropriate for full dancing regalia and partly on the observed use of plumes. The importance of plumes in decorations bears no particular correspondence to the difficulty of their acquisition. Most of the species listed in categories A and B occur either in Tsuwenkai or in nearby regions in the Jimi and Simbai.

Of the fifty-three species of birds exploited for plumes, the majority (thirty-four) are found locally in Tsuwenkai territory. The remaining nineteen are not locally available, although most are found in the Jimi and Simbai Valleys within one or two days' walk from Tsuwenkai. Only six nonlocal species are confined to more distant parts of the highlands or coastal regions, although a number of species found in or near Tsuwenkai are also obtained in these distant areas. (See app. 2 for distributions.) Table 5 shows the means of acquisition of plumes in Kundagai collections at the time of the census of valuables in 1974, in terms of the local/nonlocal distinctions just made. Locally available species that are also acquired from beyond Tsuwenkai are included only in the column for local species.

Most feathers and skins retained for decorations are obtained by gift or minor prestation, with hunting and trade of next importance. I am using gift and minor prestation as synonymous here, contrasting such exchanges with trade, as indicated in the Introduction. Further details of the way decorative plumes are obtained are given in chapter 4. As might be expected, the means of acquisition show some relationship to whether a species can be hunted locally or is available only from beyond Tsuwenkai territory.

The predominance of hunting for locally available species, and of trade and gift for nonlocal species, is to be expected. But what is noteworthy is the importance of trade in acquiring local species and of hunting in obtaining nonlocal birds. Most trade of local species involved more valuable plumes, and remains of only nine of the thirty-four locally available species represented in collections had come by trade. Most of the hunting of nonlocal birds for plumes occurred in coastal areas rather than elsewhere in the Jimi or Simbai. Young men serving two-year work contracts as plantation laborers on coastal plantations commonly kill local birds—notably the Paradise Kingfisher—or purchase them from local traders. Many Cockatoo, Hornbill, and Raggiana Bird of Paradise plumes are acquired on the coast, though they

TABLE 4. MARING HIERARCHY OF DECORATIVE VALUE OF PLUMES

English Name	Scientific Name	Maring Name
A. HIGHLY ESTEEMED AND MOST IMPORTANT		
Long-tailed Buzzard	*Henicopernis longicauda*	*rukump*
Harpy Eagle	*Harpyopsis novaeguineae*	*binam*
Papuan Lory	*Charmosyna papou*	*goli*
White Cockatoo	*Cacatua galerita*	*akaka*
Common Paradise Kingfisher	*Tanysiptera galatea*	*joli*
Hornbill	*Aceros plicatus*	*kauwia*
Black Sicklebill	*Epimachus fastosus*	*kalanc gi yondoi*
Princess Stephanie's Astrapia	*Astrapia stephaniae*	*kombam*
Superb Bird of Paradise	*Lophorina superba*	*yenandiok*
Lesser Bird of Paradise	*Paradisaea minor*	*yambai*
King of Saxony Bird of Paradise	*Pteridophora alberti*	*balpan*
B. OF LESSER IMPORTANCE		
Dwarf Cassowary	*Casuarius bennetti*	*kombli*
Domestic Fowl	*Gallus gallus*	*kloklo*
Rainbow Lorikeet	*Trichoglossus haematodus*	*gir*
Purple-bellied Lory	*Lorius hypoinochrous*	*yindama*
Black-capped Lory	*Lorius lory*	*yindama*
Fairy Lory	*Charmosyna pulchella*	*jimbonk*
Muschenbroek's Lorikeet	*Neopsittacus muschenbroekii*	*pendent*
Vulturine Parrot	*Psittrichas fulgidus*	*kopel*
Blue-breasted Pitta	*Pitta erythrogaster*	*golembeli*
Brown Sicklebill	*Epimachus meyeri*	*kalanc gurunt*
Raggiana Bird of Paradise	*Paradisaea raggiana*	*parka*
C. OF MINOR IMPORTANCE		
All other species listed in Appendix 2.		

are readily obtained closer to home also. The Papuan Lory (*goli*) is a mountain species, but most specimens in the Bismarck Range are melanistic forms. The most highly esteemed skins of red-phase birds are often bought from Koiari, Goilala, and other traders in Port Moresby's Koki Market.[1] The Koiari of the Sogeri Plateau also visit plantations to sell skins of the Lory and other birds to laborers.

Workers in coastal areas collect exotic plumes primarily for their decorative value and as gifts for kinsmen. Some of these plumes are also traded on return to the Jimi, but there is little deliberate attempt to amass stocks for this purpose. Gifts of plumes most frequently involve nonlocal species. More feathers of local than nonlocal species are found. Most such finds are picked up from dancegrounds where they have fallen from headdresses. In addition, feathers of locally occurring species are sometimes discovered in the bush, accounting for the slightly greater incidence of this form of acquisition for local species.

TABLE 5. MEANS OF ACQUISITION OF PLUMES OF LOCAL
AND NONLOCAL SPECIES IN KUNDAGAI COLLECTIONS[a]

Means of Acquisition	Local Species		Non-local Species	
	No.	%	No.	%
Trade	50	10.9	70	15.3
Gift	47	10.3	124	27.1
Loan	3	0.6	11	2.4
Shot	86	18.7	36	7.9
Found	18	3.9	13	2.8
Number of cases	204	44.4	254	55.5
Number of species	34	64.2	19	35.8

[a] For explanation of local/nonlocal categories see text. Species involved are listed in appendix 2. Any species shown in the appendix as found in habitats I or II is "local," except the White Cockatoo which is a rare visitor to Tsuwenkai. All other species are "nonlocal." Total number of birds represented in the census of valuables (from app. 2) is 490; the total in this table is less because the means of acquisition of 32 remains are unknown.

STORAGE AND LIFE OF PLUMES

The care with which feathers are stored depends largely on their value as decorations or trade items and on their age and condition, though these last two factors are themselves partly a function of care in their storage. Most feathers I saw were in rather poor condition. Few had been reserved specifically for trade at the time of the census, although many plumes were acquired subsequently which were to be traded after use in dances. Most men now own suitcases or steel or wooden strongboxes in which they keep their feathers, furs, shells, other valuables, cosmetics, and trinkets. Wings and skins of parrots and smaller birds tend to be jumbled together in trunks and quickly become bedraggled. Large flight quills of the Long-tailed Buzzard, Cockatoo, and Hornbill and of some other birds are sometimes more carefully protected between sheets of paper or the pages of old schoolbooks. Skins of the Papuan Lory and the Paradise Kingfisher may also be protected in this way. Valuables cases are usually kept locked and stored on the sleeping platform at the rear of a man's or his wife's house. Men without cases wrap their plumes in bundles of the bark of the *kemer* palm (unident.) or occasionally in bundles of pandanus

Papuan Lory (black phase), *Charmosyna papou*, Maring *goli*

leaves. The immense skins of the Black Sicklebill are kept in flat packages of bark and leaves of up to one-and-a-half meters long.

Occipitals of King of Saxony Bird of Paradise and tail feathers of the Papuan Lory and Paradise Kingfisher are sometimes stored in thin bamboo tubes. Skins of Princess Stephanie's Astrapia and the Lesser Birds of Paradise are generally stored in larger bamboo tubes, plugged with leaves and sometimes wrapped in *kemer* bark or cloth to further prevent the entry of smoke and insects. Bundles and tubes are lodged in the rafters or walls of houses where the almost continuously smoky atmosphere drives away insects and keeps plumes and their wrappings dry. Older Astrapia and Lesser Bird of Paradise plumes are simply thrown into cases with other feathers.

Although the Kundagai carefully store their more valuable decorations, these can become damaged easily during dances. The Maring generally begin dancing at ceremonies during the afternoon and continue all night. Dancing space is sometimes limited, especially at night when dancers may continue their performance in the shelter of specially constructed dance houses, *kaiko ying*. Plumes fixed to large, awkward wigs are sometimes damaged in the jostling crowds of such structures. Dancing often continues during rain, and feathers are occasionally packed away when still damp and so quickly become moldy. House rats and insects chew feathers, and children may damage them in play if they are not locked away or stored out of reach.

All these factors reduce the life of plumes, and I suspect that Narak and Kandawo plumes, for instance, which I examined in the upper Jimi, last longer than Kundagai plumes, because of more care in storage and use.

It is not easy to estimate the age of plumes in decorations. Most Lesser Bird of Paradise plumes I saw were old and faded, though many had been acquired when new. These are used for about two or three years before they become too faded and tattered to use as major decorations or as trade items. They are then worn on minor ceremonial occasions, such as bridewealth presentations. A temporary gloss can be added to old Lesser Bird of Paradise plumes by rubbing them with dry soap, and the color of faded plumes enhanced by applying yellow dye extracted from a grassland shrub. For the dances that occurred after I conducted the plume census, most men obtained new Lesser Bird of Paradise and other plumes from kinsmen and friends in the Simbai and lower Jimi, even though some already owned small or faded plumes. These were considered unsuitable for major decorations.

Feathers of other species probably last in good condition longer than Lesser Bird of Paradise, but plumes of more valuable locally obtainable species are usually traded out of Tsuwenkai soon after they are acquired. Most other plumes remain in suitable condition as decorations or trade items for a minimum of five years if stored with care.

Principal decorations for major ceremonies are acquired mainly by loan, trade, or gift from associates in other settlements or by hunting shortly before they are needed, whereas less important additions to the headdress are drawn from personal stocks of feathers. Many of these plumes acquired for a specific occasion are traded immediately after they have been used and were therefore not encountered in the census. Thus, although most Kundagai plume collections are rather unimpressive, men are able to decorate themselves with plumes of high quality.

DECORATIONS

I do not intend to give a detailed description or analysis of dress and body decorations here. My main purpose is to indicate the occasions on which plumes are used and the kinds of arrangements that are employed.

Everyday styles of dress vary in minor detail according to the social status and personal tastes of the individual. Older men mainly wear the traditional netting apron and buttock covering of *tanket* leaves. Young men usually wear shorts and shirt and express embarrassment at being reduced to wearing everyday traditional clothing. European frocks and modern Papua New Guinea styles are increasingly worn by younger women, but the majority still wear the traditional string pubic apron, bark-cloth rear covering, and a cotton cape or large net bag suspended from the forehead and covering the back. European clothing marks the wearer (or in the case of women, their menfolk) as a participant in the wider contemporary world; traditional styles are worn by those who have little direct involvement or confidence in that world and who are mainly concerned with time-honored pursuits.

It is in the numerous minor decorations that more subtle statements are made about the wearer. Most adults and adolescents wear a bead necklace, but the addition of other items signals certain personal characteristics. Extra necklaces, bead armbands, and bracelets from the seals of petrol drums received as gifts testify to the popularity of young people with the opposite sex or the ardor of their lovers. A widower may add a purse containing a locket of his wife's hair or a string from

Vulturine Parrot, *Psittrichas fulgidus*, Maring *kopel*

her apron to his necklace. A widow sometimes suspends a bound and mummified finger of her husband from her neck. One waggish man in a bizarre parody of this custom had a large pink plastic hand from a doll dangling from his necklace. Prominent supporters of the church often sport a religious medallion or crucifix. An older man in high spirits intent upon visiting may ornament his nose with spikes of bamboo bristling from little holes in the alae, and a sliver of pearlshell through the septum, or in sickness remove all his decorations. Young men and girls occasionally wear a parrot wing or skin, or colorful leaves in their hair, especially when visiting friends in other settlements.

On minor ceremonial occasions, such as feasts and bridewealth presentations, younger men and girls decorate themselves more heavily. Older participants sometimes wear feather, fur, or shell decorations also. Girls put on bright dresses or their best string aprons, wind a length of red cloth or white marsupial fur about their heads, and stick feathers—borrowed from fathers or brothers—in their hair. Young men put on neat clothes or their best colored aprons and arrange many bright bird skins and wings in their hair. Old plumes from the Lesser Bird of Paradise may project sideways from the headdress. Plumes of the Raggiana Bird of Paradise are also worn, although these are generally scorned by younger men. As a general rule, feather and other decorations are not combined with modern clothing.

Styles of major decorations have changed somewhat over the last ten to twenty years. Formerly, most adolescent males assumed a wig at the time of the *konj kaiko* ceremony culminating the ritual cycle following war. This was molded into their hair from the sap of the *gunc* tree. The wig, *mamp ku gunc* ("head stone *gunc* tree"), formed a base for feather decorations. This wig, worn high on the forehead, was stained red and was sometimes decorated with a band of the shards of the green *mimola* scarab beetle. The *mamp ku gunc* is no longer made, but in its place as a dancing wig the Kundagai have adopted the wig of their Kalam neighbors. This they variously call *mamp ku, mimola glong,* or *glong*. The *glong* is a large, bulbous, ovoid wig made of hair clippings or tree burs, formerly covered with bark cloth but nowadays with cotton cloth. It used to be worn high on the forehead, like the *mamp ku gunc,* and decorated with a few rows of *mimola* beetle heads, interspersed with vertical rows of white marsupial fur (see plates in Rappaport 1968). Nowadays the *glong* is made larger and is worn tilted forward to the eyebrows. Diagonal rows of thousands of *mimola* heads mounted on sticks zigzag around the *glong* between vertical bands of white fur or cloth. A bonnet, *kabang kai* ("bird base"), of tightly massed dark feathers of domestic fowl, Hawk, or other species, or of the white feathers of the Cockatoo, is fixed to the crown of the *glong*. Alternatively, a *kabang kangapa* may be worn here. This is a raffia circle supporting a ring of cane spikes pointing up and outward. Individual feathers of Buzzard, Eagle, Cockatoo, or Hornbill are attached to the spikes, and Lorikeet or Kingfisher skins may be added in the center. A Lesser Bird of Paradise skin is mounted on the end of a long flexible stick thrust into the crown of the *glong*. The plume waves almost a meter above the dancer's head. Some dancers, usually older men, do not wear *glong* but instead a larger *kabang kangapa* directly on the head, worn high on the forehead. The basketry framework also supports a stick for a Lesser Bird of Paradise plume. These two basic styles of headdress may be varied with skins of the Long-tailed Sicklebill or Astrapia,[2] in place of Lesser Bird of Paradise, and embellished with additional Parrot skins and wings thrust in among the bonnet or basketry framework. The occipitals of the King of Saxony Bird of Paradise or the long tail feathers of Papuan Lory and Paradise Kingfisher are worn through the nose.[3]

The *glong* style of headdress is now worn by the western Maring. The Kundagai say that some Kauwatyi are beginning to fashion inferior *glong*, although most continue to wear the more traditional *kabang kangapa* style of headdress, as do the Cenda. Eastern Maring headdresses apparently conform more to Narak than to Kalam styles. Narak headdresses are similar to Wahgi Valley styles, though less sumptuous.

Maring headdresses are in general much less elaborate than the full dancing regalia of many western highlanders, such as the Kuma or Melpa. In place of a mass of Astrapia skins or other plumes set amidst a cluster of Parrot skins and Raggiana or Lesser Bird of Paradise plumes, the Maring generally wear one or only a few plumes of these species set among a more sparse arrangement of Eagle, Cockatoo, or Hornbill feathers.

THE SOCIAL SIGNIFICANCE OF PLUME USE

The Kundagai say they use plumes only as items of decoration and trade. Except for rare occasions, feathers are not included in ceremonial payments. The amount, relative value, and quality of plumes a man holds therefore bears little relation to the degree to which he partici-

Common Paradise Kingfisher, *Tanysiptera galatea*, Maring *joli*

pates in ceremonial exchange. Further, as already noted, a man does not need to rely on his own stocks of plumes for his major decorations in dances. A man's collection of plumes cannot therefore be taken as an index of his political influence or wealth. In this connection, I have noted that political influence is not closely linked with ability to manipulate wealth items in prestations. There is no tendency for big-men to hold larger stocks of plumes than other men.

The size of plume collections varies primarily with age. Younger men generally own larger and more varied stocks of plumes simply because it is they who most keenly participate in dances.

During fieldwork in 1973–1974 the Kundagai participated in six dances. Although all these attracted considerable numbers of spectators, the contingents of participants from Tsuwenkai were small—around ten to fifteen. Total numbers of dancers at most celebrations were nonetheless quite large, with dancing teams from several communities. A much larger contingent of Kundagai planned to dance at a ceremony in Kwima in mid-1974. This dance, associated with Tugumenga preparations for a *konj kaiko,* was canceled at the last moment when a prominent man of the host community died.

Dances in which Kundagai participated included two Kalam *semi* initiation ceremonies and Christmas celebrations and the opening of a new hospital at the Koinambe mission station. Two dances were hosted in Tsuwenkai: one to celebrate the consecration of a new church, the other in connection with a *pati*. A *pati* (TP and Maring for "party") is a public entertainment hosted by a group of men who kill pigs and sell small cuts to visitors. Nearby communities are invited to send dance teams, and the hosts provide accommodation and vegetable foods. The 1974 Tsuwenkai *pati* was the first to be held by the Kundagai.

Dances, consisting of stylized movements and accompanied by songs, sometimes specially composed for the occasion and set to two basic melodies, are highly ceremonialized forms of group display and contest (see Strathern and Strathern 1971 for the Melpa). Formal warfare on a fight ground was also somewhat ceremonialized and circumscribed by conventional tactics, which led to relatively few deaths (see Lowman 1973; Rappaport 1968; Vayda 1971). Besides carrying incised and painted shields for purposes of display and defence (Lowman 1973), Maring warriors also blackened their bodies and wore headdresses of black cassowary plumes, sometimes embellished with black-and-white tails of striped possums (*Dactylopsila*), faded Lesser Bird of Paradise plumes, and white leaves. The overall effect was blackness, accentuated by the contrast of white plumes, furs, and leaves. The purpose of warfare decorations was not only to hide the identity of individuals but also to make the ranks of warriors appear forbidding and intimidating. Warfare decorations, then, were employed in one form of stylized intergroup competition.

Participants in more peaceful competitions are drawn from the same groups as warfare parties. In dances, members of each clan cluster form up in separate competing groups. Dancers may invite allies from other groups to swell their numbers. Each team performs separately on the danceground, *kaiko ren*, trying to outdo its rivals in the splendor of its decorations, the volume of singing, stamping, and drum beating, in their endurance, and the number of admiring unmarried female spectators they can attract to their ranks. These competitions can sometimes lead to violence, especially if one group attempts to charge through the ranks of another to show its strength. The dances I attended were all good humored.

As occasions for group display, dances can indicate the strength and vigor of a group, and by the number of allies present as helpers could, in the past, serve as an indication of military strength. The richness of the dancers' decorations also signals the relative wealth and economic connections of a group (see also Rappaport 1968). The Kundagai say that the dance group wearing the finest decorations, making the most noise, and which keeps dancing longest is accorded victory in the contest by public opinion, although there is no formal declaration of a winner.

The Kundagai deny that there is any competition between individuals in dancing. Nonetheless, vigorous and well-decorated individuals may gain the reputation of being fine dancers, although they are regarded as contributing to group prestige. Such men are likely to attract the attention of unmarried women, who may join the dancers and hold the wrist of the man they admire.

The Fight Magic big-man (*bamp kunda yu*) possesses spells to aid dancers and weaken competitors. Before a dance he recites spells over the dancers to give them strength and endurance and to impart brightness to their decorations, so that women will flock to them. Other spells recited over magic traps hidden on pathways leading to the danceground are designed to counteract the strength and beauty magic of rival groups. To my knowledge dancing magic was not performed on dancers attending any of the celebrations that occurred during fieldwork.

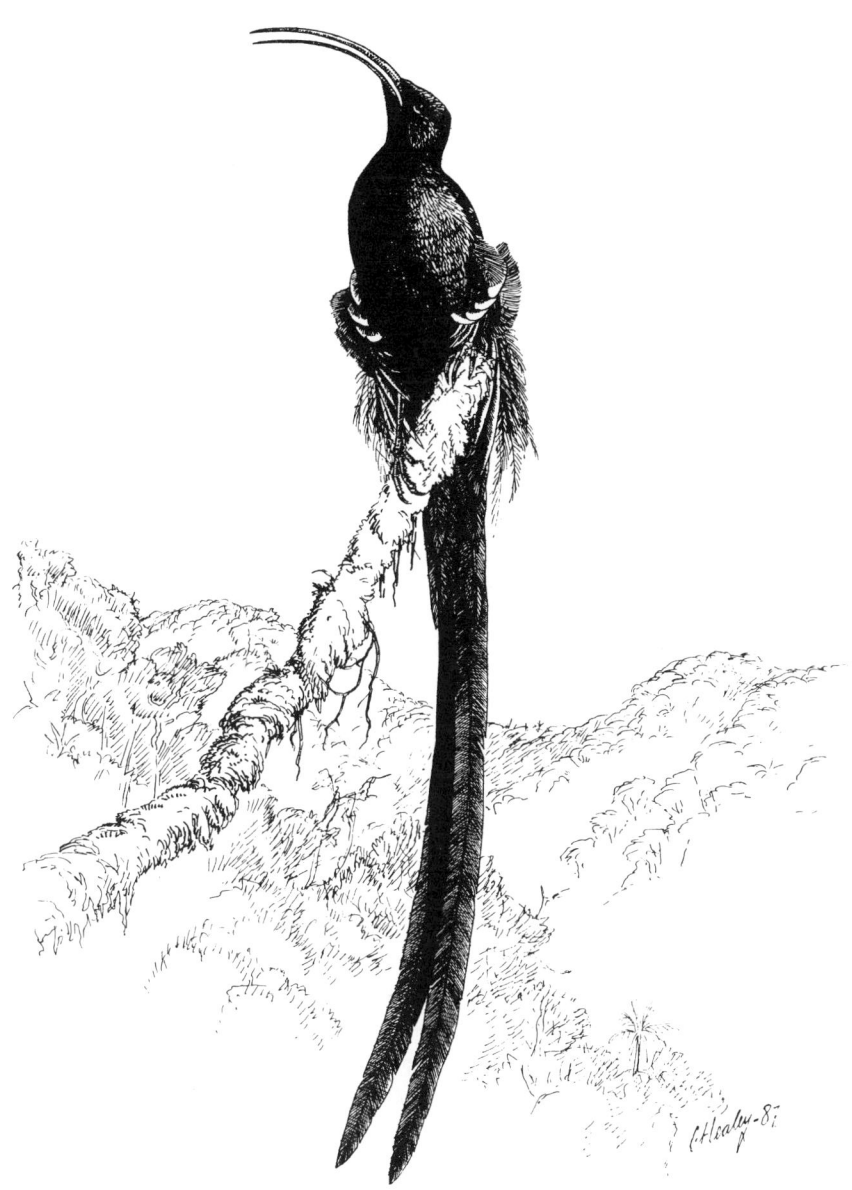

Black Sicklebill, *Epimachus fastosus,* Maring *kalanc gi yondoi*

Aside from individuals' reputations as strong dancers, decorations have further social significance for individuals as opposed to the groups in which they perform. Although a group of dancers as a whole competes to attract women from the spectators, it is to individuals that the women are drawn. At the end of dancing, girls sometimes follow home men to whom they are attracted. The qualities that influence this choice are endurance, personal attractiveness, and the wealth items the man displays. These romantic attachments may result in marriage if the man and the agnates of the girl and man are all agreeable. Sometimes the man may agree to marry the girl against the wishes of her agnates, in which case she is spoken of as being "stolen," *ku*. Such romantic marriages and short-lived attachments are generally initiated by the girl, the man taking a more passive role. The man "steals" the woman insofar as he acquiesces to the arrangement, thereby denying the rights of her agnates to dispose of her at their choice.

Several women married to Tsuwenkai men were "stolen" by their husbands after they were attracted to them at dances. Dances therefore provide occasions on which women are presented with a collection of men from which they might choose a husband, as Rappaport (1968: 193 ff.) has argued.

These remarks could apply to almost any form of display. They take for granted the particular decorative items, their combinations, and their choreographed presentation. Many questions remain: why have styles changed; why wear the *glong*; what is it that makes the Lesser Bird of Paradise the most appropriate plume to wear as a centerpiece; and so on?

The meaning of plumes as objects in themselves and as elements in an expressive performance by decorated dancers and singers is a complex subject that has received limited attention (Feld 1982; O'Hanlon 1983; Sillitoe 1988; Strathern and Strathern 1971; M. Strathern 1979). My data on the symbolism and aesthetics of decorations are scanty, partly because my attempts to engage the Kundagai in discussions on these matters were usually met with highly general and superficial statements. Men tend to respond to such enquiries simply by remarking that plumes are beautiful and it is custom to dance in this way. The issues involved in the interpretation of decorations are incidental to the main focus of this book, and I confine myself to only brief remarks.

As those ethnographers cited in the last paragraph have also observed, decorations both suppress individuality amidst the ranks of similarly bedecked performers and reveal essential qualities of the self.

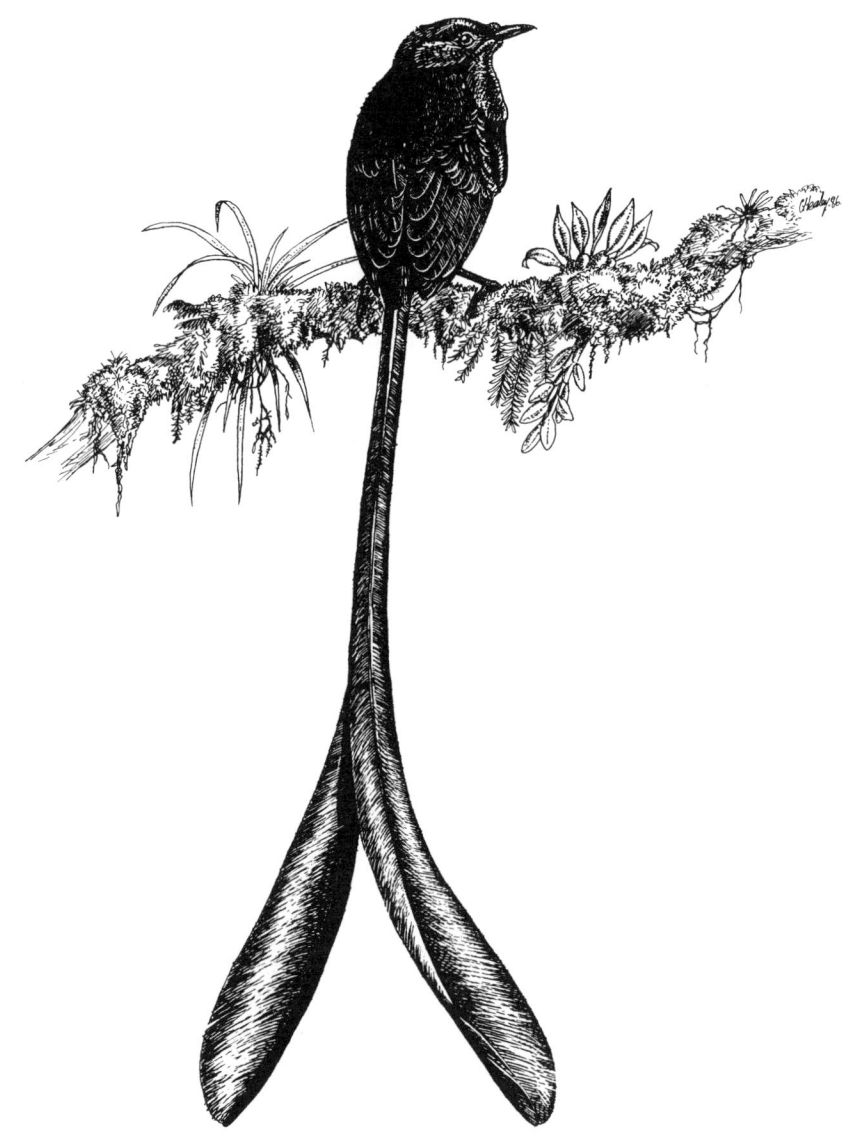

Princess Stephanie's Astrapia, *Astrapia stephaniae,* Maring *kombam*

Decorations and dance also mark gender. Only men don full dancing regalia and perform to the accompaniment of drums and songs as a group in the center of a danceground. Sometimes unmarried girls join the ranks of the dancing men, grasping the wrists of young men who attract their admiration. Women occasionally may dance in their own right, wearing decorations. Such women are generally married, and their decorations are provided by their husbands. The style of decoration is essentially the same as for men, except that a woman's tasseled apron, rather than a man's woven apron, is worn as a pubic covering. Women's dance style, however, is quite different in time, space, and movement. They appear prior to the emergence of massed male dancers, alone or in small groups, and as silent figures promenading on the periphery of the danceground. They are present only with the assistance of male guardians and as individuals.

By contrast, men dance as both individuals, signaled by idiosyncracies of decoration—though their identities may be difficult to determine—and as a coordinated, undifferentiated group of dancers performing more complex sequences of movements to the accompaniment of loud singing and drumming (cf. Strathern 1985 on aspects of gender and maturity in Hagen dance styles).

The principle elements of dancing decorations are objects of nature—birds, marsupials, plants—employed in relatively unprocessed or "raw" states. Decorations express a link between men and nature, transforming the wearer into something akin to a natural, as opposed to a cultural, being. But as a manifestly cultural action, the wearing of objects accentuating certain parts of the body—the head, chest, buttocks—masks the dancer's natural form and movement. For example, the flexible stick projecting above a dancer's head, to which is attached the waving plumes of birds of paradise, extends through the base of the headdress down the nape of the neck. The neck is held flexed against this stick, so that the head and torso move as a rigid unit. To achieve the admired undulating, beckoning movement of the plume, the dancer is obliged to master a difficult undulation of the whole body through movement of hips and knees. The effect is almost as if the plume is waving the man. By appropriating objects of nature the dancer transcends his natural properties and limitations, and becomes, as it were, an extension of his decorations.

Although I was unable to elicit any clearly articulated symbolic associations of particular species of birds that might make them appropriate as decorations, there is a clear association between birds and

Superb Bird of Paradise, *Lophorina superba*, Maring *yenandiok*

men, more particularly between plume-bearing birds and virility, itself signaled in the act of display by both birds and men (cf. Feld 1982; Sillitoe 1988). For example, one song composed for a dance during fieldwork likened the energetic young men to colorful forest parrots. For a man to dream of plume-bearing birds is a sign of future good health. Most significantly, the souls, *miny-nomani* (literally "soul consciousness") of living men may manifest themselves as colorful Fairy Lories or Papuan Lories, or as the glossy long-tailed Black Sicklebill or Astrapia Birds of Paradise, or as other large, bright, plume-bearing birds. Thus, when men bedeck themselves with plumes they are displaying their souls or essential selves. As one man remarked, this makes them look "smart." That is, it is not plumes themselves that make a man smart but the revelation of the soul through the wearing of plumes.

At a rather general level, then, plume-bearing birds are associated with vigorous masculinity. Just as it is that young, virile men display themselves bedecked in bird of paradise and other plumes, hoping to attract the attention of girls, so the Maring speak of birds of paradise that engage in elaborate displays in the forest as "young males." Decorations, moreover, refer to conceptions of the relationship of males in particular, and humankind in general, to culture and nature.

The Maring value few of the many kinds of feathers they use. Decoration styles do not require the use of many plumes, and the Kundagai themselves owned few considered to be of sufficient quality for use as major decorations.

It is reasonable to assume that suppliers of plumes will tend to have low stocks of locally available species and will retain in greater numbers only plumes of nonlocal birds. Data in appendix 2 lend support to this hypothesis, especially if only the more important species identified in table 4 are considered. Thus, for instance, we find relatively large stocks of the nonlocal Lesser Bird of Paradise and low stocks of the locally common Astrapia, Superb, and Saxony Birds of Paradise. All these species are highly regarded in many other highland societies. They have not been retained in Kundagai collections because there is a ready market for the plumes and fresh supplies are easily procured locally. As a further test of the above proposition I compare holdings of several species among the Kundagai and three settlements further up the Jimi (table 6).

The most notable point of comparison is the difference in holdings of Astrapia plumes from an average of 0.07 plumes per man in

TABLE 6. HOLDINGS OF PLUMES IN FOUR JIMI SETTLEMENTS

Species	Tsuwenkai[a]			Kwiop[a]			Koriom[a]			Bubgile[a]	
		No. of birds	Av. No. /man		No. of birds	Av. No. /man		No. of birds	Av. No. /man	No. of birds	Av. No. /man
Papuan Lory	+	33	0.6	+	75	5.0	+	18	2.25	+	91	2.0
Cockatoo	−	50	0.9	+	3	0.2	+	3	0.4	+[b]	8	0.2
Vulturine Parrot	−	8	0.2	−	16	1.06	−	23	2.9	+[b]	38	0.8
Kingfisher	−	68	1.3	−	32	2.1	−	15	1.9	+[b]	42	0.9
Hornbill	−	16	0.3	−	1	0.06	−	0	0	+[b]	1	0.02
Brown Sicklebill	+	1	0.02	−?		0.06	−	0	0	+	3	0.06
Astrapia	++	4	0.07	+	52	5.5	++	25	3.1	+	95	2.1
Superb B. of P.	++	5	0.09	+	6	0.4	+	8	1.0	+	6	0.13
Raggiana B. of P.	−	30	0.5	−	7	0.5	−	11	1.4	−[b]	1	0.02
Lesser B. of P.	−	37	0.7	+	12	0.8	+	6	0.75	+[b]	39	0.9
Saxony B. of P.	+	12	0.2	+	4	0.3	+	9	1.1	+	6	0.1

[a] A plus sign indicates the species is locally present, a minus sign indicates it is locally absent. Number of men represented: Tsuwenkai, 54; Kwiop, 15; Koriom, 8; Bubgile, 45. Source for last three settlements: own fieldwork, 1972.
[b] Present in Ramu lowland territory of Bubgile: Vulturine Parrot in small numbers only.

Lesser Bird of Paradise, *Paradisaea minor*, Maring *yambai*

Tsuwenkai, where the species is common, to 3.5 plumes per man in Kwiop where the Manga claim the species is absent. Koriom and Bubgile people say the Astrapia is uncommon in their lands. The contrast between holdings in Tsuwenkai and other settlements is probably accentuated by the greater use of this species in decorations by the Narak (of Kwiop and Koriom) and Kandawo (of Bubgile). A similar trend is found with the Vulturine Parrot, the average number of feather collections per man increasing in settlements that cannot hunt the species in their own land. Tsuwenkai stocks do not conform to the generalization, but this situation can be explained largely by a very low local demand for this species as an item of decoration, although the Kundagai trade considerable quantities of this species. The Superb and King of Saxony Birds of Paradise are probably more common in Tsuwenkai than the other areas. This is reflected in the number of Superb skins held, with lowest stocks in Tsuwenkai. Similarly, stocks of Cockatoo feathers are roughly proportional to the ease with which the species can be hunted within a population's territory, being largest in Tsuwenkai where the species is absent (except on rare occasions) and lowest in Kwiop and Bubgile where it is most common. Figures for plumes of the Lesser Bird of Paradise do not conform to the general trend. One might expect the number of Lesser plumes held to be highest in Tsuwenkai where the species is absent and lowest in Kwiop and Bubgile where it is most common, but the reverse is the case. Two factors explain this situation. First, the typical Kundagai full dancing regalia requires only a single Lesser skin, whereas those of the Narak and Kandawo require two and can accommodate several more. The Narak and Kandawo therefore have need of larger stocks of this bird. The second factor is purely fortuitous. At the time of the plume census in Bubgile, a party of men had only recently returned from a hunting expedition to the Ramu lowlands where they had collected many of the skins I saw.

The four settlements listed in table 6 lie on one of the major routes along which plumes travel to the Wahgi (Healey 1973: 153 ff.). A consequence of the concentric structure of plume trade is that with decreasing distance from the central consumption area stocks will become larger, for plumes from ever more suppliers become channeled through fewer and fewer communities in the network.

Plume collections examined in Kwiop, Koriom, and Bubgile were only a small proportion of the totals in these places. Conclusions drawn from the comparisons in table 6 can therefore only be tentative. The

King of Saxony Bird of Paradise, *Pteridophora alberti*, Maring *balpan*

data, nonetheless, do lend support to the propositions that plume suppliers tend to retain fewer locally obtainable species than exotic ones and that the size of individuals' collections tends to increase with decreasing distance from the central point of the plume-trading network—the Simbu and Wahgi Valleys. Similar data provided by the ornithologist Navu Kwapena (1985) for plume holdings in the Mendi region lend comparative weight to this conclusion.

By way of conclusion I wish to make two simple points. First, in comparing Kundagai plume collections and decoration styles with those elsewhere in the highlands (e.g., Strathern and Strathern 1971) one may gain the erroneous impression that the Kundagai are little interested in feathers. The variety alone of species used, even if only casually, belies this conclusion. Second, a consideration of the kinds of plumes retained, on the one hand, with cultural variations in decoration styles of neighboring groups and, on the other hand, with the distributions and abundance of wild birds, indicates that there is little impetus toward the accumulation of feathers among the Kundagai. Desire to retain exotic plumes is limited, and locally available kinds can be readily replaced by hunting or local redistribution by gifts or trade. The size and composition of Kundagai plume stocks says rather little about the importance or volume of hunting or trade in plumes. For the sociocultural and ecological factors influencing these activities one must look beyond the patterns of holdings at any one time and their means of acquisition.

3
Hunting and Its Regulation

Most ecological studies of production focus on subsistence activities, whereas those of trade generally take a broad-scale, regional view without adequate attention to the dynamics of production and distribution at the local level. The material in this chapter goes some way in repairing these deficiencies in a fuller understanding of Melanesian economy. Specifically, I examine activities by which objects of decoration and trade are produced. Among the Kundagai these objects are mainly wild forest resources—especially birds—so that production takes the form of exploitation or appropriation from nature. Obviously, such activity has ecological consequences for those species so exploited and, ultimately, has a constraining role on the capacity of the Kundagai to maintain their position in the wider network of trade as an important producer of desirable goods. This exploitation of natural resources is mediated by the cultural and social organization of hunting. It is therefore necessary to describe Kundagai understandings of hunting, its technical aspects, productivity, and social mode of restriction or limitation, before discussing the ecological aspects of the effects of hunting on target populations.

HUNTING METHODS AND PRODUCTIVITY

One of the preeminent male activities of the Maring is hunting, *tum koi-ma nimbe apng duk bon* ("we go to the forest to get game," literally "lizards mammals we-eat tree garden we-go"). The term for game is *tum koi-ma* or *tum kabang* (literally "lizards larger-mammals" and "lizards birds"). This is imprecise in its application, as the principal prey sought are in fact of the subcategories *apng koi-ma* ("arboreal larger-mammals") and *kabang yondoi* ("valuable plume or flesh-bearing birds," literally "birds large"). The Kundagai name at least nineteen distinct kinds of larger mammals, *koi-ma,* found in Tsuwenkai. About thirteen are classed as *apng koi-ma,* "tree or arboreal mammals," the rest as *kai koi-ma,* "base or ground mammals." The more knowledgeable naturalists split some of these lower-order taxa into pairs of terminal taxa. Ten of the arboreal mammals are marsupials—mostly cuscuses and ringtail possums, as well as the tree kangaroo, though the latter is rare in Tsuwenkai. Three species of arboreal giant rats are also common in Tsuwenkai forests. Although all larger mammals are eagerly sought for their flesh, it is only certain marsupials that are also taken for their pelts or loose fur.

Some 150 species of birds are found in Tsuwenkai, besides many more in lower altitudes. There is a general, though not complete, correspondence between species recognized by scientific zoology and the named, terminal taxa recognized by Kundagai experts in bird lore (cf. Majnep and Bulmer 1977 for the Kalam). Relatively few of the locally available species are regarded as plume-bearing birds. Included in the category are the Long-tailed Buzzard and Harpy Eagle, the Fairy and Papuan Lories, all found primarily but not exclusively in the high-altitude forest. But the most notable plume-bearing birds are the birds of paradise. There are 15, perhaps 16, species of birds of paradise among the 200 or so different birds inhabiting Maring lands. Thirteen of these live in Tsuwenkai, but some are rather nondescript, and only 5 are classed as *kabang yondoi* and hunted at all systematically. These are the Long Saber-tailed Black and Brown Sicklebills (*Epimachus fastosus* and *E. meyeri*), both rare birds of the mountain forest, the Long-tailed Princess Stephanie's Astrapia (*Astrapia stephaniae*), the Superb Bird of Paradise (*Lophorina superba*), and the King of Saxony Bird of Paradise (*Pteridophora alberti*). The last three are quite common in primary montane forest, with the Superb also numerous in forest-edge and advanced secondary-forest habitats. The golden-plumed Lesser Bird of Paradise (*Paradisaea minor*) is common in lower-altitude forests and fallow growth beyond Tsuwenkai.

In pursuit of arboreal mammals and plume-bearing birds, a man must make special excursions into the *kamungga,* high-altitude forest.

He is prepared to take other prey, such as bats, reptiles, small birds, and terrestrial mammals in the course of his search for other game.

Women and children also kill animals. The principal game sought by women, however, is quite different: frogs, *kamp,* rats, *koi,* and edible insects, *bang.* Small boys patrol homesteads, gardens, and fallow with their bows and arrows and will shoot almost anything that moves. Children also occupy themselves in play, seeking edible tidbits, animal and vegetable. One commonly encounters secretive knots of little children probing in rivulets for crabs, frogs, and insect larvae to eat. Such activities are perhaps more reasonably regarded as gathering, along with the similar collecting of wild plants and invertebrates by women and, to a much lesser extent, by men. As a consequence, children probably have a comparatively high and frequent intake of animal protein, compared with adults, and especially men, whose individual meat meals may be a good deal larger but much more intermittent, especially if they are not skillful hunters.

Hunting involves knowing an animal's habits and locating and immobilizing the prey. It often also involves the use of specialized aids, magical or material. Such aids are designed with hunting as a principal application. A further generalization I would make is that hunting is usually directed toward securing mobile and active prey.

Except for occasional nocturnal parties organized to capture frogs by torchlight, women seldom deliberately attempt to hunt or collect animals. Most of their actions arise from chance encounters. For instance, while weeding or harvesting women will stun rats they find nesting in their gardens. A further limitation of women's hunting and collecting is that nearly all game they secure is within the zone of human habitation. Women do not venture into the high forest for the sole or major purpose of seeking game as men do, though they may be alert for rats nesting under tree roots or in low bushes or young pandanus palms while collecting plants for specific purposes. Women and girls occasionally accompany their husbands or fathers to the forest in the fruiting season of the pandanus palms to collect nuts. They search for rats or bird nests on these occasions or help their male companions kill marsupials thrown down to them from tree holes. Most animals killed by women, whether on their own or when helping men, are on or within reach of the ground, for it is considered improper for females to climb trees.

Since the principal game sought by men is arboreal, much of their hunting involves climbing trees to inspect holes for mammals, or to

Hunting and Its Regulation 89

wait in blinds for birds.[1] It is men, too, who alone use specialized hunting aids.

I do not know whether hunting and collecting by males or females is the more productive in terms of the return of prey for the time and energy expended in securing it. Although much hunting by males occurs on excursions to the forest specifically to secure game, men also often attempt to kill birds or mammals they encounter in the zone of human habitation or in grassland while they are pursuing other tasks. There is no doubt that most men spend a larger proportion of their time in hunting than do women and that the number of animals and total weight of meat they catch over time is larger than that caught by women. It is quite possible, however, that they expend a much greater amount of effort in hunting by trekking to the forest and climbing trees. In terms of energy expenditure, then, women's hunting may be more efficient or productive, even though they contribute very little animal protein to the diet. The results of women's hunting are consumed almost entirely by women and children within the household. Game killed by men may be shared more widely, though not invariably, in accordance with principles of reciprocity, and so may be more socially significant.

The principal hunting aids are bows and arrows, axes, bushknives, spears, clubs, and traps. Most males over about ten years old own at least one bow (*rim*) and several arrows. Bows are made from the black palm (*bina*) and vary in length from about 1.5 to 1.9 meters, averaging around 1.6 meters. Small bows for boys are made of bamboo. Bowstrings are of bamboo, cut from a locally abundant wild variety with long internodes. *Bina* palms apparently do not occur naturally in Tsuwenkai, and only a few have been planted in the lower reaches of the Kant Valley. Tsuwenkai men obtain ready-made bows or unshaped lengths from friends and relatives in other settlements where the palm grows at lower altitudes.

Arrows come in varied forms but are of three main types: multipronged for birds and other small game, pointed or barbed, and broadbladed. The last two kinds are used for larger game and, formerly, in war. Many men and boys carry bow and arrows on visits to gardens or when they expect to pass through patches of forest.

Spears are seldom used in hunting, except in pursuit of cassowaries, feral pigs, or domestic pigs that have run wild or become garden raiders. There is at least one shotgun in most Jimi and Simbai settlements, but no one owns a gun in Tsuwenkai. One man has unsuccessfully applied to the Jimi Local Government Council for a gun license. The number of licenses issued is pegged at a ceiling set by the Council, ostensibly in the interests of game conservation.

A lack of weapons does not deter the would-be hunter. Sticks are used as probes to flush game or as bludgeons. An unarmed hunter may hurl stones to good effect.

There are five main types of trap, or *keren*: springes (*keren*) for giant rats, phalangers, and cassowaries; pitfalls (*kau*) for pigs; deadfalls (*kepo*) for ground birds, smaller marsupials, and rats; bird traps (*kapongga*) used especially for birds of paradise; and eel traps (*klem keren*).

Besides these direct tools for killing game, the Maring use a variety of blinds and lures. Depending on the desired prey, blinds are built on the ground, by pools, or in trees. Some blinds are little more than leafy screens, others are sturdy structures that may be refurbished with camouflage and used for years. From tree blinds located in fruiting or flowering trees the hunter shoots parrots, doves, and birds of paradise. The latter are also shot from blinds built in or near their display trees.

Lures of the jen vine (*Trichosanthes*) and of the giant wild banana, *jiki*, are hung at traps or in front of blinds. They are particularly used to attract certain birds of paradise.

The Kundagai appear to rely mainly on their considerable pragmatic knowledge and skill in hunting. Few admitted to the use or even knowledge of hunting magic, although this may have been an expedient to preserve secret knowledge. There are, however, a number of charms a man may carry to attract game or make his aim true. Some men who own display trees where the Astrapia and Lesser Bird of Paradise gather communally over generations, bespell the trees to make adult birds congregate in large numbers. Another magical device, *kabang ranggo* ("bird ginger"), involves rubbing a leaf of a kind of ginger (*ranggo*) onto the trunk of the display tree, then inserting it in a cut in the bark. As the wound heals and traps the leaf, so the tree becomes hot or spicy (*rik*), drawing birds irresistibly to the tree.

The spirits are associated with certain categories of game, which are spoken of as the spirits' "pigs." Men say that if game is plentiful and the spirits are pleased with the living, they will permit hunters to meet with success.

The Piakai Ambra (Above Woman spirit) may actively hinder hunters if she wants to protect her pigs, by showering dry moss into the upturned faces of those searching the treetops for signs of prey. One man

Hunting and Its Regulation

related how he and his father heard female laughter from the treetops as they unsuccessfully sought game. They reasoned that this was the Piakai Ambra mocking their lack of success and, afraid, they hurried home.

To remain in the favor of spirits a hunter should sacrifice a pig periodically to the spirits in return for the game he has already killed and might kill in the future. In practice, it seems that the Kundagai seldom sacrifice specifically for this purpose, but pigs killed for other reasons, such as in times of sickness, may also be specified as a return for game. If such sacrifices are neglected, men say the spirits may kill a hunter's pigs or cause him or his family sickness in retribution.

When going hunting a man should be unobtrusive, lest many people see him, for these people will then think of him, and the spirits of the forest, divining these thoughts, will hide game. The Kundagai, however, consider that they are able to exert some measure of control over the spirits by deceit or magic. Occasionally a hunter makes up a bundle of banana or cordyline leaves to resemble a package containing pork. He carries this to the forest edge where he addresses the spirits, telling them that he has killed a pig and brought them its head—a choice cut, cooked in a ritual oven dedicated to the spirits, and normally eaten in a small communion feast by the close male agnates of the pig-killer. He invites the spirits to gather, telling them that he will return to share the feast with them later. The man then enters the forest to hunt, confident that the distracted spirits will not discover his true intentions and so will neglect to hide their "pigs." When I asked how the spirits reacted, people presumed they either do not discover the deception or are not angered if they do. Were this the case, they say, the hunter or his family or pigs would be stricken with sickness. The Kundagai are vaguely amused by the simple-mindedness of the spirits in being so easily deceived.

Magic is used only to control the *menjawai* demon, regarded as the most dangerous of the spirits of the high forest. Before going hunting a man may light a small fire and bespell the smoke. The *menjawai*, smelling the smoke, is frightened and flees so that the hunter may search the forest without fear of attack. This practice seems to be a magical reenactment of an incident told in a myth concerning the origin of crops. In the myth a group of women, who live by hunting, destroy a demon in a forest fire they had lit to flush game. No one admitted to knowing the appropriate spell.

The strategies employed in hunting depend largely on the kind of weapons at hand and the expected prey. Most men set out on a hunting expedition with the aim of securing particular kinds of prey: marsupials for their fur and for the pot, a particular bird of paradise that has established a territory in the forest, and so on. The bow and arrows and a bushknife or axe are the standard equipment for a planned hunt. They can be used in most strategies for approaching and capturing game.

Bulmer (1968) has reviewed hunting methods used in New Guinea at some length and I follow his terminology here. One of the most commonly employed and simplest strategies is stalking: the covert approach of mobile prey. This method is frequently adopted opportunistically when a man encounters birds. Most small birds, and the occasional cassowary and bird of paradise, fall to the hunter using this method. Men also successfully stalk mammals on moonlit nights, when they can be located by the sound of their feeding, squabbling, or progress through the treetops.

Ambushing, involving a stationary hunter waiting for game to approach, is a more productive strategy. The hunter waits, usually concealed in a blind, at feeding places of mammals or birds, at forest pools, or at display sites of birds of paradise. He may entice his prey into the ambush by the use of lures. Several species of birds of paradise are attracted to fruit lures, and some marsupials can be drawn along horizontal branches laid out as lanes by the hunter to baits of edible bark. Birds can also be attracted by noise. Loud squeaks, similar to the calls of nestlings, sometimes attract the inquisitive Parotia and Superb Birds of Paradise, and the latter species will also flock within bowshot range in response to the alarm calls of a chick taken from the nest. The Astrapia is sometimes attracted to its display site or a fruit bait by imitating its call.

Trapping is essentially a form of ambush in the absence of a hunter. Traps for mammals or cassowaries are set up on their customary runs. Birds are usually trapped at pools, where the devices provide convenient perches, or at fruit baits, often set near display sites of birds of paradise where they are more likely to be noticed by the birds.

Nocturnal animals are usually obtained in daylight by besetting, involving a stealthy approach upon the known or presumed resting place of the quarry. An excursion into the forest is usually punctuated by many halts when a tree hollow or large clump of moss is discovered. The hunter may inspect the nearby ground and tree trunks for droppings, fur, fallen nesting material, and scratches. A skilled hunter can distinguish fresh from old marks, the probable species, and its age. Even in the absence of any clear signs, a man will attempt the sometimes perilous climb to investigate a tree hollow. Once there, he must act with speed and boldness. Clinging to the slippery mossy trunk with one hand, he must plunge the other into the hole, find his quarry's tail, heave the animal out, and fling it to a companion waiting below, or dash it against the treetrunk before the beast has a chance to savage his hand. Giant rats and larger marsupials have formidable incisors that can shear right through a man's hand. Some birds, especially the Harpy Eagle and Long-tailed Buzzard, are taken at the nest in similar style. Having discovered a nest a man prefers to wait until the chicks are ready to fly before killing them, thereby maximizing the yield of flesh and valuable feathers. Raids on a nest are usually made at night in order also to kill the sitting bird. Some birds are taken by hand or shot on their roosts at night.

Many attempts to kill animals by the strategies outlined above degenerate into a chase when the prey attempts to elude the hunter. All but larger birds and mammals quickly disappear in the forest, however, and the chase is seldom protracted or successful. Dogs, *cena,* are sometimes used in pursuing and bringing to bay wallabies, the terrestrial cuscus, pigs, and cassowaries. There were only four dogs in Tsuwenkai during fieldwork and, to the best of my knowledge, none was used in the hunt in this time, although one old man took from his bitch the carcasses of marsupials that it brought back for its puppies. The Tsuwenkai dogs appeared true to the endemic wild dog *Canis familiaris hallstromi,* being terrierlike animals with short legs and bushy tails. Wild dogs (and recently introduced cats turned feral) are apparently quite common in the forest, and domestic bitches are sometimes impregnated by wild dogs. Migrant workers occasionally bring back dogs of European stock, but these animals invariably succumb to disease and are poor hunters besides, an essential skill, as dogs are not systematically fed by their owners.

The ideal time for hunting, according to the Kundagai, is during the *wula* or dry season. At this time conditions in the forest are most congenial for hunting, and the more frequent cloudless nights encourage hunting by moonlight. During the wetter season, *kembonda,* the heavy banks of moss on forest trees become waterlogged, and there is a very real danger of limbs or whole trees being brought down by the weight, even in windless conditions. Men also find it difficult and dangerous to climb wet and slippery trees in search of game. The cold temperatures coupled with the absence of dry firewood for warmth and cooking make conditions too unpleasant for most men to bear. Some enthusiastic hunters, nonetheless, occasionally venture into the forest by day, but seldom spend the night there.

All birds of paradise are said to breed in about November to January, during the wetter season. By the early part of the dry season their ornamental plumes are old and damaged by wear and insect parasites. They are molted during the dry season, and the new feathers are in their best condition by about July or August, toward the end of the dry season. This is therefore considered the best time to hunt for valuable birds. Kundagai opinion conveniently complements the agricultural cycle, as the earlier part of the dry season is a time of intense activity with new gardens to clear, burn, and plant.

The main species sought during the wetter season is the cassowary. When cucumbers and corn are ripe in new gardens, mainly in about December to February, it is said the cassowary chicks will have hatched. It is then, when the chicks are still small and unable to keep up with fleeing adults, that men seek out cassowaries in the forest.

Seasonality of hunting is revealed in variations in the intensity of hunting from one period to another. At no time is there a total absence of hunting in relation to the seasons. There is, however, a variation in the main strategies employed in wetter and drier seasons. Trapping is of greater importance during the wetter months, for the hunter can set his traps on a clear day and return to examine them later, thereby minimizing the time he must spend in the forest. Other forms of hunting are more widely employed during the dry season, although trapping remains an important method.

There is much variation in the hunting abilities of individuals. This hinges on the skill of the hunter in applying hunting methods, the extent of his knowledge of the habits of his prey, and on his personal inclinations. Several men told me that they rarely went hunting. Others frequently journey to the forest, sometimes spending several days and nights there, either alone or in the company of male friends or relatives, or with their wives and children. Such differences in the amount of hunting a man may do are, I believe, simply a matter of taste. Some men gain evident enjoyment and fulfillment in spending long periods in the forest, whereas others find the experience arduous, uncomfortable, and fruitless.

A highly successful or prominent hunter is called *yu tum kabang gwio aumba yundo*, "the strong-armed shooter of game" (literally "man lizard bird bone strong he-shoots"). Such a hunter is said to have energy, knowledge about the natural environment, and success in killing many valuable plume-bearing birds. On these grounds informants named eight such hunters, although three are now old and seldom if ever hunt. Several more men who are renowned for their hunting of mammals and birds in general were suggested as possible prominent hunters. The reputation carries no particular implications of status, although such men may receive some notoriety and respect for their skills and become repositories of specialist knowledge.

Contrary to what one might expect in a society where meat is eagerly sought but irregularly eaten, the major Kundagai criterion of the successful hunter does not center on the contribution a man makes to the diet of his family or the community at large. Indeed, game is usually shared by the hunter only with members of his own household, except on certain ritual occasions, or when his bag is large or bigger game (pigs and cassowaries) is killed, though periodically a successful hunter makes small gifts of game to his affines. Rather, a reputation as a prominent hunter lies in a man's publicly displayed ability to secure prey of value in the nonsubsistence sector of the economy. As such, any material benefits of success are largely personal, as the hunter can exchange the plumes acquired for valuables to increase his own stocks of wealth.

Animal protein from game typically makes only a limited contribution to the diet in the New Guinea highlands (Heider 1970: 55; Pospisil 1963: 231; Rappaport 1968: 71 ff.; Salisbury 1962: 44). Hunting is nonetheless an activity of greater cultural and dietary significance among the sparse populations of the highland fringe, such as the Wopkaimin (Hyndman 1979), Mianmin (Morren 1986), Gadio Enga (Dornstreich 1973), and Etolo (Dwyer 1983). There have been few quantitative studies of the productivity of hunting or trapping. Dwyer, Hyndman, Morren, and Dornstreich give considerable data on the frequency of hunting, the gross weight and edible portions of meat obtained, and its nutritional value, arguing that hunting in the highland fringe is highly efficient in energetic terms. Of course, hunters themselves do not see their activities in quite this light, but rather in relation to perhaps vaguely articulated notions of reasonable returns of kind and quantity of game for time and effort expended, and the favorable disposition of spirits. Such evaluations are culturally and contextually specific, so that it becomes meaningless to assign any absolute values to what one might call a "coefficient of disinclination," whereby hunting is liable to decline once perceived yields fall below certain critical levels. A comparison between the productivity of hunting among the Kundagai and other populations, nonetheless, gives some indication of the relative capacity of the Kundagai to secure game for the pot or for decoration and trade.

In table 7, I list those men whose hunting times I was able to estimate with reasonable confidence and whose total bag size I knew. All but Aikupa did their hunting while accompanying me as assistants on trips to the high forest. Their hunting time was thus somewhat limited during the day (even though we made many stops to investigate tree holes for phalangers and giant rats), but my companions were free to hunt at night. These constraints make my data roughly comparable to Dwyer's (1974) more extended sample of hunting by his Rofaifo (Siane) assistants. Similar data on the Wopkaimin were collected by Hyndman (1979: 214–227), accompanying hunting expeditions as a spectator rather than as an organizer. Hyndman's data therefore more accurately reflect the potential of hunting than do my own or Dwyer's material on the Rofaifo. Recently, Dwyer (1983) has provided the most exhaustive study yet available on New Guinea hunting performance and energetics in his analysis of the Etolo (or Etoro) of the Great Papuan Plateau. Unfortunately, he discusses only hunting for mammals, which make these data not strictly comparable to other studies cited in terms of the total number and weight of prey secured in the hunt. He does note, however, that frogs, reptiles, birds, and small rodents were taken incidentally in hunts focused on medium-sized mammals. Although such captures account for less than 1 percent by weight of all prey (Dwyer 1983: 153), there is no indication of how many incidental prey species are involved.

Among Kundagai hunters Aikupa is considered a prominent hunter, although Yekwai and Gum showed themselves to be much more productive. Wepo, Amang, and Deimang (who is not a Kundagai and unfamiliar with local conditions) are not, by their own testimony, particularly successful or skillful hunters.

Dwyer's Rofaifo assistants only killed at night, but Dwyer includes in the total number of hunting hours of each man the time spent during the day in selecting or preparing ambush sites for night hunting. His assistants had at least two days' free time on each forest trip in which to hunt. My own companions' time was more limited. Table 7 indicates that the Kundagai showed a preference for diurnal hunting. The Wopkaimin in Hyndman's sample also favored hunting during the day,

TABLE 7. PRODUCTIVITY OF KUNDAGAI HUNTING

Day/Month (1974)	Hunter(s)	Hunting Estimated Hours	Day/Night	Prey	Weight[a] (kg)
27/5	Yekwai	2	N	-	-
28/5	Yekwai	2	D	*Alisterus chloropterus* (Papuan King Parrot)	0.162
28/5	Yekwai & Amang	1	D	*Uromys anak* (Giant Rat)	0.54
28/5	Deimang	1	D	-	-
29/5	Yekwai & Deimang	1	D	-	-
29/5	Amang	1	D	-	-
1/7	Aikupa	10	D,N	*Pteridophora alberti* (Saxony Bird of Paradise)	0.100*
8/7	Yekwai	2	D	-	-
8/7	Yekwai	3	N	*Pseudocheirus cupreus* (Ringtail Possum)	1.509
				Rattus verecundus (Small Rat)	0.060*
9/7	Yekwai	3	D	*Pteridophora alberti*	0.100*
9/7	Yekwai	1	D	*Pteridophora alberti*	0.100*
10/7	Yekwai	3	D	*Ducula chalconota* (Pigeon)	0.800*
22/7	Wepo	1	D	-	-
23/7	Wepo	4	D	*Pachycephala schlegelii* (Small bird)	0.022
23/7	Wepo & Yekwai	1	D	-	-
25-26/8	Yekwai	20	D,N	*Pteridophora alberti* x 2	0.200*
				Charmosyna papou (Papuan Lory)	0.120*
28/8	Yekwai	1	D	*Ptilinopus ornatus* (Pigeon)	0.163
28/8	Gum	2	D	*Pseudocheirus corinnae* (Ringtail Possum)	1.052
29/8	Gum	3	D	*Phalanger vestitus* (Silky Cuscus)	1.957
				Pipistrellus imbricatus x 3 (Small Bats)	0.009*
29/8	Gum	3	D	*Mallomys rothschildi* (Giant Rat)	1.277
29/8	Gum & Yekwai	2	D	-	-
30/8	Yekwai	5	D	-	-
6/9	Yekwai	3	N	*Pseudocheirus cupreus*	1.509
				Phalanger vestitus	1.957
28-29/9	Aikupa	15	D,N	*Pseudocheirus forbesi* (Painted Ringtail Possum)	0.577
				Phalanger vestitus	1.957
TOTALS		90			14.369

[a] Weights for most mammals are averages computed from Dwyer's (1983) data on Etolo hunting, except for the rat, *Uromys,* taken from Dwyer (1974). New Guinea mammals vary in weight by region and altitude, and Bulmer (personal communication) considers mammals in the nearby Kaironk Valley to be much heavier than in the Rofaifo area (compare Dwyer 1974 and Bulmer 1976). Weights of birds are taken from Diamond (1972). Weights indicated by an asterisk are my own estimates.

mainly because of bad weather at night. The Etolo by preference hunt almost exclusively during daylight (Dwyer 1983).

Table 8 compares the productivity of Kundagai, Rofaifo, Etolo, and Wopkaimin hunting. Among the Wopkaimin and Etolo, hunting and collecting are of considerable subsistence significance, but negligibly so among the Kundagai and Rofaifo. It is therefore not unexpected to find that Wopkaimin and Etolo hunting is the more productive in terms of the weight yield for time spent. Somewhat unexpectedly, however, Kundagai hunting is more productive in terms of the number of prey killed for time expended. This is because the Kundagai are prepared to bag small mammals and birds, whereas the Rofaifo, Etolo, and Wopkaimin hunters clearly discriminate in favor of larger, meatier prey at the expense of frequency of kills (cf. Dwyer 1974: 279). The Wopkaimin illustrate the strategy well: on one expedition of 70 man hours of hunting, four men killed one feral pig, two cassowaries, and a large phalanger at the rate of 17.5 hours for each kill. However, this represents a weight yield of one kilogram per 0.6 hours of hunting (Hyndman 1979: 222–224). Wopkaimin also tend to select larger game that is not subject to dietary taboos. The Etolo's active hunting is focused on larger marsupials. Feral pigs are seldom encountered on expeditions, and although cassowaries are present they are usually caught in traps, and so are not considered in Dwyer's presentation. It is not clear from Dwyer's account whether the Etolo combine techniques of trapping with more active assaults on prey, and whether, therefore, yields from trapping should properly be included in his analysis. Dwyer (1974: 288) notes that in respect of smaller mammals the Rofaifo seem to have lost some hunting skills through concentration on larger prey. His data also suggest that younger men have declining skill in securing large game, as hunters under thirty years old spent, on average, almost four times as long to kill each mammal as older men. A similar trend in hunting success by age is evident among the Etolo. Dwyer (1983), however, attributes increased productivity among older Etolo hunters to accumulated skill, experience, and greater endurance, rather than to a loss of skill and knowledge by young men. That is, whereas one might expect young Rofaifo to continue as poor hunters as they age, young Etolo hunters are likely to become more successful, until old age saps their endurance, reflecting the continuing subsistence and ideological significance of hunting among the Etolo, against its decline among the Rofaifo. In this regard, the Kundagai are more likely to hold to the

TABLE 8. HUNTING PRODUCTIVITY IN FOUR HIGHLAND SOCIETIES[a]

	Total hours	No. prey	Weight (kg)	Hours /kilo	Hours /prey
Kundagai	90.00	23	14.369	6.26	3.9
Rofaifo	497.17	37	19.792	25.10	13.4
Etolo	2,899.60	592	1,004.400	2.89	4.9
Wopkaimin	401.00	68	187.800	2.10	5.9

[a] Data for other than Kundagai from Dwyer (1974; 1983); Hyndman (1979).

Etolo pattern. Certainly I discerned no loss of skills among younger Kundagai hunters.

Dwyer (1983) offers another explanation for variations in hunting productivity in different societies and regions. In a comparison of the Etolo, Gadio Enga, and Rofaifo, he attributes declining yields to the effects of a depauperate mammalian community with increasing altitude, compounded by the effects of increasing population density. Although this argument may account for the lower productivity of Rofaifo hunting, the Kundagai do not fit the pattern. Certainly there is a decline both in the availability of the variety of mammal species and in the range of size of prey. Significantly, feral pigs are absent at the higher altitudes in which the Kundagai hunt. There is, however, no simple relation between increasing population density with altitude for the highlands as a whole or for the Maring in particular. And, although Dwyer notes that Etolo and other hunters do seek a wide range of prey species, as already indicated, there is nonetheless a clear preference for selecting a limited range of heavier prey.

Comparison of hunting productivity is hampered by the small sample size of the Kundagai material. The relatively high productivity of Kundagai hunting, however, measured as a ratio of time to weight yield, and especially as time to number of prey caught, seems to be a function of a willingness to take most game that is encountered rather than selecting heavy prey. High levels of skill, at least among more enthusiastic hunters, may also be a factor. This willingness stems in part from the objectives of hunters. Among the Rofaifo, Etolo, and Wopkaimin, the primary concern of hunters is to obtain meat. Although this is a prime aim of the Kundagai as well, it is not the sole objective; they also seek decorative plumes and furs for personal use or as items of trade.[2] But above all else, for the more enthusiastic Kundagai hunter at least, hunting is a sport and a pleasurable pastime.

HUNTING RESTRICTIONS

In the past any Kundagai could ideally shoot or trap game, including valuable plume-bearing birds, anywhere within the clan cluster territory from the Jimi to the Simbai River. Within this area individuals laid claim to particular localized resources, such as nests or bird of paradise display trees. Although Tsuwenkai remained uninhabited, Bokapai and Kinimbong Kundagai hunted there, though Bokapai residents infrequently because of the distance from their settlement and easy access to forests nearer the Jimi. Similarly, Kinimbong and Tsuwenkai residents seldom hunted in Bokapai land.

Initial government patrols sought to formalize settlement boundaries. As noted in chapter 1, the Kundagai recognize the official boundary between Bokapai and Tsuwenkai but not between Tsuwenkai and Kinimbong. Although early kiaps told the Kundagai to confine their activities within their three official territories, following traditional precedent any Kundagai is still accorded the right to harvest natural resources in any part of the clan cluster territory, without permission, provided the resource is not considered to be of value in the nonsubsistence sector of the economy (see table 9 for a list of restricted items). In line with the kiap's ruling on boundaries, and the subsequent affirmation of this by the Local Government Council, the Kundagai say that residents of Bokapai and Tsuwenkai should not hunt for valuable birds on one another's territory. Despite the kiap's ruling on the Kinimbong–Tsuwenkai boundary, members of these two settlements, as members of a single clan subcluster, say they are free to hunt valuable birds in both areas without territorial restriction. Kundagai territory is thus divided into two major subterritories in respect of hunting valuable birds. These territories conform to the two Kundagai clan subcluster territories.

Clan clusters are the largest units owning rights to the resources of a territory. Rights within this area may be further restricted at more exclusive structural levels. Members of other local groups have no rights to these resources. There are, however, several situations in which people are permitted to hunt on land of other clan clusters. Travelers

TABLE 9. RESTRICTED GAME

Species that may not be hunted in areas in which other individuals or groups have more exclusive hunting rights.

English Name	Scientific Name	Maring Name

A. Most commonly named species: Almost all informants agree that hunting rights to these species are restricted.

English Name	Scientific Name	Maring Name
Dwarf Cassowary chicks	*Casuarius bennetti*	*kombli*
Papuan Lory	*Charmosyna papou*	*goli*
Brown Sicklebill	*Epimachus meyeri*	*kalanc gurunt*
Black Sicklebill	*Epimachus fastosus*	*kalanc gi yondoi*
Stephanie's Astrapia	*Astrapia stephaniae*	*kombam*
Superb B. of P.	*Lophorina superba*	*yenandiok*
Lesser B. of P.[a]	*Paradisaea minor*	*yambai*
Saxony B. of P.	*Pteridophora alberti*	*balpan*

B. Less commonly named species: Fewer informants agree that hunting rights to these species are restricted.

English Name	Scientific Name	Maring Name
Dwarf Cassowary adults	*Casuarius bennetti*	*kombli*
Fairy Lory	*Charmosyna pulchella*	*jimbonk*
Parotia Bs. of P.	*Parotia* spp.	*kiawoi*
Blue B. of P.	*Paradisaea rudolphi*	*aweng*
Macgregor's Bowerbird	*Amblyornis macgregoriae*	*kombek*
Feral Pigs[a]		*konj demi*

[a] Not found in Tsuwenkai.

may shoot game of no special value that is encountered in foreign territories, but such hunting should occur only as opportunity permits, and a hunter should not stray far from paths. Anyone from another clan cluster found wandering away from paths is assumed to be poaching valuable game or on hostile business. Some Kundagai nonetheless say that a man is free to hunt within the clan cluster territory of his matrikin, *bapa-wambe,* and affines, *latse-imatse.* According to some, it is even permissible to shoot valuable birds in the territory of these kin, although it is polite to seek permission first. The extension of hunting rights so close matrikin and affines might be regarded as a form of the ideal of generalized exchange that the Maring consider should be maintained with these kin. Such hunting of valuable game is seldom done, unless in the company of matrikin or affines, and would not be condoned by unrelated members of foreign clan clusters.

Within the constraints noted above on hunting in territory to which one has no primary-use rights, only a few species of valuable game are forbidden quarry. With the exception of feral pigs and cassowaries the restricted species are the more valuable plume-bearing birds. There is no complete agreement on restricted game, but table 9 indicates those species generally listed by informants.

On land seldom used either for gardening or hunting and gathering, hunters from other groups may be tolerated, even if they have no close kinship ties with the landowners. Even valuable birds might be taken on such land, which is usually at such a distance from the settlements of the owners that they may be unaware of the extent of hunting by outsiders. For instance, the Kundagai hunted on former Cenda land in the upper Pint Valley (see map 3) long before they gained ownership of it.

A clan cluster would only tolerate hunting on its land by members of other friendly clan clusters or *nokomai*, "allies." Members of major enemy groups, *cenang yu*, were in the past in danger of being attacked if found hunting beyond their territory. A further factor inhibiting infringements of enemies' hunting rights was (and remains) the fear that the spirits of these groups resident in the forest would attack intruders, causing serious sickness or even death.

Boundaries of clan cluster territories in the primary forest are not always clear. For instance Mount Yirua on the Bismarck crest to the east of Kundagai territory is not clearly within the territory of any one clan cluster. Formerly the Kundagai, Manamban, Kanump–Kauwil, and Tuguma all hunted on the slopes of Yirua, and no one group claimed exclusive ownership to the area.

Within the Tsuwenkai–Kinimbong subcluster territory there is a further subdivision of land in respect to the hunting of valuable birds. A small area is the exclusive hunting territory of the Kolomp (1) clan, whereas all the remaining forested land may be hunted in by members of the Wendekai–Amankai–Atikai cognatic cluster (map 3). This Kolomp (1) hunting territory was established only a few years ago. Prior to contact any Kundagai was permitted to hunt valuable birds here as elsewhere. These became restricted game after the kiap ordered the Kundagai to confine their activities to their ancestral lands, and it seems that little hunting of valuable birds occurred here by non-Kolomp clansmen after the kiap's order. Several years ago, however, two Wendekai clansmen shot valuable birds on this land. The ensuing dispute was brought before a moot or *kot* (TP: "court") adjudicated by the Local Government councillor. The case is summarized here.[3]

CASE 1: RIM VERSUS AIKUPA AND CENGITAI

Aikupa and Cengitai of Wendekai clan went hunting together on Kolomp (1) land at Wumenakema, where Aikupa shot an Astrapia and Cengitai a Saxony Bird of Paradise. Rim objected to this infringement of his clan's hunting rights and, as the instigator of the dispute on behalf of his clan, demanded compensation for the birds killed. The consensus of opinion at the *kot* was that compensation should be given. Aikupa exchanged the Astrapia for a male piglet, which he gave to Yunai of Kolomp (1), a classificatory father of Rim. Cengitai gave K2 compensation for the Saxony Bird of Paradise to another classificatory father of Rim resident in Bokapai. Although Rim did not receive compensation himself he says he was satisfied that suitable recompense had been made.

During the dispute Kolomp (1) clansmen announced that a portion of clan land was to be marked out as an exclusive hunting preserve, within which only Kolomp (1) clansmen would have rights to hunt valuable birds, though any Kundagai would still be free to hunt for other birds or mammals. As a reminder of exclusive Kolomp (1) rights to the valuable resources of the land a Kolomp man planted two sets of cordyline shrubs and stakes about one kilometer apart on Kondokoi ridge in the forest.[4] All restricted game (table 9) found in the area running down to the valley floor from between the marks erected on the ridge may be hunted only by Kolomp (1) clansmen.

The Kolomp (1) of Tsuwenkai extend hunting rights to fellow clansmen living in Bokapai. These Bokapai Kolomp (1) and the Baikai (1) allied to Atikai are the only Bokapai clans with full hunting rights in Tsuwenkai. The issue of Baikai (2) clansmen (allied to Wendekai) hunting in Tsuwenkai has not arisen as far as I am aware.

In chapter 1, I noted that certain individuals are "fathers" of land in Tsuwenkai gained by grant from the Tsembaga and Tuguma. These individuals have extended full hunting rights to fellow members of the Wendekai–Amankai–Atikai cognatic cluster. These hunting rights relate only to the Kundagai and are not identical with rights in other settlements. Not all Maring and related populations claim the same type of hunting rights, although there are similarities in the basic principles involved.

By right of discovery members of territory-holding groups may claim individual ownership of resources on their land. By claiming particular trees attracting or sheltering animals, building traps or blinds, or hanging fruit lures, a hunter also establishes exclusive rights to harvest any game found in association with these objects. The basis for sole rights is that the claimant has expended time and effort in locating prime hunting sites or preparing structures and that he should therefore have primary access to the proceeds of his labor. Any man who capitalizes on the labor of others is liable to meet with a demand for compensation from the owner of the hunting rights. Most men say, however, that they would tolerate such infringements by close agnates, matrikin, and affines, and few men refuse requests to hunt at individually claimed sites.

Although any Kundagai may claim temporary rights of harvest at fruiting or flowering trees, or build hunting aids anywhere in Kundagai territory, he may only harvest restricted game in areas held by the smallest corporate landholding group of which he is a member. To hunt the more valuable birds (category A in table 9), men claim rights of harvest to flowering trees where Papuan Lories feed, to the nests of cassowaries, and to the display sites of birds of paradise. All these claims are temporary, lasting only until trees cease flowering, the cassowaries disperse, or the single birds of paradise occupying display trees are shot by the claimant. A hunter may not always be able to locate a display tree, even though a bird of paradise haunts a limited area. In this case he makes it known that he regards the bird as his by right of being the first person to locate its customary range. Such claims are not as outlandish as they might seem. Male birds are sedentary in habits and not infrequently have minor differences in plumage making them distinguishable to the practiced eye. Ideally a man should announce the location of any display tree or other sites he claims, so that others will not inadvertently shoot his birds and be asked to surrender the skin or pay compensation. In practice this is not always done, for two reasons. First, some men fear that poachers might deliberately shoot the birds. Second, it is tacitly agreed that valuable birds occurring in particular regions are owned by certain men who therefore have no need to make their specific claims known. For instance, Superb Birds of Paradise frequenting the forest edge near homesteads are assumed to be claimed by the owner of the nearest house. Again, as will be discussed shortly, some men confine their hunting to definite tracts of forest, and others assume that a hunter familiar with the area has already found and claimed all valuable birds there. Thus, in many parts of the forest most valuable birds are regarded as the property of individuals, and their rights of ownership are generally respected, even if they have not been announced publicly.[5]

The basis of concepts of individual property or ownership warrants further attention here. It is noteworthy that claims of individual rights to harvest birds at particular natural or man-made sites, or of ownership of birds in particular areas, apply in land held under collective tenure. Sites or particular birds come to be accepted as individual, as opposed to collective, property by the investment of personal labor. Kundagai point to the importance of what they refer to as *hat wok* (TP: "hard work"; Maring: *konggiang*), applied to building blinds, setting lures, and searching the forest. But this concept of labor is only incidentally concerned with its objective manifestations in the form of built structures, such as blinds and traps. More fundamentally, it is through "hard work" that one achieves specialist knowledge. A hunter builds his blinds or searches for birds, display trees, and fruiting trees on the basis of the personal knowledge he has accumulated over a long period of intense association with a particular tract of land. It is this familiarity, privileged knowledge and, indeed, emotional attachment, distilled over frequent visits, that prompts a man to speak of a particular tract of forest as "my land," *ren nan*. By this means he has acquired a richly textured understanding of the local environment—the conformation of the land and the particularities of the plant and animal communities it supports.

The unique knowledge a man may build up over time of a particular locality is the product of his own physical and intellectual efforts, even if it is grounded on a more general, less-detailed collective knowledge of the environment. Such specialist knowledge gives a man the potentiality to harvest the resources of his favored locality by conscious design, whereas those less familiar with the region depend more on chance. It gives a man privileged access to wild resources: valuable game is in a very real sense the product of unique knowledge, and hence it is the rightful property of the individuals who have worked at acquiring knowledge.

Specialist knowledge that yields material or other benefits of one kind or another is clearly a valuable resource. Detailed knowledge of natural history tends to be highly particular, rather than general: certain individuals are deeply knowledgeable about particular localities; some are acknowledged experts on high-forest birds, others on cassowaries, and yet others on phalangers and giant rats, and so on. There is, in short, a tendency toward specialist areas of expertise, although the range and depth of general knowledge of natural history among enthusiasts is impressive. This kind of specialist knowledge is akin to magical knowledge, in the sense that both are private, personal, and particular possessions. Certain individuals (men or women) are credited with knowing particularly efficacious magic for specific purposes, like promoting the growth of pigs or curing particular ailments. Individuals are reluctant to divulge details of their knowledge indiscriminately, though they readily apply their knowledge to assist others. Thus, a man may take a friend hunting in his favorite haunts or make a gift of a bird skin or meat to kin of affines—the product of his specialist knowledge—just as he will willingly perform secret magic he possesses on behalf of someone else.

The males of two species of birds of paradise gather to display communally at traditional sites in the Jimi. The most widespread and common is the Lesser Bird of Paradise of lower-montane forest, which is present in perhaps all middle-Jimi territories except Tsuwenkai (Healey 1978b). The other species, Princess Stephanie's Astrapia, is common in the Tsuwenkai high forest. There are four known display sites of this bird in Tsuwenkai. Some of the display trees have been in use up to sixty years by generations of birds. Three of these sites were found by Yekwai and his father Kemba, but they lost ownership of two to other men (see case 5 below). Yekwai and another tree owner are well known as eager hunters. In view of their frequent visits to their Astrapia trees, other men assume that these two hunters have discovered and claimed all other valuable birds in the vicinity and so generally refrain from seeking such birds in these regions.

Since sites where birds display communally may remain in use for so long, they are the most valuable of hunting claims an individual can make. In 1973–1974 none of the original discoverers of Astrapia display trees in Tsuwenkai had died, although Yekwai had effectively inherited his father's site as the old man was no longer an active hunter. Lesser Bird of Paradise display trees are usually inherited patrilineally, like other individual property. Occasionally, rights to harvest at trees are transferred in exchange for small payments of a pig, shells or, nowadays, money. Kinsmen may help a purchaser with small contributions hoping to be invited to hunt at the tree or rewarded with skins of birds shot there by the new owner. A Tsuwenkai man helped a Bokapai relative in such a purchase but never received any reward.

In principle, the Kundagai say that a man who claims ownership of display trees and the birds associated with them may demand that any plumes obtained at or near these sites by a non-right-holder be surrendered to him. The owner has the right to take possession of these skins even if the hunter was unaware that the bird shot was already claimed by another. In practice, few men who through either ignorance or intent shoot another man's birds do relinquish the plumes. In this case the rightful owner of the birds can expect to receive compensation amounting to the generally accepted value of the plumes in cash or other goods. Some men say that if the plumes are handed over by the poacher it is proper and wise for the owner of hunting rights to make at least a small return payment of cash or trade goods. It is considered proper because the poacher has worked hard to shoot the bird, just as the owner worked hard to establish his prior claims to ownership; it is wise because he may be a witch and, angered by compensation demands, may seek revenge through witchcraft if no payment is made to mollify him. The following cases illustrate some of these points.

CASE 2: KOM VERSUS YEKWAI

Without seeking permission Kom shot an Astrapia at the Bombong display tree formerly owned by Yekwai. Although Kom is his classificatory father, Yekwai demanded compensation. Kom, however, argued that although he had shot the bird it had escaped and died in the forest, where its decomposed remains were later found. Since he had worked hard to kill the bird but had not profited, Kom reasoned that he was not liable to pay compensation. Yekwai agreed with the argument and dropped his claims.

CASE 3: CENGITAI VERSUS MENEK

After the last case, Menek gained ownership of the Bombong site (see case 4). Here his clan brother Cengitai shot one adult male Astrapia and trapped an immature male close to the display site in mid-1972. Menek claimed that the birds visited his site and that by right they were his own, and demanded that Cengitai hand over the skin of the adult bird. Cengitai refused, saying he wished to exchange the skin for a pig. He agreed, however, to give Menek one of the progeny of the pig he obtained. In September 1974 Cengitai gave Menek a piglet in settlement.

During the *kot* on the issue some men told Cengitai and his brother that since their father was an Ambrakwi (who sought refuge with his Kundagai matrikin and affines after a violent dispute with other Ambrakwi), they had no right to hunt on Kundagai land. They were told to confine all their hunting to Mena, a tract of land bought by the Bokapai Kundagai from the Ambrakwi in the late 1960s. The two men have not complied with this directive, which has not been pressed further.

I have noted above that some men customarily hunt in certain tracts of forest. Other men seldom seek valuable birds there, on the assumption that they have already been claimed. In short, informal personal hunting territories can be identified, within which other members of the group holding corporate hunting rights to valuable game in that region seldom hunt, in recognition of the intensive hunting activities of one man. Such men thereby gain de facto exclusive rights to hunt valuable birds occurring on the land, even if they have not been claimed previously or discovered by the hunter. Some men who are regarded as holding these informal territories speak of the land as their own, *ren nan* ("land mine"). Kinsmen sometimes share personal hunting domains. There are no formal principles of ownership of domains. Rather, they are recognized on the basis of the current most-intensive users of the land for the purpose of hunting valuable birds. In addition, as the following case shows, vague notions of inheritance may also be entailed in defining personal territories.

CASE 4: YEKWAI VERSUS AIKUPA AND MENEK

Yekwai and his father Kemba found two Astrapia display sites: at Gandakai and Bombong. They shot several birds at each place. Kemba subsequently ceased hunting actively and Yekwai retained ownership of the sites. Aikupa disputed Yekwai's right to the Gandakai site and declared ownership himself. He justified his claim by noting that his father's father had for a time lived at Bokapai, from where he and his coresidents had hunted at Gandakai.

Menek took possession of the Bombong site, arguing that his father's mother was of Aiwaka clan of Bokapai and that the Aiwaka had formerly hunted at Bombong. Both men, in short, claimed to inherit informal hunting territories held by groups of men two generations ago.

Yekwai agrees that he has relinquished rights to these sites but still regards his claims of ownership to be stronger than those of their present owners. He supports these claims by stating that as the original finders of the sites he and his father have superior rights of ownership. He further argues that Gandakai and Bombong were included in the grant of land from Kolomp (2) to his own clan (Atikai; see chap. 1) and that Wendekai and Amankai are entitled to garden the land and harvest its resources only on sufferance. (Aikupa and Menek are of Wendekai clan.) He ceased to press his claim because he says Aikupa and Menek are more persuasive and aggressive talkers than himself. Both are politically influential—Aikupa a *tep yu* big-man and former *luluai* and kaunsil, Menek the present kaunsil.

The following table (table 10) lists the six personal hunting territories identified by informants. The areas are not clearly demarcated, but each is composed of a core ridge or ridges where the principal hunter or hunters concentrate their activities.

TABLE 10.   PERSONAL HUNTING TERRITORIES
IN TSUWENKAI, 1974

Hunter(s)	Relationship	Territory[a]
1. Aikupa[b]		Dukema, Gandakai
2. Dukumpwai & Gela	Brothers	Yongga
3. Kemba & Yekwai[b]	Father-son	Gonggia, Gacambo ridges 1, 2, 3, & 4
4. Kima		Anggelep & upper Anyen
5. Menek[b]		Anggelep
6. Rim		Wumenakema, Mindindepe

[a] See map 3 for locations
[b] Astrapia display tree owners. The fourth site owner, Planc, is too old to hunt and seldom did so when younger. His surviving sons are absent, and no personal territory is associated with his tree (now abandoned).

I am not sure how widely these territories are recognized, but certainly the individuals named are the most active hunters in the regions listed, according to records in hunting histories. Rim, as senior Kolomp (1) clansman, is regarded as the local "father" of the area in his domain, while Dukumpwai and Gela are the sole acknowledged "fathers" to the former Kwibukai land at Yongga (see chap. 1). As such, these three men would have primary use rights to these areas even if they were not active hunters. The other personal domains are on land of the Wendekai–Amankai–Atikai cognatic cluster.

Menek seldom hunts at Anggelep, but informants (including Menek) list him as retaining a personal territory because he owns an Astrapia display tree there. Kima frequently hunts there and at Anyen and was, therefore, included as a domain holder even though he neither owns Astrapia trees nor is a "father" of land. These two men, therefore, share parts of their domains. They are classificatory brothers, firm friends, and political allies.

The largest single domain is that of Kemba and Yekwai. With Kemba's advancing age Yekwai is now the most active hunter in this area. Their hunting territory was larger in the past when they owned Astrapia display sites at Gandakai and Anggelep (case 4).

Of the eight men listed in the table, Aikupa, Dukumpwai, and Kima are regarded by informants as *yu tum kabang gwio aumba yundo* (prominent hunters). Kemba had been such a hunter in the past. Although Yekwai owns an Astrapia display site, he does not consider himself to be a successful hunter, though some others class him as one.[6]

There are a number of taboos on the eating of game which pertain to various categories of persons or particular stages in the ritual cycle. Hunters do not deliberately seek out tabooed game, but they may kill such an animal when encountered and give it to someone else to eat. Many younger Kundagai profess an ignorance of dietary taboos or simply do not observe them. Various ritual states that formerly involved restrictions on the diet no longer occur. Nonetheless, such taboos undoubtedly influenced hunting intensity and selectivity of prey in the recent past. The most significant and widely observed taboos on the eating or killing of game occurred in the context of war and its aftermath.

During periods of hostilities warriors assumed taboos on the consumption of a variety of animals and crops, including several marsupials, eels, cassowaries, and certain other birds associated with water or the night. Fight Magic men, *bamp kunda yu,* assumed a wider range of taboos, many of which they maintain for life. For other fighters some dietary taboos were abrogated on the cessation of fighting and others at the uprooting of the *yu miny rumbim,* "men's souls' cordylines," which were planted immediately after establishing a truce in order to give protection to warriors. The uprooting of the *rumbim* occurs several years after the termination of a war and is one ceremony of the ritual cycle culminating in the *konj kaiko.* During this period there is also a ban on trapping mammals in the forest, and Rappaport (1968: 151) suggests that this allows mammal numbers to increase. It is not clear, however, if these taboos act as a general disincentive to hunting, or if men turn their attention to other prey, including plume-bearing birds.

The Kundagai consider that the spirits can restrict hunting success by hiding their "pigs"—game mammals and birds—from the hunter. However, men themselves should exercise restraint in the number of animals they kill in a single day to avoid the anger of the spirits. This notion may be invoked to explain subsequent misfortunes, but I doubt that a man cuts short a hunting trip if it proves unusually successful, as good fortune itself can be interpreted as a sign of benevolence on the part of spirits who remove protection from their "pigs." They are especially likely to do this if the game is intended for ritual feasts in their honor or plumes are to be used in dances associated with the *konj kaiko.*

As well as the various jural and supernatural restrictions that limit hunting, some Kundagai also accept a number of voluntary restraints. I have already noted that few men shoot birds in the informal, personal domains of other men. This is a jural restriction if the birds have been claimed publicly, but a voluntary restraint if the territory owner is assumed to be unaware of the presence of some birds in his area. Movements and reproduction of the birds will ensure that from time to time the numbers of birds in a personal territory will change, and the non-territory-holder is free to harvest these if he finds them first. In practice, few men are prepared to exercise this right, lest the customary hunter of that area claim that the birds killed are his own.

Some Kundagai consider that, aside from avoiding the anger of spirits, it is advisable to exercise restraint in the number or frequency of valuable birds killed. They argue that hunting rates should be moderated to give bird populations a respite for regeneration. Some men say that as a rough guide one should kill no more than half the males of valuable species occurring in a given area, or half the number of Astrapia displaying at a single site.

In the past, female-plumaged birds of paradise[7] were commonly shot and trapped for food, but many hunters now state that this practice is unwise. Since contact, they say, the volume of plumes traded has increased, and they claim that this has been sustained by increased hunting rates, to the extent that if female-plumaged birds are killed the reproductive potential of valuable birds will be reduced. By sparing female-plumaged birds the Kundagai argue that the resulting increased reproductive pool can accommodate the higher predation by man on adult male birds. Several men told me that they do not shoot female-plumaged birds, and if they find them alive and unharmed in their traps they may even release them. Most Kundagai, however, say that no such restraint need be exercised on the Superb Bird of Paradise as this species is abundant. In fact, some men seldom killed female-plumaged birds even before the presumed increase in predation and trade in plumes following contact. These last two restraints on hunting are deliberately applied as conservatory measures, so that the continued survival of valuable birds to be exploited for decorations and trade is enhanced.

Hunting is somewhat seasonal, being more intensive during the drier season. The Superb and Saxony Birds of Paradise are generally silent in wet weather and, since they are often located by their calls, hunting them in the rain is not only uncomfortable but difficult. Astrapia are said to visit display sites even in the rain and can therefore be hunted profitably at any time. Even in the drier season most hunting occurs only during fine weather, for rain makes hunting uncomfortable and less productive.

Shortly preceding and during the annual molt (about June to August), plumes are in poor condition or only partially developed. By reducing hunting activities at this time the Kundagai minimize loss of plumes from their stocks by shooting birds with inferior plumes that would not be acceptable as valuable trade or decoration items.

Older men told me that toward the end of the ritual cycle they went hunting especially to obtain plumes to wear on the last day of the *konj kaiko*. Nowadays it seems that hunting is seldom increased before particular dances in connection with the *kaiko* or other occasions. Certainly I discerned no such intensification prior to the several dances that occurred while I was in the field, nor did informants suggest that this occurred nowadays.

Although one might conclude that intensification of hunting to secure plumes for specific occasions in the past was probably of only minor significance in altering predation rates,[8] there is little doubt that during periods of hostilities hunting was considerably reduced. The assumption of taboos on the eating of a large variety of marsupials and certain other animals, many of them esteemed for their flesh, meant that there was little incentive for hunting in this period. A further disincentive was the fact that the solitary hunter or small party was vulnerable to attack by enemy raiders who usually traveled through the forest for concealment. For this reason, any hunting done during periods of hostilities mostly occurred away from areas where the enemy or bribed assassination parties from other settlements were likely to appear.

Big-men of all categories, but especially *tep yu* ("Talk Men") and *bamp kunda yu* ("Fight Magic Men") were particularly sought by raiding parties, and these men were cautioned by their comrades never to venture beyond the areas of homesteads and gardens without companions. Several big-men told me that their hunting activities had been constrained by fear of attack. Nowadays the Kundagai evince no fear of attack while hunting, except from witches.

The Jimi Local Government Council was established in 1966. At various times since then the councillors in session have affirmed the clan cluster boundaries established by early kiaps and echoed kiaps' injunctions to confine all gardening and hunting of valuable birds to the land of the smallest territory-holding group of which one is a member. Although the Kundagai formerly held joint and exclusive rights to the exploitation of resources throughout their estate, the Council rules on territories have shifted ownership of hunting rights to more exclusive structural levels. This conforms to traditional restrictions in many of the constituent wards of the Council, although there is some variation between individuals' conceptions of hunting rights within and between settlements.

The Council has also affirmed the right of individuals to claim ownership of particular display sites that a man might find on territory in which he has full hunting rights.

Case 5: Aikupa versus Yari

> Aikupa often went hunting at Aiyonju in Bokapai territory. Here he found an Astrapia display site where over a number of years he shot several birds. Yari of Baikai (1) clan at Bokapai disputed Aikupa's claim of ownership. Both men agreed that the land had formerly belonged to the Went–Kai, now of Rinyimp. Yari claimed that he had the right to own the tree in preference to Aikupa because his sister was married to a Went–Kai man and that he was free to hunt on his affines' land. Aikupa justified his claim by pointing out that use rights to Aiyonju had been given to his father and father's brother as part of affinal exchanges (see chap. 1). The land therefore belonged to his own clan, Wendekai. Aikupa and Yari both continued to claim superior rights of ownership, until in about 1967 Yari felled the tree in anger.
>
> Up to this point it appears that each man recognized the other's right to hunt at Aiyonju. The dispute was rather over who had the strongest claim to the tree. At this stage, however, other Bokapai residents entered the dispute and introduced a new issue. They pointed out that Aiyonju is within Bokapai territory as determined by annexation after a war with the Went–Kai and as affirmed by the kiap and the Council. As a resident of Tsuwenkai Aikupa therefore had no right to hunt valuable birds there. This argument was accepted by other Tsuwenkai residents (who had no particular stake in the issue), and the Tsuwenkai kaunsil warned Aikupa that he should cease hunting at Aiyonju. Aikupa still claims hunting rights there and, although he continues to visit the area and has recently shot Astrapia there, he has not been involved in any further disputes on the issue.

Although restraints on the hunting of female-plumaged birds were formerly a matter of choice for individual hunters, the Council has now declared that all hunters must observe this rule. No one could tell me how such a rule could be enforced since, according to Maring legal conceptions, an offence that can be sanctioned by the living, as opposed to spirits, only occurs when the rights of another person have been infringed. Shooting female-plumaged birds does not constitute such an infringement, as no one claims to own them.

The only rule introduced by the Council which has no traditional basis relates to the use of shotguns. Councillors have been told in Tok Pisin by government officers that it is illegal throughout Papua New Guinea to shoot *kumul* with a gun. To Jimi people *kumul* means only the Lesser Bird of Paradise and not the wider category of birds of paradise in general. It is therefore permissible, they say, to shoot other valuable birds of paradise[9] with a gun, provided this is done only by the licensed holder of the gun and that he hunts only in areas where he has rights to kill valuable birds. This misconception, the result of inadequate communication between government officers and councillors,[10] has resulted in at least one unfortunate prosecution under national hunting laws.

CASE 6: ANC KILLS A BIRD OF PARADISE WITH A GUN

This case, which does not involve any Kundagai, illustrates the misinterpretation of official court decisions that while officially punishing one offence appear to sanction informal Council rules.

> Anc (a pseudonym) is the kaunsil of a Jimi Maring settlement and a prominent figure in the Local Government Council. He used his shotgun to shoot a Sicklebill on the land of a Simbai Valley community. Someone complained to the Simbai kiap about this infringement of their territorial hunting rights. The Simbai kiap informed his Tabibuga counterpart who convicted Anc on a charge of using a shotgun to kill a bird of paradise. Anc was fined and his gun impounded in Tabibuga, while the bird skin was confiscated in the Simbai where it joined a display of murder weapons on the courthouse walls.
>
> According to Kundagai informants, however, Anc was entitled to shoot the Sicklebill with his gun but was punished for hunting on the land of another group where he had no rights.

No Kundagai own guns, nor is there any strong desire to do so. The leading Kundagai *tep yu* big-man told me he has forbidden the Kundagai to own guns. It is doubtful that his injunction would be heeded if the opportunity to obtain a gun license arose, but his objections to guns seem to be accepted by many. He argues that guns make hunting easier and that there would therefore be a real danger of rapidly exterminating valuable birds locally. This would disrupt trade and Kundagai ability to acquire valuables in exchange for plumes. He notes that bows and arrows and traps have hitherto proved sufficient to secure game. Guns are also dangerous, and he cites several incidents in other parts of the Jimi where men have borrowed guns and injured themselves and others through misuse. Finally, he says, it would be easy for a witch to find a hunter in the forest by following the sound of his gun; the solitary hunter would make an easy victim.

All informants see these restrictions on hunting as safeguarding their *bisnis* interests. A common statement throughout the north Jimi is that plumes are *bisnis bilong mipela* (TP: "our commercial enterprise"). Council rules on territories and individual ownership of birds or display sites safeguard holders of hunting rights from poaching of birds to which only they have rights of access. Similarly, rules forbidding the killing of female-plumaged birds and shooting the Lesser Bird of Paradise with a gun are accepted for their value of conserving valuable species. The Kundagai recognize that it is in their own long-term *bisnis* interests to preserve bird populations at sufficient densities to permit sustained exploitation to provide plumes for trade, especially as there are very limited opportunities for entrepreneurial activities. I return to the issue of conservation of bird populations in the following section.

Where an individual's hunting rights are infringed he may bring the resulting dispute to a *kot* adjudicated by the kaunsil or komitis. Often these officials take no active part in the proceedings if public opinion crystallizes quickly and parties to a dispute agree to any decisions arrived at. Ideally a settlement is not reached until the principals to a dispute and the spectators have reached a consensus of opinion as to where the guilt for any wrongdoing lies and what recompense must be made to the injured party. Anyone is free to speak, and in the course of a dispute other grievances may be aired. Often these further complicate a dispute, opinion becomes divided, and no settlement is reached. In such situations, *kots* may drag on for days until an agreement is reached. Occasionally, to effect an early settlement, the kaunsil may threaten to take the disputants before the kiap, whose courts are seen as swift, intransigent meetings.

By law, councillors had no authority to deliver judgments in *kots*. Neither they nor their constituents were aware of this, and kiaps have encouraged councillors to settle minor disputes in order to leave the official courts free to conduct what kiaps see as more serious cases. Such encouragement by kiaps and their occasional upholding of rulings given by councillors in disputes referred to official courts certainly appeared to the Jimi people to support councillors' claims that they have the power to give judgments in *kots*.

Intervention by the kiap in disputes is interpreted as sanctioning the power of the kaunsil and therefore as legitimizing Council rules (TP: *lo*). None of the *lo* relating to hunting territories and rights set down by the Council have been forwarded to the Office of Local Government in Port Moresby for ratification. As such, they do not constitute formally recognized by-laws of the Council, and so transgressions legally cannot be punished either by local *kots* or the formal courts of the kiap. But by claiming and appearing to receive the endorsement of Council *lo* and local *kot* decisions, councillors and their followers created a situation where unofficial courts based on a blend of traditional and introduced conceptions of dispute settlement became integrated into the official national legal system.[11]

INTENSITY AND EFFECTS OF HUNTING

This analysis of the ecology of plume production rests on a detailed examination of aspects of bird population dynamics which moves from strictly anthropological concerns to ornithology. Since this analysis and supporting data are dealt with elsewhere (Healey 1986) and may be of little interest for many readers, I simply draw on the relevant conclusions from that study, rather than detailing the research strategy and analysis.

Although Kundagai hunting appears to be more productive than in some highlands societies, it is unlikely that traditional strategies are much more efficient. Productivity of hunting partly depends on the game sought. As I have indicated, although Kundagai hunting is focused on a limited range of arboreal mammals and plume-bearing birds, the hunter is less discriminating in the prey he takes than some hunters elsewhere. Productivity also depends on the number of active hunters in an area and the abundance of game. Clearly, these factors may be closely linked.

Where there is a high ratio of hunters to a given area of hunting land, their effects on prey populations will tend to be greater than where there is a lower ratio. Many hunters combing the area for game are more likely to secure a higher total bag than a few hunters. This may even be the case where each individual has limited success as game becomes scarcer through intensive predation. By contrast, where the ratio of hunters to area of hunting land is low, individual hunters can achieve high productivity while the total bag of all hunters remains relatively low. Predation, in short, may be extensive rather than intensive.

These propositions can be examined by a comparison of hunter to land-area ratios in several Maring territories (table 11). Areas of hunting land in the table include only primary forest, and in all places other

TABLE 11. RATIO OF HUNTERS TO HUNTING LAND IN MARING TERRITORIES[a]

Population	No. Hunters	Area forest (km²)	No. Hunters/ km²
Tsuwenkai Kundagai[b]			
a.	58	16	3.8
b.	89	16	5.6
Tsembaga	68	3.9	17.4
Tuguma	81	5.9	13.7
Kanump-Kauwil	125	4.4	28.4
Kandambent-Namikai	97	4.3	22.6
Tsenggamp-Mirimbikai	57	5.6	10.2
Bomagai-Angoiang	32	0.9	35.5
"Gunts"[c]	89	6.2	14.3
Kauwatyi	315	c 2.7	c 116.7
Total[d]	913	49.9	18.3
Mean[d]	101	5.5	29.4

[a] For sources see Healey (1977: 235). See appendix 4 and map 1 for locations.
[b] Entry a, resident population in November 1974; entry b resident population plus absentee males. The latter entry to be compared with other populations.
[c] Includes Bomagai-Angoiang and Funggai-Korama communities.
[d] Only entry b. for Kundagai included. For Total entry, no. hunters/km² = no. hunters/area. For Mean entry, no. hunters/km² = mean of vertical column.

than Tsuwenkai this includes lower-montane forest. All males over the estimated age of fifteen years are taken to represent the number of potential hunters.

The actual ratio of hunters to forest land will be lower than indicated for two reasons: population figures include small numbers of absentees, as well as old men who seldom if ever hunt. I can correct for these factors only in the case of Tsuwenkai. Assuming that the proportion of male nonhunters is similar in each population, these ratios serve as a rough index of the maximum potential hunting pressure expressed as the number of hunters operating in a given area.

A more useful ratio for comparative purposes would be the number of hunters within a radius of half a day's walk of settlements—that is, forest that can be exploited in a one-day trip from settlements. All Tsuwenkai forest is within this distance and, since Tsuwenkai includes within its borders the largest known area of forest of all Maring territories, I would estimate that the area of accessible forest of all populations listed in the table within which settlement members have primary hunting rights is also within half a day's walk. The Bomagai–Angoiang of the Gunts area are an exception, for they have access to a vast, unpopulated tract of primary forest to the southeast beyond their territory (Buchbinder 1973: 133). For this group it is likely that the number of hunters to the square kilometer of hunting land (whether in absolute terms or within half a day's walk from Gunts) is well below the figure for the Kundagai.

Even if game is equally numerous in all territories listed, it must be subjected to less intensive predation in Tsuwenkai as measured by the density of hunters operating in a given area. The inference is that each hunter in Tsuwenkai, having a larger area in which to hunt, competes less with his fellows and may thereby be capable of securing larger amounts of prey in a given time. Men of all settlements probably have roughly equal demands on their time to participate in social and subsistence activities.[12] This places an upper limit on the amount of time they are able to devote to hunting. Kundagai and Bomagai–Angoiang hunters may be more inclined to approach the maximum amount of time possible in hunting, as the returns from this activity will be greater, making hunting a more rewarding activity.

Since the amount of time available for hunting is limited, it also follows that game is subjected to less hunting pressure where the density of hunters is low. For example, 6 Kundagai per square kilometer of hunting land will have to work much harder to exert the same hunting pressure in the same period of time as 117 Kauwatyi. It is in this regard that the differential rights of clans and individuals to hunting land or specific sites become particularly important in reducing overall hunting pressure, although these restrictions do not apply to all categories of game.

Aside from the time available for hunting and competition from other hunters, the efficiency of a hunter is further limited by his personal knowledge of game, skill in hunting techniques, and efficiency of his weapons. Available time and other limitations set an upper limit on the productivity of hunting. Where the ratio of hunters to hunting land is high these additional limitations become less significant in reducing hunting pressure. Where the ratio of hunters to hunting land is low, as in Tsuwenkai, additional limitations become more important in reducing overall hunting success, so that although each hunter may be highly productive, the sum of all hunters' efforts may have a lesser effect or pressure on their prey. This may be so even if the total number of prey killed exceeds the total killed by populations with a high hunter-to-area ratio, because prey species may remain more numerous, in turn sustaining continued high productivity of hunters.

Game, of course, is not equally numerous in all territories, while the preferred prey also varies in relation to what is locally available. Feral pigs and large lower-montane marsupials are especially sought by the non-Kundagai listed in the table. These animals are absent from Tsuwenkai where hunters concentrate on montane marsupials and birds. I have no good data on the relative abundance of game in different territories. Informants' subjective opinions and the results of a dietary survey by Buchbinder nonetheless offer a rough guide.

Kauwatyi men told me that birds of paradise were less numerous in their territory than in Tsuwenkai. In a survey of the contribution of game to the diet, Buchbinder (1973) found that little meat had been eaten in most populations during the week prior to her investigation, and that had been mainly from small animals rather than the preferred larger prey. The Kandambent–Namikai and Tsenggamp–Mirimbikai said small game was common, but the Kanump–Kauwil, with the highest ratio of hunters to land, said there was little game available and apparently had difficulty in locating it. Only the Gunts people had caught large quantities of game, including larger animals. Their hunter-to-land ratio is no doubt lower than the table suggests because of access to uninhabited forest in the Ramu lowlands.

Buchbinder's data suggest a gradient of game availability from least where overall population densities are highest to where densities are lowest. The Tsuwenkai Kundagai conform to this pattern; with their low hunter-to-land ratio they appear to have access to much game. The Kundagai consider that their preferred prey are mostly quite common and, although a competent hunter may not always find what he is searching for, he seldom has much difficulty in locating game of some sort. His problem, rather, is actually killing it. These observations are inconclusive but lend some support to the hypothesis that game is more plentiful and an individual's hunting productivity is greater in those territories where there is a low ratio of hunters to land area.

Demographic factors may limit the intensity of hunting but have no necessary and direct conservatory impact by imposing absolute limits on levels of predation. Although hunting contributes to subsistence, though marginally and erratically, the motivations to hunt are very different from those of subsistence hunter–gatherers, whose levels of predation are intrinsically limited by the finite demands of modest and immediate subsistence targets (Lee 1979; Sahlins 1972). For the Kundagai, hunting is subservient to the demands of subsistence production, rather than being a component of such production, and as such, although wild meat is a welcome addition to the diet, it is not considered a culturally "necessary" component. Nor is success in hunting ideologically necessary for the achievement of masculine identity. Thus, as far as I am aware, women and children do not nag men of the household to go hunting for meat, nor is there any suggestion that unsuccessful hunters are deficient in masculinity. In this the Kundagai contrast with some hunter–gatherer societies, such as the Kalahari San (Lee 1979) and hunter–horticulturalists, such as the Amazonian Sharanahua (Siskind 1973).[13] A proficient hunter may gain some notoriety, but a poor hunter suffers no loss of esteem. Many men rarely go on deliberate hunting excursions, and only a few are skillful and knowledgeable hunters making extended trips into the high forest at all frequently.

Under these circumstances hunting serves as a diversion from everyday pursuits rather than a materially and ideologically "necessary" undertaking. It provides a welcome source of meat but is hardly an imperative. The tangible fruits of hunting can be readily absorbed by the nonsubsistence exchange economy, as the finite objectives of subsistence have no bearing on the activity, except to supress hunting in times of intensive agricultural labor demand.

This means, on the one hand, that active hunters are self-limited to those with sufficient skill and inclination. On the other hand, those who do choose to hunt tend to focus their activities on plume-bearing birds and marsupials valued for their pelts and fur. Notwithstanding the Kundagai hunter's willingness to take a range of prey, his search strategies are thus directed to securing products that can be accumulated almost without limit. As such, there is no intrinsic factor beyond personal disinclination which will limit the intensity of hunting by ardent hunters. Potentially, then, the survival of birds and marsupials valued primarily for feathers and furs is endangered by overexploitation to satisfy a highly elastic demand for trade goods, in addition to the threat of habitat destruction that threatens all forest game.

I have already argued that habitat destruction is unlikely to pose an absolute threat to most valuable game animals (see also Healey 1986). Various practices and belief also limit hunting pressure and may therefore have some conservatory value.

Taboos on hunting and eating certain favored game animals associated with ritual states, notably in times of war, undoubtedly reduced hunting intensity in the past, as did fear of ambush in the lonely forest during hostilities. The occurrence of war followed a long cycle of periodicity ranging from about eight to twenty years. With the cessation of war such long cycles of fluctuating hunting intensity no longer occur. The short, seasonal cycle of decreased hunting intensity in the wetter months remains important, however. Since most birds, including plume-bearing birds of paradise, breed in the wetter season, the seasonality of hunting facilitates the annual recovery of populations of deep-forest birds.

Dietary taboos affecting particular individuals permanently or collectivities periodically may make hunting a less attractive pursuit for the gourmet, since most tabooed species are favored larger game mammals. Plume-bearing birds, however, are not subject to such taboos. Nonetheless, the reduced range of potential prey may serve as a disincentive to hunt at all.

The observance of hunting restrictions in relation to corporate territorial rights or the rights of individuals to harvest valuable birds at flowering trees, blinds, display trees, or in de facto personal hunting reserves reduces the number of hunters active in certain localities. This in itself does not necessarily mean that hunting intensity is comparably reduced. However, fewer hunters will concentrate their active search for game on more numerous, desirable prey. Should such game decline in numbers from overhunting or other causes, hunters will turn to alternative prey or cease hunting altogether.

In combination with factors reducing the number of active hunters the technology of uncertain reliability is of particular importance in limiting predation. Despite often considerable knowledge of his prey and skill in hunting techniques, the simple technology of hunting often leads to failure: wind or leaves deflect the unfletched arrow; bowstrings snap at inopportune moments; or a bird darts from its perch on hearing the twang of a bowstring. Traditional hunting weapons and, of course, traps are only effective at a close range many prey will not tolerate. These limitations make the shotgun an attractive alternative. The success of a hunting expedition is never a foregone conclusion—and therein no doubt lies part of the attraction for some men.

Although limits on hunting intensity, supported by legal principles, religious belief, and a disinclination to persist in unproductive activity may have beneficial consequences for the conservation of game, it is important to recognize that such consequences are not necessarily intended. Further, although it is possible to hypothesize, as Rappaport (1968) has done for the Tsembaga, that cultural and social factors reduce hunting pressure absolutely or periodically, thus enabling game numbers to build up to optimum levels, it is difficult to demonstrate that this circumstance actually occurs synergistically (cf. Dwyer 1982: 179).

Many Kundagai and other north-Jimi people consider that trade in forest products is an important *bisnis* or cash-earning activity, and they recognize the need to limit their hunting to conserve bird populations for continued harvest. Voluntary restraints on killing female and immature male birds of paradise and on leaving some adult males alive at communal display sites are explained by hunters as having deliberate conservatory value. To the extent that these restraints are actually observed, so confining hunting to adult male birds, they would undoubtedly have beneficial effects. Sparing female and immature male birds helps maintain the reproductive pool of females in polygynous breeding species (including all valued birds of paradise) and the number of immature males to reach maturity for later harvest. Such practices are nonetheless intended to further the short-term exploitative interests of individual hunters rather than for the benefit of the community at large, much less the preservation of wild animals as an end in itself (cf. Bulmer 1982).

Various Kundagai hunting rights and practices and mystical beliefs amount to an integrated system of conservatory value. There is, however, no direct evidence for the positive benefits of hunting techniques and restrictions in limiting the intensity of predation. The Kundagai, however, regard most valuable birds to be quite common in their territory. The two exceptions are the Black and Brown Sicklebill Birds of Paradise whose present rarity may well be due partly to past hunting pressure. There is some circumstantial evidence for reduced hunting pressure at communal display sites of the Astrapia as a consequence of de facto personal hunting preserves of those claiming exclusive rights of harvest, and of restraints on killing females, young males, and all adult displaying males (Healey 1986). However, in the absence of comparative material from other communities that do not observe the restrictions outlined here, it is possible only to infer the conservatory benefits of these beliefs and practices.

On purely intuitive grounds one might suppose that among birds lacking pair bonding, as with the more ornate birds of paradise, selective hunting of mature males will only endanger local populations if all or nearly all such birds are killed. This is because a few surviving males mate with an undiminished stock of females, so that annual breeding rates remain unaffected (see Healey 1986 for a fuller discussion of this issue as it relates to Tsuwenkai). Given that Kundagai hunting of birds of paradise is, by their own testimony, sex selective for males, one would expect an unbalanced sex ratio in favor of females in the few species subjected to intensive hunting. In fact, hunting records indicate that predation is not as markedly age and sex selective. This may go some way to explaining why sex ratios in Tsuwenkai bird populations appear close to equality.[14]

The Kundagai claim, correctly, that they have intensified trading since the government peace was established in the mid-1950s. They also claim that hunting rates have increased to sustain a greater volume of trade. If this is so, one might presume that hunting now poses a greater threat to the survival of wild birds, and so to the Kundagai's continued participation as major providers of trade plumes. To evaluate the situation one must therefore compare predation rates with rates of recruitment in bird populations. This is a difficult exercise. Obviously one cannot reconstruct past predation figures because many former hunters are now dead.

Estimating annual recruitment rates for birds is a problem of a different order, involving concepts and methods of the animal population ecologist. I have attempted this elsewhere (Healey 1986) and will not repeat the exercise. Suffice to say that the conclusions I summarize are merely approximations on a thin data base and refer only to three species of birds of paradise intensively hunted for their plumes.[15] Predation rates of individual hunters vary considerably over time, but since the numbers of hunters, their identities, and skills also vary, any fluctuations in predation rates by individuals are not necessarily reflected in their combined rates. Contrary to Kundagai opinion, an analysis of the fifty-seven hunting histories I collected, which extend back to the 1920s, shows that there has been no appreciable increase in predation rates of the more commonly killed valuable birds. How greater rates of trade are sustained in the face of no significant change in local production will be examined in chapter 5.

The following table (table 12) provides an index of annual predation rates in the years before and after 1956. Obviously, these figures are not based on the total number of birds killed but on total remembered kills by men still living. Absolute numbers of kills would be higher for both periods, but most especially so for the pre-1956 years because rec-

TABLE 12. INDEX OF ANNUAL PREDATION RATES ON BIRDS, PRE- AND POST-1956

Species	No. birds killed	Pre-1956 Period of records in years	Rate/ year	Post-1956[a] No. birds killed	Rate/ year	1973/74 No. killed	Annual recruit-ment rate males[b]
Cassowary[c]	13	20	0.65	19	1.0	0	?
Buzzard	5	15	0.33	4	0.2	1	?
Harpy Eagle	1	15	0.07	2	0.1	0	?
Papuan Lory	27	30	0.9	16	0.8	1	?
Fairy Lory	97	15	6.5	19	1.0	2	?
Astrapia	16	25	0.6	19	1.0	2	5
Superb B. of P.	24	25	1.0	29	1.5	8	12-17
Saxony B. of P.	28	25	1.1	22	1.1	5	11

[a] All records over nineteen years.
[b] From Healey (1986). These are deliberately minimum rates; actual rates must be higher, but by an unknown factor.
[c] Live chicks caught.

ords for that period are based on the testimony of fewer surviving men who were actively hunting then. I add figures for the number of birds killed during fieldwork, which represent as close to absolute numbers as is possible to show. Clearly, annual rates can fluctuate within limits without seriously endangering the long-term survival of local bird populations, but I have no way of determining whether 1973–1974 records are anywhere near average rates. Also, I cannot be certain that I heard of all kills during the year, though I am confident that few escaped my channels of information. Similarly, it is not possible to even suggest how much higher annual predation rates for pre- and post-1956 should be. Given these limitations of data, what the table does suggest is that predation rates have remained fairly constant over time, even if they have fluctuated in the short term.

It is, in fact, quite possible that pre-1956 predation rates were not only higher than suggested but actually exceeded post-1956 rates. If this was so, the decline in hunting rates might be a consequence of either increased rates of trade through Tsuwenkai replacing hunting as a means of acquiring plumes, or a response to increasing scarcity of birds, or both. The opinion of Kundagai hunters certainly does not support the latter suggestion. That predation rates for three of the birds listed are within estimates of minimum annual recruitment rates suggests that these bird populations are safe from the threat of serious depletion or extermination by present levels of hunting. There is no way of knowing, however, whether present recruitment figures are representative of past reproductive potential. Given the recency of large-scale Kundagai settlement of Tsuwenkai, it is quite likely that many bird species were more numerous in the past and could sustain higher rates of hunting.[16] In other words, although some present bird populations seem to have achieved homeostasis, there are no good grounds for presuming that there has been a static equilibrium. This conclusion has important consequences for the wider ecological framework of this analysis: although the cultural organization of territoriality, rights to resources, and restraints on hunting can be interpreted as tending toward limiting hunting pressure, it is not actually possible to specify any positive links between these practices and the population dynamics of birds. In other words, the relationship between belief and hunting practice and their consequences as manifested in bird populations through production for plume trade and use can only be inferred; the parameters cannot be integrated operationally. One cannot, therefore, assume that the relationship between hunting and bird recruitment necessarily tends toward homeostasis. By contrast, it is reasonable to conclude that hunting rates over time have remained within the limits set by rates of bird reproduction.

Although the ecological data on bird populations does not lend itself to definite conclusions, the collective wisdom of Kundagai hunters deserves a place in the analysis of the impact of hunting on the population dynamics of birds. From the perspective of the Kundagai hunter what ultimately counts is the ready availability of plumed male birds. Hunters of the current generation quite clearly have an appreciation of the potential impact of their activities on bird numbers. They can articulate strategies hunters should adopt to reduce that impact while maintaining yield. Whether they systematically apply strategies of restraint and conservation is another issue. The point is that in the light of their clear appreciation of critical ecological insights into their impact on their prey, Kundagai hunters express no concern over diminishing availability of favored prey. The available evidence on the population ecology of the birds does not contradict Kundagai evaluation of the impact of their hunting. Notwithstanding my cautionary comments on the interpretation of ornithological data, it seems to me quite reasonable to arrive at a more definite conclusion: under current regimes of exploitation the Kundagai are able to maintain long-term production of feathers (and other forest products) on a sustained-yield basis. In short, their particular place as producers in a wider network of trade can be maintained.

This chapter has examined the local ecological basis of Kundagai production of certain valuables that in part sustain local participation in trade. In succeeding chapters I turn to an examination of the articulation of distribution in various forms of exchange with levels of production and consumption of valuables.

4
Valuables and Prestations

TRADE AND PRESTATION

Melanesians have been represented as preoccupied with the exchange of material goods.[1] In many instances the stereotype is undeserved and serves to mask a fuller understanding of the nature and meaning of transactions. Nonetheless, many ethnographers have pointed to broad distinctions between classes of transactions involving material items, variously contrasting trade, barter, commodity exchange, or "economic exchange" with ceremonial exchange, prestation, or gift. Others have made such distinctions from more theoretical perspectives (e.g., Gregory 1982; Sahlins 1972).

The passage of goods between parties to an exchange is one of innumerable forms of transaction as that notion may be broadly understood (Kapferer 1976). As I have argued in the Introduction, it is misleading to distinguish trade from prestations on the basis of descriptions of their conduct. This is an exercise in typologizing that must crumble in the face of intermediate cases. Rather, I argue that these forms of exchange should be distinguished in terms of actors' primary interests or intents. This is not to say that a label can be attached definitely to any particular transaction one may witness. Multiple social and cultural factors are involved in any transaction which are capable of manipulation and variable interpretation by the actors (cf. Bourdieu 1977).

This approach has the advantage of conforming to some theoretical arguments developed by Sahlins (1972), and also to the conceptions of the Maring themselves. The Maring make a terminological distinction between two general forms of exchange which I gloss as "trade" and "prestation." Each term entails an understanding of reciprocity, but the social and material contexts of the exchanges may vary widely. The term *munggoi rigima,* literally "valuables exchange," which I translate as "trade," refers to transactions explicitly concerned with the acquisition and distribution of goods. As stated by informants, the overt focus of such transactions is on the reciprocal movement of dissimilar objects of value. Trade transactions may occur between individuals—never groups—standing in any relationship to one another.

The term *munggoi awom,* literally "valuables give," I translate as "prestations" or "gifts." In these transactions the participants are explicitly concerned with the establishment, continuation, or discharge of social relations, rights, and obligations. The flow of material objects is not necessarily reciprocal but may entail the transmission of valuables in exchange for the gift of a woman in marriage, military aid, or settlement of insult. Maring exegesis points to the more restricted nature of *munggoi awom* exchanges: they occur only between particular categories of persons or collectivities in certain circumstances.

As a consequence of these different orientations of modes of exchange, the interests of transactors shifts from the appearance of a dominant concern for objects and the self in trade to a concern for the other in prestations. I say "appearance" of material self-interest since, in the final chapter, I argue that in the praxis of trade there is a potential for the expression of a central concern for sociability. Further, although the Maring characterize trade as centered on objects, it would be a misleading oversimplification to treat it as an essentially materialistic pursuit. It is also important to note that, in the absence of overt haggling or bargaining, trade does not involve competition within or between groups of "buyers" and "sellers," nor is it geared to the making of profit (cf. e.g., Thurnwald 1932). These issues can only be noted here but will be dealt with further in later chapters.

Trade transactions tend to be unremarkable events, involving only a pair of individuals. The actual exchange of goods is a relatively private event, unencumbered by elaborate codes of conduct. They are therefore hard to see, and many ethnographers whose attention was focused elsewhere may have gained the false impression that trade is of little significance. Prestations, by contrast, run the whole gamut from the commonplace, private exchange of minor valuables between individuals as a sign of courtesy or intimacy to the rare and glorious spectacle of the dances and distribution of salted pork to allies in the final stages of the *konj kaiko* ceremony.

The various forms of prestations in fact can be grouped into two broad classes that I gloss as major and minor prestations. There is no general term for major prestations. Usually, they are highly public events involving groups of transactors. They consist of several named categories of ceremonialized exchange to mark specific events in the life cycle of individuals or the fortunes of collectivities. Such transactions usually involve strict codes of conduct relating to participants and the appropriate nature and quantities of goods. The various kinds of major prestations are detailed below, but examples include bridewealth and death payments. Minor prestations or gifts are known collectively as *munggoi aure awom* ("valuables nothing give"). The various forms and circumstances are not named. They are uceremonialized exchanges, usually between individuals, expressing solidarity, reconciliation, or intimacy attending numerous social events for which no named ceremonial exchange is obligatory. There is no set code of conduct relating to the occasions when gifts are appropriate, or to the kind and quantity of goods involved. Examples include mutual gifts between visiting matrikin or affines, or small prestations as expressions of sympathy in times of misfortune or as appreciation of past kindness.

There may be some objection to collapsing into a simple dichotomy the variety of transactions empirically present among the Maring and others (for which both the participants and anthropologist can provide distinctive labels). Mauss (1954: 28–29) provides some justification for such an exercise implicit in his complaint of the proliferation of Trobriand terms for different kinds of prestations, which masks the common features of all forms of the "gift."

To characterize trade as primarily "economic" in focus and prestations as social, political, or religious in orientation is misleading.[2] Clearly, both forms of exchange have important economic implications for the production of exchangeable items, their distribution, and consumption. A trader, nonetheless, may be motivated by a desire to acquire a particular item that he can use in a social and political transaction, such as bridewealth in exchange for rights to a woman's productive and reproductive powers and the political support of her agnates, or a religious transaction, such as the sacrifice of a pig to the spirits in exchange for health and protection. Even trade transactions with an apparently self-interested and materialist, "economic" focus may also involve strong social and political motives. For instance, trade between affines may be pursued partly because the transaction has some utilitarian benefit for the participants, but also because it expresses a commitment to maintain their social and political links. By the same token, parties to a prestation may be conscious of the practical utility of the exchange as a means of redistributing useful or desirable goods.

These considerations indicate that trade and prestations as pure forms occupy the poles of a continuum and that they intergrade in some intermediate region. I stress that the distinctions, which derive from a particular ethnographic context, lie in actors' perceptions or interpretations of particular events and motives. The labeling of any specific transaction therefore cannot be based on mere observation by the ethnographer but requires attention to transactors' evaluations of their activities. This scheme thus serves as an advance on a similar continuum of forms of exchange proposed by Sahlins (1972) in terms of generalized through balanced to negative reciprocity, in which a priori assumptions about kinship distance are held as important determinants or covariants of the form and conduct of transactions. In Sahlins's scheme, what I call prestations fall toward the generalized reciprocity pole, typically involving relatives, and trade transactions toward the negative reciprocity end typified by self-interested, potentially hostile relations between unrelated persons.

Maring prestations occur between kin and affines, but parties to trade transactions run the spectrum from unrelated strangers to close relatives—even true brothers—and transactions may be completed immediately or delayed for up to several years. The conduct of trade transactions will be examined in chapter 8. Here I wish merely to note that although trade and prestations may be difficult to disentangle theoretically, to the Kundagai the distinctions in practice are clear, and must be so, if they are to react appropriately by normative standards in any particular transaction. Of the several thousand cases of exchanges that I collected, my informants were nearly always quite certain whether any one was to be understood as *munggoi rigima* or *munggoi awom*.

Since the goods and persons involved in Maring prestations are also those engaged in trade, neither form of exchange can be examined in isolation. Both are forms of the distribution of goods and of intergroup relations. Although the focus of this study is on trade, it becomes obvious from the foregoing remarks that one cannot understand the movement of goods in trade in isolation. The last chapter showed how the production of plumes destined for trade is embedded in the relations between humans and the environment, between groups and individuals, and between humans and the spirit world. Here I identify the major goods involved in trade and prestations, their ownership, and the flow of goods in prestations, before making a detailed examination of trade in subsequent chapters.

VALUABLES

In common with many other New Guinea societies the Maring class a range of goods in a named category, *munggoi*. The term has two meanings. In a general sense it refers to any object that is described in Tok Pisin as *samting pulim pe,* something that "pulls pay" or has exchange value. In this sense it may refer to any good passed in trade or major and minor prestations. In a more restricted or focused sense it is confined to "valuables" or "prestige goods." Paradigmatically, valuables in this narrow sense embrace items passed in major prestations: pigs, cassowaries, certain shells, stone and now steel tools, and paper money. Some high-value bird plumes and marsupial skins are also classed as *munggoi* in this restricted sense, although they are not used in major prestations among the western Maring. The Kundagai explain that they are "valuables" because they are of comparable exchange value to pigs, the preeminent object of ceremonial exchanges. Indeed, many such plumes and skins are used to acquire by trade pigs later killed for prestations. In all, some thirty-six objects fall into the category of "valuables" (although some informants are inclined to expand the list). Only twelve of these, however, are valuables in the restricted sense and are or were regularly employed in major ceremonial exchanges, and *only munggoi* are so used. Although traditionally the western Maring, including the Kundagai, did not use plumes in major prestations, the eastern Maring and the Narak and Kandawo have always done so. The Kundagai, however, have recently received some Red Bird of Paradise, Hornbill, and Paradise Kingfisher feathers in bridewealth, mainly from eastern Maring communities, although they do not include feathers in any major prestations they make.

The category *munggoi* as valuables includes items that may also be used as decorations, *mokiang,* but not all *mokiang* are also valuables. Many non-*munggoi* decorations are also traded, though less commonly than are *munggoi* and generally at lower exchange rates. There is no doubt that the introduction of money has facilitated trade in these lesser goods and that, although some of these goods were formerly obtained by the Kundagai from beyond their territory, this was mainly in minor prestations from kinsmen rather than by trade. A few items are neither *munggoi* nor *mokiang* and are occasionally exchanged for money; these, however, were probably seldom if ever traded in the past.

Appendix 3 gives details of over seventy goods transferred in trade. The catalogue of items actually traded in any one period of time has varied as indicated in the appendix. Most things no longer traded are not used for any other purpose, such as decorations, or even retained as mementos of the past. For instance, to my knowledge no Kundagai now owns a dog-tooth necklace or pack of native salt.

Over one hundred items, animal, vegetable, and mineral, provide decorations, but I recorded only forty-seven used in trade. Of the fifty-three species of birds used in decorations, twenty-seven are or have been traded.

Goods passed in trade can be classed broadly either as more or less ubiquitous or as specialized and localized in origin. Here I classify goods relative to their availability in Tsuwenkai. Items found in both Tsuwenkai and many other areas of dissimilar environment are not of specialized origin. Things found only in Tsuwenkai or a limited number of other similar environments, or widely distributed goods absent from Tsuwenkai, are classed as being of specialized origins. By this reckoning twenty-three, or somewhat less than half of the items ever traded, are the products of ecologically or technologically distinct areas. In most cases items are peculiar to high or low altitudes, although salt, stone, and some pigments are derived from localized deposits that are distributed with little relation to altitude.

The Maring grade valuables into broad hierarchic categories of order of value. Unlike, for instance, the Mae Enga (Meggitt 1971: 200), the Maring hierarchy does not involve rigid restrictions on the interconvertibility of items of different hierarchic levels. The Kundagai say that ideally items of one level can be exchanged for those in any other level. Mae Enga valuables normatively can be exchanged only with items of the same or immediately adjacent levels. Nonetheless, on the one hand, exchanges of goods with widely divergent value would not be contemplated by the Maring. On the other hand, convertibility between Maring levels is enhanced insofar as items within any one level are not of equal exchange value. The levels of value therefore do not conform to a scale of exchange value but are, rather, a hierarchy of "worth or desirability" (Meggitt 1971: 199).

Scales of value have altered over time as items available for use in prestations have changed. Table 13 lists hierarchies of valuables around the year 1900 (as related by an old man born around that time) and in the present. Opinion varies somewhat as to the number of levels and the allocation of specific items in the contemporary hierarchy.

Some informants list money in the same category as pigs, shells, and steel tools, because, like those items, it is a major component of prestations. Those who place money in a separate category of superior value do so because they say that since money can be converted to any other item more freely than other valuables it is the most valuable. It is therefore the most desirable of all goods.

Other categories crosscut these hierarchies: all shells are glossed *mengr,* bird plumes as *kabang an* (feathers) or *kabang wak* (skins), and marsupial fur as *koi-ma an* and skins as *koi-ma wak*.

Ethnographers frequently record quantities of valuables transferred in ceremonial exchanges. Except for pigs, however, there are few published details available on valuables stocks retained by individuals. A major aim of the following discussion is thus to document patterns of ownership of valuables among the Kundagai and show how the means of acquiring valuables varies. It must be conceded immediately that custodianship of valuables does not necessarily mean ownership, as one may hold temporary stewardship over, say, shells that belong to others. Nonetheless, the great bulk of valuables I saw during a census of valuables collections were identified by their custodians as their personal property.

I did not discern any reluctance on the part of the Kundagai to show me their plume and shell collections. It is possible that some men had stored separately shells that they had received in, or were about to give in, prestations, and that they preferred to keep the fact secret from my assistants and spectators in case their display should provoke claims or comments. In the absence of signs of evasiveness, however, I am confident that I saw most shells and plumes owned by resident Kundagai. I also saw some valuables belonging to absentees which were stored with resident kinsmen. In their general willingness to display and discuss valuables collections the Kundagai clearly contrast with some other societies—such as the Mae Enga, at least in respect of pigs (Meggitt 1974)—where such information is sensitive and secret.

TABLE 13. HIERARCHY OF VALUABLES

Order of Value	Items

A. ABOUT 1900

1. Greensnail shells
2. Pigs, live cassowaries, plumes of Astrapia, Sicklebill, Superb and Saxony Birds of Paradise, Vulturine Parrot, Fairy Lory, Goura Pigeon, Hornbill and Buzzard[a]
3. Stone axes
4. Dog- and marsupial-tooth necklaces
5. Nonema bead necklaces
6. Marsupial tails and pelts
7. Job's Tears necklaces

B. IN 1973-1974

1. Money
2. Pigs, cassowaries, kina and greensnail shells, steel tools
3. Plumes of Astrapia, Sicklebill, Lesser, Superb, Saxony, and Raggiana Birds of Paradise, Vulturine Parrot, Papuan Lory, Cockatoo, Paradise Kingfisher, Hornbill, Buzzard, and Harpy Eagle; marsupial skins
4. Loose fur, chickens, minor shells

[a] Other plumes, for example, of the Lesser Bird of Paradise, probably fell in this level.

As noted in chapter 2, most plumes and furs are owned by younger men, as it is they who more keenly participate in dances. Plumes and skins are not used by the Kundagai and other western Maring in major prestations, so that older men who are uninterested in dancing do not generally retain such goods except as trade items. In table 14 I give details of how animal remains recorded in the census of valuables were acquired.

The most common means of acquiring plumes and marsupial skins retained in valuables collections was by gift, followed by trade. By "gift" I mean minor prestations as outlined above. All the marsupial skins listed in the table are low-altitude species unavailable to Tsuwenkai Kundagai hunters by virtue of territorial hunting rights. Concerning bird plumes, trade and loans are more important means of acquiring valuable, or *munggoi,* plumes than those regarded only as decorations. This is as one might expect, for *munggoi* items, being more desirable, are more likely to be sought by a trader than are non-*munggoi,* as they can be used not only for decorations but exchanged for other valuables. In other words, they become commodities as well as decorations and, as such, can be converted into other desirable items. Non-*munggoi*

TABLE 14. ACQUISITION OF ANIMAL REMAINS IN VALUABLES CENSUS, 1973–1974

Total No. sets	Trade	Gift[a]	Loan	Shot	Found
A. BIRD PLUMES					
All Species 458	120(26.2)[b]	171(37.3)	14(3.1)	122(26.6)	31(6.8)
Non-valuables 187	29(15.5)	76(40.6)	1(0.5)	69(36.9)	12(6.4)
Valuables 271	91(33.6)	95(35.0)	13(4.8)	53(19.6)	19(7.0)
B. MARSUPIAL SKINS					
45	20(44.4)	23(51.1)	2(4.4)		
C. BEETLE SHARDS					
17	5(29.4)	5(29.4)		7(41.2[c])	

[a] Refers exclusively to minor prestations.
[b] Numbers in parentheses are percentages of row totals.
[c] Collected by present owners in swarming season.

goods do not enjoy such free exchangeability. Gift is almost as important a means of acquiring *munggoi* as non-*munggoi* plumes, but hunting is of relatively minor importance in acquiring *munggoi* plumes, though in large part this is because six of the fifteen *munggoi* species are not found in Tsuwenkai.

The pattern of acquisition of shells differs from that of other animal products. Partly this is because shells are not of local origin and also because their uses and the categories of men owning them differ. Shells are transferred in large numbers in major prestations in which older men participate. Tables 15 and 16 give details of the ownership of 210 kina and 250 greensnail shells recorded in the collections of all 55 resident adult males. I have not reordered data on the distribution of ownership by age for other shells, as the numbers recorded are small and these shells are now very rarely used in prestations. Gross holdings of these other shells were as follows: 28 sets of *Nassa* dogwhelk headbands and ropes, most acquired in bridewealth, 3 sets of *Cypraea* cowry ropes, 8 *Conus* shell disks, mostly obtained in gifts, and one *Melo* bailer-shell fragment, acquired in bridewealth.

TABLE 15. OWNERSHIP OF SHELLS IN VALUABLES COLLECTIONS, BY AGE GROUP, 1973–1974

Age:	15-25	25-35	35-45	45-55	55-65	65-75	All ages
Number of men:	7[a]	22[b]	11[c]	5[c]	7[d]	3[e]	55
A. KINA							
No. men owning	2	21	9	5	4	2	43
No. shells	6	111	45	21	23	4	210
Range owned	0-4	0-13	0-9	1-8	0-14	0-3	0-14
Av./total men	0.8	5.0	4.1	4.2	3.3	1.3	3.8
Av./men owning	3.0	5.3	5.0	4.2	5.8	2.0	4.9
B. GREENSNAIL							
No. men owning	3	17	11	5	4	2	42
No. shells	28	109	59	19	24	11	250
Range owned	0-15	0-13	3-12	3-6	0-16	0-7	0-15
Av./total men	4.0	5.0	5.4	3.8	3.4	3.7	4.5
Av./men owning	9.3	6.4	5.4	3.8	6.0	5.5	5.9
C. KINA AND GREENSNAIL COMBINED							
No. men owning	3	22	11	5	4	2	47
No. shells	34	220	104	40	47	15	460
Range owned	0-19	1-25	3-17	5-11	0-30	0-10	0-30
Av./total men	4.9	10.0	9.4	8.0	6.7	5.0	8.4
Av./men owning	11.3	10.0	9.4	8.0	11.7	7.5	9.8

[a] Only one of these men is married; he and two others owned all the shells.
[b] Four of these men are unmarried.
[c] All men have at least one living wife.
[d] Includes two widowers.
[e] Only one man with surviving wife.

Although plumes and skins are retained primarily for use in decorations or trade, shells are required as major components of prestations. They are also commonly traded but are only minor items of decoration. Consonant with these different social utilities, patterns of ownership and means of acquiring shells differ by age groups from holdings of plumes and skins.

In general one might anticipate that young and old men will own fewer shells as they will tend to be less involved in ceremonial payments, requiring fewer shells for prestations and receiving less. Young unmarried men are not considered to be fully adult, partly because they have not assumed responsibilities for dependents and for the maintenance of amicable relations with affines. As such their need of shell valuables is not great. Old men similarly are often little involved in

TABLE 16. MEANS OF ACQUISITION OF SHELLS IN VALUABLES COLLECTIONS, BY AGE GROUP, 1973–1974

Age	No. owning[a]	No. shells[a]	Means of Acquisition[b]							
			1 Bride-wealth	2 Death payment	3 Bride-wealth return	4 Death payment return	5 Gift	6 Prestations combined (1–5)	7 Trade	8 Other
A. KINA										
15-25	2	6	3(50.0)[c]				1(16.6)	4(66.6)	1(16.6)	1(16.6)
25-35	21	83	16(19.3)	10(12.1)	25(30.1)	3(3.6)	5(6.0)	59(71.1)	20(24.1)	4(4.8)
35-45	9	41	11(26.8)	4(9.8)	13(31.7)	6(14.6)	1(2.4)	35(85.4)	6(14.6)	
45-55	5	12	7(58.3)	1(8.3)		2(16.7)	1(8.3)	11(91.7)	1(8.3)	
55-65	4	23	16(69.6)	2(8.7)	2(8.7)			20(87.0)	3(13.0)	
65-75	2	4	3(75.0)		1(25.0)			4(100.0)		
B. GREENSNAIL										
15-25	3	28	4(14.3)	6(7.1)	8(28.6)	3(3.6)	8(9.5)	12(42.9)	14(50.0)	2(7.1)
25-35	17	84	19(22.6)	6(10.3)	21(25.0)	3(5.2)	8(13.8)	57(67.9)	19(22.6)	8(9.5)
35-45	11	58	20(34.5)	3(18.7)	14(24.1)	3(18.7)		51(87.9)	7(12.1)	
45-55	5	16	5(31.3)		1(6.3)			12(75.0)	4(25.0)	
55-65	4	24	11(45.8)		2(8.3)		1(4.2)	14(58.3)	10(41.7)	
65-75	2	11	3(27.2)	2(18.2)			3(27.2)	8(72.7)	3(27.2)	
C. KINA & GREENSNAIL COMBINED										
15-25	3	34	7(20.6)	16(9.6)	8(23.5)	6(3.6)	1(2.9)	16(47.1)	15(44.1)	3(8.8)
25-35	21	167	35(21.0)	10(10.1)	46(27.5)	9(9.1)	13(7.8)	116(69.5)	39(23.3)	12(7.2)
35-45	11	99	31(31.3)	4(14.3)	27(27.3)	5(17.8)	9(9.1)	86(88.9)	13(13.1)	
45-55	5	28	12(42.9)	2(4.3)	1(3.6)		1(3.6)	23(82.1)	5(17.8)	
55-65	4	47	27(57.4)	2(13.3)	4(8.5)		1(2.1)	34(72.3)	13(27.7)	
65-75	2	15	6(40.0)		1(6.7)		3(20.0)	12(80.0)	3(20.0)	
TOTALS	46	390	118(30.3)	34(8.7)	87(22.3)	20(5.1)	28(7.2)	287(73.6)	88(22.6)	15(3.8)

[a] Totals in these columns do not equal totals that can be calculated from table 15 since means of acquisition of some shells is unknown.
[b] For explanation of categories see text.
[c] Numbers in parentheses are percentages of row totals.

prestations. In part this is the result of their declining interest and ability to participate through age and ill health, but also because sons, on reaching middle age, assume the exchange responsibilities of their fathers. It follows that married men of middle age can be expected to be most involved with prestations and so to handle larger amounts of shells. This does not necessarily mean that they will hold larger stocks.

Data on shell holdings of fifty-five men are arranged in ten-year-interval age groups in tables 15 and 16. Some clarification of certain tabulated means of acquisition is required. Informants usually specified whether a shell was received in a major prestation—mainly bridewealth and death payment—or as a return gift for such a payment they had made or contributed to. In the first instance, shells were acquired directly from donors or indirectly in redistributions from major recipients. Return payments include three subcategories: direct returns for earlier major prestations by current shell owners; as indirect returns in redistributions from other major recipients; as returns for helping kinsmen make their own major prestations. That is, figures for bridewealth and death payments, and for returns for these two prestations, include shells both distributed between groups making prestations and redistributed within recipient and donor groups. The inclusion of several types of distribution under one heading conforms to Kundagai presentation of information. The "gift" column includes shells passed in minor prestations (*munggoi aure awom*) that were not counted as reciprocation for aid in amassing prestations associated with marriage or death.

As suggested, the average number of shells owned by individuals in different age groups varies as does the relative importance of means of acquisition. Most shells are acquired in prestations, although relative proportions vary with age. Trade assumes greater significance as a source of shells for young and, to a lesser extent, old men, with prestations being most significant for men aged between thirty-five and fifty-five. The few shells listed as acquired by "other" means include several taken live from the sea, then cut and polished by their present owners while working on coastal plantations. One man also inherited nine shells from his father. Several dogwhelk collections had also been inherited. Inheritance of shells seems uncommon; on death a man's valuables are normally distributed to kinsmen as part of a death payment.

It is appropriate to note briefly how the age groups employed in the analysis relate to the developmental cycle of men and their households.

Lucien Yekwai in full dancing regalia. He wears a *mamp ku glong* wig, decorated with lines of scarab beetle heads, cuscus fur strips, and plumes of eagle, fowl, and parrot, and carries a bow in his left hand.

Looking north up the Kant Valley to Gendupa Pass on the Bismarck Crest. The buildings on the nearer ridge include the ethnographer's house (center) and the *haus kiap* (government rest house) located on the edge of the census ground (left). Note the planted casuarina trees around the census ground, graded walking track on flank of farther ridge. Newly cleared gardens can be seen at the forest edge at the head of the valley where the Kant River turns sharply westward. Fallow growth in the middle altitudes obscures several homestead sites.

Looking south across the Pint Basin grasslands. The long ridge sloping down from the right is the north face of Komongwai near the southern border of Tsuwenkai territory. Kompiai settlement is located on the ridge to the left. The Sepik-Wahgi Divide lies on the skyline. Note the landslip scar on the flanks of Komongwai and horizontal marks attributed by the Kundagai to old garden terraces cleared in grassland before the arrival of steel tools in the 1940s.

Mount Dundunk on the heavily forested Bismarck Crest, seen from a homestead yard.

Kumbwamp in 1974, aged about 65. She wears a traditional bark cloth cape and necklace of greensnail shell fragments.

Wande planting a newly cleared garden cut from advanced secondary forest. Burnt rubbish is still smoking in the background.

Kamkai returning home from work in his gardens. He carries harvested tubers and other produce in a bilum (string bag) and improvised bundle carried in the male fashion slung from the shoulder. Because he has been working in a bush area, he carries a bow and hunting arrows in case he encounters game. He has hitched up his apron for ease of movement in thick undergrowth.

Bird hunting blind at a pool in the high altitude forest. The blind has been abandoned for some time and is in disrepair, with its heavy leafy covering largely rotted away revealing the domed structure. A bark tube to guide an arrow to its mark protrudes through the blind wall bound to the top of the pole that serves as a perch.

Sacrifice of a large pig for a bridewealth presentation in a *raku,* sacrificial grove and cemetery.

Spectators at a bridewealth presentation in 1974. The low, turtle backed house in the background, roofed with pandanus fronds, is typical of Tsuwenkai houses.

Part of a bridewealth presentation on display, 1974. Greensnail shells are arranged at the far end, kina, flanked by lines of paper money on the left (the arrows are to prevent the money from blowing away, and are not part of the presentation), axs and bushknives to the right. Joints of cooked pork are on display in a separate pile out of the photo.

After presentation of bridewealth the bride and her companion emerge from seclusion. She is heavily decorated, mainly with parrot feathers. In her left hand she waves a Lesser Bird of Paradise plume and carries a joint of pork in her right hand as gifts for her husband's kin. This practice of presenting a heavily decorated bride has been adopted recently from Kuma-speaking areas of the upper Jimi.

Giewai displays Harpy Eagle feathers he hopes to exchange for money with a party of visiting traders from the upper Jimi.

Kemba (left) displays money (folded on his thigh) to a group of fellow Kundagai. He has been given the money by a trade partner in the Simbai Valley who asked Kemba to get him a pig.

John Kandemungu (left) ponders the merits of a piglet a visiting trader from Togban (right) wishes to exchange for money. The visitor holds a stick of sugarcane he has been offered in hospitality.

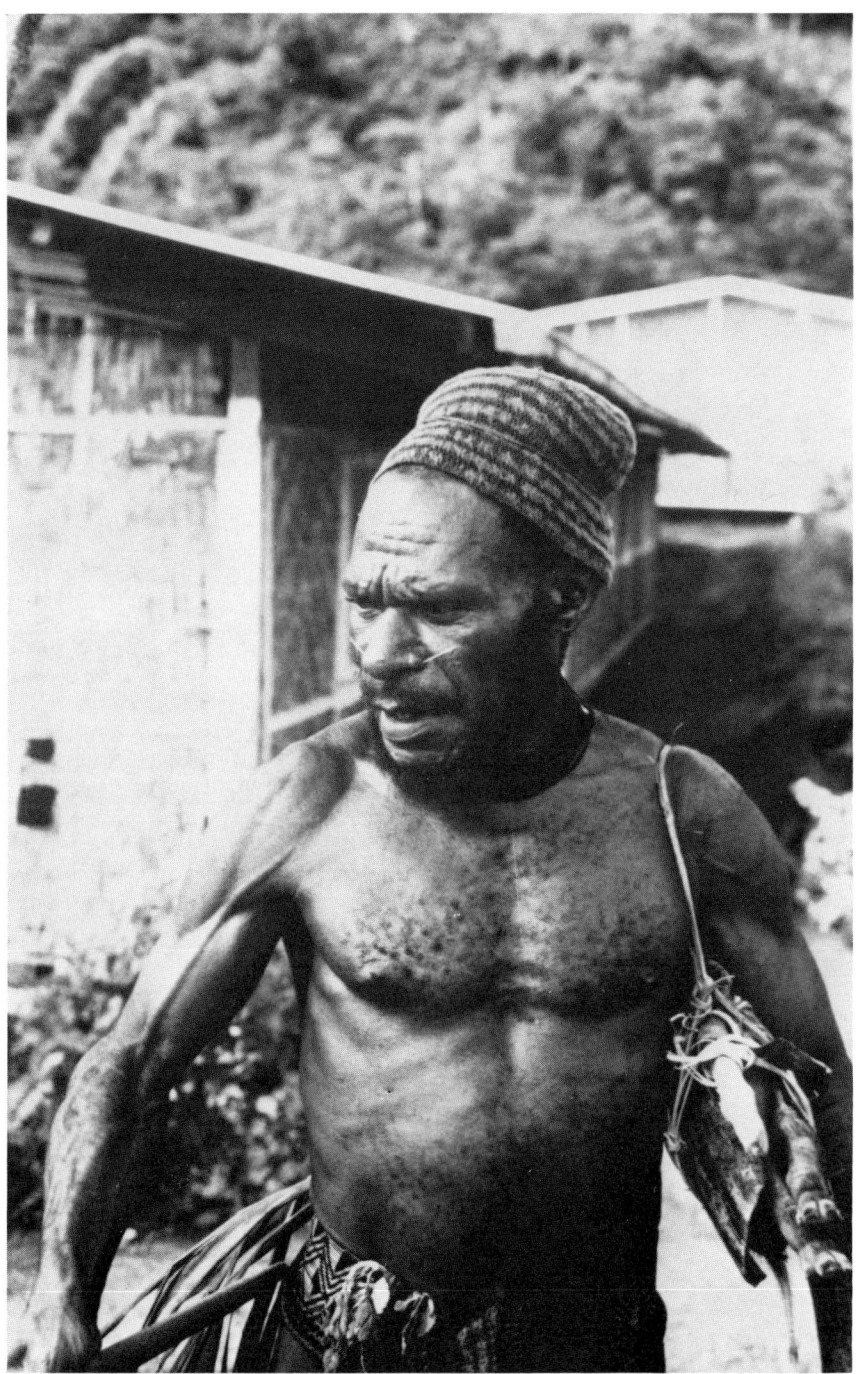

Itinerant pig trader from south of the Jimi River at festivities hosted by the Anglican Mission at Koinambe, Christmas 1973. Note his traditional decorations of netted cap, slivers of bamboo in nose, and woven belt. He carries the piglet he wishes to exchange for plumes slung in a bark roll from his shoulder. The piglet's trotters can be seen protruding from its wrapping.

Dance contingent and spectators at a *pati* held in Tsuwenkai, 1974. The building in the background is a temporary shelter for visitors. The man in the right foreground has a Lesser Bird of Paradise plume in a bamboo tube he wishes to trade.

Valuables and Prestations 139

The fifteen to twenty-five age group represents young adults, the bulk of whom are bachelors attached to the households of their fathers, elder brothers, or other senior cognatic or affinal kin. The next three age groups (from twenty-five to fifty-five) represent predominantly married men with responsibilities for one or more wives, growing numbers of children, and perhaps unmarried siblings, widows of kinsmen, aging parents, and other kin. As a man approaches middle age his responsibilities for dependents tend to increase and he becomes more involved in a network of exchanges flowing from both his own marriage as well as those of other clansmen. By the time he is in his late forties or early fifties a man's conjugal family will begin to break up, with the marriage of his children. Relatively few men in their late fifties have continuing responsibilities for young children, and their exchange obligations and care of dependents have frequently been assumed by sons or younger brothers. Thus, the last two age groups represent old men, most of whose households have dissolved and who have been incorporated into the households of a younger generation of mature men.

A large proportion (all unmarried) of men under twenty-five own no shells at all. Of those that do, their stocks of kina are lower than of any other age group, although holdings of greensnail approximate the average for all age groups combined. Bridewealth forms the most important means of acquiring kina, whereas trade is the major means of obtaining greensnail shells. Most greensnail coming by trade were bought while their owners were on contract labor near Rabaul. Men of this youngest group are a significant source of new greensnail brought from beyond the locally based spheres of exchange. Kina are less often brought home in this way. It is mainly such younger men who go to work in distant areas.

Men of the twenty-five to thirty-five age group retain the largest stocks of shells. Bridewealth and trade are the most significant means of acquisition. Men in the thirty-five to forty-five age groups gain most shells in bridewealth and death payments but rely least heavily of all ages on trade for their supplies.

In the forty-five to fifty-five age group the average size of shell stocks is below the mean for all age groups combined. Receipt of bridewealth and death payments and return gifts for these are the most important means of acquiring shells. These means become more marked for the oldest two age groups.

There are two peaks of the average number of shells owned: in the fifteen to twenty-five and fifty-five to sixty-five age groups. The peak in the younger group can be explained by their acquiring shells by trade, whereas the older group receives some by trade but most (57.4 percent) in bridewealth, mainly for their daughters. Most women are probably married when their fathers are in this age group.[3]

If average shell stocks are calculated on the basis of all men in an age group, rather than the number of men owning shells, then the largest collections are held by the twenty-five to thirty-five age group, with stocks decreasing thereafter with age. This pattern may be accounted for as follows. Men between twenty-five and thirty-five are amassing shells for their own initial bridewealth payments. Indeed, at the time of the valuables census, several men in this group stated that they had many shells because they were about to give bridewealth. Although this group receives only 21 percent of their stocks in bridewealth, mainly for clan sisters, they are evidently receiving many shells in return for their own bridewealth payments and in return for helping kinsmen, mainly agnates, in making bridewealth payments. Of all age groups, they receive the largest proportion of their stocks in the form of return gifts associated with bridewealth.

Bridewealth increases in importance as a means of acquiring shells up to the age of sixty-five, but return gifts associated with bridewealth decrease in importance. This is because the major contributors to bridewealth payments tend to be younger men, whereas older men give smaller and receive larger proportions of shells by this means. Men between forty-five and fifty-five, by contrast, are the major recipients of death payments and return gifts for death payments. Such payments are mainly received for deceased married sisters and their children and for their father's sisters and father's sisters' sons and unmarried daughters. Men in the oldest age group, who are often real or classificatory fathers to men of the forty-five to fifty-five age group, are also the main recipients of death payments for the latter category of deceased males and unmarried women, who are sisters' children.

These data concern only shells currently held in personal collections. I have no comparable material on the number of shells or other valuables that men may have distributed in prestations or contributed to major exchanges of other men, and for which returns are outstanding. Indeed, this would be a fruitless exercise of computation for the ethnographer and Kundagai alike, as one can never be certain that valuables will be reciprocated in equal quantities and worth, or when, if at all. Some shells I saw in collections were already earmarked to settle existing debts. The number of shells a man may expect to exercise relatively autonomous control over therefore is indeterminate and does not necessarily include all in his possession but may include some in the custody of others.

Notwithstanding these considerations, the material on existing shell stocks can be used as a basis to suggest the means of loss of shells. Although men aged twenty-five to thirty-five receive relatively few shells in bridewealth, they receive the largest proportion of all age groups in return gifts for bridewealth. Men of these ages are most active in giving bridewealth, and the large amounts they receive in return gifts reflect this. Similarly, men aged forty-five to fifty-five are not only receiving large proportions of shells in death payments but pay out substantial death payments for parents and young children. In the census of valuables, return gifts for death payments exceed receipt of death payments. As not all death payments are countered by a return gift (see below), it is probable that many of the return gifts listed are from other men whom shell owners have helped to make payments, rather than as returns for presentations their owners have made as principal donors. Men over fifty-five years old have received no shells as return gifts for death payments, and few as return gifts for bridewealth payments, which suggests that they contribute little to such prestations. This conclusion is borne out by my observations on contributions to such prestations that occurred during fieldwork.

Bridewealth becomes increasingly important with age as a means of acquiring shells, but the fact that the size of shell stocks decreases with age indicates that losses of shells, mainly in death payments in middle age and as contributions to sons' bridewealth payments which are not replaced by return gifts,[4] exceeds the acquisition of shells with advancing years. Accumulation through trade is most important for younger men and of secondary importance for men over forty-five. The latter are perhaps attempting to replenish their stocks, which are declining through prestations that are not fully reciprocated.

Regardless of age, bridewealth and associated return gifts are the most important means of acquiring shells (55.6 percent combined), with trade being next in importance. Shells received in death payments and associated return gifts are of lesser numbers, if only because death payments are smaller than bridewealth.

Nine of the fifty-five men whose shell collections I examined are big-men. Two of these (in the forty-five to fifty-five and sixty-five to seventy-five age groups) are politically influential *tep yu* ("Talk Men"). The other big-men are *bamp kunda yu* ("Fight Magic Men") and *mengr yu* ("Shell Men") who are not outstanding in political affairs. The older *tep yu* owns more shells than the average for his age group and slightly more than the average for all shell owners irrespective of age. The younger *tep yu* owns fewer shells than these averages. Most remaining big-men own stocks approximating averages for their age groups. Greatest variations are two men owning no shells and one owning thirty shells. There is, then, a wide range in the collections of big-men, but there is no strong evidence to suggest that they tend to possess more shells than other men. I doubt that big-men as a category have created more outstanding debts by contributing to other men's prestations than have other men, although the younger *tep yu* may have done so. It is reasonable to conclude that big-man status of itself does not necessarily correlate with personal wealth.

I obtained no ordered data on the ownership of steel tools. Most men own several axes and knives, but they are often all used for everyday tasks, even if one tool is favored above others. Thus, steel tools are seldom stored in separate bundles like other valuables and, if not in immediate use, are propped up inside doorways or wedged into house walls. One man aged about thirty had a bundle of thirteen axes stored in his house. Another man of about forty-five had five axes. While on contract labor in coastal centers most men buy several steel tools for use in their own bridewealth payments or to distribute as gifts to male and female kin. Steel tools are also bought from stores in Tabibuga, Koinambe, and Simbai Patrol Post and are usually purchased by younger men collecting bridewealth payments. Steel is also commonly traded between settlements. Most such tools, however, change hands in prestations.

I attempted to determine the size of the Kundagai pig herd on two occasions: during the population census at the beginning of fieldwork and again in late September 1974. During the population census I simply asked men the number of pigs they owned. I did not see all animals, therefore, and, although I know at least some men gave accurate figures, some errors were inevitable by this method. The Kundagai do not appear to be secretive about the number of pigs they own, unlike, for instance, the Mae Enga (Meggitt 1974: 168, n. 8). Nor do kinsmen in other settlements agist pigs for the Kundagai to any significant extent.

A man generally divides his pigs among his wives and older unmarried daughters to care for. If his herd is larger than these dependents can care for on their own, he may assign some pigs to the care of married sisters or his mother resident in Tsuwenkai, or to male kin who in turn assign them to their own female dependents.

In January 1974 the Kundagai pig herd was counted at 243 animals, which is no doubt an underestimate. At the end of September 1974 the number of pigs was 311. This latter count is more accurate.[5] It excludes pigs agisted outside Tsuwenkai, though probably no more than 12 animals are involved. The total includes piglets, but I do not know the age or sex structure of the pig herd. Table 17 shows the distribution of ownership of pigs by age and sex as of September 1974.

All males over about fifteen years old are potential pig owners, though few adolescents actually own beasts. Almost every male over the age of twenty-five owns at least one pig, whatever his marital status. Women do not normally own pigs over which they can expect full rights of disposal. Of the three women owning pigs, the youngest is a remarried widow whose husband lives in Bokapai with his first wife. The older woman is a vigorous and independent co-wife of a *mengr yu* big-man. Her two pigs were a gift from a daughter's husband. The remaining woman is a non-Kundagai widow with several young children. She lives in the homestead of her husband's brother.

All married men owned at least one pig, while one man owned as many as fourteen. On marriage a man will often be given a pig by his father or an elder brother for his wife to care for. A woman with no pigs under her charge will complain to her husband.

The size of an individual's pig herd shows an increase up to the forty-five to fifty-five age group, after which the size of herds falls. Two of the twenty-two unmarried pig owners are likely to remain permanent bachelors, as informants say no woman would consent or be expected to marry them. One, aged about thirty, is considered *plim,* "mad," the other aged forty to forty-five, a notorious *kwimp,* "witch."

Men between thirty-five and fifty-five own the largest pig herds. This may be explained by the tendency of men of these ages to support the greatest number of female dependents who can care for their pigs. Most polygynists with both wives surviving are in this age range. It is also between these ages that a man generally will have the greatest number of unmarried younger sisters or daughters to help his wife or wives and widowed mother to care for his pigs. Once a man's sisters or daughters are married they will be caring for their husband's pigs and, even if they remain within their natal settlement, the number of further pigs belonging to agnates which they can care for decreases. Thus, older men are often unable to find sufficient guardians to maintain large pig herds.

TABLE 17. PIG OWNERSHIP, SEPTEMBER 1974

Age	A. No. potential owners	B. No. owning	No. pigs	Average owned per A	Average owned per B	Married No. owning	Married Av. owned	Unmarried No. owning	Unmarried Av. owned	Widowed No. owning	Widowed Av. owned
A. MALES											
15-25	27	15	46	1.7	3.1	1	5.0	14	2.9		
25-35	31	30	130	4.2	4.3	23	4.6	7	3.4		
35-45	13	13	69	5.3	5.3	12	5.7	1	1.0		
45-55	5	5	29	5.8	5.8	5	5.8				
55-65	7	5	19	2.7	3.8	4	4.5			1	1.0
65-75	3	3	11	3.7	3.7	1	4.0			2	3.5
SUB TOTAL	86	71	304	3.5	4.3	46	5.0	22	3.0	3	2.7
B. FEMALE[a]											
25-35		1	1		1.0	1	1.0				
35-45		1	4		4.0					1	4.0
45-55		1	2		2.0	1	2.0				
SUB TOTAL		3	7		2.3	2	1.5			1	4.0
C. TOTALS[a]		74	311		4.2	50	4.6	22	3.0	4	3.0

[a] It is unusual for women to own pigs in their own right, and so potential number of female pig owners has not been shown.

Younger unmarried men are in a similar position. They rely upon unmarried sisters, mothers, or brothers' wives to care for their pigs. All these women may also have responsibilities for other men's pigs. There seems to be only a minor tendency for big-men to own slightly more pigs.

The average number of pigs per owner (male and female) is 4.2. This compares well with data Meggitt (1974: 168, n. 8) gives on Mae Enga pig holdings, where the average number of pigs per owner varies from about 1.9 for bachelors to 5.4 for married men, with a mean of 4.1 for all owners. (The equivalent figures for the Kundagai are 3 pigs for bachelors and 5 for married men.) Meggitt suggests his ratios are underestimates, as the Mae Enga are reluctant to reveal the number of pigs they own.

The ratio of Kundagai pigs to the total resident human population is also high by highland standards. In September 1974 there were 1.1 pigs to 1 person. This compares with 0.83 to 1 among the Tsembaga when the pig herd was at its maximum prior to their 1963 *konj kaiko* (Rappaport 1968: 93) (see table 19 for other Maring ratios). Ratios in the central highlands range from about 1 to 1 to 3 to 1 (Feachem 1973). It is clear, then, that the Kundagai cannot be considered poor in pigs. Although the much denser human populations of the central highlands mean that their pig populations are also much larger, it is unlikely that Kundagai husbandry practices and the work burden of women would permit a much larger pig herd. Nonetheless, informants were of the opinion that the Kundagai herds were larger prior to the last *konj kaiko* in 1960, although I cannot evaluate this statement. The herd is maintained at a lower level now, they say, as pigs are more frequently killed for damaging food and coffee gardens and are killed periodically to be butchered and sold for cash within Tsuwenkai. Such killings are now an important means of depleting the pig herd. Major prestations often include joints of cooked pork from one or more large pigs, while celebratory feasts and sacrifices to the spirits to cure sickness account for most other pigs. Table 18 lists the number of pigs killed during fieldwork and the principal reasons.

In addition, at least five adult or subadult pigs died of sickness or were killed by other pigs during fieldwork. An unknown number of piglets died, mostly from apparent intestinal infections. Several of the larger pigs were eaten, two being cut up for sale.

To the time of the September pig census fifty-nine pigs were killed, or nineteen percent of the then total population. If no further pigs were

TABLE 18. PIG KILLS, TSUWENKAI, NOV. 1973–NOV. 1974

Principal Reason for Killing	Number
1. Bridewealth & other affinal prestations	16
2. Death payments	2
3. Termination of widow's mourning	6
4. Removal of food and fire taboos (in association with widow remarriage)	1
5. Sacrifice in sickness	3
6. Adultery compensations	2
7. Celebratory feasts	
a. return of migrant workers	6
b. for Bishop on opening of new Tsuwenkai church	2
c. for Healeys on departure from field	3
8. Garden or house raiding	10
9. Run wild	3[a]
10. For killing other pig	1
11. For butchering and sale	11[b]
TOTAL	66

[a] One agisted in Tsuwenkai for a Kinimbong man.
[b] All or part of at least 10 pigs killed for other reasons also put on sale.

acquired before November (as I suspect was the case), the loss rate of pigs by killings was 21.2 percent. The number of live pigs lost from the Tsuwenkai herd was small. Most such losses were of piglets imported by trade and then quickly exported again.

Buchbinder (1973: 131) gives figures for the number of pigs killed by several Simbai Maring populations in 1968. Comparative data are given in the following table.

These data indicate that the size of the Kundagai pig herd relative to human population is similar to ratios in other Maring settlements. The Simbai Maring are further comparable with the Kundagai in that none were collecting pigs for a *konj kaiko* (Buchbinder 1973: 130). A ratio of about one pig per person therefore appears to be the general size of contemporary Maring pig herds. In 1968, however, no Maring population approached the Kundagai slaughter rate. The collective kills of the Bomagai–Angoiang and Funggai–Korama clan clusters of Gunts made up the highest slaughter rate. The average proportion of pig herds killed annually for the nine Simbai populations was 9 percent.

The greater rate of killing in 1973–1974 no doubt reflects an increase in the number of pigs killed for butchering and sale. Money was still scarce in the Simbai in 1968. My presence in Tsuwenkai as a ready source of cash undoubtedly encouraged the killing of pigs for sale. If

TABLE 19. ANNUAL PIG KILLS IN TEN MARING POPULATIONS[a]

Population	Resident human population	Pig population	Pig-per-person ratio	No. pigs killed	Percent of herd killed
Tsuwenkai Kundagai	273	311	1.1	66	21.2
Kinimbong Kundagai	113	148	1.2	14	9.5
Tsembaga	206	209	1.0	16	7.6
Tuguma	253	232	0.9	24	10.3
Kanump-Kauwil	342	354	1.0	15	4.2
Kandambent-Namikai	321	319	1.0	14	4.4
Ipai-Makap	220	197	0.9	17	8.6
Tsenggamp-Mirimbikai	90	180	2.0	23	12.8
Bomagai-Angoiang & Funggai-Korama	293	297	1.0	51	17.2
Kono	121	113	0.9	10	8.8
MEAN	223.2	236	1.1	25	10.6

[a] Data other than for Tsuwenkai from Buchbinder (1973).

these animals are excluded from the table, then 17.6 percent of the Tsuwenkai herd was killed. This is only slightly above the highest rate of slaughter in the Simbai in 1968. If kills for such rare events as celebratory feasts for the diocesan bishop and other visitors are also excluded, then 16.1 percent of the herd was killed. This is still a high slaughter rate.

To maintain their pig herd in the face of high slaughter the Kundagai would need to increase the recruitment rate of the herd. The major means of achieving this are by import of live pigs and a reduction of export of locally raised pigs.[6] Medicines are sometimes acquired from agricultural officers at the Tabibuga government station, which help reduce pig mortality through sickness. Considerably increased import of young pigs has probably been the major factor in allowing greater rates of slaughter. I doubt, however, that pigs are often kept until they reach full size, and this may be important in permitting a sustained rapid turnover of the pig population. Indeed, a feature of the present pig herd is that it appears to be maintained at near-maximum size. Formerly, and still so among those Maring populations yet to stage *konj kaiko* ceremonies, pig herds went through long cycles of slow increase to maximum densities followed by massive slaughter at the end of the ritual cycle (Rappaport 1968). The present Kundagai strategy may have serious ecological consequences yet to be determined. However, assuming that fewer pigs are allowed to reach maximum size (and certainly I saw few very large pigs), the overall live-weight of the herd at maximum numbers permitted by the capacity of women's labor to sustain them may be considerably less than that of a herd immediately prior to a *konj kaiko*. In short, the demographic pressure of the Kundagai and their pigs may be less than that of a comparable population approaching a *kaiko*.

Small numbers of live piglets are lost from the herd in trade, gifts to affines or occasionally as return gifts for bridewealth or death payments. Most pigs are nonetheless lost as pork rather than live. The same holds for the Narak and Kalam neighbors of the Maring. Unlike many parts of the central highlands where ceremonial payments may include relatively large numbers of live pigs, losses from a Maring herd do not swell the herds of recipients.[7] One is led to conclude, therefore, that notwithstanding the periodic large pig kills among central highlanders, there is probably a more rapid turnover of pigs among the Maring and their neighbors. Even if Maring pig fertility is similar to that in the central highlands it is unlikely that reproduction is sufficient to maintain the Kundagai pig herd at its present size without considerable import of live pigs, mainly effected through trade,[8] a matter to which I return briefly in chapter 7.

Kundagai stocks of other livestock are low. Two men owned one cassowary each during the period of major fieldwork. One of these birds was killed as a sacrifice to the spirits during the illness of the owner's wife. Three men owned four dogs, two of which had litters. Most householders own fowls, but their numbers are few.

PRESTATIONS

So far I have identified those items traded and variables affecting the ownership of valuables. I now turn to a discussion of how these goods are distributed in prestations between groups and the geographic patterns of these movements.

Here I focus on those transactions labeled *munggoi awom*, "prestations," by the Kundagai. Being concerned with the establishment, maintenance, or discharge of obligations and rights, these transactions are a form of social relations grounded largely in kinship. The categories of individuals or groups making or receiving prestations are determined mainly by the patterns of past or present marriages linking donors and recipients. To this extent, one can speak of exchange as defining groups, as Wagner (1967) argues for the Daribi (Healey 1979; LiPuma 1988).

As I have shown in chapter 1, the distribution of marriage ties has a strongly directional component and, to this extent, it follows that prestations flowing between individuals or groups related by marriage (in the same or different generations) must also be directional. If these prestations are balanced by an equal flow of similar goods in the reverse direction, then the movement of goods in prestations becomes symmetrical. In that event, prestations would effect a circulation of valuables among intermarrying communities. Where the flow of women between communities is not symmetrical, however, there will also be an unequal flow of valuables in prestations, such that prestations will serve to drain valuables from those communities receiving more wives than they themselves give in marriage.

The following payments are those that the Kundagai class as *munggoi awom*. In the Kundagai view the principal prestation is bridewealth, and it is invariably mentioned first in any list of payments sought from informants. This is understandable in that not only are bridewealth payments generally the largest prestations a man makes, but they should ideally continue as long as a marriage lasts. Contingent on the presentation of bridewealth and the legitimation of a union that it effects, various other prestations follow. Thus, for instance, the recipients of death payments are determined by the direction of bridewealth.

The analysis of trade in subsequent chapters is based on detailed case material of individuals' recall of trading histories. The same numerically based analysis of individuals' involvement in prestations is not possible, for informants were generally unable to remember precise details of prestations they had made. I believe this "amnesia" to be genuine, not an attempt at evasion. A few men claimed to recall quantities of valuables in major bridewealth and death payments they had made, though most could give only vague indications. It is, of course, possible that men feigned forgetfulness—especially when witnesses were present—for fear that disclosures might open them to claims on their resources by exchange partners. Yet, willing public disclosure of the composition of prestations by some men does not support such an interpretation.

There is an ideal of equivalence and balance rather than competitive increment in Maring prestations (see also LiPuma 1988: 148, 151). Contrary to the pattern observed in certain other highland societies, Maring big-men do not gain status through the management of wealth in competitive exchange (Rappaport 1968; Lowman-Vayda 1971; Healey 1978a). Social relations stress egality rather than inequality, although this does not rule out the occurrence of imbalances over a series of prestations. This ethos of egality makes the absence of strict accounting of prestations explicable as a subversion of any certain means of evaluating individual performances against others; prestations are expected to conform loosely to a general ideal rather than to be evaluated against specific transactions of other individuals. Thus, men can give statements about the general size and composition of different kinds of prestations in particular periods while maintaining ignorance of details of their own transactions—the number of items and the identity of those who contributed to a prestation.

Although most major prestations are made in the name of a particular individual, he receives assistance from a range of kinsmen, so that they are essentially collective transactions expressing the state of particular social relationships at specific moments in time. Despite the ideal of egality and conformity to conventional composition, there is, nonetheless, scope for a degree of negotiation on the part of donors and recipients, and for generosity in giving larger prestations than customarily expected. For example, a representative of bridewealth recipients may be present when a donor amasses valuables in his homestead prior to the ceremonial presentation. In veiled speech he may indicate the recipients' expectation of a larger prestation or try to prevent too large a bridewealth being made if he feels his group's resources will be unduly strained in providing a return gift. The possibility of generosity in major prestations introduces elements of tension into particular transactions which the collective suppression of memory prevents from developing into invidious comparisons of performance over time.

By contrast, most men show remarkable recall of the details of trading transactions. The reasons for this lie in the Maring view of trade as explicitly focusing on reciprocal and strictly equivalent transfers of objects rather than on the nature of social relationships. This is so even though trade may be an expression of, and a means of, constructing ongoing social relationships, as I argue in the final chapter. Unlike prestations, trade transactions are exclusively the private affairs of individuals, not of collectivities in public. As explicitly balanced transactions regardless of the state of social relationships linking transactors, trade exchanges are rigorously equalitarian. Further, although particularly vigorous traders may gain some notoriety, men do not compare performances, and no status attaches to differential involvement in trade. Full recall of trading activities is thus no real or potential threat to the equalitarian social order.

Although account is not kept of the composition of prestations given and received, men do recall details of many specific items involved. Thus, in recording trade histories, I often learned of a shell or an axe that had been acquired by trade, contributed to a prestation a kinsman was amassing, and reciprocated in a return gift. The point is, however, that such accounting is keyed to specific *items,* not the *events* in which they moved in prestations. I found it as fruitless an exercise to ask men to list others who had contributed to their prestations as it was to recount the composition of prestations. For example, on one occasion I asked separately a man who had given bridewealth and his brother, who was a major contributor, to detail the composition of a prestation a few days after I had observed its ceremonial display and presentation. Their opinions differed, and neither account tallied with my record. Once assistance has been received and reciprocated the details of an event are forgotten.

In this general lack of recall of the details of major prestations the Kundagai are in marked contrast to other societies, such as the Kaulong (Goodale 1978), Wola (Sillitoe 1979), and Melpa (Strathern 1971). Significantly in such societies the social identity and status of men (and, for the Kaulong, of women also) or groups is inextricably linked to prowess in the skilled manipulation of valuables in competitive ceremonial exchange.

It is noteworthy that by the mid-1980s the situation in regard to the recall of major prestations was changing. In respect of at least bridewealth, men were beginning to claim good recall of bridewealth payments they had made, and often the composition of prestations was written down. The stated reason for this change in attitude toward recall of bridewealth was so that a donor could gain full return of the prestation in the event of divorce. Though never common after the payment of major bridewealth, divorce occasionally occurs nowadays when a young man feels that his young wife is not attending to his entrepreneurial interests. These revolve around the production of parchment coffee, as well as a man's interests in such ventures as trade stores and alluvial gold works (see chap. 6). Concern to record exact amounts given in bridewealth does not seem to be general, however, but mostly confined to younger and more entrepreneurially ambitious men.

Bridewealth

Bridewealth payments, *ambra poka* ("woman price"), are often delayed until the birth of a child, by which time it is generally regarded that a marriage will endure. There seems to be a tendency nowadays for bridewealth to be given with less delay, and often before the birth of a child. Of the several bridewealth payments a man usually makes to his wife's agnates during her life only the first or second are substantial. In making the major presentation a man generally requires assistance, as he seldom owns sufficient valuables of his own. Fellow subclan members provide the most aid, with other clan members and, to a lesser extent, matrilateral kin providing smaller amounts. Bridewealth received by a man for his sister or daughter is shared out among the same kin, and such distributions are often specified as returns for aid in making the recipient's own bridewealth payment, or, if he has not yet given bridewealth, they may be counted as creating debts that can be canceled by contributions to his later bridewealth. A woman's brothers are the principal recipients of bridewealth for her, though her father may receive it if there are no true brothers of sufficient age to receive and redistribute the bridewealth.

Informants say that the amount of bridewealth given is decided by the husband. One of the bride's agnates, however, often comes to watch the husband make a final count of valuables on the day preceding the presentation. The purpose of this visit is to gauge the amount of valuables bridegivers will have to amass for the return gift, but if the bridewealth is less than expected the visitor may intimate to the husband that he must collect more valuables.

Bridewealth presentations are divided into two portions, the *gi poka* ("black price") of nonreturnable valuables that may be "eaten" by the recipients, and the *jika poka* ("return price") of valuables to be reciprocated in a return gift. This, however, must not include any items that were received in the bridewealth, so that recipients cannot rely on the prestation to finance their return gift. Even return gifts of money are made up of notes (coins are not used) that have been collected within the receiving group. The same rule applies in making return gifts for other payments. Return gifts of valuables from the bride's agnates

Valuables and Prestations

to the husband may be made the day after bridewealth is ceremonially presented or delayed for many months. Nowadays, a return gift of money is often made with little ceremony immediately after bridewealth is received. Return gifts of other valuables are usually delayed longer. The size of return gifts varies from about 25 percent to 75 percent of the bridewealth received. Table 20 gives details of the composition of bridewealth payments since the turn of the century.

Bridewealth for previously married women, mostly widows, occasionally divorcees, is less than for unmarried women.

Additional bridewealth payments generally consist of a single cooked pig and/or a few shells and steel tools and money. These additional payments are often made after the birth of children and are sometimes called *wamba poka*, "child price."

Whatever the reason for a marriage, bridewealth should be given; failure may be a cause for divorce, initiated either by the wife who feels her worth is unacknowledged and her agnates not compensated for losing her, or by the wife's agnates who prefer to reassign her to someone more likely to be conscientious in making affinal prestations.

Bridewealth received from the Kalam is usually smaller than that given by the Maring. The Kalam, however, do not expect a return gift although their Kundagai affines sometimes offer one.[9] In making bridewealth payments to Kalam the Kundagai give customary Maring amounts and receive return gifts.

It is clear from the table that there has been considerable inflation in bridewealth values, as well as changes in their composition since around the 1930s. There was a sharp increase in the number of shells, steel tools, and the amount of money passed in bridewealth in the 1960s and early 1970s, while the number of pigs increased also. Thereafter, the numbers of shells—especially kina—and steel tools included in bridewealth fell off considerably, while the number of pigs and sums of money increased yet further. Marginally more pigs were included in bridewealth in 1974–1978 than in the subsequent period, but the variation in numbers in individual transactions was lower: from two to six pigs in 1974–1978, against five to eleven in 1979–1985. It has become more common to include at least some live pigs in more recent bridewealth presentations.

Death Payments

Death payments, *munggoi gwio wele awom* ("valuables bones break give"), or *munggoi kump-kent awom* ("valuable bones give"), for

TABLE 20. COMPOSITION OF BRIDEWEALTH

Period[a]	Pigs	Cassow-aries	Money (K)	Axes (S=stone)	Bush-knives	Kina	Green-snail	Dogwhelk/cowry ropes, head-bands	Other
A. MAJOR BRIDEWEALTH, PREVIOUSLY UNMARRIED WOMAN									
1900-1910 (1)	1			10S		1 or 1		2	
1930*	1	1		12S				2	1 tooth necklace
1935-1940 (2)	1.5			8.5S		6.5	2.5	2.5	
1955-1960*	1-2			5-20	5-20	5-20	5-20	10-20	
1965-1970 (5)	2	0.2	26+[b]	9.6+	6.8+	19.8	18.2+		
1973-1974 (8)	2.6	0.1	240	17.5	12.4	30	29.8	0.1	1.3 Kingfisher skins
1974-1978 (8)	8	0.8	937	+	+	+	+		
1979-1985 (5)	7.4		1,720	4.8	3.4		7.4		
B. MAJOR BRIDEWEALTH FOR REMARRIED WIDOW/DIVORCEE									
1973-1974 (2)	1		123	4.5	12	13.5	14		
1974-1978 (2)	2		605	+	+	+	+		
1979-1985 (2)	1.5		550	7.5	7.5	6	7.5		

[a] A figure in parentheses indicates number of cases; entries in columns are mean amounts. An asterisk denotes general statement in absence of specific cases.
[b] A + denotes additional amounts given, but precise details not remembered.

males and unmarried females are given by the deceased's agnates to the group that ceded rights in the deceased's mother to that group. In most cases the transfer of rights is effected through bridewealth payments.[10] In the case of married females, the payment is made from the woman's husband to her agnates. As the Kundagai explain the direction of these prestations, death payments for all males and unmarried females are made to the deceased's *ama cen,* or matrikin. Specifically, the recipients are the deceased's *bapa,* mother's brother, and *wambe,* mother's brother's son. If the deceased is still a child his father makes the payment. Death payments for a married woman are given to her agnates by her husband, if he is alive, and by her sons if they are adult. Death payments are therefore clearly related to patterns of marriage.

A return gift is not always made for death payments. The practice of sister exchange and repeated intermarriage between two clans means that there will be many death payments flowing in both directions between two clans. Donors of a death payment may tell recipients not to make an immediate return gift but to count the death payment for a specified wife or member of the recipients' clan as a later return. Ideally such paired death payments should be of equal value. If this is not the case, a return gift should be made to balance the payments.

Unlike bridewealth only a single death payment is usually made. However, several smaller prestations are sometimes made to different recipients.

Informants say that death payments for people of either sex or any age are the same. Since few informants could recall exact amounts given in particular cases the statement is difficult to evaluate (see table 21). It seems, however, that death payments for young children are generally smaller than for adults and are often counted by their donors as doubling as a further bridewealth prestation.

A general inflationary trend since the mid-1960s at least, similar to that shown by bridewealth, is suggested by the small number of cases listed in table 21.

GIRLS' PUBERTY PAYMENTS

The term "girls' puberty payments" seems the most appropriate translation of the Kundagai, *munggoi am yundem,* "valuables breast assemble." This payment is given by a girl's father to his wife's brother, the girl's *bapa,* when she reaches puberty. It is generally made when the girl is between about fifteen and eighteen years of age. The donor

TABLE 21. COMPOSITION OF DEATH PAYMENTS

Period[a]	Pigs	Money (K)	Axes	Bush-knives	Kina		Green-snail	Dogwhelk /cowry ropes head-bands	Other
1930*	1				1	or	1	2	1 tooth necklace
1955-1960 (1)	1	32					4		
1965-1970 (1)	1	45	3		5+		15		
1970-1974 (2)	1	60	3.5	2	5		10.5		
1974-1978 (1)			2	2	6.5		2		
1979-1985 (2)	3	394	4.5	4			9.5		

[a] Figures in parentheses indicate number of cases; entries in columns are mean amounts. An asterisk denotes general statement, no specific cases remembered.

receives aid from fellow subclan and to a lesser extent clan members. The Kundagai rationale for the prestation is as follows. The girl's *bapa* has received much bridewealth for his sister and thereby relinquishes his rights to share in bridewealth received for his sister's daughter. It is the girl's brothers or, if they are still young, her father, who are the principal recipients of her bridewealth. Yet the mother's brother has "planted" the girl in another clan,[11] and her father has benefited from her labor, and her brothers will not only receive her bridewealth but may themselves obtain a wife in sister-exchange for her. On the girl's marriage the *bapa* also loses rights to receive a death payment for her. The *am yundem* is therefore given to the *bapa* to compensate him for his loss of rights to share in bridewealth and death payment for the girl. At the same time the prestation discharges any further obligations the girl's father and brothers have toward her *bapa* in respect of her. Males retain obligations and rights of mutual aid with their *bapa* throughout their life.

This kind of prestation does not seem to be widely known as *am yundem* among the Kundagai, and it is apparently unknown in at least some other Maring groups including the Tsembaga (Roy Rappaport, pers. comm.) and the Tugumenga (Neil Maclean, pers. comm.). Many Kundagai regard such a prestation as an additional substantial bridewealth and name it accordingly. Significantly, *am yundem* payments approximate the value of a major bridewealth, but no return gift is received. Informants suggested that the approximate size of a prestation in the mid-1970s would be one or two pigs, K100, and twenty each of axes, bushknives, kina, and greensnail shells.

CHILD RECLAMATION PAYMENTS

Young widows often return to their natal homes or remarry into different clans if their husbands' agnates do not exercise their right to marry the woman in widow inheritance. Any children they take with them tend to become assimilated into their mother's or her new husband's clan. Occasionally a deceased man's agnates may wish to retain or reclaim his children as members of their own clan while allowing their mother to depart. This may be done by a *wamba munggoi lem* prestation ("child valuables give"). Such a "reclamation payment" is made to whoever assumes guardianship of the children—usually the widow's agnates or new husband. In practice the payment seems seldom given and informants could not recall any cases. They considered that a payment of several hundred Kina and one to three pigs would be an appropriate amount.

PAYMENT TO MILITARY ALLIES

On the final day of the *konj kaiko* festival hosts distribute salted belly-fat of pork, *konj kura* ("pig salt"), to those who have helped them in the last round of hostilities. Since recruitment of allies in war is an individual enterprise, these highly ceremonialized prestations pass between individuals. Allies, *nokomai,* are drawn exclusively from consanguineal and affinal kinsmen. They are always of different settlements, as all members of a local population participate as a single unit in warfare with major enemies.

I asked fourteen men to list the *konj kura* prestations they made in the last, 1960 *konj kaiko*. The sample comprises almost 60 percent of surviving men who were of fighting age in the last war the Kundagai fought as major enemies. One of these men had never given *konj kura,* while four of them had also fought in the 1943–1944 war with the Tsembaga and rewarded their allies in the 1952 *konj kaiko*. The man who made no prestations, long regarded as a witch, had not recruited allies, because he was either unable or unwilling to do so. The remaining men made a total of 59 prestations or an average of 4.5 each (range 1–15). In the 1952 *kaiko* four men made 27 prestations or an average of 6.75 each (range 2–12). Combining the two sets of prestations, seventeen men (counting those who gave prestations on both occasions twice) gave 86 prestations or an average of 5 each. The categories of kin to which prestations were made, and the distribution of their settlements of residence, are shown in table 22. Kinsmen of the same generation provide the greatest amount of aid (68.6 percent). Brothers-in-law are the single most important category of kin who provide aid, classificatory brothers, mainly mother's sister's sons, being next-most important. All recipients are related to ego through women in either the same or first ascending or descending generations. The distribution of allies in relation to marriage, however, is tempered by the areal distribution of these kin. Settlements closest to Tsuwenkai generally provide the greatest number of allies. Five allies recruited from Kinimbong were all wife's brothers in Aikupa and Kwibukai clans. Both these clans were autonomous until recently, although they participated with the Kundagai as major enemies rather than as allies in war against the Tsembaga. Informants say the *konj kura* prestations to these kin were

TABLE 22. KUNDAGAI SALT PORK PRESTATIONS TO ALLIES, 1952 AND 1960 COMBINED

Residence of recipient[a]	Relationship of recipient to donor[b]								TOTALS	
	WB/ZH	WF/DH	MB	MBS	ZS	'F' FMZS	MZS	'S' MZSS	FZH	No.	%
Bokapai	12	3	1	1	2	4	8	4		35	40.7
Kinimbong	5									5	5.8
Kompiai	6		2	3	1		7	1	2	22	25.6
Kupeng							2	2		4	4.6
Kandambiamp	1				1		1			3	3.5
Ginjinji							1			1	1.2
Gai	4		1	2	1		2			10	11.6
Nimbra						1	1			2	2.3
Nembenakump	2									2	2.3
Kumbruf	1							1		2	2.3
TOTALS:	31	3	4	6	5	5	22	8	2	86	
PERCENT:	36.0	3.5	4.7	7.0	5.8	5.8	25.6	9.3	2.3		

[a] Allies from Tuguma and Cenda are not represented in this sample, and informants' statements suggest that they were few in number.
[b] Maring terminologies for the nine categories, from left to right, as follows: *latse, imatse, bapa, wambe, wai wump nako, anya* or *wowa, gwite, wai nako, alianggai*.

made as affinal prestations rather than as discharging obligations to allies in war.

Ideally a *konj kura* prestation should consist of the salted belly-fat of a single pig. Other portions of the cooked carcass are often given in addition. In fact, each prestation varied from one-third to one whole carcass. The number of pigs killed by each donor in 1960 ranged from 1 to 5, with an average of 2.8 per donor. The number of Tsuwenkai men who fought in the last war and survived to 1960 was about thirty-two, which means that at least 90 pigs were killed in 1960. This compares with 96 pigs killed by the slightly smaller Tsembaga population in 1963 (Rappaport 1968: 213). The figure for the Kundagai is an underestimate as an unknown number of additional pigs were killed to discharge debts of deceased men. At an average of 5 prestations per donor there would have been a minimum of 160 transactions. In their 1963 *kaiko* the Tsembaga made at least 163 prestations (Rappaport 1968: 214). Tsembaga and Kundagai prestations were thus of roughly equivalent composition.

In the sample there is a tendency for both older men and big-men to make more prestations. Older men have firmly established affinal ties by repeated affinal prestations as well as having increased the number of such ties through the marriages of their sisters and daughters. Older men also have more same-generation consanguineal kin of fighting age if the latter are sons of younger sisters. Big-men, because of their prominence in the fields of ritual and magic, politics and fighting may be able to attract more allies simply because of their status. Such men with specialized knowledge, influence over their fellows, or prowess in fighting will also be particularly useful allies when those who aid them in turn wish to recruit allies of their own.[12]

Failure to reward allies is regarded as a serious renegation of obligations. In their last *konj kaiko* the Kanump–Kauwil allegedly refused to reward their Kundagai allies. The Kundagai were only just restrained from starting a fight on the ceremonial ground to press their claims for reward.

If a man dies before giving *konj kura* his sons assume responsibility for the prestation. Similarly, a man's sons inherit the right to receive *konj kura* due to their father. His widow may advise the heirs of their rights and obligations. If the sons are still boys their mother may receive *konj kura* on behalf of her dead husband.

Other prestations are often given at the time of *konj kura*. Of the sample of thirteen men giving *konj kura* in 1960, six gave additional bridewealth payments, and one of the four men who gave *konj kura* in 1952 gave an additional prestation, again bridewealth.

REFUGEE PAYMENTS

Two prestations are involved, given by groups of refugees who have usually fled from their former home after rout in warfare or following fighting within their natal clan cluster. The first payment may be made several years after the arrival of refugees, when they give a payment called *munggoi wunt-piye yanggale mia,* "valuables sleeping-mat sit-down remain," to their hosts. I could not discover the precise amounts involved, but the payment includes several cooked pigs, shells, and steel tools. In about 1955 three agnatically related Tuguma men sought refuge in Tsuwenkai after an interclan fight at Mondo. The refugees were cognates of Wendekai Kolompepe men. After about five years' residence with the Kundagai they made the above payment to their Wendekai hosts and a few men of other clans who had publicly welcomed them. Two of the refugees later married Kundagai women, thus consolidating their links with those who had offered them refuge. All three men and their children are now regarded as members of Wendekai Kolompepe by virtue of the payment and their continued residence and full participation in clan affairs (see Healey 1979).

Shortly prior to the 1960 *kaiko* a group of Kalam refugees of Tawanjen clan of Kumbruf fled from feuds at home and took refuge with kin of Atikai Kolompepe. They did not make an arrival payment, but they did make the second payment given by refugees on their departure. This departure payment is called *munggoi wunt wele mule yemp wi,* "valuables sleeping-mat break fold put come." The Atikai hosts gave a return gift, and as an earnest of their continued friendship, a woman in marriage to Tawanjen.

VENGEANCE PAYMENTS AND
HOMICIDE BRIBES

Both types of payment are called *munggoi kupi lem,* "valuables homicide give," and are given to those who avenge the death of a close kinsman and to those hired to assassinate a selected victim. Ideally a man's death by violence should be avenged on the killer's group by the dead man's close kinsmen. Sometimes they are unable or unwilling to do this, but another man may do so, either by ambush or on a fight ground during war. The victim of vengeance need not be the killer himself and is sometimes selected for his superficial resemblance to the dead man. Such vengeance payments apparently do not exceed a few shells. They are now seldom if ever made among the Jimi Maring, as the presence of the government deters vengeance killings and encourages claims for compensation instead.

Kupi lem payments are also offered as a bribe for the assassination of selected victims, generally witches or enemy big-men. The payment, consisting of shells, is often secretly displayed to possible homicides to induce them to join an assassination party.

Compensation Payments

Collectively, compensation payments are known simply as *munggoi awom* or *munggoi lem*, "valuables give." The most substantial payments are those made to the agnates of an ally killed in warfare and to those of a victim of accidental killing or murder. The former payment, classed as a death payment by the Kundagai (and so named), is said to have consisted of up to twenty pigs and other valuables. Informants suggest that the present monetary equivalent would be about K800–K2,000. These amounts may be exaggerated, but at the least they indicate that such payments for the deaths of allies are the most substantial that the Kundagai make. No one could recall any such payments given or received by the Kundagai since the 1930s.

The only cases of compensation for deaths not resulting from hostilities between enemy populations that I learned of followed a murder and an accidental killing within the clan cluster. Such payments, known as *munggoi yu mamp lem*, "valuables man head give," include cooked pork, shells, steel tools, and money. The amount given is said to be more than for death payments and less than for bridewealth, though no one could remember precise amounts. The killer's clan should also give a woman in marriage to the dead man's clan. Her first son is considered to be a replacement for the dead man and usually bears his name.

A further named category of compensation payments is for illicit sexual relations. The payment, *ambra duai konj awom*, "woman penis pig give," or *ambra ku konj*, "woman steal pig," is given by the offender to the woman's male guardian. Two such payments occurred in 1974. One consisted of a medium-sized dead pig and K8, the other a dead pig, one axe, one kina, one greensnail shell, and K8. No compensation was given in a third case that came to public notice, as informants explained that the woman involved was a widow with no male guardians to be affronted at an infringement of their rights in the woman. Compensation given in more recent times has risen to between K100 and K200 and at least one pig.

Other compensation payments generally involve lesser amounts and are paid in reparation for damage done to another's property, for insult, or to settle quarrels. In the latter case both parties generally exchange the same items simultaneously.

Minor Prestations

These transactions are called *munggoi aure awom,* "valuables nothing give." There are no set forms and occasions for such gifts. Although they are regarded as creating debt, *menga,* and an expectation of reciprocity, there is no injunction that specific gifts must be reciprocated. Sometimes men make reciprocal minor prestations of equivalent goods at the same time. Often, however, a donor explicitly abjures any specific return for his action. These transactions are instances of what Sahlins (1972) calls generalized reciprocity.

Minor prestations frequently involve single *munggoi* items and other more valuable trade goods, as well as luxury foods and exotic manufactures. They usually pass between individuals in comparative privacy. A common form of gift is the sharing of special foods as a sign of friendship, solidarity, and hospitality with visiting kin and affines. On returning from contract labor young men distribute gifts of money, shells, steel tools, decorations, and cosmetics to consanguines, male and female. More substantial gifts include providing fowls or pigs for sacrifice in the event of an affine's or matrikin's serious illness. Matrikin and affines often favor one another with gifts of *munggoi* items when visiting. Such transactions, whether reciprocated immediately or after a delay, may take on the appearance of trade, yet are rarely confused as such by those involved.

PRESTATIONS IN RELATION TO MARRIAGE PATTERNS

Marriage patterns have altered over time. Consequently the flow of valuables in prestations has also changed. Bridewealth, death payments, *am yundem, konj kura,* and compensation payments for allies killed in war are the most important prestations in the redistribution of valuables between local populations, in terms of the frequency of their occurrence or the size of prestations. Parties to these transactions are all connected by ties of marriage in their own or ascending generations. Affinal and matrilateral ties also predominate in relating parties to various minor prestations.

Several prestations related to marriage ties are mandatory, in that ideally they must (and in practice almost always do) follow the establishment of a stable marriage. These are bridewealth; death payment for a wife, her sons, and unmarried daughters; and *am yundem* for her daughters. Other payments, such as *konj kura* or compensation for death of allies in war, are only contingent on the voluntary decision to recruit matrilaterals or affines for aid in war.

Ideally, a reasonable picture of the patterns of flow of valuables in and out of Tsuwenkai over time could be obtained by collecting complete case histories of all prestations given and received by a sample of men whose affinal and matrilateral connections are representative of the population as a whole. Besides procedural difficulties in obtaining such a sample, the exercise would be fruitless because of the Kundagai's insistent claims to be unable to remember the details of numbers of different items transferred in prestations. Further, such a sample would relate to a much shorter timespan than is available in records of marriages contained in genealogies.

Less precise but operationally feasible methods must therefore be used to outline the movements of valuables in relation to marriage patterns. Mandatory prestations related to marriage will only continue as long as at least one of the following conditions hold for a married woman:

1. She is alive—so that bridewealth payments are still periodically made and her agnates are yet to receive her death payment.
2. Or, if she is dead: her sons are alive—so that her agnates are yet to receive death payments for them.
3. And/or: her daughters remain unmarried—so that her agnates are yet to receive puberty payments for them, or death payments if they die before marriage.

The payments result in an unequal flow of valuables. If the bride givers who receive these payments are themselves bride receivers from donors of prestations (as in sister exchange), then the net flow of valuables may be equal. But only death payments are subject to deliberate attempts to effect a balanced reciprocal flow of valuables. The full range of mandatory prestations set in train by a marriage may take seventy years or more to run its course. For example, such prestations relating to the marriage of the oldest Kundagai's mother are complete except for the death payment for that man to his matrikin. Other series of prestations are only just beginning with the marriages of young men and women, and may stretch as far into the future.

Once all of the above conditions are no longer met, that is, once the woman is minimally a deceased grandmother of living men or unmarried women, her marriage may still be a basis for prestations,[13] but there are no mandatory life-crisis payments patterned by that marriage. Such relationships are ideally concerned with mutual aid, and any prestations are usually in the form of *munggoi aure awom* resulting in an ideally equal flow of goods, if the relationship is maintained through gifts at all. A common form of exchange between such kin is the balanced flow of dissimilar goods in trade.

In determining the flow of valuables in mandatory prestations patterned on marriage only the following marriages need to be taken into account:

1. Living in- and out-marrying women (husband surviving or dead).
2. Deceased in- or out-marrying women whose sons and/or unmarried daughters are surviving.

I cannot apply this method of analysis fully, as it requires complete genealogical records of offspring of all women married within Tsuwenkai, those arriving as wives from elsewhere, and Tsuwenkai women sent out in marriage to other settlements. Such records are available for the first two categories but not for the non-Kundagai offspring of the last category. If, however, the number of children for whom death payments and *am yundem* have been or will be given are excluded (on an assumption that there is an even distribution of the number of offspring by region), then the material can be presented in respect of those marriages where the wife survives, that is, where it is clear that at least death payments for the woman are yet to be received (table 23). This table gives only a partial indication of the geographic distribution of Kundagai marriages patterning the flow of valuables in mandatory prestations, as transactions are continuing in respect of affinal and

TABLE 23. DISTRIBUTION OF KUNDAGAI MARRIAGES TO 1974 PATTERNING MANDATORY PRESTATIONS

Area	Women From		Women To		Imbalances	
	No.	%	No.	%	Received	Sent out
Up-Jimi	10	34.5	21	56.8		11
Down-Jimi	7	24.1	6	16.2	1	
Cross-Jimi						
Up-Simbai	5	17.2	4	10.8	1	
Down-Simbai	7	24.1	6	16.2	1	
Subtotal	29	99.9	37	100.0	3	11
Bokapai	16		10		6	
Kinimbong (including Aikupa)	6		6			
Subtotal	51		53			2
Tsuwenkai	23					
TOTAL MARRIAGES: 127						

matrilateral ties through women now dead (see map 4 for locations of regions listed).

The table indicates that sixty-one or 48 percent of all marriages where the wife survives (to 1974) are within the Kundagai–Aikupa population. Prestations related to these marriages largely remain within the population as a whole but, since Tsuwenkai has received more women than it has sent out in marriage with Bokapai, there is a net drain of valuables in prestations to Bokapai. Clearly, given a marked excess of Tsuwenkai women sent in marriage to settlements further up the Jimi (principally Kompiai), there will be a net inflow of valuables in prestations from that region, which will be redirected to Bokapai and, in a minor way, to the lower Jimi, the upper Simbai, and the far (north) wall of the Simbai.

Given the reservations already outlined concerning the utility of this material, more detailed interpretation of the table would be misleading. Some rather impressionistic views, however, of changes over time in patterns of movements of goods in mandatory prestations can be gained by reference to material on marriages presented in appendix 1 (see also chap. 1).

Over time, genealogies indicate that the Kundagai have received

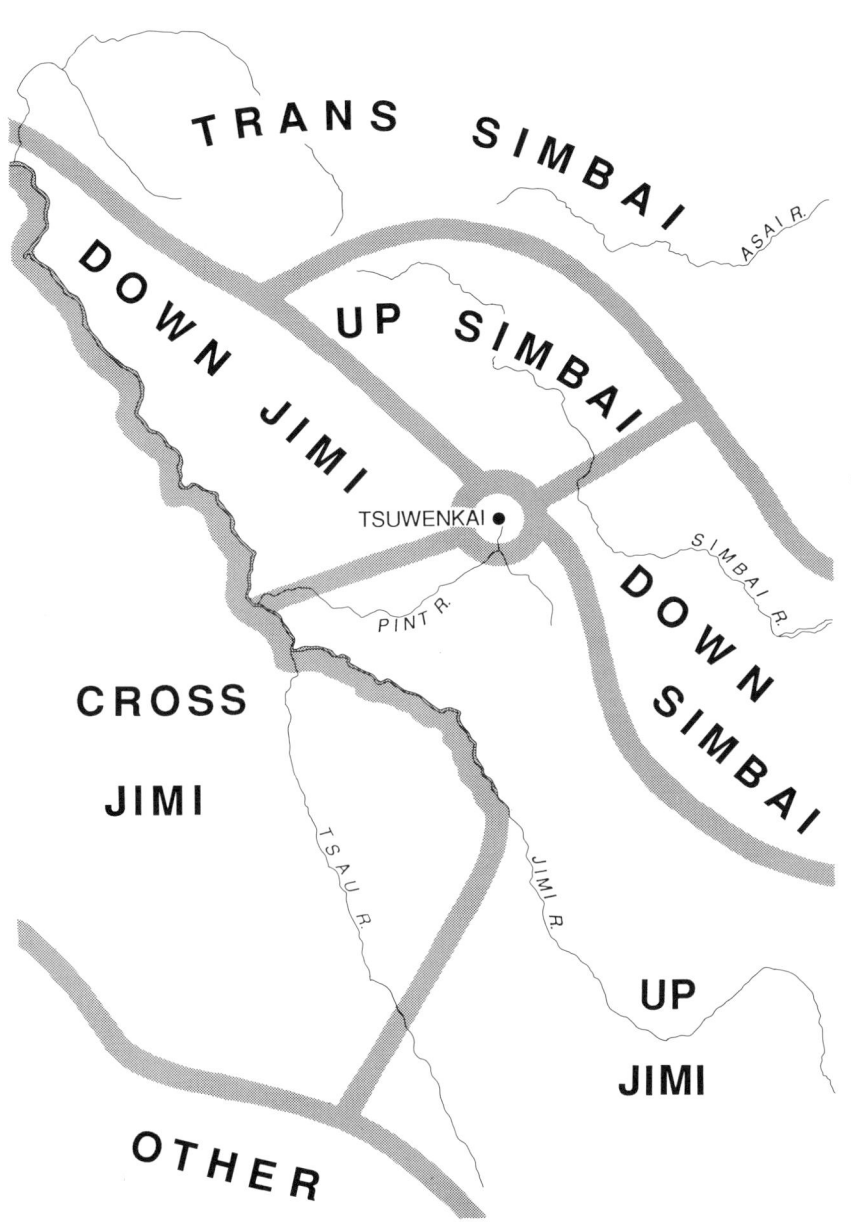

Map 4. Trade Regions

more women in marriage than they have sent out. This is largely an artifact of the structure of genealogies, which tend to omit female agnates in distant generations: there are no records of out-marrying Kundagai women before about 1915. After this date the number of non-Kundagai women recorded as received in marriage approximate the number of Kundagai women sent out in marriage. The pattern of marriages is uneven by region, however. Excluding records for pre-1915, the flow of women between Tsuwenkai and upper-Jimi settlements was roughly even until about 1955 when a dramatic excess in the number of out-marrying Tsuwenkai women developed. Until 1955 the Simbai, especially the upper valley, sent more women than it received, a trend that has been weakly reversed since that date. Marriage ties across the Jimi all but ceased in the mid-1930s. Many marriages contracted prior to 1955 are still patterning mandatory prestations. The general trend, however, is that there is an increasing flow of valuables from the upper Jimi moving against Tsuwenkai women sent out in marriage. Much of this wealth will be lost in prestations to the upper Simbai, but such losses will diminish in the face of changed patterns of marriage. With a trend toward greater endogamy within the Kundagai–Aikupa population, valuables received from the upper Jimi will increasingly accumulate within the greater population but will be drained out of Tsuwenkai to Bokapai, which provides more wives than it receives.

In short, there is currently a general trend for wealth to flow in mandatory prestations from nearby upper-Jimi settlements through Tsuwenkai to Bokapai and the upper Simbai, with smaller net outflows to the lower Jimi. This conclusion can be qualified. The amount of wealth passed in mandatory prestations depends partly on the number of children a woman bears and also on the customary items and size of prestations. Neither factor is necessarily stable for the large geographic area encompassed by Kundagai marriage relations. Buchbinder (1973: 96) gives evidence to indicate that family sizes in the Simbai vary between settlements in relation to environmental factors that affect fertility. There are no comparable data for the Jimi.

The size of prestations does vary by area. Payments received from the Kalam (from Up-Simbai and Down-Jimi) are generally smaller than those received from other Maring groups, whereas Kundagai payments to the Kalam are usually of customary Maring amounts. Thus the inflow of valuables from Down-Jimi will be small and may well be exceeded by prestations in the reverse direction. Similarly, the outflow of valuables to Up-Simbai may be greater than table 23 would suggest, given that the Kundagai will receive smaller prestations from these Kalam groups. The flow of valuables, therefore, may be even more strongly directional from Up-Jimi to Up-Simbai than the table suggests.

Increasing intermarriage with Up-Jimi communities, and especially the excess of women sent from Tsuwenkai, is related to the Kundagai view of this region as being a major source of valuable exotic imports. Some men have sent sisters and daughters in marriage to upper-Jimi settlements specifically to forge close affinal ties that can be used to gain access to the wealth of the region. On their own account, some women are also attracted to men of this region whom they regard as more sophisticated than Simbai, lower Jimi, and Tsuwenkai men, with their reputation for rusticity. As far as I can tell from the few detailed cases collected, bridewealth received from Up-Jimi groups is not consistently larger than such prestations from other Maring populations.

I suggest, then, that there is a rather small net inflow to the Kundagai of valuables in prestations. At the same time, there is a distinct directional flow of valuables in prestations from Up-Jimi to Up-Simbai and, to a lesser extent, Down-Simbai. The flow of valuables is therefore from the direction of ultimate plume consumers toward primary plume suppliers: from the center to the periphery. There is an infrequent flow of plumes of the Raggiana Bird of Paradise, a product of the major plume-consuming areas, in the same direction but, except on rare occasions, plumes do not go in prestations in the reverse direction. Prestations, then, do not directly affect the flow of plumes between communities. As will be seen in subsequent chapters, however, the overall directional flow of valuables in prestations affects the power to obtain plumes in exchange for other valuables from communities situated toward primary plume suppliers.

This flow of goods in prestations parallels movements of some of the same items, specifically shells and steel, in trade. This means that there are two major means of obtaining exotic goods: in exchange for women by prestations and in exchange for forest products by trade. In fact, as will become clear in subsequent chapters, the size of prestations is such that the Kundagai are unable to rely on goods received in such exchanges to fund their own prestations. Trade and prestation as modes of conveyance thus become functionally integrated and interdependent for various aspects of their maintenance and operation. The remaining chapters are devoted to describing the structure of trade and specifying the nature of the interdependence between spheres of trade and prestation.

5
The Structure of Trade

TRADE TRANSACTIONS

In this chapter I am concerned with giving an overall description of the network of trade centered on Tsuwenkai. The focus here is on the geographic and ecological dimensions of the trade, as a prelude to an analysis of more sociological aspects in later chapters. I conclude, however, with a discussion of mechanisms of maintenance of the trade which foreshadows material on social relationships to be discussed in more detail in chapter 8.

There have been important changes in the items and patterns of trade in precolonial and more recent times. Some of these changes are indicated here, but a more detailed discussion is reserved until later chapters. Importantly, although the Kundagai increasingly encountered strangers from distant areas after the imposition of colonial authority in the Jimi, they continued to conceive of trade as maintaining its aboriginal economic and social organization. Whatever the motives of visiting traders from the central highlands, trade did not become more "commercial," "materialistic," or characteristic of market exchange as far as the Kundagai were concerned. It is only in the 1980s that this sense of continuity with past practices of trade has begun to crumble.

This description is based partly on general statements by informants about past and present patterns of trade, but I rely heavily on detailed case histories of individual men. By the time I left Tsuwenkai in 1974 I had interviewed all but one of the men who lived there for the full period of my fieldwork or returned during that time. That one exception was an old man whose speech had been rendered unintelligible by what was probably a stroke (attributed to a witch attack). I also interviewed a number of men who left for work contracts during my time in Tsuwenkai. I collected fifty-eight such case histories.

My informants claimed that these accounts covered every instance of trade they could remember. In addition, I learned of the odd transaction of a further twenty-seven men, either dead or absent, and of two Tsuwenkai women. In all, these histories and additional accounts deal with 2,382 separate trade transactions by Tsuwenkai residents. Some of these had occurred between coresidents, and I was told of them by both men. Such exchanges within the settlement, whether of goods that remained there or of items originally imported or subsequently exported, amount to 9.6 percent of all transactions.

In subsequent fieldwork I collected further case-history material from nonrandom samples of men. In 1978 I gathered details from twenty-three men of 217 trading transactions conducted since 1974. In 1985, fifteen men provided details of 210 transactions occurring since 1978. I have full trade histories for all three periods of fieldwork for only six men. All told, trade histories deal with 2,809 transactions.

Case histories cover a timespan of about sixty years, extending back to a few transactions conducted in the 1920s by men in their seventies in 1974. There is no way of knowing how complete a record of the trading activities of informants these accounts represent. Certainly a few older men confessed that they had forgotten some of their dealings. In terms of an average number of transactions per year, older men's rates are lower than those of younger men, although this in itself does not indicate an expected increase in forgetfulness with age and lengthened trading period. Such lower rates are explained in large part by a decline in trading activity as men pass their prime. Old men have also been trading for longer periods before the establishment of the colonial order, after which time trading saw a general increase throughout the highlands. Nonetheless, I consider that case histories represent the bulk of the transactions ever completed by my informants, especially since 1974. Those forgotten are most likely to involve items of relatively low value which the trader merely handled on behalf of someone else without retaining for his own temporary use.

For the purposes of this analysis, however, it is not important to claim near-total recall on the part of informants. I do consider it reasonable, nonetheless, to take these transactions as representative of the trade history of each individual, and also the combined trading patterns of all Tsuwenkai Kundagai over the last five or six decades.

The total of cases does not include numerous incomplete transactions unless the parties involved had already agreed upon the final arrangements and were awaiting the delivery of the goods. Some quantified material derived from case histories is given in accompanying tables.[1] The following analysis of case material is based primarily on data gathered in 1973–1974, and unless otherwise indicated the "ethnographic present" refers to this period of major fieldwork.

A note is in order on what I take to be a trade transaction for the purposes of tabulating numbers. Put simply, given the definition I have already proposed (chap. 4), a transaction involves the exchange of one or more items as a discrete unit for another such unit. Thus, a man may exchange a bird plume for an axe. But in Maring practice the exchange of two bird plumes for two axes (or other objects), even if between the same men, is invariably two transactions because two separate assessments of appropriate exchange rates are involved. The Kundagai and their trading partners, however, commonly trade some items in variably sized bundles or in multiples in exchange for single items. For example, eagle feathers may be traded in large or small bundles at different rates of exchange. Or again, the Papuan Lory may be passed as a single skin or in multiples—commonly five or ten in one set. When describing exchanges involving several goods informants were generally quite clear whether the items were transferred as a single or as several separate transactions, even if they were all taken by the same individual. Essentially, then, my view of any particular transaction follows Kundagai opinion.

Each transaction, of course, involves a reciprocal flow of items. The 2,809 separate transactions deal with 2,866 imported items and 3,153 exports (some imports counted again as exports). Obviously, many transactions involve the transfer of multiple items in the one direction.

Exports exceed imports by about 9 percent. This is accounted for mainly by local production of trade goods rather than by diverting goods received in prestations into trade, as will be discussed below.

DIRECTIONS OF TRADE

I have divided the Kundagai trading sphere into seven geographic regions with reference to Tsuwenkai as a focal point. The divisions are the same as those used in the earlier discussion of marriage patterns (map 4).

The Jimi and Simbai are divided by a line running along the Bismarck crest. A second line intersecting this at right angles and running through Tsuwenkai divides the Jimi and Simbai into Up- and Down-regions. Areas to the north of the Bismarck crest axis and lying beyond the Simbai Valley I call Trans-Simbai. The Kaironk, Asai, and Kinenj Valleys are included in this region. The south bank of the Jimi River is labeled Cross-Jimi. I include, however, areas south of the Jimi River but upstream of a line running south from about Togban to the Tsau River in the Up-Jimi region. These divisions roughly follow Kundagai directional categories. In Tok Pisin they refer to Up-Jimi—including such settlements as Karap on the south of the river—as *antap* (on top, upstream) and to Down-Jimi as *daunbilo* (below, downstream). Cross-Jimi is referred to as *hapsait long Jimi* (other side of Jimi). Areas to the north of the Bismarck crest are similarly distinguished. Orientation terms in the vernacular are more complex. Two cardinal points are recognized—east, *rungga kemi mingge ya,* "sun below it-comes to-see," and west, *rungga yure po,* "sun it-turns it-goes." An intersecting axis is also recognized: north is referred to as *keno* or *kiyo,* "toward the head of the valley," and south as *kemi,* "below." The latter terms are specific to Tsuwenkai's location in a north–south valley, and different ones would be used in settlements situated on other topographic features. Crosscutting these cardinal points is a more complex system of referents based on topography—valleys, ridges, mountain flanks, and altitude, and the location of places in relation to these features—on the same ridge system, across a ridge or river, or across at the same, higher, or lower altitude.

The line separating the upper and lower Jimi relative to Tsuwenkai places the settlement of Bokapai in the Down-Jimi region and the nearby settlements of Yimpigema and Koinambe in the Up-Jimi region. The Kundagai refer to all three places as *kemi,* "below." This, however, is a reference to their altitude rather than to their position on a roughly east–west axis. Some further remarks on the limitations of the boundaries of the trade areas will be made in the course of this chapter. In the main, however, the areas identified allow for the discussion of the directional movement of goods in trade in terms of the model of trade outlined in the Introduction.

All six regions are within about two days' walk of Tsuwenkai and are now regularly visited by the Kundagai. Visitors from these regions also periodically journey to Tsuwenkai and are encountered by Kundagai traders in other settlements, at ceremonies, government stations, or community projects such as roadbuilding. Where transactions are conducted away from the homeground of both parties involved (for instance, where men of Tsuwenkai and Karap trade at Kompiai), I determine the place of origin of the non-Kundagai trader by reference to Tsuwenkai as a focal point, not the place where the actual exchange took place.

Since contact, a further trade area that I simply label "Other" has been exploited by the Kundagai. This "area" consists of any point beyond the Jimi, Simbai, or Trans-Simbai which the trader must make special efforts to reach. Included are the Wahgi Valley, the Simbu region, coastal centers of Madang, Rabaul, and Port Moresby, and any other area with which the Kundagai might have trading relations.

Settlements of each trade area which have at any time been linked to the Kundagai by trade are given in appendix 4.

In the course of analysis in this and subsequent chapters it is convenient to group the geographic regions just identified into a dichotomy in terms of a center–periphery model of trade outlined in the Introduction. It should be stressed at this point that the model specifies a spatial structure; it does not entail any propositions about political–economic domination. In that sense, my use of the terms *center* and *periphery* does not entail the kind of conceptual loading associated with "worldsystems" analysis (e.g., Wallerstein 1974). (Chap. 6, however, takes up some recent transformations in center–periphery relations and argues for the emergence of ties of dependence and domination.)

In terms of the model of trade the "center" constitutes that region of the central highlands designated as "ultimate plume consumers," whereas the "periphery" encompasses the highland fringes, occupied by "primary plume suppliers." Any of the seven local regions can then be designated as peripherally or centrally located relative to Tsuwenkai. Those regions lying toward the periphery are Down-Jimi, Up-Simbai, and Trans-Simbai, whereas those lying toward the center are Up-Jimi, Cross-Jimi, and Down-Simbai. The Wahgi Valley, which has been included in the "Other" residual trade region, also can be classed as more centrally located.

In this chapter I am concerned only with intercommunity transfers of goods; trade within Tsuwenkai, which amounts to less than onetenth of all recorded transactions, is not considered here.

The Structure of Trade   175

Although all the transactions recorded in case histories were conducted by present Tsuwenkai residents, many were made while traders lived in Kinimbong, when Tsuwenkai was only lightly settled. Most transactions, however, have been conducted by Tsuwenkai residents. The present sample, therefore, cannot be regarded as representative of the trading patterns of inhabitants of any other settlement. It is unlikely that the trading patterns of Tsuwenkai men formerly resident in Kinimbong were appreciably different from patterns centered on Tsuwenkai. These men formed only a part of the total Kinimbong population. The overall pattern of trade centered on Kinimbong may differ from patterns outlined below, if only because the distribution of marriages, and hence of potential trading partners, may differ from Tsuwenkai marriage patterns. The difference in location and distance from other settlements would have relatively little effect on trading patterns of the two settlements. Certainly, trading patterns of men who have lived in both places do not appear to have changed with their shift in residence.

I begin this description of trade by detailing the movement of major locally obtained goods, over which the Kundagai and their neighbors have a large degree of control in the process of production. These goods, which I refer to as forest products, include almost all plumes, many animal skins and furs, live cassowaries and, formerly, various minerals and stone products. Trade in goods sent in exchange—mainly shells, pigs, and steel tools—is then described.

BIRD PLUMES

The ornamental plumes, skins, or loose feathers of at least twenty-seven different species of birds have been traded (app. 3). Only about seventeen of these are valued as decorations or trade items, the rest are merely curiosities of little significance and seldom regarded as worthwhile trade items. The numbers of more valued plumes that are traded largely reflect the availability of wild birds rather than their exchange values or appropriateness as decorations locally. Plumes can be grouped into three major categories: those locally available in Tsuwenkai forests, those locally absent but regionally available to trading partners of the Kundagai, and exotic plumes of distant origins. All local birds are also regionally available, and trading patterns in both categories are essentially the same.[2] Some local birds, and rather more lower-altitude regional birds, are also available from exotic regions. Besides the odd curiosity the only truly exotic species regulary imported from distant regions is the Red Bird of Paradise of the Wahgi Valley and the southern and eastern lowlands. Although present in the lower-Jimi and Simbai Valleys, most skins of the Common Paradise Kingfisher are also obtained from coastal regions.

Hunting, of course, is an important source of locally available plumes. Since the critical period of the mid-1950s,[3] when the government presence and imposed peace were consolidated, trade has assumed increasing significance as a means of acquiring plumes. Only for the Long-tailed Buzzard and the Black Sicklebill have trade imports always exceeded hunting as a supply source for export, but the numbers involved are low. Table 24 summarizes the patterns of trade for eleven species: seven local and four regional.[4]

Whether one considers the number of transactions involved or the number of skins traded (since some species are commonly passed in multiples), the pattern is clear. The great bulk of plumes have always come from the upper Simbai (around 50 percent) together with the lower Jimi (up to 25 percent), with about the same proportion (75 percent) sent on to the upper Jimi. This pattern has remained remarkably stable through the timespan covered in trade histories. Minor variations in the quantitative data are increasing imports from the Trans-Simbai over time, additions of "Other" sources, and increasing exports to Cross-Jimi settlements since about 1956. In fact, Kundagai testimony indicates that Cross-Jimi exports were formerly more numerous than suggested by data from trade histories, with much exchange of plumes for stone axes with Wum–Tsenga people.

The overall flow of plumes is markedly toward ultimate plume consumers from more peripheral regions. Since there is a drain of plumes along the Wahgi toward the east, the flow of plumes Cross-Jimi constitutes an arm of the general orientation toward the central Simbu–Kuma area. Most known Wahgi destinations of plumes sent Cross-Jimi are to Melpa areas and the Banz region.

The dominant pattern of trade is highlighted by the very minor counterflow of plumes from the upper Jimi. This has involved only two species, the Red Bird of Paradise (excluded from the table) and the Lesser Bird of Paradise. Plumes of the latter mainly came from Kompiai, and largely in the pre-1956 period (see below). Counterflows to the Down-Jimi region are more marked. The great bulk of these transactions, however, are with Bokapai Kundagai partners. Smaller Up-Simbai counterflows have mainly been to the Kinimbong Kundagai. In many cases my informants knew that feathers sent to Bokapai and

TABLE 24. PATTERNS OF TRADE IN MAJOR PLUMES[a]

Time/Region	Imported From		Exported To	
	No. transactions	%	No. transactions	%
PRE-1956:				
Up-Jimi	7	5.6	143	75.3
Down-Jimi	28	22.6	18	9.5
Cross-Jimi	5	4.0	7	3.7
Up-Simbai	64	51.6	12	6.3
Down-Simbai	18	14.5	8	4.2
Trans-Simbai	2	1.6	2	1.1
TOTAL	124		190	
1956-1974				
Up-Jimi	2	0.4	416	78.2
Down-Jimi	107	23.4	24	4.5
Cross-Jimi	3	0.7	59	11.1
Up-Simbai	252	54.9	6	1.1
Down-Simbai	47	10.3	8	1.5
Trans-Simbai	25	5.5	-	-
Other	21	4.6	19	3.6
TOTAL	457		532	
1974-1978				
Up-Jimi	1	1.7	53	76.8
Down-Jimi	16	26.7	5	7.2
Cross-Jimi			5	7.2
Up-Simbai	25	41.7	3	4.3
Down-Simbai	7	11.7	3	4.3
Trans-Simbai	9	15.0		
Other	2	3.3		
TOTAL	60		69	
1979-1985				
Up-Jimi			44	66.7
Down-Jimi	2	8.9	2	3.0
Cross-Jimi	2	3.6	14	21.2
Up-Simbai	30	53.6		
Down-Simbai	10	17.9	4	6.1
Trans-Simbai	9	16.1		
Other			2	3.0
TOTAL	56		66	
ALL TIME				
Up-Jimi	10	1.2	787	75.9
Down-Jimi	190	23.6	58	5.6
Cross-Jimi	11	1.4	92	8.9
Up-Simbai	438	54.4	25	2.4
Down-Simbai	88	10.9	51	4.9
Trans-Simbai	45	5.6	2	0.2
Other	23	2.9	22	2.1
TOTAL	805		1,037	

[a] Summary of inflow-outflow by species and period listed below. Figures in parentheses indicate number of skins or birds represented where multiple skins are passed in a transaction. The "In" entry list the number of transactions by which plumes are imported to Tsuwenkai; "Out" entry lists transactions by which plumes are exported from Tsuwenkai.

TABLE 24. PATTERNS OF TRADE IN MAJOR PLUMES (continued)

Species	Pre-1956	1956-1974	Period 1974-1978	1979-1985	All time
A. LOCALLY AVAILABLE BIRDS					
Long-tailed Buzzard					
In	6	10		4	22
Out	9	7		3	19
Papuan Lory					
In		14(84)	1(5)	3(21)	19(111)
Out	7(42)	26(101)	4(21)	3(19)	68(232)
Fairy Lory					
In		2(16)		1(5)	4(61)
Out	17(152)	6(34)		2(25)	31(273)
Black Sicklebill					
In	10	20	5	6	48
Out	9	21	6	7	51
Stephanie's Astrapia					
In	12	38	10	11(13)	86(88)
Out	27	64	11	15	137
Superb Bird of Paradise					
In		12(13)	1	1	16(25)
Out	17	53(54)	3(4)	6	104(114)
King of Saxony Bird of Paradise					
In	8(30)	23(64)	6(12)	6(19)	50(147)
Out	14(40)	44(118)	5(12)	8(26)	97(245)
B. BIRDS NOT LOCALLY AVAILABLE					
White Cockatoo					
In		16			16
Out	2	2			4
Vulturine Parrot					
In	39	147	28	18	291
Out	38	146	25	16	280
Hornbill					
In	9	5			16
Out	8	4			14
Lesser Bird of Paradise					
In	40	170	9	6	237
Out	42	159	15	5	231

Kinimbong were redirected to Up-Jimi settlements, while Cross-Jimi links from Bokapai are also important. The Bokapai Kundagai have long maintained marriage and trading relations Cross-Jimi, especially with Kwibun. In other words, most transactions against the dominant trend actually preserve the pattern of movement from the periphery toward the center via the upper Jimi or south across the river to the central Wahgi Valley.

Two significant anomolies remain, nonetheless: some exports to the

The Structure of Trade   179

Up-Simbai involve Papuan Lory skins to Kalam partners, for special cultural reasons. Two-way movements of plumes assume greatest proportions between Tsuwenkai and the lower Simbai. This area is geographically closer to the center than Tsuwenkai, yet it is the third most significant source of plumes for the Kundagai. Imports from the lower Simbai have always exceeded exports to that area. I discuss both these departures from the predominant pattern further below.

For the eleven species listed in table 24, a total of 1,600 plumes, skins, and feather collections have been exported from Tsuwenkai over time, with 1,062 imported. Exports thus exceed imports by 1.5 to 1. Just over half of these imports (560) are of regionally occurring species not available to the Tsuwenkai hunter. Since the 1920s I recorded only four kills of such species by Tsuwenkai men, hunting on land of affines or cognates elsewhere in the Jimi or Simbai. In contrast, lesser proportions—about a third of these plumes (429 of 1,600)—are subsequently exported. In other words, most exported plumes are of locally available birds. This is not to say that all such plumes were acquired by hunting in Tsuwenkai forests; indeed, almost half of them (502 of 1,071) were acquired by trade, mainly from the upper Simbai and lower Jimi. Small numbers came as gifts from kin and affines in other areas.

Although over time nonlocally available species have accounted for about 53 percent of all plume imports to Tsuwenkai, patterns of export of local as against nonlocal species have changed. Prior to contact almost 77 percent of exports were of locally occurring species. From 1956 to the late 1970s this proportion dropped to about 56 percent, climbing to around 80 percent in the 1980s. In other words, since contact there was until recent times an increased traffic of plumes through Tsuwenkai: proportionately greater amounts of nonlocal plumes have passed Up-Jimi through Kundagai hands. As I will show later, this development also involved an increasing volume of trade.

There have been some slight changes in the volume of certain kinds of plumes or skins traded over time. This is most clearly evident for the Raggiana Bird of Paradise, unknown to the Kundagai before about the early 1960s, although it was occasionally obtained by people further up the Jimi well before that time. Plumes of this bird have never been very highly regarded. In the 1970s it was obtained from Up-Jimi and southcoastal areas, but it seems to have been abandoned since then. Similarly, skins of the lowland Purple-bellied and Black-capped

Lorys and the Common Paradise Kingfisher, though regionally available, have only been obtained in significant numbers in the 1960s and 1970s, mainly from the coast. In contrast, certain kinds of feathers now considered dull, such as of the Goura Pigeon, Hornbill, and White Cockatoo, have decreased in popularity as decorations and trade items in recent years. These variations partly reflect changes in decoration styles among the Maring and their neighbors. A degree of innovation and an attraction for bright and contrasting colors characterizes decorations. Perhaps significantly, there is little evidence of fluctuations in trading rates of other plumes that have always been more important items of local decoration, and also in high demand by distant traders. I now give brief details about trade in a few species that exemplify particular aspects of the overall trade in plumes.

Patterns of trade in the handsome black and red feathers of the Vulturine Parrot, *Psittrichas fulgidus* (Maring: *kopel*), are little affected by local decoration styles. These feathers are considered only minor decorations by the Maring and are rarely worn. They are, however, very popular with the Narak, Kandawo, and other upper-Jimi and Wahgi groups, who construct halolike headpieces and elaborate forehead plaques from flight and body down feathers. The Kundagai handle large numbers of feather packets of this bird, which is among the most highly valued of trade goods. In terms of the number of transactions in which it is involved, this species is the most commonly traded bird and the third most frequently traded object after pigs and money.

The birds are killed by the Kopon of the lower Kaironk and Jimi Valleys, the Kalam of the Asai Valley, and the Maring and Gainj of the lower Simbai. Local people of the last area are allegedly resisting plans to build a road through their lowland forest territory to link Simbai and Aiome Patrol Posts. The Kundagai report that these Simbai Maring fear the road will attract hunters to poach parrots in the forests.

Prior to contact only the flight and larger body feathers, known as *kopel banka,* were traded. Bicolored down feathers are now included in trade packages, which are usually larger than in the past. Most packages contain feathers from a single bird, although they are sometimes divided into two bundles in their passage toward the Wahgi and Simbu.

Throughout the period of records most Vulturine Parrot imports (50–70 percent) have come from Up-Simbai settlements, especially Kinimbong, Tekerau, and Kumbruf. Down-Jimi settlements, mainly Ginjinji, are the second major source (15–19 percent). Considering it is a source area for the species, Down-Simbai has provided relatively

The Structure of Trade   181

few collections. Most exports from this area are probably sent to Jimi settlements upstream of Tsuwenkai. Recently a few collections have been obtained from the Kinenj and Asai Valleys beyond the Simbai, and from Port Moresby. People called "Goilala" by the Kundagai are said to be the main source of Vulturine feathers in the markets in and around the national capital.

Exports from Tsuwenkai are predominantly Up-Jimi, ranging from 90 percent before 1956 to 50 percent in the 1980s. Prior to contact 73.5 percent of these exports went to the large neighboring settlement of Kompiai. This is still an important destination, though exports to other settlements have increased. Exports to Cross-Jimi, previously often in exchange for stone axes, have been next in importance, amounting to almost 40 percent in the 1980s. In recent years, visiting Kuma-speakers from the upper Jimi and Simbu traders have purchased collections.

Trade in this species exemplifies the general pattern for most other commonly traded plumes passing through Tsuwenkai from more peripheral areas, including those species that are also procurable from local forests.

Patterns of trade in the Papuan Lory, *Charmosyna papou* (Maring: *goli*), do not conform to this general pattern. This parrot is widely distributed in mountain areas, including the Owen Stanley Ranges inland from Port Moresby. Most birds in the Jimi–Simbai area are of the melanistic form, being starkly black and green with only small touches of red and blue. The predominantly red-colored forms seem to be more common near Port Moresby, where many skins are now obtained by Jimi men working on the rubber plantations of the Sogeri Plateau, and from itinerant traders—perhaps Goilala, Kunimaipa, and Orokaiva people—visiting the city's market and outlying rubber estates.

I have no record of imports of this species prior to contact, although men say small numbers were obtained from the lower Jimi and the Simbai. In this period exports were rather infrequent but roughly balanced between Up-Jimi and Up-Simbai. Since contact, imports have exceeded local production by hunting as a source of plumes for trade, with most skins coming from upper-Simbai settlements. Exports have also been intensified, predominantly to Up-Jimi settlements, although Up-Simbai forms a much more important destination of skins than in any other species. Over time, imports from Up-Simbai have doubled trade in the reverse direction, so that the net drain of skins to the upper Jimi is preserved. Nonetheless, the relatively high proportion of trade in opposition to the main flow requires explanation.

The Kundagai note that Lory skins have ritual significance in Kalam *semi* initiation festivals for boys. As a festival draws near Kalam fathers seek decorations for their sons, and their Kundagai trading partners offer skins, sometimes obtained from Up-Simbai in the first place. After the dancing that follows the emergence of the newly initiated boys, dancers often offer their plumes to visiting traders, and the skins resume their passage toward the upper Jimi. Particular cultural factors thus intervene to deflect trade patterns in this species from grosser ecological and cultural forces.

Perhaps the most important species for local decorations, and the second-most commonly traded bird, is the Lesser Bird of Paradise, *Paradisaea minor* (Maring: *yambai*). Although absent from Tsuwenkai it is found in lower-altitude forest in all surrounding areas, but only as far upstream in the Simbai as Nembenakump. Precontact records of trade reflect this central location of Tsuwenkai as a minor local importer and consumer of Lesser plumes. Prior to about 1945 the dominant flow of these plumes was from nearby Up-Jimi settlements and the lower-Jimi to Up- and Trans-Simbai areas—largely a reversal of patterns for other species. Most plumes from Up-Jimi came from Kompiai in exchange for salt packets (see below). Kompiai trading partners acquired many Lesser Birds of Paradise in exchange for the Kundagai salt from their Kwibun (Cross-Jimi) partners. After 1945 trade patterns in these plumes changed to conform to general trends, with the great bulk of plumes passing from Up-Simbai and Down-Jimi to the upper Jimi.

The location of Tsuwenkai in relation to Lesser Bird of Paradise–supplying communities replicates in microcosm the geographic pattern of trade outlined in the Introduction. That the plumes now do not converge on Tsuwenkai, where there is a high demand, but pass through in the same way as other plumes requires explanation. Lesser Bird of Paradise plumes are only one item of a larger category of goods. Only very rarely are different types of plumes exchanged for one another. As a class of goods, plumes are therefore exchanged only for sets of dissimilar items. There are no specialized products of Tsuwenkai that neighboring communities, also supplying Lesser plumes, do not have themselves. Tsuwenkai, therefore, does not hold a monopoly in relation to neighboring communities on a desired exchange item. Like most nearby areas the major specialized products of Tsuwenkai are animal remains. Because these are not interexchangeable, they can only be offered in return for other goods, which, except in the case of pigs, salt, and stone axes, are not produced by their neighbors either. The desire to acquire exotic goods and use them in exchanges with other communities necessitates the Kundagai, and their neighbors who provide Lesser plumes, to direct their plume trade toward the source of these goods. In this connection it is probably significant that the dominant flow of Lesser plumes was reversed in the early 1940s when shells exchangeable for these and other feathers began arriving in increasing numbers from Up-Jimi rather than the Simbai (see below). Until this time, Up-Jimi and Wahgi communities that now obtain at least some of their Lesser Bird of Paradise plumes via Tsuwenkai may have relied on skins from wild populations of birds in the upper-Jimi and Ramu Valleys.

MARSUPIAL FURS

Phalangers or cuscuses of the species *Phalanger maculatus* and probably *P. orientalis* come in a variety of forms—dark, white with dark or ginger blotches, and all-white (see app. 3 for Maring taxa). Pelts of these forms, exclusively obtained from lower altitudes, are highly valued. Tail skins of the tree kangaroo, *riawe*, are also valued, and it is the only species in high demand which is present in Tsuwenkai. It is, however, rare. Several locally occurring species of phalanger and ringtail possum[5] also yield loose fur (used to decorate men's dancing aprons, women's best aprons, and good string bags), fur strips for headbands and armbands, and skins prepared as drumheads. Trade in such locally available products is relatively unimportant in terms of both volume and exchange value but has increased since the mid-1950s under the stimulus of a steady demand for fur from newly contacted and distant people Up- and Cross-Jimi. One Tsuwenkai man who is particularly skilled in hunting marsupials has made several special journeys to Banz in the Wahgi Valley to sell fur bundles in the town's market.

Few locally obtainable furs have been imported. Exotic furs, by contrast, predominantly come from the lower Jimi, where phalangers seem to be fairly common, and from Up- and Down-Simbai. Most Up-Simbai furs probably originated in the lower-Jimi, Kaironk, Kinenj, and Asai Valleys; the lower Simbai is also a source area.

The great majority of exports are to the upper Jimi, with Cross-Jimi next in importance. There are no evident changes in trade patterns in furs over time. The flow of furs in trade is thus similar to that of plumes. The incidence of trade in furs and skins, however, seems to have diminished from the late 1970s.

MINOR ANIMAL PRODUCTS

The only other local animal remains still traded are green scarab beetles. Whole exoskeletons are woven into yellow-orchid fiber headbands, and beetle heads are threaded onto sticks about fifteen centimeters long. Hundreds of these sticks are then attached in zig-zag patterns to the wig to give a beaded effect. Beetles are collected by the Kundagai when they swarm in the drier season in lower altitudes. They are also obtained infrequently by trade, mostly from more peripheral areas.

Until the 1940s animal-tooth necklaces were one of the most important items of prestation. The most valuable necklaces were made of dog canine teeth. Incisors of marsupials and rats were sometimes interspersed among dog teeth, and necklaces of lesser value were composed entirely of these.[6]

Dogs and other mammals were widely distributed so that no community had a monopoly on the ability to make necklaces, although the number of teeth required probably meant that necklaces were a long time in the making, and scarce items. Those with access to plentiful game may have had an advantage over less favorably endowed communities. The Kundagai say that the upper-Simbai Kalam made the finest necklaces, and these were obtained in exchange for stone axes, pigs, cowry, and dogwhelk shells. The last two items, say the Kundagai, ultimately replaced tooth necklaces in the 1940s. In turn, necklaces were occasionally exported toward the center in exchange for the same items. No records of trade in necklaces occur in the trade histories collected, from which I infer that it was infrequent.

LOCAL LIVE ANIMALS

Pigs are the most important live animals traded, but I reserve discussion of them until later, as patterns of trade are quite different from those of other animals, and the Kundagai see themselves more as consumers (literally and metaphorically) of pigs than as producers.

The next-most important species of local animal traded live, and the only wild animal treated thus, are adult and immature cassowaries. Of ninety-seven birds acquired, only seven have come by trade, one from Nembenakump (Up-Simbai), four from Bank and one from Konggerau (both Down-Simbai, near the transition to Up-Simbai), and one from Tsembant (Down-Jimi). The remainder were all caught as chicks in the Tsuwenkai forests. Of these, thirty-five or 36.1 percent have been lost through mortality and occasionally as gifts to kinsmen or in sacrifice. The cassowary trade can be regarded as a high-risk, labor-intensive pursuit. Chicks require careful tending even though they forage much of their own food. Adult birds are caged because they may become dangerous and must be fed daily, mainly on bananas and cooked sweet potato. Improper or inadequate feeding and housing, neglect, or killings by pigs and dogs are the main causes of mortality.

Prior to contact most exports were Up-Jimi. Since then Cross-Jimi exports have increased following direct contact with the Melpa and Kuma. Kuma visitors from Up- and Cross-Jimi periodically visit Tsuwenkai seeking cassowaries for use in bridewealth.

Cassowaries are sometimes caught by laborers from the Jimi in forests near Port Moresby and are sold to Melpa and Southern Highlanders in the city. Some of these birds are airfreighted to the purchasers' home areas.

Wild dogs are allegedly common in Tsuwenkai forests and sometimes breed with domestic bitches. As far as I am aware the Kundagai do not capture wild puppies. Since contact at least, puppies have sometimes been traded. I recorded ten such cases: six to Up-Jimi, two to Down-Simbai, and one each to Bokapai (Down-Jimi) and Up-Simbai. All dogs traded were of the feral New Guinea form, which seems to be a hardier beast than dogs derived from European breeds. I do not know if this Up-Jimi trend in trade is an established pattern or merely an artifact of a small number of cases. Feral dogs, however, appear to be less common in parts of the upper Jimi, where I saw few domesticated animals other than emaciated and sickly beasts brought in from the coast. Tsuwenkai may therefore be a minor local source area of dogs.

Most families own a few fowls. Sales of birds occur occasionally within settlements, but I know of only three live hens being brought to Tsuwenkai by trade.

Recently, a few cats have been obtained from feral litters and missionaries. Cats are well regarded as edible curiosities and useful ratters but seldom stay long with their masters. There are odd sales of homebred kittens.

OTHER MINOR LOCAL PRODUCTS

Several vegetable products have been traded very infrequently. I have records of intercommunity trade involving a drum, an orchid fiber belt, and a string bag. Particularly well-made or decorated arrows are sometimes sold for about twenty Toea to visitors. Before shells became common, bead necklaces made from the seeds of the *nonema* shrub were important items in prestations. They were only rarely traded. All such goods were widely manufactured, and trade was clearly on an ad hoc basis related to individual's particular desires, but with no clear relation to resource differences.

Various exotic and luxury goods are infrequently bought from settlements in lower altitudes where crops grow better. Thus the Kundagai sometimes buy breadfruit, pawpaws, or European cabbages, even though they usually receive them in gifts from kinsmen. Bundles of cured tobacco are regularly sold within Tsuwenkai and less often between settlements. One man exchanged tobacco for a Red Bird of Paradise plume in Tabibuga.

Some of the first coffee seedlings acquired by the Kundagai came by trade from the upper Jimi and lower Simbai in exchange for money, furs, and minor plumes.

SALT

Trade in native salt ceased in the 1960s when salt bought in stores and received in payment from Europeans stationed in the Jimi and Simbai became freely available. Prior to contact trade in salt was of considerable importance. Rappaport (1968) has stressed the utilitarian, nutritional value of salt, though McArthur (1974) suggests he overestimated the importance of salt to Maring survival.[7] My own impression is that the Kundagai neither traded in salt to the extent that the Tsembaga seem to have done from Rappaport's remarks nor valued salt as much for its addition to the diet. Rather, it seems to have been valued for its use as a trade good. Indeed, as I argue below, it is misleading to categorize trade goods as utilitarian and nonutilitarian when the goods may be used both to sustain life (if indeed that was the case with salt) and to exchange for other items of no direct subsistence value.

The Kundagai obtained six salt products. Five of these were mineral salts, the last, *kiyop*, was produced from the ash of a plant of the same name (*Polypodium* sp.). The salts *timbi* and *rengen* (glossed:

bunk) were produced from pools near streams of the same names near Bank (Down-Simbai). *Wum* salt was refined from pools at Gai (Down-Simbai), while *kanji* came from a pool, apparently in Melpa territory, near Timbunki (Cross-Jimi). The exact origin of the last salt type, *aka*, is unknown. The Kundagai only rarely obtained it, in exchange for plumes and furs, mainly from nearby Up-Jimi communities said to have acquired it from Wum–Tsenga and other Cross-Jimi areas. *Aka* possibly came from Enga or Wahgi salt factories (see Hughes 1977).

Aka and *timbi* were considered to be superior in taste, followed by *rengen,* then *wum* and *kanji,* with *kiyop* least esteemed. Poorer-quality salts were sometimes improved by mixing them with better kinds.

Of the different salts only *kiyop* was probably widely produced in the Jimi and Simbai. I have only one record of trade in this salt, exported Up-Jimi in exchange for a pig.

The *bunk* varieties, from Down-Simbai, were often processed by the Kundagai. They traveled to Bank and collected saline water with the permission of kinsmen there. This was carried home in bamboo cylinders. The water was then evaporated slowly in clay vats built over a fire, and the salt residue collected. *Bunk* salts were also imported from Up-Simbai neighbors of the Bank salt-pool owners and, less frequently, from the lower Jimi. In turn, *bunk* salts were exported Up-Jimi in exchange for pigs, stone axes and, prior to 1945, Lesser Bird of Paradise plumes. Much salt sent Up-Jimi, especially to Kompiai, was redirected Cross-Jimi to the Wum–Tsenga axe makers. Some was also sent Down-Jimi to Bokapai and from thence Cross-Jimi to Rinyimp—that is, toward axe-making communities.

I have no case records of trade in the other three salt types, which were only rarely acquired by the Kundagai. Salt from Gai and Timbunki is said to have been extracted occasionally by the Kundagai, although since better-quality *bunk* salts were readily available it is unlikely that the Kundagai traded in these salts to any great degree.

PIGS

The pig is the preeminent exchange item, and because of constant slaughter for prestations and other purposes the Kundagai have a continuous demand for them. Table 25 shows patterns of trade in pigs. Prior to contact almost 80 percent of imports were from Up-Jimi. Since all Jimi and Simbai communities were pig producers, insofar as herds were at least in part maintained by reproduction, this marked direc-

TABLE 25. PATTERNS OF TRADE IN PIGS

Time/Region	Imported from		Exported to	
	No. transactions	%	No. transactions	%
PRE-1956				
Up-Jimi	67	79.8		
Down-Jimi	6	7.1	8	19.5
Cross-Jimi	3	3.6		
Up-Simbai	7	8.3	19	46.3
Down-Simbai	1	1.2	13	31.7
Trans-Simbai			1	2.4
TOTAL	84		41	
1956-1974				
Up-Jimi	255	70.2	1	0.6
Down-Jimi	26	7.2	41	23.8
Cross-Jimi	59	16.3		
Up-Simbai	5	1.4	112	65.1
Down-Simbai	15	4.1	18	10.5
Trans-Simbai				
Other	3	0.8		
TOTAL	363		172	
1974-1978				
Up-Jimi	50	66.7		
Down-Jimi	7	9.3	15	57.7
Cross-Jimi	15	20.0		
Up-Simbai	1	1.3	7	26.9
Down-Simbai	2	2.7	3	11.5
Trans-Simbai			1	3.8
Other				
TOTAL	75		26	
1979-1985				
Up-Jimi	28	33.3		
Down-Jimi	2	2.4		
Cross-Jimi	8	9.5		
Up-Simbai	1	1.2	10	76.9
Down-Simbai	5	5.9	3	23.1
Trans-Simbai				
Other	40	47.6		
TOTAL	84		13	
ALL TIME				
Up-Jimi	484	67.8	1	0.3
Down-Jimi	48	6.7	86	26.2
Cross-Jimi	93	13.0		
Up-Simbai	17	2.4	197	60.1
Down-Simbai	29	4.1	41	12.5
Trans-Simbai			3	0.9
Other	43	6.0		
TOTAL	714		328	

tional component of trade is highly significant. Down-Jimi (mainly Bokapai) and Up-Simbai (mainly Kinimbong) have provided small numbers of pigs in the reverse direction. Almost 60 percent of pigs imported remained in Tsuwenkai to be disposed of other than by trade. By contrast, only about 15 percent of pigs exported were locally raised, the rest having been first imported. Tsuwenkai was a significant consumer area of pigs, then, exporting just under half as many as it imported. The major destinations of pigs sent on from Tsuwenkai were more peripherally located communities. Since contact up to the late 1970s imports from Up-Jimi decreased slightly in importance at the expense of Cross-Jimi. Down-Jimi remained an important source, although since 1956 the great majority of such pigs were from Bokapai. Many of these animals were known to have reached Bokapai from both Up-Jimi and Cross-Jimi. Imports from Up-Simbai were of minor importance. Down-Simbai imports increased in importance and came from six settlements as against one in the precontact period. The counterflow of pigs to Down-Simbai slightly exceeded imports from the same region, with six settlements receiving pigs. Pigs imported from "Other" regions came from Mala and Banz in the Wahgi, that is, essentially the same direction as Cross-Jimi.

Postcontact exports were predominantly Up-Simbai and to a lesser extent Down-Jimi. Imports from Bokapai exceeded exports to this settlement, while exports to other Down-Jimi settlements far exceeded imports from them.

The pattern of trade in pigs thus remained little changed over the almost sixty years to 1978. The dominant flow was from the center toward the periphery and was therefore very much like a mirror image of the patterns of plume trade in the same period.

From the late 1970s some significant changes in the trade of pigs occurred. The implications of these changes are taken up in the next chapter. Up- and Cross-Jimi remained important source areas, but on a much-diminished scale. Almost half of all pigs, however, imported in the six years prior to my last fieldwork in 1985 were acquired from itinerant traders usually identified by the Kundagai as Minj–Banz or Minj–Wahgi people. Consequently, there has been a dramatic increase in imports from a region designated "Other" in the table. Exports have been exclusively to the Simbai, especially the upper valley. In many respects the most recent pattern of trade in pigs is an accentuation of previous patterns, since the Minj–Wahgi region lies geographically beyond both Up- and Cross-Jimi, and closer to centrally located ultimate plume consumers.

Another major change in pig trade is the size of animals traded. Until the late 1970s almost all pigs traded were shoats. These were easily transported over foottrails, trussed up and immobilized in a folded palm spathe or sheet of tree bark slung from the shoulder. In the 1980s, however, Wahgi traders often bring well-grown beasts by truck to the roadhead at the bridge linking Kwima to the south bank of the Jimi. Here they wait for local men to arrive or lead pigs on foot to more distant settlements.

The number of exports for the last period for which records are available is small but suggests that large pigs of Wahgi origin are mostly retained in Tsuwenkai, exports being mainly of small, locally raised animals or those imported from traditional sources.

Although patterns of pig trade have remained essentially the same for the whole period for which records are available—notwithstanding the recent dominance of the Wahgi as a source area—the relative volumes of exports, expressed as a proportion of imports, and the proportion of exports derived from locally bred pigs, have shown consistent trends of change (table 26). Essentially, there has been a growing retention rate of pigs acquired by trade: lesser proportions of pigs imported have been subsequently exported in trade. At the same time, a growing proportion of the diminishing exports have come from local stock rather than from trade imports. This suggests that Tsuwenkai has increasingly accumulated pigs, and at an accelerating rate. Since pigs are mortal this accumulation is obviously not unlimited, but it does suggest that the Kundagai have increased the availability of pigs for disposal in means other than trade. From the discussion of prestations in the last chapter it is clear that increased numbers of pigs have entered the prestation sphere. The consequences for the exchange system as a whole of the increasing availability of pigs is discussed in subsequent chapters.

SHELLS

Before about the 1920s few if any marine shells reached the Kundagai. The first kinds obtained were cowries and dogwhelks, which quickly replaced dog-tooth and *nonema* seed necklaces as valuables. Although in 1974 these shells were still kept as valuables by some

TABLE 26. CONTRIBUTION OF IMPORTS AND LOCAL BREEDING TO EXPORTS OF PIGS

Period	Proportion of imports subsequently exported (%)	Proportion of exports funded by local breeding (%)
Pre-1956	48.8	14.6
1956-1974	47.4	15.1
1974-1978	34.7	26.9
1979-1985	15.5	46.2

men, they had largely been replaced by the more numerous kina and greensnail shells. By the 1980s, however, these shells had themselves become scarce and were seldom traded, and they passed in only limited numbers in prestations. Table 27 gives details of patterns of trade in the more important shells.

KINA

By the 1970s kina (pearlshell, *Pinctada maxima*; Maring: *anggani, kinya*) was one of the most important shells and was an essential component of bridewealth and most other ceremonial exchanges.[8] There are mentions of kina in trade histories relating to the 1930s, and old informants stated that on rare occasions shells were acquired even earlier.

Kina initially reached the Kundagai from Up-Jimi and Cross-Jimi and, rather surprisingly, from the Simbai Valley. The shells must have filtered their way along aboriginal trade routes up through the Bosavi–Lake Kutubu axis in the southern highlands and along the Wahgi to spill over into the lower Jimi toward the Ganz and Tsenga axe makers and the upper Jimi. Shells reaching the Kundagai from the Simbai may have crossed over from the upper Jimi in the vicinity of Bubgile (see below) or across the Bismarcks from the Simbu area to the middle Ramu Gende people.

In the late 1930s and 1940s kina became more readily available, reaching the Kundagai from such places as Rinyimp (Cross-Jimi) and Kompiai (Up-Jimi). A notable acquisition was from a distant Por

TABLE 27. PATTERNS OF TRADE IN SHELLS[a]

Time/Region	Imported From No. transactions	%	Exported To No. transactions	%
PRE-1956				
Up-Jimi	72	75.8	4	7.0
Down-Jimi	5	5.3	11	19.3
Cross-Jimi	3	3.1	2	3.5
Up-Simbai	3	3.1	33	57.9
Down-Simbai	9	9.5	6	10.5
Trans-Simbai	3	3.1	1	1.7
TOTAL	95		57	
1956-1974				
Up-Jimi	183	73.2	3	3.2
Down-Jimi	3	1.2	32	34.0
Cross-Jimi	27	10.8		
Up-Simbai	4	1.6	45	47.9
Down-Simbai	19	7.6	9	9.6
Trans-Simbai	5	2.0	5	5.3
Other	9	3.6		
TOTAL	250		94	
1974-1978				
Up-Jimi	5	62.5		
Down-Jimi			6	28.6
Cross-Jimi				
Up-Simbai	1	12.5	8	38.1
Down-Simbai	2	25.0	3	14.3
Trans-Simbai			4	19.0
Other				
TOTAL	8		21	
1979-1985				
Up-Jimi	3	75.0		
Down-Jimi			2	22.2
Cross-Jimi				
Up-Simbai	1	25.0	7	77.8
Down-Simbai				
Trans-Simbai				
Other				
TOTAL	4		9	
ALL TIME				
Up-Jimi	302	72.6	8	3.6
Down-Jimi	10	2.4	69	30.8
Cross-Jimi	34	8.2	3	1.3
Up-Simbai	11	2.6	111	49.5
Down-Simbai	42	10.1	23	10.3
Trans-Simbai	8	1.9	10	4.5
Other	9	2.2		
TOTAL	416		224	

[a] Summary of inflow-outflow by type and period listed below. "In" entry lists number of transactions by which shells are imported to Tsuwenkai; "Out" entry lists transactions by which shells are exported from Tsuwenkai.

TABLE 27. PATTERNS OF TRADE IN SHELLS (continued)

Shell Type		Pre-1956	1956-1974	1974-1978	1979-1985	All time
Kina	In	26	113[b]		1	165[b]
	Out	16	23	1	1	59
Greensnail	In	37	125[b]	8	2	201[b]
	Out	26	68	20	8	147
Cowry ropes	In	14				14
	Out	5				5
Dogwhelk ropes/headbands	In	18	12		1	36
	Out	10	3			13

[b] One transaction involved passage of two shells.

(Cross-Jimi) trader met at a Cenda *konj kaiko* ceremony in about 1940. Clearly, this influx of kina and other shells followed the massive distributions made by Europeans in the central highlands in the 1930s and 1940s, where shells had formerly been uncommon (see Hughes 1978).

Nonetheless, kina filtered through from new centers of supply in the Simbu and Wahgi areas rather slowly. They did not arrive in any numbers until the Kundagai *konj kaiko* of the early 1950s, when Cenda visitors brought many to trade. Cenda trade relations are strongly oriented south across the Jimi. Since this time, most kina—around 75 percent—have come from Up-Jimi, with Cross-Jimi becoming an important secondary source since contact. Most kina were exported Up-Simbai and Down-Jimi. Since contact up to the mid-1970s there was a shift from a predominant flow to the former area to one favoring the latter. Possibly in earlier times Down-Jimi communities obtained more of their shells from south-bank Melpa groups. Since the mid-1970s the greatly reduced exports have focused on the upper Simbai.

As with many other goods, there has long been a two-way flow of kina in trade with Down-Simbai, although case histories suggest that exports to that area have predominated slightly.

It is noteworthy that the great majority of kina shells in the 1970s appeared to be smaller specimens than those used in the central highlands. The middle and lower Jimi were for a time something of dumping grounds for shells deemed unsuitable by the Simbu, Kuma, and Melpa, who until recently valued shells highly. Kina remained readily available in the Jimi in both trade and prestations into the mid-1970s.

Thereafter, the shell became scarce quite rapidly, rarely passed in trade, and was used only in small numbers in prestations. In 1985 few men retained kina shells and considered them of little utility, other than to be burnt as a source of lime for betel chewing. I consider changes in the availability of shells further in chapter 7.

GREENSNAIL SHELL

Like kina, most greensnail (*Turbo marmoratus*; TP: *trambum*;[9] Maring: *jenja*) originally came infrequently from the Simbai and Cross-Jimi, but by the late 1930s shells began to arrive in greater numbers. Patterns of imports have been similar to those for kina except that Down-Simbai has been a slightly more important source and Cross-Jimi less so. Since the 1960s imports from Simbu and Rabaul, including uncut shells collected by migrant laborers, have been significant sources of supply. Most exports have been to the lower Jimi and the upper Simbai, with the latter predominating. That is, although greensnail and kina come from the same sources, most greensnail are exported to the Simbai and, till the mid-1970s, most kina to the lower Jimi.

Since at least 1935 the Kundagai have been consistently importing and exporting more greensnail shells than kina. Further, greensnail stocks in valuables collections in 1974 also exceeded holdings of kina (table 15). An explanation for this is hard to suggest with the data at hand. Both shells are traded at roughly equal exchange rates (see chap. 7) and have much the same use value as objects of decoration and prestation. Despite this equality in terms of the usual concepts of value employed by anthropologists, Kundagai behavior suggests that value has another facet, that of aesthetics, which is at least partially independent of exchange and use values. Greensnail captures the interest of the Kundagai, who consider it more beautiful than kina. Aesthetic reasons may go some of the way in explaining a preference for greensnail, but factors of availability may also be involved. Aesthetics and cultural meanings of objects are considered further in chapter 7. Greensnail seems to be even less regarded in much of the central highlands and upper Jimi than kina, so that there may be a greater pool of shells that have no use value other than as trade goods in dealings with the Maring and Kalam.

From the mid-1970s greensnail suffered a similar massive decline in supply to kina, yet it is still well regarded by the Kundagai and their

Kalam trading partners and is still a desirable component of major prestations.

OTHER SHELLS

Cowries (Cypraea moneta/annulus; TP: *girigiri;* Maring: *mengga, ambapo).* Ropes and necklaces of cowries were first acquired in the 1920s from the Simbai in exchange for pigs and stone axes. Some also came from the upper Jimi. The shells were presumably from the north coast, reaching the Maring and Kalam via the Ramu. They were apparently passed on toward the Melpa, for Vicedom and Tischner (1983: 263) record them reaching the Hagen area from the Dorfer (Jimi) Valley. From the 1930s most cowries came from the upper Jimi and were sent on mainly to the upper Simbai and Down- and Cross-Jimi. I recorded few cases of trade, and none after about 1956.

Dogwhelks (Nassa sp.; TP: *tambu;* Maring: *gram, yamapiak).* The Kundagai obtained their first dogwhelks in the early 1920s from Down-Jimi and Up-Simbai groups. Until about 1940 the shells came up along the lower Jimi from the coast (cf. Clarke 1971: 97; Hughes 1977: 187) and were passed on Up-Jimi and across the Jimi to axe makers and ultimately the Hagen region (cf. Vicedom and Tischner 1983: 263). After about 1940 the flow was reversed, with relatively large collections of shells, sewn onto ropes and headbands, coming from the upper Jimi. From Tsuwenkai they were sent Down- and Cross-Jimi and to Up-Simbai. Trade in dogwhelks all but ceased in the mid-1960s. The rapid alteration of the trade flow was no doubt a result of the introduction of shells by Europeans in the central highlands.

Bailer Shell (Melo sp.; TP: *gam;* Maring: *mendema).* Bailer shell is rarely obtained by the Kundagai. Coming only as a cut forehead ornament, it is regarded as a curiosity of little value. The first bailers were apparently acquired from early kiaps who gave them out in exchange for pigs. It seems to have been only rarely traded, from the upper Jimi.

Conus Shell (Conus sp.; Maring: *wurawura).* Conus anuli or disks, used as nose pendants, and shell bracelets probably of this species, are said to have come, though rarely, from Cross-Jimi in exchange for plumes. This pattern is consistent with that shown by Hughes (1977: 197), with conus traded north by the Melpa to the middle and lower Jimi. Always a minor object of trade, most conus shells are now bought from street vendors in coastal towns by migrant laborers.

CUTTING TOOLS[10]

STONE AXES/ADZES

Older men identified seven or eight different types of stone axe blades, *cenang*. One of these, called *goipaiku* or *kandenai*, was made from boulders found in Goipai Creek in the upper Kant Valley within Tsuwenkai territory during the 1920s.[11] A second, *kira*, was from stone quarried from outcrops in the Pint Gorge by the Cenda and Ambrakwi. Both locally made axes were of poor quality, liable to split and chip, and were seldom traded and then mainly to the Simbai. According to the Kundagai, the remaining five or six types of blades[12] were made by the Wum–Tsenga people. Comparison of blade names with the petrographic groups to which they refer (listed by A. and R. Rappaport in Chappell 1966) suggests that most nonlocal blades came from the Ganz and Tsenga factories, with others originating from the Abiamp and Dom quarries in the Wahgi and a quarry at Mala Gap on the Sepik–Wahgi Divide. Maigmol, near Tsenga, was probably also a source of some Kundagai axes.

The Kundagai abandoned the use of stone tools by the late 1940s or early 1950s, although they continued to trade in stone occasionally: a Tsuwenkai man traded a stone axe to Ginjinji (Down-Jimi) in about 1956.

Most stone came to Tsuwenkai from Kompiai, Koinambe (Up-Jimi), Bokapai, and Kandambiamp (Down-Jimi). All these communities maintained close trading links with Cross-Jimi settlements, including the Wum–Tsenga area. Tsuwenkai Kundagai occasionally accompanied Bokapai kinsmen to trade directly with axe-makers at Wum. The odd blade obtained from the lower Simbai may have been from Wahgi Valley quarries, reaching the Simbai via a pass near Bubgile in the upper Jimi (cf. Hughes 1977: 176 ff.).

Although some blades (from Ganz–Tsenga and the Wahgi) came to Tsuwenkai from Up-Jimi settlements, especially Kompiai, trade in the reverse direction probably predominated. With some accuracy the Kundagai see themselves as having been distributors of axes in all directions except Cross-Jimi, receiving salt, plumes, and furs in return from

Down-Jimi and the Simbai, and shells and pigs from Up-Jimi and Down-Simbai.

STEEL TOOLS

The first steel to reach the Kundagai came as fragments of hoop iron, plane blades, or broken knife blades in the 1930s, mounted as adzes, *kopiama*. The Wahgi was undoubtedly the source of these tools, which the Kundagai acquired in small numbers from Up-Jimi. Even fewer were exported: my only records refer to nearby Up-Simbai settlements.

By the late 1930s axes and knives, distributed by Europeans in the central highlands, began to filter through to the Kundagai. Trade patterns in steel tools have not appreciably changed over the years (table 28). Around 75 percent of all steel comes from the upper Jimi, with lesser amounts mainly from Cross-Jimi, especially settlements close to the Tabibuga government station, and Down-Jimi (almost exclusively from Bokapai). Exports are mainly to Up-Simbai (about 50 percent) and Down-Jimi (about 32 percent), with the balance mainly going to Down-Simbai.

The number of axes traded exceeds knives by about two to one at all times. Patterns of trade in both commodities are much the same, except that knives have been more frequently sent Down-Jimi than axes.

Although the predominant flow has remained strongly from the center toward the periphery, there is a much more marked flow in the reverse direction than for most other goods. This is probably the result of a more even distribution of tools, stemming from early distributions by kiaps and other visitors, and the now dispersed sources of trade store–purchased axes and knives at government, mission station, and village trade stores in the Jimi and Simbai. As with shells, there has been a marked decrease in the passage of steel tools in trade from the mid-1970s.

PIGMENTS

In the past the Kundagai acquired a variety of mineral pigments, and their trade was probably more significant than their absence from case histories might suggest (cf. Hughes 1977 for highlands pigment trade in general).

Red *kalom* earth pigment came in exchange for dogwhelks, plumes,

TABLE 28. PATTERNS OF TRADE IN AXES AND BUSHKNIVES[a]

Time/Region	Imported From		Exported To	
	No. transactions	%	No. transactions	%
PRE-1956				
Up-Jimi	42	77.8		
Down-Jimi	6	11.1	12	31.6
Cross-Jimi	1	1.8	2	5.3
Up-Simbai	2	3.7	20	52.6
Down-Simbai	3	5.6	4	10.5
Trans-Simbai				
TOTAL	54		38	
1956-1974				
Up-Jimi	51	78.5		
Down-Jimi	3	4.6	16	31.4
Cross-Jimi	8	12.3	2	3.9
Up-Simbai	2	3.1	26	51.0
Down-Simbai	1	1.5	4	7.8
Trans-Simbai			3	5.9
Other				
TOTAL	65		51	
1974-1978				
Up-Jimi	3	100.0		
Down-Jimi				
Cross-Jimi				
Up-Simbai			2	50.0
Down-Simbai			1	25.0
Trans-Simbai			1	25.0
Other				
TOTAL	3		4	
1979-1985				
Up-Jimi	1	100.0		
Down-Jimi			1	33.3
Cross-Jimi			2	66.7
Up-Simbai				
Down-Simbai				
Trans-Simbai				
Other				
TOTAL	1		3	
ALL TIME				
Up-Jimi	126	74.6		
Down-Jimi	13	7.7	40	32.3
Cross-Jimi	9	5.3	6	4.8
Up-Simbai	6	3.5	58	46.8
Down-Simbai	15	8.9	16	12.9
Trans-Simbai			4	3.2
Other				
TOTAL	169		124	

[a] Summary of inflow-outflow by type and period listed below. "In" entry lists number of transactions by which steel tools are imported to Tsuwenkai; "Out" entry lists transactions by which items are exported from Tsuwenkai.

TABLE 28.   PATTERNS OF TRADE IN AXES AND BUSHKNIVES (continued)

Tool Type		Pre-1956	1956-1974	1974-1978	1979-1985	All time
Axe	In	35	36[b]	3		103[b]
	Out	27	43	2	3	100
Bushknife	In	19	29[b]		1	66[b]
	Out	11	8	2		24

[b] One transaction involved two items.

and furs from Up-Jimi. The Kundagai themselves extracted another red pigment, *klimkoi,* from a lode at Kumbruf (Up-Simbai), or obtained it in exchange for dogwhelks. A dark-blue pigment, *muk,* thought by the Kundagai to come from Kol, was obtained from Up-Jimi in exchange for plumes and furs. Several other pigments were either collected locally or from deposits in territories of nearby communities, or obtained by gift. The only pigment said to be exported was *kalom,* sent Up-Simbai and Down-Jimi for dogwhelks, plumes and furs.

Except for the use of charcoal and locally occurring white and orange clay used in mourning, the Kundagai now rely on store-bought paints, which they favor for their brightness and better range of colors. Not long after contact, when such paint was not easily available, a few sets of paints came to Tsuwenkai from Up-Jimi in exchange for plumes.

OTHER MINOR GOODS OF EUROPEAN MANUFACTURE

In the years immediately before and after contact trade in beads and small porcelain disks assumed some importance. Beads came from Up- and Cross-Jimi and Up-Simbai, that is, from areas previously traversed by early government patrols. A few collections were exported Up- and Down-Simbai. Trade in beads quickly fell off once they became freely available from kiaps and missionaries, in return for small services, and from stores. Bead necklaces and armbands are continually distributed as gifts today and are a standard component of exchanges between lovers.

I recorded a number of instances of trade in shovels and metal cooking pots. These items are usually fairly easily available in stores in government and mission stations, and migrant laborers often bring them home from coastal towns. Trade in these items, to Down-Jimi and Up-Simbai, has been to settlements at some distance from the Tabibuga and Simbai stores. Plumes and pigs were given in exchange.

Various other items of European manufacture are traded infrequently, if special requests are made. The only records I have are single cases each of Kundagai men exchanging matches (Down-Jimi) and soap (Down-Simbai) for minor plumes at a time when these goods were exotic items rather difficult to acquire. They are now freely available, even in most of the smaller and poorly stocked local trade stores.

MONEY

Money[13] occupies a special place in the Maring catalogue of valuables. It has a dual quality and use, first as a general measure of the value of commodities. That is, it is used as a standard of value subject to division and multiplication—as currency. But in addition, money is a category of valuables, like pigs, plumes, or shells. Much the same point has been stressed by other ethnographers, among them Clark (1989), Harding (1967: 57), Newton (1978), Nihill (1989), Rappaport (1968: 189), and Salisbury (1962).

That this dual character of money prevails is shown by the retention of superseded notes and coins. Old Territory of New Guinea shillings, strung on cords through the hole minted for that purpose, are kept by some men as mementos. More significantly, the odd one-pound note, dating from the period to 1967 when Australian decimal currency was introduced, are to be seen, and in 1978 Australian notes were still common after the introduction of national currency in 1975. What is important for my argument is that the three kinds of notes are all equivalent and acceptable in prestations, at least until recently, even though the Kundagai know that Australian pounds and dollars are no longer acceptable in monetary transactions in stores.

Money as a valuable is passed in standard amounts, the most desirable units being K2, K10, and multiples of these. These sums may be made up of Australian $1 and K5 notes, but *blu not* [TP: "blue (i.e., green) K2 notes"] are favored. (National K1 coins are not widely accepted in major prestations.)

Money passed in prestations is, of course, being used as a valuable rather than as currency revealing a price. Further, money functions as a valuable in most trade exchanges in which it is involved, with notes passing in standard amounts. In that sense, I consider it misleading to refer to such transactions as cash sales. The point probably can be generalized to many other societies in New Guinea and elsewhere. Failure to appreciate the double capacity of money to function as a valuable and a currency has led some anthropologists unreasonably to assume that the value of all commodities can be expressed in monetary terms, or that rates of exchange can be reduced to a monetary equivalent.

Most younger men are familiar with the use of money as currency, but many older people are not. I was often asked to change undesirable brown Australian dollar notes and later K1 coins for an equal number of preferred green $2 or K2 notes. Individual notes are treated as if they have a particular identity, rather than being substitutable for notes of equal face value or for sets of lesser-value notes and coins. For instance, some people write their names or other cryptic signs on notes, so that they retain a residual claim on that particular note even when it leaves their possession (cf. Nihill 1989 for similar practices among the Southern Highlands Anganen). The singular identity of notes is further indicated by the way they are passed in prestations. Where a return gift for a ceremonial prestation is being made the donors are careful to avoid using any notes received in the main prestation. Thus, the money received cannot be used to fund the return gift. Precisely the same rule operates for return gifts of shells and steel tools. These observations further support the identification of money as a valuable.

Even in transactions with the appearance of cash sales, money is used in a way that belies its theoretical capacity to be freely multiplied and divided. For example, in transactions at village trade stores the Maring tend to pay for each item they buy separately, rather than adding up the bill and making only one cash transaction.[14] Similarly, people bringing several foodstuffs for my household supplies preferred to receive separate payments for each bundle instead of a handful of coins for the total offered.

The Kundagai first acquired money in the early 1960s, but cash did not flow through Tsuwenkai in any great quantity till about 1966, after which date the increasing number of men signing up for contract labor, mainly on coastal plantations, began to inject larger amounts of cash into the economy on the laborer's return. Smaller amounts were also earned working for mission and government personnel in the Jimi and

Simbai. Since roughly the mid-1970s the expansion of local government activities has provided some further opportunities for employment, especially for such trained people as medical orderlies.

Patterns of trade in goods so far discussed have proven remarkably stable. Major changes have involved decreasing incidence of trade rather than significantly altered patterns in terms of flows toward a regional center in the major highland valleys and a distant periphery. Since money is acceptable in exchange for a wide range of goods it has tended to be used in transactions with all regions. Unlike other trade items besides pigs, money is more or less ubiquitously present in all regions within the Kundagai trading sphere. It is not, of course, evenly distributed, since certain areas, notably the upper and south bank of the Jimi Valley, have been favored with better access to markets for labor and coffee and for assistance from local development projects. Although other trade goods tend to pass from areas of local abundance to those of relative scarcity, the flow of money in trade is more complex, as indicated in table 29.

The comparatively richer areas closer to the central highlands have always provided just over 75 percent of all money imported by trade. But these same areas are major recipients of money in trade from the Kundagai. At the same time, money has always been channeled through Tsuwenkai to more peripheral areas. Nonetheless, the most significant changes have occurred in dealings with regions located toward the central highlands. The proportion of exports (figured as the number of transactions) sent in this direction has risen from about half in 1966–1974 to almost three-quarters in the 1980s. The number of exports against the number of imports in the reverse direction has risen from about 1 to 1 to 2.2 to 1 over the same period. Yet more dramatically, the center has attracted ever-increasing amounts of money from Tsuwenkai, as indicated by the rise in the average value of transactions (pt. B, table 29). In 1966–1974, 63.2 percent of all money exported went toward the center. The proportion in 1974–1978 was 78.7 percent, and in 1979–1985 it had risen to 85.4 percent. In other words, the central highlands has increasingly become the focus of trade involving cash, and the Kundagai increasingly spend more money in trade in that direction than they receive in trade from more peripherally located regions. Although in the period to 1974 there was only a slight excess of the amount of money exported over the amount imported, amounting to K1.10 for every K1 imported, the ratio changed in 1974–1978 to K4.80 to K1 and in 1979–1985 to K3.70 to K1. The decline in the ratio in the last period is attributable to the rising average value of transactions received from more peripheral areas.

Clearly, after an initial period when the flow of money in and out of Tsuwenkai was roughly balanced, the use of money in trade has altered considerably, so that there is now a considerable drain of cash out of Tsuwenkai toward the central highlands. The causes and wider significance of these changes are examined in succeeding chapters.

SUMMARY OF THE FLOW OF GOODS IN TRADE THROUGH TSUWENKAI

There are strong continuities through time in trade patterns of some goods. These are best seen in the passage of plumes, skins, and furs, and one of their major exchange items, pigs. Plumes introduced into the trade system by Tsuwenkai hunters have predominantly always been exported to Up-Jimi settlements and, to a lesser extent, Cross-Jimi. Imported plumes—other than Red Bird of Paradise from the Wahgi Valley—have almost exclusively come from the upper Simbai and the lower Jimi, and less importantly from the lower Simbai. Many of the feathers and furs received from the upper Simbai are not of local provenance but are from lower altitudes. Upper-Simbai Kalam obtain these in trade from a wide catchment area in the lower Jimi and its tributaries, the Kaironk and Kinenj, but also from such places as the Asai in the Ramu drainage. Pigs travel through Tsuwenkai in a reverse pattern that closely mirrors the passage of plumes. Steel tools also show relatively stable trade patterns, mainly paralleling the trade in pigs. Discontinued trade patterns in salt and stone axes, which were articulated on an axis at right angles to the major "plumes–pigs" axis, were also relatively stable, as were, apparently, the minor flows in pigments. Such a picture, however, was rather complicated by the widely scattered points of manufacture of stone and salt, even though the Bank salt pools in the Simbai and the Ganz–Tsenga quarries were the dominant centers of production within the Kundagai trade orbit. The Tsuwenkai Kundagai's direct links with Cross-Jimi axe-makers were minimal, so that the reciprocal flow of axes and salt tended to be mediated by Tsuwenkai traders in short-haul movements to nearby Up- and Down-Jimi settlements before resuming directions to and from centers of axe and salt production.

It is in the trade in shells that patterns of movement have shown the most dramatic changes. Earlier patterns probably represent more truly

TABLE 29. PATTERNS OF TRADE IN MONEY

A. BY REGION

Time/region	No. transactions	Imported From Amount (K)	Av./ transaction (K)	No. transactions	Exported To Amount (K)	Av./ transaction (K)
1966-1974						
Up-Jimi	122(53.3)[a]	657.50(41.1)	5.39	116(33.9)	819.90(48.0)	7.07
Down-Jimi	22(9.6)	133.40(8.3)	6.03	61(17.8)	260.30(15.2)	4.27
Cross-Jimi	10(4.4)	120.00(7.5)	12.00	12(3.5)	85.10(5.0)	7.09
Up-Simbai	31(13.5)	232.00(14.5)	7.48	90(26.3)	304.20(17.8)	3.38
Down-Simbai	8(3.5)	66.00(4.1)	8.25	42(12.3)	153.80(9.0)	3.66
Trans-Simbai				19(5.6)	64.00(3.7)	3.37
Other	36(15.7)	392.50(24.5)	10.90	2(0.6)	22.00(1.3)	11.00
TOTAL	229	1,601.40	6.99	342	1,709.30	4.99
1974-1978						
Up-Jimi	17(63.0)	108.50(42.0)	6.38	13(31.0)	706.00(56.9)	54.31
Down-Jimi	6(22.2)	123.00(47.6)	20.50	5(11.9)	158.00(12.7)	52.00
Cross-Jimi	2(7.4)	4.00(1.5)	2.00	8(19.0)	200.00(16.1)	25.00
Up-Simbai				10(23.8)	80.00(6.5)	8.00
Down-Simbai	1(3.7)	20.00(7.7)	20.00	2(4.8)	70.00(5.6)	35.00
Trans-Simbai				4(9.5)	26.00(2.1)	6.50
Other	1(3.7)	3.00(1.2)	3.00			
TOTAL	27	258.50	9.57	42	1,240.00	29.52
1979-1985						
Up-Jimi	26(60.5)	582.00(49.2)	22.38	13(12.7)	492.00(11.3)	37.85
Down-Jimi	5(11.6)	119.00(10.1)	23.80	3(2.9)	110.00(2.5)	36.67
Cross-Jimi	6(14.0)	172.00(14.5)	28.67	7(6.9)	342.00(7.8)	48.86
Up-Simbai	5(11.6)	210.00(17.8)	42.00	16(15.7)	238.00(5.5)	14.87
Down-Simbai				14(13.7)	444.00(10.2)	31.71
Trans-Simbai				9(8.8)	288.00(6.6)	32.00
Other	1(2.3)	100.00(8.4)	100.00	40(39.2)	2,447.00(56.1)	61.17
TOTAL	43	1,183.00	27.51	102	4,361.00	42.75

B. BY DIRECTION

Time/direction[b]	No. transactions	Income From Amount (K)	Av./transaction (K)	No. transactions	Expenditure To Amount (K)	Av./transaction (K)
1966-1974						
From Center	176	1,236	7.02	172	1,080	6.28
From Periphery	53	365	6.89	170	628	3.69
1974-1978						
From Center	21	135	6.43	23	976	42.43
From Periphery	6	123	20.50	19	264	13.89
1979-1985						
From Center	33	854	25.88	74	3,725	50.34
From Periphery	10	329	32.90	28	636	22.71

[a] Numbers in parentheses are percentages of column totals.
[b] The direction of the center includes Up- and Cross-Jimi and Down-Simbai and the Wahgi (part of Other) regions. The direction of the periphery includes Down-Jimi, and Up- and Trans-Simbai.

the aboriginal trade in shells in this part of the highlands, although only small numbers were involved. Shell valuables did not arrive in any great numbers until the advent of Europeans in the central highlands, and the marked influx of shells coming mainly from the upper Jimi, and to a lesser extent from Cross-Jimi, was undoubtedly a result of the flooding of central-highlands exchange networks with shells.

Before about the 1930s, then, when steel tools and shells were rare or not available at all, trade patterns were characterized by a dominating flow of plumes, furs, and live cassowaries out of Tsuwenkai toward the upper Jimi, with some imports from the Simbai and the lower Jimi. Small amounts of dogwhelk shells followed this pattern. Goods flowing in the reverse direction were mainly pigs, with the odd kina and greensnail shell.

A second strong set of trade relationships, linking plume- and salt-producing communities of the Simbai with axe-makers and shell providers Cross-Jimi complicated the Kundagai trading patterns. In the pre-1930 period trade patterns were more complex partly because areas of supply of some goods—mainly axes and salt—were highly localized and widely separated, and because some particularly rare goods—mainly shells but perhaps also dog-tooth necklaces in even earlier times—filtered into the Kundagai trade sphere from a variety of directions.

Once Europeans introduced large numbers of shells and steel tools, and later, money, into the central highlands these objects replaced traditional valuables and utilities both functionally and aesthetically. These goods came along preexisting trade routes from the Simbu and Wahgi areas down the Jimi, and across the Jimi from the Banz and Mala area.

This change in patterns meant that a greater variety and overall quantity of goods now came from the central highlands. In terms of the model of trade used here, the Kundagai received increasing amounts and kinds of goods from the direction of centrally located ultimate plume consumers, which in turn they passed on to more peripheral communities. In exchange the Kundagai received plumes, furs, and live cassowaries from the periphery, added the same products by local hunting, and sent them on toward the center.

Since salt and stone ceased to be major objects of trade, the only locally available products in wide demand—especially in the central highlands—have been bird plumes, marsupial skins, and live cassowaries. Although demand for plumes and skins in trade has diminished somewhat in the 1980s (see chap. 6), as a class they remain the second-most commonly traded goods after money. For the Kundagai and their neighbors these local forest products provide the dominant structure to the overall pattern of trade; dominant in terms of the gross number of objects traded and also of the limited directions in which they are passed. It is the local production and exchange of these forest products which are the articulating force in Kundagai trade. This is perhaps most clearly demonstrated in the exchange of plumes for pigs. Pigs are almost ubiquitous in distribution, although local variations in population dynamics must be expected. All communities produce pigs, even if some, such as in the upper Jimi, Wahgi, and Simbu have greater productivity because pigs are not always killed for prestations as they commonly are among the Narak, Maring, and Kalam. Not all communities, however, produce plumes in general, or particular kinds of plumes, and the closer one approaches the central highlands, the less variety is locally available—valued lowland species are totally absent. It therefore appears that the strong pattern of pig trade from plume consumers toward plume suppliers is determined more by the distribution of plumes than of pigs.

This crucial role of the location, production, and distribution of forest products, especially plumes, justifies the focus of attention on the place of feather decorations in highland cultures and on the organization of hunting, which in turn structures the nature of trade in plumes.

Although the dominant directions of trade in most goods are quite marked, there is some two-way movement of many goods. Such reciprocal flows are least evident in the Up-Jimi and Cross-Jimi trade, and most pronounced in the Down-Simbai trade, but there are marked two-way movements in Up-Simbai and Down-Jimi connections. As I will argue further below, the relation between Tsuwenkai and Down-Simbai is a special case, with the lower Simbai forming an alternative and parallel route to the upper Jimi. Much of the trade in the Simbai is channeled into the Jimi via Tsuwenkai and Aindem (north of the Bismarcks from Bubgile). Jimi–Simbai connections between these communities, conveniently located at low passes across the mountain range, are much fewer, carrying relatively little trade.

Much of the trade in particular items in opposition to the dominant pattern that occurs between Tsuwenkai and Down-Jimi is actually with residents of Bokapai. Trade with Bokapai appears in the tables as with Down-Jimi. Much of this involves imports of forest products and exports of major exchange objects—pigs, shells, steel—and is therefore in accordance with the dominant flow of goods. Significant numbers of these various goods, however, pass between Tsuwenkai and Bokapai in the opposite directions, thus weakening the dominant patterns of trade. But such a weakening is more apparent than real, because many of the goods flowing contrary to the major flow are actually channeled through Bokapai to or from Up-Jimi or Cross-Jimi settlements. Thus, for instance, many pigs reaching Tsuwenkai from Down-Jimi have come from Kompiai or Tabibuga via Bokapai and are thus only momentarily appearing to move in reverse to the dominant pattern.

Much of the trade apparently at odds with the predominant flow of goods between Tsuwenkai and Up-Simbai centers on Kinimbong and can be viewed in much the same way as trade with Bokapai. Trade between Tsuwenkai and neighboring Bokapai and Kinimbong amounts to lateral movements at right angles to the dominant axis of trade. These settlements may best be viewed as staging points from which goods received from Tsuwenkai are redirected to other areas that preserve the general directional flow of goods.

A certain amount of trade occurs within Tsuwenkai: up to 1974, 9.6 percent of all transactions were of this type, the proportion being 14.3 percent in 1974–1978 and 9.5 percent in 1979–1985, or 10 percent for the full period of records. These internal transactions usually involve more valuable items, such as Vulturine Parrot feathers or pigs. Such exchanges effect a redistribution of goods within the community. Factors influencing a man to trade with a member of his own community rather than with an outsider include constraints on his willingness to travel, such as his age, health, or fear of being the victim of vengeance killing; a desire to obtain a specific item owned by a fellow resident; and the knowledge that a fellow resident is to journey to a place where a desired object may be obtained.[15]

Trade between Kinimbong and Bokapai and Tsuwenkai is, in essence, much like trade within Tsuwenkai. The inhabitants of each settlement are Kundagai and so are accorded kinship status; they are people whom one frequently visits and with whose possessions and travels one is most familiar. They are therefore the people to whom one is most inclined to transfer trade goods if one is unable or unwilling to travel elsewhere to exchange them. The three settlements therefore constitute a core area within which goods are redistributed before they are directed elsewhere. Not all trade with these settlements, however, amounts to a first step in the subsequent disposal of goods to other settlements, for both Kinimbong and Bokapai Kundagai have access to different goods, either in their own territories or by virtue of slightly different trading patterns, to which the Tsuwenkai Kundagai lack access. Thus they are also source areas of certain objects desired in Tsuwenkai, such as Lesser Bird of Paradise or Cockatoo plumes. Although there are apparently no birds or marsupials yielding valuable plumes or furs in Tsuwenkai which are not found elsewhere in Kundagai land, some of these resources, such as Princess Stephanie's Astrapia, may be more common in Tsuwenkai. The Tsuwenkai Kundagai may also have access to different goods or quantities of them in other settlements because of different trading patterns.

MAINTENANCE OF THE TRADE SYSTEM

Having described the ecological and geographic dimensions of trade it is appropriate here to outline some of the sociological parameters. This anticipates the focus of later chapters, and I confine myself to a brief summary.

Most exchanges are initiated by parties lying further away from plume consumers than their trading partners; thus, Down-Jimi or Up-Simbai traders tend to initiate trade with the Kundagai, who in turn travel up the Jimi to trade. Because of this directional component in initiating trade, one party to a transaction is often unprepared or unable to make an immediate return. Consequently, the majority of exchanges are delayed—most such transactions occurring between kinsmen. Trade with unrelated partners has increased greatly since contact and predominates in relations between the Kundagai and areas closer to the center.

Rates of exchange are conventionalized, with little haggling or variation depending on relationships between traders. The exchange value of most forest products has remained unchanged for over fifty years, despite greater availability of most plumes since the mid-1950s.

The trade system as briefly characterized lacks classic market forces of supply and demand. Given such an organization of trade, which is not built on the basis of individual gain, notions of profit, impersonality of transactors, and so forth, one central problem of analysis emerges: what keeps the trade system operating more or less continually?

The material—economic and ecological—conditions of local insufficiency of certain goods (however that is defined) are not enough to *induce* trade. Need, or desire for goods, lies with those who do not have enough. Being materially at a disadvantage they cannot be the force that compels exchange, unless their chosen trade partners are also disadvantaged in some other goods. Although the ecological structure of Maring trade tends to lead toward such reciprocal disadvantage (since most goods are of specialized regional origin), it is expecting too much that this circumstance always and solely is enough to ensure that both parties to a transaction see themselves as equally in need of the other's goods (cf. Pryor 1977: 158).

Although material forces may be implicated in the desire of an individual to initiate trade in order to satisfy a demand for goods, the forces that compel both parties to conclude a transaction must lie outside the realm of the goods themselves, in social and cultural forces. In that sense, there is a marked sociable dimension to trade. This sociability need not necessarily rest between the transactors; a third party may be involved with the trade transaction feeding into that external sociable relation, as when one man trades on behalf of another.

Although these sociological dimensions are critical in the maintenance of trade, they occur in a system significantly structured on material factors of discontinuous distribution and/or exploitation of resources for ecological and cultural reasons. This material structure to the trade system is thus also of critical importance in understanding the continuity of passage of goods through time, and I now turn to an analysis of this structure.

Trade passing through Tsuwenkai converges on the settlement from a limited number of more peripheral locations fanning out to numerous points lying toward the center,[16] so that it is convenient to see Tsuwenkai as a focal point of numerous lines of trade directed roughly toward ultimate plume consumers and fewer lines directed toward primary plume suppliers. These lines may be regarded as trade chains of differing lengths, composed of varying numbers of links between settlements in each direction. Trade chains of other settlements are arranged in a similar pattern, so that a complex interlacing results producing a web of trade links, along which it is possible for a good to be transferred in a zigzag path. Informants described such flows, where, for example, a plume was traded from the upper Simbai to the Jimi, back to the Simbai, then across the divide to Tsuwenkai before being sent Up-Jimi.

Such a weblike structure of links facilitates the movement of goods, since it increases the number of chains converging on each point in the web and the paths goods may follow. Take the example of a simple web (fig. 2) where a man of place A seeks a pig from B in exchange for

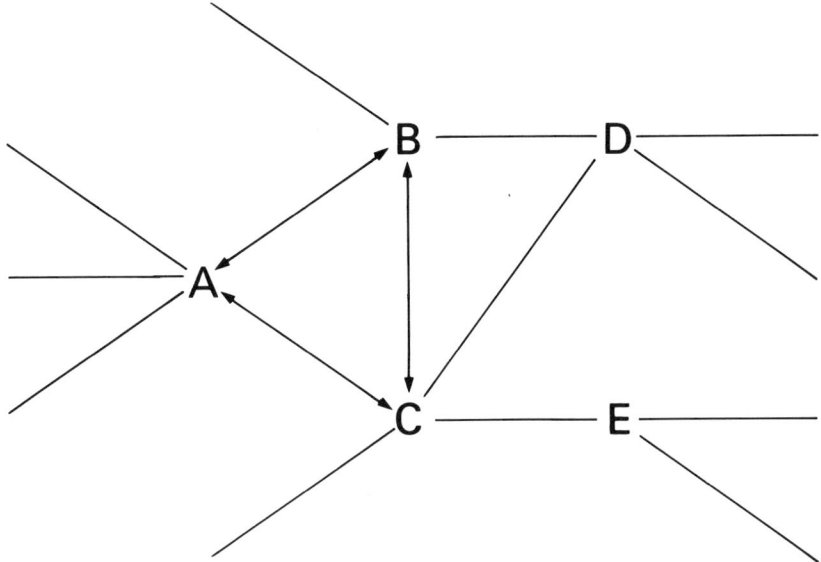

Figure 2. Simple Trade Web

a plume. If B is unable to provide a pig and if A and B are points on a trade chain not further elaborated into a web by crosslinks, A's desire will remain unsatisfied. B, however, may be willing to part with a pig in exchange for a stone axe that A is unable to provide. But A may exchange his plume for an axe with C, then exchange the axe with B for a pig. Alternatively, B might accept the plume, giving a pig in return, and exchange the plume for an axe with C. Again, A may give his plume to C and ask for a pig. C then keeps the plume for his own use and exchanges his own axe for a pig with B, and sends the pig back to A. If B and C have neither axes nor pigs, they can engage in similar exchanges with their other trading partners D and E, and so on.

In his discussion of Maring trade, Rappaport (1968: 105–109) begins with the premise that a set of transactions forms a closed system. The present study shows that trade cannot be regarded as a closed system. Elsewhere I have identified the boundary of the system of trade in plumes—a system that encompasses much of the highlands and surrounding foothills (Healey 1980). Even this system cannot be viewed as closed, as the presence of marine shells and Swedish steel axes in the highlands testifies. It is more realistic to view trade in New Guinea as a series of overlapping regional complexes, with some goods transferred within each region also being passed from one to another (cf.

Hughes 1977). Rappaport further assumes that in the precontact situation both salt and stone working axes were "necessary for survival" and that though they were exchangeable the demands for them were limited (Rappaport 1968: 107). If only salt, from the Simbai pools, and axes, from the Ganz–Tsenga quarries, were exchangable he remarks that it is unlikely that supply could be maintained over the intervening links in the trade connections between the two points of production, for not only were the producers isolated from one another, but each producer could be expected to manufacture only as much salt or as many axes as he needed for his own uses and to exchange for his own limited needs of the other product. Thus, axe-makers would go hungry for salt if salt producers for the moment had sufficient axes for their needs. But shells, plumes, and other valuables are exchangeable for both axes and salt, and there is an unlimited demand for them. The reason for this is not spelled out but would seem to lie in a utilitarian/nonutilitarian dichotomy. Lacking a materially necessary utility, the amount of plumes and so forth that might be accepted is not conditioned by limits of practical sufficiency. In Rappaport's terms, then, nonutilitarian items are exchangeable for utilitarian ones. Because of this, a constant supply of salt and axes can be maintained since, if salt producers have sufficient axes, axe producers can be assured of a supply of salt by offering plumes or shells in place of axes. Salt producers can assure their supplies of axes by similarly offering other goods in place of salt. Similarly, those groups producing neither salt nor axes but requiring them, can maintain their supplies by substituting other, nonutilitarian valuables in their dealings with salt or axe providers if they have insufficient supplies of axes or salt to exchange.

Rappaport suggests that the substitution of nonutilitarian items would not be necessary if salt and axe producers were joined by a web of trade links. It would then be possible to transfer the goods over alternative routes if an exchange could not be effected in one part of the web because of a lack of local demand for one of the products. He argues, however, that the Jimi–Simbai axe and salt trade is composed of chains and that if one link in the chain is unwilling or unable to exchange salt for axes, moral pressure transmitted from one link to another may be insufficient to ensure that the exchange is completed. Although Rappaport's suggestion is addressed specifically to describing the nature of Tsembaga trade, some ethnographers have noted the applicability of his explanation to other areas (e.g., Heider 1970: 28; Strathern 1971: 112; see also Wright and Zeder 1977).

This model, however, can be criticized on a number of ethnographic and theoretical counts. In the first place, I have argued above that Maring trade relations are composed of a weblike structure (see also Hughes 1977). Each settlement maintains chainlike links with several other settlements, and the various chains make up a complex web. Each community has a different pattern of chains radiating from it, and the interconnections with chains centered on other settlements allows a multiplicity of paths along which goods can be passed. For instance, the Kundagai obtained salt from several Simbai communities. At times they also processed it themselves. They obtained axes from several Jimi settlements but only rarely from axe-makers directly. If there were no axes available in, say, Koinambe, they moved on to Bokapai, Kandambiamp, or Kompiai—that is, across the general axis of the axe trade along lateral links in the web stretching between salt and axe producers. Although this weblike structure may facilitate the distribution of goods, it does not of itself overcome the problem posed by Rappaport concerning the motives of localized producers of goods for which demand is limited, unless, as is the case among the Maring, goods are readily interconvertible. That is, in maintaining supplies of desirable goods, it is not just the web of trade links that is important but also the cultural code determining the exchangeability of goods.

I would also suggest that Rappaport has underestimated the strength of moral pressure in ensuring the acquisition of a desired good. His comments on the inability of moral pressure to be sustained over an extensive chain of trade implies that as the number of links between the end-points multiply moral pressure correspondingly diminishes. That is, the strength of a trader's demand for a specific exchange item fades as one moves further away from the point at which that good is to be consumed. Since men in intervening links will not benefit from owning the objects exchanged they make less effort to ensure that the desired goods are provided.

Kundagai statements indicate that moral pressure can be sustained over several links—certainly a sufficient number to ensure the supply of axes to the Tsembaga if no substitutions of goods occur in intervening links. In place of Rappaport's scheme I suggest that at each link moral pressure to supply a particular item is renewed. Informants recounted many instances in their trade histories. For example, one Tsuwenkai man received a plume from Kumbruf that came originally from an Asai man wanting a pig in exchange. From Tsuwenkai the plume was sent to Kompiai and then Kwibun. At each of the four links the request for a pig was reaffirmed, and a pig duly passed from Kwibun to the Asai. The majority of transactional sequences of this kind occur between kin or affines. Kinship, involving the ideal of generalized reciprocity, cooperation, and fair dealing, may form a basis of the moral pressure brought to bear on trading partners (see chap. 8). In a large proportion of their transactions, therefore, the Kundagai have had moral pressure put upon them to procure a desired item. This pressure does not always work as smoothly, but failure to comply with a request is uncommon. Sometimes, with the best intentions, a trader is unable to obtain a requested good. In such cases, he may accept an unwanted exchange item and either return this to the initiator of the sequence of exchanges with an explanation of the situation or keep the item and supply the desired good from his own stocks.

There appear to be two major practical reasons why moral pressure can be effective over many links. First, to neglect providing a requested item marks a man as an unreliable trading partner, and the relationship may be terminated. There is a danger, then, of losing contact with a valuable supplier of goods. Even when a man is only one link in a longer sequence of transactions he may temporarily retain a trade item for use in decorations before trading it on. Thus, a man may be given a plume in trade and use it in a dance before exchanging it for a pig. Occasionally he may retain the pig until it breeds and return one of its piglets to complete the sequence. Such a practice is rare today, though apparently more common in the past. Generally, however, a pig is not kept until it breeds unless the initiator of the exchange sequence invites his trading partner to do so.

Moral pressure is also strengthened by the fear that failure to comply with a request may leave one open to a witchcraft attack if the unsatisfied trading partner is a witch. According to the Kundagai, witches are great dissemblers. It is therefore unwise to cause offence lest those whom one offends are witches. The only well-known and universally feared male witch in Tsuwenkai has traded very little. Friends said that this was because he was uninterested in trade, but one discreetly suggested that few people would be prepared to trade with him for fear that he might be dissatisfied with an exchange and revenge himself through witchcraft on his trading partners.

I have noted McArthur's (1974) suggestion that salt may not have been critical to Maring survival. The Kundagai also do not seem to regard salt as nutritionally essential. It was, however, ritually and ceremonially necessary in salt-pork prestations to allies, just as pigs and pearlshells are essential in affinal payments, or plumes for decorations in dances, which may attract brides. It is questionable, therefore, whether salt was a utilitarian item, as Rappaport claims. Similarly, I would question the value of labeling axes (either stone or steel) as utilitarian items. Undoubtedly they are essential to survival, given highlands horticultural tradition. But not only could at least some Maring communities, including the Kundagai, make their own, albeit inferior, axes from local stone, but they also employed axes in prestations. Both work and "bridal" axes, *cenang ambra poka,* were used in prestations. Most bridal axes were of such delicate workmanship as to be useless tools. A man also often owned more axes than he needed for subsistence tasks. These were useful as a reserve in case of breakages or for trade or prestation. This is the case with steel axes too. Although the Maring certainly acquired axes for their utility, they also sought to amass an excess to distribute in trade and prestation. Like other valuables, axes are individually esteemed, aside from their utility, for their size and weight, their shape and proportions, their markings, length, and color, and smoothness of their handles. More care is often lavished on a favorite axe than is required simply to keep it in good cutting condition.

I do not wish to suggest that axes or salt are nonutilitarian items, but rather that the distinction between utilitarian and nonutilitarian is misleading. To the Kundagai all valuables have a utility. The value of axes in subsistence seems to be taken for granted, whereas the utility of axes and other valuables as items of exchange and prestation is explicit. All this is not to say that Rappaport's hypothesis of the importance of plumes, shells, and other valuables in effecting the distribution of other goods is unfounded, but rather that he has introduced an unnecessary distinction of the utility of goods traded. Rappaport (pers. comm.) has suggested in response to this criticism that the utilitarian/nonutilitarian contrast might better be represented as elastic/nonelastic or more elastic/less elastic. Although I would agree that such terminology goes much of the way in overcoming the "utilitarian" aspects of the model of trade, I consider that this revision still represents trade as subject to the capacity of the economy to absorb goods whose use-value primarily lies outside the sphere of exchange. On the contrary, I would argue that the trade and prestation spheres of exchange have the capacity to absorb goods on an essentially "elastic" basis. Relative elasticity does not lie in distribution and consumption (that is, once goods have entered the trade/prestation spheres), but in the productive process, before they become objects of exchange. Thus, for example, what limits the numbers of pigs or axes passed in exchange is not the numbers that subsequently may be consumed but how many may be produced.

In his discussion of trade in the central highlands Hughes (1977: 213) also expresses some reservations about Rappaport's hypothesis, but he accepts the utilitarian/nonutilitarian dichotomy. He remarks that even if shells and plumes were not exchangeable for "utilitarian" goods the latter would nonetheless have been circulated sufficiently to meet subsistence needs, but he concludes that "valuables stimulated the production of utilitarian goods, increased the quantities and rates of flow through the network and assisted their transfer by acting as supplementary . . . media of exchange." Such a statement accepts the "functions" of trade as the supply of utilitarian goods. On the contrary, Kundagai evidence indicates that plumes, shells, and steel are primary rather than supplementary media of exchange.

The substitution of items to ensure the supply of other goods might be invoked to explain trade occurring in directions other than the dominant axes, for such substitutions may not always be possible within a settlement if stocks are low. Yet, since the flow of a wide variety of goods is strongly directional along a northwest/southeast axis and between areas of specialized resource differences, one would expect the necessity to seek substitutions for trade items in different directions to be slight. Nonetheless, I have noted the fairly prominent flow of goods to and from the lower Simbai (8.1 percent of all imports coming from Down-Simbai, 8.3 percent of all exports sent in return).

Down-Simbai relative to Tsuwenkai lies closer to the center and near and parallel to the main axis of trade. Simply in terms of geography trade with this area is not unexpected. Down-Simbai is ecologically similar to Tsuwenkai and Down-Jimi, however, and its major specialized products are the same as those produced in Tsuwenkai and Down-Jimi. Import of these goods thus constitutes a reversal of the dominant flow. Many of these things are also produced Up-Jimi, yet trade of these to Tsuwenkai is virtually nonexistent, and exports from Tsuwenkai to Down-Jimi are mostly to Bokapai from where they are redirected Up- or Cross-Jimi. Down-Simbai, being closer to the center, sends specialized highlands goods—pigs, shells, and steel tools—to Tsuwenkai, as is expected in terms of the trade model, but there is also a smaller reverse flow. The two-way flow of goods between Tsuwenkai and Down-Simbai is at variance, then, with the dominant flow of goods. It also conflicts with Hughes's (1977) conclusion, based on data from an extensive part of the highlands, that the basis of highlands trade lies in ecological differences. The situation therefore calls for some special consideration.

Of value here are some remarks of Kelly (1977: 13–14) in his discussion of trade between the Etoro and their Onabasulu neighbors of the Great Papuan Plateau. Kelly notes that there is

> ... little basis for trade between the Etoro and Onabasulu derived from differential resources, cultural needs, or structural position in the larger trade networks. Both tribes have equivalent access to Highlands goods through trade with the Huli, and both have much the same items available for exchange ...

Nonetheless, trade in tree-oil, shells, and other items occurs between the two groups, with goods moving in both directions. Both groups also trade with the Huli, the major providers of highlands goods such as shells. Kelly explains this two-way trade as follows. All Etoro are regarded as kinsmen, with whom trade is not permitted, an injunction shared by the Onabasulu (Ernst 1978). Two Etoro desiring one another's goods cannot exchange them. They can, however, effect the exchange through an Onabasulu intermediary. "The ban on internal trade thus necessitates external exchange relations and, more specifically, exchange with a tribe that possesses a nearly identical repertoire of goods."

In fact, there are resource differences between the Etoro and Onabasulu [and within Onabasulu territory itself (Ernst 1978)]. Significantly, only the Onabasulu produce cosmetic tree-oil, which is such an important trade item in the southern and western highlands. As Kelly himself notes, the Etoro obtain their tree-oil for the highlands trade from the Onabasulu. The local Onabasulu monopoly on the production of tree-oil must therefore result in that tribe maintaining rather different trade patterns from the Etoro and thus possessing different types or quantities of exchange goods as a consequence. Etoro and Onabasulu resources, cultural needs, and structural position in the larger trade networks are therefore not as similar as Kelly suggests.

Despite these reservations Kelly's explanation of a particular ethnographic situation would also seem to apply in its broad outlines to the Kundagai/Down-Simbai trade. Although there is no moral ban on trade within the Maring area as a whole or between kinsmen of any population that is not a major enemy, this need not hamper the applicability of Kelly's conclusions to the Maring.[17] The essential point of comparison is that both Etoro/Onabasulu and Kundagai/Down-Simbai trade occurs between regions of similar (though not identical) ecological and resource zones. The structural positions of the Kundagai and Down-Simbai groups in the wider trade system differ somewhat as I have indicated above. Some trade between the two areas is therefore in goods over which one area possesses greater opportunity of access than the other. Despite similar locally occurring resources, the catalogues of trade goods must therefore differ somewhat.

The advantage to the Kundagai and Down-Simbai groups of trading with each other is that since they both command roughly similar access to locally available and imported resources they can offer each other a wider range of goods. Men of both areas are prepared to pass products of primary plume suppliers and of ultimate plume consumers in both directions. This pattern is not as acceptable to traders in different resource zones, as they are less able to exchange goods of dissimilar origins.

Down-Simbai and Tsuwenkai may therefore be seen as retaining a pool of goods that are redistributed between the two areas, along a side-arm of the major highlands–foothills trade route, without unduly altering the catalogue of goods, since any product may move in either direction. Such substitutions of goods with other areas necessarily result in different repertoires of goods because of strongly directional trade flows.

At any particular time a trader may seek a certain item within this Tsuwenkai/Down-Simbai pool of goods if the item is not currently available in his own community or the wider collection of all Kundagai. Such exchanges need not be to the disadvantage of one of the partners, if each is seeking what the other offers or is able to pass the goods on to another partner.

The Kundagai do not describe trade with Down-Simbai in these terms but see it as essentially similar to trade with other areas. They are aware of the strongly directional flow of goods through Tsuwenkai to Up-Simbai and Down-Jimi, and Up-Jimi; and although they rightly regard their trading relations with Down-Simbai as being of lesser importance than trade flowing between the upper Jimi and the upper Simbai or lower Jimi, they tend to present the lower Simbai as a source area of pigs, shells, and steel tools, and, to a lesser extent, of plumes and furs.

With the Kundagai located between primary plume suppliers (somewhere in the lower-Jimi/Yuat Gorge area and the middle-Ramu lowlands) and central-highlands plume consumers, one expects them to be able to export more plumes than they import by adding to the flow by hunting. This is indeed the case for most locally available species. But the same pattern holds for regionally available birds and other products which are absent from Tsuwenkai territory. We are therefore left with the need to explain why exports of locally occurring and nonlocal but regionally available forest products exceed imports. Although the Kundagai export more regional (but nonlocal) resources obtained from the periphery than they import, they export fewer goods coming from the center (mainly pigs, shells, steel) than they import. This is not unexpected, but since exchanges do not always involve reciprocal flows of single items these two features of Kundagai trade are not simply mirror images. To refine the assumption made above I suggest that the proportion of excess of export over import of a good is a function of the amount of local production of that good.

Table 30 summarizes the contribution of local production to the total number of items obtained by local production or trade of the most commonly traded birds (seven species listed in table 24), marsupials, and live animals (cassowaries and dogs), all locally obtainable by the Kundagai.

Exports of all locally obtainable goods exceed imports, and local production is such that except for plumes in the 1980s and marsupial furs and skins figured over time the total amounts obtained by production and trade together exceed exports by trade. In short, there is an excess of goods obtained which is either consumed within Tsuwenkai or disposed of by means other than trade.

The second-to-last column in the table shows the proportion of exports that can be met or funded solely by local production. Not every locally produced item is actually exported, however, so that the figures refer to the maximum proportion of recorded exports that could be permitted by local production; they are an index of capacity, not actuality. A locally produced good need not be exported to fund exports.[18] It may be used as a replacement for an imported good, thus augmenting local stocks so that the import can be exported without any deprivation to its owner. In only two goods, Superb Bird of Paradise plumes and live cassowaries, has local production yielded numbers in excess of total exports. All plume species combined come closest to this situation, followed by local marsupial furs and skins.

Except for plumes in the period 1979–1985 and marsupial furs,

TABLE 30. IMPORTANCE OF LOCAL PRODUCTION AND TRADE IN ACQUISITION OF LOCALLY OBTAINABLE GOODS

Time Period	Local Production No.	Local Production % of total obtained	Import No.	Import % of total obtained	Total obtained	Total export	Contribution of local production to exports (%)	Total obtained exceeds imports by (%)[a]
A. PLUMES								
Pre-1956	281	82.9	58	17.1	339	297	94.6	14.1
1956-1974	241	49.6	245	50.4	486	400	60.25	21.5
1974-1978	24	42.1	33	57.9	57	54	44.4	5.6
1979-1985	23	25.0	69	75.0	92	103	22.3	-[b]
All time	745	59.7	502	40.3	1,247	1,073	69.4	16.2
B. LIVE ANIMALS (Cassowaries and dogs)								
Pre-1956	15	100.0			15	13	+[c]	15.4
1956-1974	57	93.4	4	6.6	61	41	+	48.8
1974-1978			3	100.0	3	2	0	50.0
1979-1985			7	6.5	108	61	+	72.1
All time	101	93.5						
C. MARSUPIALS								
All time[d]	65	86.7	10	13.3	75	92	70.7	

Time Period	Local Production No.	Local Production % of total obtained	Import No.	Import % of total obtained	Total obtained	Total export	Contribution of local production to exports (%)	Total obtained exceeds imports by (%)
D. TOTALS								
Pre-1956	296	83.6	58	16.4	354	310	95.5	14.2
1956-1974	298	54.5	249	45.5	547	441	67.6	24.0
1974-1978	24	42.1	33	57.9	57	54	44.4	5.6
1979-1985	23	24.2	72	75.8	95	105	21.9	-
All time	911	63.7	519	36.3	1,430	1,222	74.5	17.0

[a] (Total obtained-Export)/Export, as percentage.
[b] Export exceeds import.
[c] Production totals exceed imports, but cassowaries that subsequently died in captivity are included in production totals.
[d] Datable records up to 1974 too few to warrant comparisons by period.

local production alone is sufficient to account for the excess of export over import. The magnitude of the excess is shown in the last column of the table. Local production coupled with small amounts of these goods obtained in minor prestations from other settlements is also obviously sufficient to replace any losses that occur within Tsuwenkai through damage or age. It is also sufficient to defray the small amount of loss that occurs in the form of minor prestations from Tsuwenkai to other settlements.

The importance of local production in sustaining exports, however, has altered over time, although the reliability of data makes assessment of the magnitude of this change difficult. Figures for the period to 1974 are derived from case histories for the near-total male population during the major period of fieldwork. Figures for later periods, however, are based on smaller, nonrandom samples and must therefore be treated with more caution. For example, the absence of records for 1974–1978 of capture or trade in live animals should not be taken to indicate that cassowaries or dogs were necessarily not traded in this period. At least in respect of bird plumes, nonetheless, there is a clear-enough trend of diminishing importance of local hunting as a means of acquiring goods and sustaining exports. But although hunting fell from providing over 80 percent of all locally available plumes prior to contact to providing 25 percent in the 1980s, this still represents a significant level of local production.

The excess of the total number of goods obtained by production and trade over the total exported by trade gives some idea of the maximum proportion of acquired goods that are available for loss by means other than trade. This loss will take the form of damage and age (that is, local consumption), minor prestations and, in the case of cassowaries, major prestations and religious sacrifices. Only with marsupial skins and furs does export exceed both tabulated means of acquisition. Local hunting of marsupials is probably more important than the table suggests, as I failed to discover how a number of fur bundles exported were first acquired. Most of these were probably made up from animals killed in Tsuwenkai forests, and their number is sufficient to give a figure for the total obtained in excess of the number exported. For other classes of goods the percentage excess of acquisitions over exports has increased after contact but then declined sharply from the mid-1970s. The excess for live animals, mostly cassowaries, is exaggerated by the inclusion in the production column of chicks that died in captivity. Up until the late 1970s as much as nearly one-quarter of stocks of all forest products remained after exports had been funded. This excess fell sharply in the late 1970s, consonant with the declining importance of local hunting in procuring goods. The excess of goods obtained over exports was available for the replacement of goods retained for personal use and consumption but which were lost in damage or age (or in the case of cassowaries, eaten) and for disposal in prestations. The actual figures for these other means of loss of stocks are harder to determine. By the 1980s hunting had declined sharply as a means of acquiring trade goods, but exports exceeded totals acquired. This excess suggests a growing importance of gift as a means of obtaining subsequently traded goods.

It is, however, difficult to assess the numerical importance of prestations in contrast to trade as a means of acquiring or disposing of goods. This is because, as noted in chapter 4, the Kundagai were reluctant or unable to recount full details of prestations in similar detail to their trading activities.[19] By full details I mean such information as the kind of exchange; its approximate date; the relationships between donor and recipient, donor and helpers (in the case of prestations made by an individual), recipient and his beneficiaries (in the case of prestations received by an individual); and the objects involved in all these ramifying exchanges. I therefore was unable to compile a sample of minor and major prestations, which, in conjunction with trade histories, would allow me to develop a profile of the total transactions of any one individual. By contrast, in recounting trade histories I learned of many items obtained or disposed of in prestations. In other words, I am only able to make some comparison about how goods moving in trade relate to the movement of goods in prestations. I must stress that the focus is on particular items, not on the number of transactions (trade or prestation).

On the basis of these data I evaluate the relative importance of local production, trade, and prestation in the acquisition and disposal of major kinds of trade objects (see table 31). I am concerned with only those goods that at some stage find their way into the trade system and so were mentioned in trade histories. Clearly, larger numbers of shells and steel tools were until recently transferred in prestations than by trade, and many of these probably never entered the trade sphere. Pigs, in contrast, move in significant numbers by trade, but not in prestations, since in the latter form of exchange they are usually passed as pork.

Only exotic goods received from the direction of the center have

TABLE 31. IMPORTANCE OF DIFFERENT MEANS OF ACQUISITION AND DISPOSAL FOR CLASSES OF GOODS

		Forest Products		From Center		Goods from[c] Periphery Center	
		Locally available[a] (A)	Non-local[b] (B)	Shells (C)	Steel Tools (D)	(A + B)	(C + D)

A. UP TO 1974

		(A)	(B)	(C)	(D)	(A + B)	(C + D)
Incoming Items:							
Shot	No.	848	4				
	%	66.6	0.7				
Trade	No.	417	557	406	172	974	578
	%	32.8	94.2	98.1	96.6	96.2	97.6
Gift	No.	8	30	8	6	38	14
	%	0.6	5.1	1.9	3.4	3.8	2.4
TOTAL		1,273	591	414	178	1,012	592
Outgoing Items:							
Trade	No.	1,053	512	194	119	1,565	313
	%	98.8	99.2	72.1	88.1	98.9	77.5
Gift	No.	13	4	75	16	17	91
	%	1.2	0.8	27.9	11.9	1.1	22.5
TOTAL		1,066	516	269	135	1,582	404
Passed Within Tsuwenkai:[d]							
Trade	No.	136	88	39	23	224	62
	%	71.6	95.7	52.0	74.2	79.4	58.5
Gift	No.	54	4	36	8	58	44
	%	28.4	4.3	48.0	25.8	20.6	41.5
TOTAL		190	92	75	31	282	106

B: 1974-1985

		(1)	(2)	(3)	(4)	(5)	(6)
Incoming Items:							
Shot	No.	56					
	%	33.5					
Trade	No.	105	67	12	4	172	16
	%	62.9	85.9	85.7	100	91.0	88.9
Gift	No.	6	11	2		17	2
	%	3.6	14.1	14.3		9.0	11.1
TOTAL		167	78	14	4	189	18
Outgoing Items:							
Trade	No.	165	68	30	7	233	37
	%	97.6	94.4	96.8	100	96.7	97.4
Gift	No.	4	4	1		8	1
	%	2.4	5.6	3.2		3.3	2.6
TOTAL		169	72	31	7	241	38
Passed Within Tsuwenkai[d]:							
Trade	No.	7	19	4	1	26	5
	%	41.2	90.5	80.0	50.0	68.4	71.4
Gift	No.	10	2	1	1	12	2
	%	58.8	9.5	20.0	50.0	31.6	28.6
TOTAL		17	21	5	2	38	7

[a] Includes the seven species of plume-bearing birds listed in table 24, plus figures for cassowaries and marsupials. The relevant figures for these last two goods are as follows: for the period to 1974: cassowaries: 90 caught; 4 imported and 49 exported by trade; 1 out by gift; 2 traded and 6 by gift within Tsuwenkai; marsupials: 57 killed; 12 imported and 84 exported by trade; 5 traded within Tsuwenkai; and for the period 1974–1985: cassowaries: 3 imported and 2 exported by trade; marsupials: 8 killed; 1 imported and 8 exported by trade; 1 out by gift.

[b] Includes the four species of plume-bearing birds listed in table 24 plus figures for marsupials as follows: for the period to 1974: 53 imported by trade, 1 by gift; 39 exported by trade; 8 traded within Tsuwenkai; and for the period 1974–1978: 6 imported and 7 exported by trade.

[c] Figures exclude local production so that means of acquisition between the two columns are directly comparable. Pigs are excluded because different forms of distribution (as reproducible piglets or as only immediately consumable pork) means their deployment is not strictly comparable with other trade goods.

[d] Includes only items first imported and/or later exported by trade.

been transferred in large numbers in prestations. Plumes and furs are very rarely included in major prestations, and then only in small numbers. Small quantities, however, are often distributed in minor prestations.

Local production was the major means of acquiring locally available forest products up until 1974, when trade assumed greater significance. In fact, the table masks a more gradual shift in the relative importance of trade and hunting, which had assumed rough parity around the mid-1950s. The great bulk of locally procurable items have always been disposed of by trade, although the significance of minor prestations has grown. Locally unavailable forest products have also predominantly moved in and out of Tsuwenkai by trade, though again, prestations have grown in importance. Overall, then, prestations are of minimal if increasing significance in acquiring forest products—mainly plumes— which are later traded, or in disposing of goods first acquired by trade.

These figures are dramatically at variance with figures for the means of acquisition of decorations in current plume collections (table 14), where minor prestations exceed trade in importance. The conclusion, borne out by informants' statements, is that items of decoration and trade received by gift are seldom traded but are usually kept until they wear out or are given away.

Of the goods obtained from the direction of the center most shells and steel tools came in prestations, especially major ones, but were then redistributed within Tsuwenkai and sent to other communities in prestations again. Most pigs given in prestations are in the form of cooked pork, and so can only be redeployed materially to a limited extent. Shells, steel tools, and Red Bird of Paradise plumes, however, are relatively durable. Very few of these goods first acquired in prestations were later passed in trade (about 3 percent of exports to 1974). By contrast, exports by trade are much reduced, and almost one-quarter of goods obtained by trade are disposed of in prestations. The inference is clear: imports by trade were an important means of accumulating shells and steel for prestations; acquisitions through trade were syphoned off into the ceremonial exchange sphere. The Kundagai themselves make the same point. There is an overall movement of shells and steel tools in prestations from Up-Jimi to Up-Simbai. Thus, these goods move in the same directions in different contexts of exchange, the number of items moving by prestation being topped up by additions drawn from the trade system. The greater transfer of these goods by prestations within Tsuwenkai indicates that the same process operates within the settlement. I suggest that the transfer of valuables from the trade to the ceremonial exchange systems has maintained the relative scarcity of these goods in the trade system (see chap. 7). More recently, as I have already indicated, shells have become scarce in an absolute sense, and numbers passed in prestations have dropped dramatically in the 1980s. Nonetheless, although the incidence of trade in shells and steel has greatly declined from the mid-1970s, greensnail and to a lesser extent axes and bushknives are still highly desired items for inclusion in prestations.

That items coming from ultimate plume consumers are withdrawn from the trade sphere to a greater extent than those from primary suppliers is understandable, given that no products traded toward the center, with the uncommon exception of cassowaries, are used in ceremonial exchange, whereas only goods coming from the center are used in major prestations, at least among the western Maring and the Kalam. Exports toward the center therefore serve the double function of drawing exotic goods in exchange that can later be used to replace by trade plumes and other products for personal use and to acquire goods to be drawn off into prestations.

The conclusion seems clear that the Kundagai rely most heavily on trade in acquiring valuables, whatever their region or origin, a conclusion that finds some support in Kundagai claims of poor recollections of their involvement in prestations against often enthusiastic recall of trading activities. Some specific examples lend further support to this contention.

A total of 276 Lesser Bird of Paradise plumes had been acquired by the Kundagai by the end of fieldwork in 1974, 222 or 80.4 percent by trade, 52 or 18.8 percent by minor prestation, and 2 or 0.7 percent by hunting. Only 215 or 77.9 percent of these incoming plumes were disposed of from Tsuwenkai, 211 (98.1 percent) by trade, and 4 (1.9 percent) by minor prestation. Of the 52 plumes acquired by gift, 23 (44.2 percent) were subsequently disposed of from Tsuwenkai, all by trade. The remainder had been discarded or were still retained by their original owners at the time of fieldwork. Trade is therefore the most significant means of acquiring and disposing of Lesser Bird of Paradise plumes.[20]

More valuable species, such as the Vulturine Parrot, are less likely to be acquired in prestations. Only 6 collections of feathers, or 2.4 percent of all incoming plumes to 1974, were obtained by gift, and none had been disposed of from Tsuwenkai by this means. Only 2 of the collections in the sample were never exported. Several other collections were retained at the time of fieldwork, but their owners anticipated trading them. Of all Vulturine feather collections imported, then, 2 or 0.8 percent had been lost. The loss rate for this species, which is seldom used in Kundagai decorations, is therefore 8 per 1,000, a remarkably low figure. Loss rates for other exotic species are undoubtedly higher.

Table 32 allows for a comparison of rates of increase or loss of stocks *in trade* between the seven commonly acquired locally available species and the four commonly traded nonlocal but regional birds (listed in table 31).

Local hunting provided 701 plume sets to 1974, more than sufficient to account for the increase in exports over imports. In fact, combining figures for hunting and imports by trade, 1,606 plumes were acquired. This means that a total of 213 plumes were accumulated or consumed within Tsuwenkai, or of all plumes obtained by these two means 13.3 percent, or 133 per 1,000, were lost from the export trade. Since 1974 hunting has diminished greatly and is insufficient to sustain levels of export in excess of levels of import. The increasing incidence of gifts then becomes of significance in maintaining a high, if somewhat reduced, rate of gain of plumes available for export. Although the excess of exports of locally available plumes over imports has fallen, the relation between levels of imports and exports of nonlocal plumes has become balanced, rather than showing a small overall loss rate. In other words, local hunting and receipt of gifts enabled the Kundagai to export more plumes than they imported, and also to augment their own stocks for personal use by replacing old decorations and maintaining a relatively high rate of through-flow of nonlocally available plumes by "consuming" local plumes.

Trade imports of more durable items (shells and steel tools) flowing in the reverse direction to forest products far exceeded exports sent toward primary plume suppliers up to 1974. Given that the Kundagai exported more plumes than they imported, this situation is not unexpected, since the Kundagai obtained in exchange for local products shells and steel for which they had no prior commitment to pass on to partners in other communities. Since 1974 trade in shells and steel diminished sharply and exports exceeded imports. Since acquisitions in prestations also diminished in this period, it seems likely that exports were substantially funded by shells and steel accumulated prior to the decline in supplies of these goods from the upper Jimi.

For the period to 1974 figures for the import and export of shells,

The Structure of Trade

TABLE 32. RATES OF ACCUMULATION OR LOSS IN TRADE FLOW OF PLUMES[a]

	No. Imported		No. exported		Net loss (-) or gain(+)		Loss (-) or gain(+) rate/1,000	
	I	II	I	II	I	II	I	II
A. NUMBER OF ITEMS TRANSFERRED								
Local species	401	102	920	157	+519	+55	+564	+350
Nonlocal species	504	61	473	61	- 31	- 0	- 62	- 0
Combined	905	162	1,393	218	+488	+55	+350	+252
B. NUMBER OF TRANSACTIONS INCLUDED								
Local species	191	55	438	73	+247	+18	+563	+247
Nonlocal species	504	61	473	61	- 31	- 0	- 62	- 0
Combined	695	116	911	134	+216	+18	+237	+134

[a] Figures in columns I for period before 1,974, in columns II for period after 1974.

steel tools, and pigs (the principal goods received in return for local products) total 1,129 imports and 608 exports. Imports exceeded exports by 521 or 46 percent. There was, therefore, an increase rate in Tsuwenkai of 460 of these items per 1,000 traded. This is well in excess of increase in plumes for the same period. This suggests that there is a regional gradient of wealth in items given in exchange for plumes, from a maximum at the center of the trade networks to a minimum at the periphery. The scale of the excess accumulation of shells, steel, and pigs over plumes exported is further magnified by the fact that many transactions involve the exchange of several plumes for a single return item. Since most such transactions involve plumes from parrots, and the Superb and Saxony Birds of Paradise which were commonly shot in Tsuwenkai, the Kundagai (and similar plume producers) were able to accumulate durable goods at a greater rate.

Hughes (1977: 213) has remarked that an advantage of the use of shells and axes in trade is that they are relatively durable and therefore have low loss rates. Pigs are durable in the sense that they reproduce, whereas plumes, furs, and cassowaries are quickly perishable. To communities such as the Kundagai, who export more plumes than they import, the perishability of plumes is an advantage rather than a liability, for plume consumers maintain a high desire and must therefore send a continual flow of goods in exchange. Because the latter goods are more durable, Kundagai stocks of them increased at a faster rate than plume consumers' feather stocks increased. Although some of these imports of durables served to replace exotic plumes lost from collections through damage and age, and to sustain continued exports to ultimate plume consumers, much of the remainder was diverted into the prestation sphere of the economy, as argued above. Thus, of the 406 shells recorded as obtained by trade, at least 111 (27.3 percent) and probably more were redistributed within Tsuwenkai and to other settlements in various prestations. Of the 187 stone and steel tools imported by trade, 27 (14.4 percent) or more were redistributed in prestations. By contrast, of 194 shells exported only 8 (4.1 percent) were originally obtained in prestations and, of 126 stone and steel tools exported, 8 (6.3 percent) were obtained by the same means. These figures, of course, are only bare minima, since the total number of these goods transferred by means other than trade is unknown. In all, a minimum of 138 (23.3 percent) shells, axes, and knives mentioned in trade histories were withdrawn from trade and redeployed in prestations, whereas only 16 (5 percent) have made the reverse transition. In short, durable goods do not move relatively freely back and forth between these two modes of exchange but tend to remain within the sphere of major prestations and gifts once they have been introduced into this type of circulation.

Trade import of these goods therefore funded prestations, and since smaller numbers were withdrawn from prestations than were introduced into them, stocks available for such transfers must have constantly increased. This obviously occurred since shells were not obtained regularly by the Kundagai until the 1920s at the earliest, and even then only in small numbers. That the number of shells and steel included in major prestations continued to rise well into the 1970s is further evidence for the accumulation of these goods in the Narak, Maring, and Kalam areas. This accumulation occurred at the same time as various central-highlands groups were divesting themselves of shell stocks, and it cushioned the Kundagai against the effects of the sharp decline in the availability of the goods in the later 1970s. By drawing on accumulated stocks acquired in trade the Kundagai and other more peripherally located groups could sustain continued use of large numbers of shells and steel in prestations for some years after upper-Jimi people had largely replaced them with money.

Pigs have been largely left out of consideration so far. Though durable in the sense of reproducible, there are obvious limits to the numbers of pigs that can be accumulated, given the finite resources of land and labor available at the household level. Table 33 shows the disposi-

The Structure of Trade 231

TABLE 33. DISPOSAL OF KUNDAGAI
PIGS OBTAINED BY TRADE TO 1974

	No.	%[a]
Trade	243	67.9
Major prestation	37	10.3
Minor prestation	9	2.5
Died	39	10.9
Killed (not for prestations)	30	8.4
Subtotal:	358	100.0
Still Living	37	
Unknown	160	
TOTAL	555	

[a] Percentage of subtotal only; that is, of pigs whose disposition by owners has been finalized. This includes undated transactions; hence percentage of disposal by trade differs from proportions listed for dated transactions only in table 26.

tion of the 555 pigs recorded in case histories as imported by trade up to 1974. In all, 289 pigs were exported, only 46 or 15.9 percent being Tsuwenkai-bred animals.[21]

These figures, drawn from cases dating from the 1920s onward, show that trade was by far the most important means of disposing of pigs initially acquired by trade. Major prestations and mortality were of next importance. Most deaths occur within a few months of a piglet being obtained in trade. Many such animals were destined to be re-exported to trading partners, and the Kundagai trader was forced to substitute a pig from his own herd. Minor prestations are the only significant means of redistributing live pigs.

Prestations are probably of much greater significance than this table suggests (and other forms of disposal correspondingly less important). Figures for trade in pigs to 1974 show a net increase of 312 beasts, or a rate of increase of 562 per 1,000. Until the early 1960s the Kundagai pig herd went through cycles of slow growth and rapid decline in relation to the ritual cycle. Since that time the herd has been allegedly maintained around a steady figure. In other words, most of the growth of the pig herd by trade must be balanced by loss other than trade (assuming informants remembered most of their pig-trading ventures).

Rates of loss by other means must therefore be considerably higher.[22] One might presume that a large proportion of pigs acquired by trade must be diverted into the prestation sphere, if only because they make this transition as pork and therefore cannot be redeployed in further exchanges.

CONCLUSION

The patterns of Kundagai trading relations amplify the model of trade sketched in the Introduction. I have suggested structural features, such as trade webs, and the mechanisms for substituting one good for another within or between populations with access to similar resources, which facilitate the continual flow of goods.

The rapidity with which early trade patterns in shells were reversed to bring large numbers of shells from Up-Jimi shows the responsiveness of the trade system to distribute goods from areas of abundance to those of scarcity. With the influx of European-introduced shells from the central highlands by way of the upper Jimi, former shell providers in the Simbai and lower Cross-Jimi effectively became deprived of shells in relation to growing stocks in the upper Jimi, and trade patterns were altered to meet their deprivation. With the substitution of steel for stone tools a similar change in trading patterns of cutting tools resulted. Despite these changes, the pattern of trade in plumes, live cassowaries, and marsupial skins and furs remains little altered, though volumes of traffic in forest products have decreased in recent years. That the trade system could adjust to affect the supply of goods (both new and of long-standing) from new sources, without disrupting the flow of forest products from the periphery to the center, shows the strong ecological and resource-difference basis for trade.

I have devoted considerable attention to these ecological and economic dimensions of trade. In part, this is justified by common assertions in the literature that these aspects are critical to an understanding of trade. Hughes (1977), Harding (1967), and Keil (1974) provide detailed ethnographic studies of the ecological structures of regional trading systems, while Brookfield with Hart (1971) gives a more general perspective. The material presented in this chapter is broadly in agreement with these earlier analyses and adds a critical dimension to them in the provision of quantified data covering several decades, so far lacking for Melanesian trade.

Most analyses of exchange in Melanesia focus on its ceremonialized forms. On the assumption that trade has firm pragmatic bases, the explanations of its conduct become self-evident from an implicit materialist and utilitarian perspective. Hence, the maintenance of trading relations is treated in terms of "need" on the part of consumers for goods to be disposed of in material fashions. The bulk of this chapter has been devoted to showing just how the reciprocal flow of goods through Tsuwenkai is sustained, by a consideration not only of aspects of distribution but of the related structures of production and consumption.

Yet, more is involved in trade than mere ecologically or culturally specialized goods and equivalence of valuations of material items. There is also a marked social dimension. This is seen in the application of more or less standard rates of exchange regardless of relationships between traders, which creates a form of equality between transactors. It is also to be seen in such factors as hospitality given to traders or the timespan agreed upon for the completion of a transaction. In addition, I suggest that the particular cultural meaning attached to exchanges and the symbolic significance of the goods involved must also be taken into account in any analysis of mechanisms of trade. The social and cultural meaning of exchange, however, lies in historically specific contexts and is subject to changing influence. Before exploring such aspects of trade it is necessary to consider the historical development of trade.

6
The Development of Trade

Material presented in the last chapter indicates a number of changes in trade in the Jimi–Simbai area. Many of these changes are the indirect consequence of the pattern of colonization of the highlands, which saw a consolidation of colonial authority among central-highlands plume consumers predating the incorporation of the Jimi–Simbai area into the colonial state by twenty years or more. The colonial penetration of New Guinea had a profound impact on the kinds and directions of passage of goods. Changes in patterns of distribution, however, were less dramatic for the organization of Kundagai trade than were changes in the relative contribution of local production to the flow of goods, the rates of flow of goods relative to one another, the exchange value of objects, and the social relationships of partners. The last two factors will be given more detailed consideration in succeeding chapters. In the present chapter I concentrate on an analysis of the historical reshaping and expansion of the Kundagai trade universe and the variable rates of transfer or "turnover" of goods. I conclude with a discussion of the growing dependence of the Kundagai on the central highlands, which has developed with the transformation of traditional trading networks and the uneven intrusion of capitalism into the highlands.

OVERVIEW OF CHANGE

On purely logical grounds it would be wrong to assume that the organization of trade over roughly sixty years, such as it can be re-

The Development of Trade

constructed from the memories of a few old men, represents some stable condition. It may well be a reflection of aboriginal trade—that is, exchange unaffected by European or other outside influence, in the form of the kinds of products traded or their directions. But it must be conceded that the European presence, thinly spread in coastal regions from the late nineteenth century, as well as earlier sporadic contacts by Southeast Asians, may have had a very indirect impact, however slight, on Kundagai trade (cf. Hughes 1977). Nonetheless, all trade goods remained indigenous in origin. What is more certain is that trade inventories and patterns were not stable. The archaeological and oral historical evidence from widely scattered parts of the highlands of radical changes in agricultural practices, demography, and ecology suggest important transformations in the social and economic environment in which trade occurred (see e.g., Feil 1987). Just how these changes affected the Maring and their neighbors is not clear.

About 1920, then, remains the cutoff point in our present picture of Maring trade founded on case material. Beyond that date remains conjecture based upon the opinion of informants. While those opinions are generally consistent there is no independent evidence to substantiate them.

As noted in the previous chapter there have been changes in the catalogue of trade items and alterations in the directions of trade in some items. Some of these changes predate European penetration of the highlands in the 1930s and the fairly rapid impact on local production and exchange that resulted, with indirect consequences for the Kundagai. It is particularly noteworthy that the Simbu expanded their use of plumes as valuables and decorations, in terms of species used and quantities desired, in the 1950s (Hide 1981: 115 ff).[1] Since the Kundagai plume trade is significantly directed toward the Simbu and has given a dominant structure to their overall patterns of trade for at least several decades, we may conclude that the whole Kundagai trade sphere had a different structure before this time, in terms of the objects traded, their directions, and exchange rates. Evidence from the Kundagai on this point is largely inferential, but what does seem to be the case is that before shells became widely passed in trade and prestations the inventory of trade and prestation goods was somewhat impoverished.

In fact, it seems reasonable to divide the development of trade in the Jimi–Simbai area into five phases on the basis of the principal goods passed in trade, the major orientations of trade routes, and the relation between the passage of goods in trade and prestations. These phases were not sharply demarcated but rather merged into one another. The dates given here are thus only approximations.

The earliest phase characterized the period prior to the turn of the century. The major items of trade were Simbai Valley salt and Wum–Tsenga stone axes. Plumes and furs were also used in trade toward axe-makers. Trade was probably rather weakly developed, nonetheless, as axes and salt also were widely redistributed in prestations and filtered into the area from other sources besides those just mentioned. Axes were also manufactured from local, albeit inferior stone. Beside axes, major items of prestations were mainly of local provenance: pigs, *nonema*-seed necklaces, and necklaces of dog and marsupial teeth. The nexus between trade and major prestations was at this time weak, with the stress on locally produced goods.

The second phase spanned the first three decades of this century. This period saw the development of trade in shells, with dogwhelks and cowries reaching the Kundagai from the north and northwest. Small numbers of kina and greensnail also came in trade, from several directions, but perhaps mainly from the upper-Jimi and Cross-Jimi areas. The salt and axe trade still provided a dominating structure to trade webs oriented across the grain of the country, but the importation of pigs and, toward the end of this phase, shells from the upper Jimi in exchange for plumes grew in importance. Shells largely replaced seed and dog-tooth necklaces in major prestations. Trade thus became increasingly important as a source of valuables for redeployment in prestations, and exchange activities became oriented toward the use of essentially exotic, imported objects.

The next phase extended from the late 1930s or early 1940s to the mid-1960s. Imports of steel tools from the central highlands led to the collapse of the old salt–stone axe trade. In addition, shells, most particularly kina and greensnail, began to flood into the region from the Simbu and Wahgi Valleys, where massive amounts had been introduced by colonial authorities, missionaries, and prospectors who first entered the central highlands in the early 1930s. Pigs also were increasingly imported from the upper Jimi. Trade became firmly oriented along a northwest–southeast axis, with forest products, especially plumes, being sent toward the central highlands in return for shells, steel, and pigs. This pattern became consolidated as the Simbu–Kuma area emerged as a major center for the consumption of plumes and other forest products, providing a dominant focus for a radial and concentric network of trade paths linking the center to a widely dispersed periphery. The Jimi–Simbai area was one sector of the peripheral zone.

This phase saw a considerable intensification of trade and of variety of goods traded, especially from the mid-1950s when the colonial presence afforded greater security to traders. Exotic shells, steel, and pigs predominated in major prestations, and the Jimi–Simbai region therefore became dependent upon the central highlands for supplies of these goods. Although the net excess of women sent in marriage from Tsuwenkai to Up-Jimi settlements meant that significant volumes of shells and steel were acquired in prestations, trade assumed considerable importance as another means of accumulating valuables.

The fourth phase, from the mid-1960s to the late 1970s, saw the general maintenance of existing patterns of trade, although there was some reduction in the variety of goods traded, with such things as Goura Pigeon plumes, cowries, and dogwhelks all but abandoned. Importantly, however, money was added as a trade item. Initially, money flowed in roughly equal amounts through Tsuwenkai toward and away from the central highlands. From the mid-1970s, however, money was increasingly drawn from relatively impoverished peripheral regions toward the monetarily richer central highlands. However, money was assimilated into the traditional scheme of valuables rather than constituting a price-revealing currency. By this means, Maring trade exhibited considerable resilience to the penetration of capitalist relations of production (Healey 1985*a*). This period saw the addition not only of money to the prestation sphere but general inflation as well in most major prestations.

The final phase extends from the late 1970s into the 1980s. The prospects of trade for the future are unclear, but this period might best be characterized as one of incipient collapse. Trade in shells and steel has all but ceased, while pigs are increasingly acquired for money rather than forest products. But the changes in this last phase have been less in patterns of trade than in relative volumes of different goods, and most especially in the social organization of transactions and the rates of exchange. These are issues that I reserve for attention in later chapters.

Within this broad framework of the development of trade over almost one hundred years, further dimensions of change can be explored. The following discussion concentrates on quantified data relating to the period from the mid-1920s.

I have noted an increasing focus on trade directed toward the central highlands once shells, followed by steel tools, came predominantly from that region. The beginning of this shift in focus chances to correspond roughly with the limits of good case material derived from trade histories.[2] It is therefore not possible to specify a more precise or quantified impact of this change.

Despite these reservations it remains possible to give some further characterizations of precolonial trade that apply at least as far back as the early 1900s, and possibly even further.

Before the early 1950s the geographic range of Kundagai traders seems to have remained roughly constant. Tsuwenkai was situated toward the southeast corner of this range. Traditionally the Kundagai rarely traveled further upstream in the Jimi than Kompiai and Kupeng, although occasional visits were made to Kwima and even beyond in the company of friends and relatives from these Up-Jimi settlements. The great majority of transactions from this period were with partners in Kompiai—a large settlement with correspondingly extensive connections Up- and Cross-Jimi. Upstream, the Kundagai trading range extended no more than about fourteen kilometers,[3] a fairly easy day's walk over narrow trails. By contrast the Kauwatyi of Kompiai trading range upstream extended some twenty-five kilometers to Kol in the upper Jimi, though it is unlikely that they often made the journey. By virtue of their well-established trading links with the Kauwatyi, the Kundagai were therefore indirectly linked to an extensive trading area. They could leave trade items with Kauwatyi friends to pass on upriver or deal directly with upriver visitors to Kompiai and other settlements, most of whom were Tugumenga from Kwima, Yomban from Togban, or Manga from Kwiop. In turn, of course, the Kauwatyi and others were indirectly linked to larger trading networks through their own trading partners.

Prior to contact direct links with Cross-Jimi people were few. The Tsuwenkai Kundagai occasionally accompanied Bokapai or Cenda friends to Wum in search of stone axes, and rather more often they journeyed to Rinyimp across the Jimi from Bokapai. The greatest distance covered in a single transaction before contact that I learned of was about 25 kilometers, when a Kundagai exchanged a cassowary for a kina with a man from Por (Cross-Jimi). This transaction, however, occurred when both men attended a *konj kaiko* in Koinambe. In the lower Simbai, few Kundagai journeyed further than Nimbra, ten to twelve kilometers away. One man, who lived as a child in Nimbra for a number of years, went as far as Pogaikump several times to trade with classificatory kinsmen there, but this is only some fifteen kilometers from Tsuwenkai.

Up-Simbai the Kundagai traveled as far as Simbai about twenty-two kilometers away, and beyond to the Kinenj and Asai. Probably the greatest distance traveled was Down-Jimi, occasionally to Waim some twenty-five to thirty kilometers away. Networks of trade therefore extended furthest toward the periphery.

Although the Tsuwenkai Kundagai were not major enemies of the Ambrakwi, trade between the two populations was rare. Trade between the Kundagai and the Tsembaga ceased after the outbreak of hostilities in the 1920s. The cessation of other forms of previously established exchange relations, and taboos on commensality and sharing the products of enemy territory, effectively prevented any form of nonhostile contact. Trade has only recently been revived with the Tsembaga, though with little effort to seek out trading partners. The relatively short distances traveled Up- and Cross-Jimi can probably be attributed in large part to fear of attack in those regions. The Kundagai say that a stranger in those parts was in danger of being killed as a known or suspected ally of an enemy group. For this reason, they say, a stranger engaged in trade was not often asked his clan cluster affiliation, for if this information were known someone might be tempted to kill him if he were found to be a member of an enemy clan cluster, or of a group standing in the major-enemy category to allies. There was, then, an etiquette of anonymity in trade, adopted to preserve peace so as to avoid the possibility of disrupting trade. Ancestral spirits of enemy groups were not so easily avoided, however, and many men feared exposing themselves to mystical attack.

Although the Kundagai traveled much greater distances among the Kalam than among the Maring, they say that this also involved dangers. Generally the Kundagai maintained friendly relations with the Kalam. Informants could cite only one war with any Kalam group, which occurred before my oldest informants in 1974 were born. Since then the Kundagai have aided Kalam in feuds and, because of this and kinship ties with Kalam groups, they were at times in danger of revenge attacks as members or relatives of feuding parties.

Hughes (1977) notes that there was a regional gradient of fear of sorcery attack from strangers from high to low country. He suggests that this fear was a major constraint on the frequency and distance traders were prepared to penetrate into lower-lying areas. Although such fears probably limited the distance Narak traders traveled into the

Maring area, the Kundagai did not admit to fear of the sorcery or witchcraft of Kalam in the lower Jimi. Possibly this was because the Kundagai themselves considered (and still consider) themselves to be subject to a high incidence of witchcraft attacks from fellow Kundagai and allies.

The lower Jimi was apparently first visited by Europeans in 1930 or 1931. In 1933 Leahy and Taylor visited the Jimi between the Ganz and Tsau Rivers (Hughes 1977; Leahy, in press). European intrusions into the Jimi appear to have had no effect on intercommunity relations until the early 1950s, when several government patrols were mounted from Minj to investigate reports of unrest (Vayda 1971). At about this time trade histories suggest an increase in trading activities (see below), almost certainly stimulated by the peace-making government presence in the upper-Jimi. In the early 1950s the Kundagai met with traders from as far Up-Jimi as Kelunga and with men from Kauwil across the Jimi (both over twenty kilometers away).

In 1956 Tabibuga Patrol Post was established, the Tsuwenkai Kundagai contacted for the first time, and the government-imposed peace in the Jimi consolidated. Almost immediately traders from Karap and Kol seeking plumes were contacted fairly regularly.

Since the early 1960s the then Highlands Labour Scheme influenced the extension of Kundagai trading networks, as well as opening up new and distant source areas for plumes. On coastal plantations the Kundagai befriend men of Up-Jimi and Simbai communities with the direct result that some agree to establish trade partnerships on their return home. Such friends can now be called on to provide hospitality while a man is traveling. Having learned Tok Pisin on the coast, younger men are able to converse with Narak, Kandawo, Kuma, Melpa, and other people with whom communication was formerly difficult. Most Kundagai are bilingual, but only in Maring and Kalam.

The number of settlements and the total population with which the Kundagai have maintained most-frequent trading links have increased greatly since contact (see app. 4). Prior to contact regular trade linked the Kundagai to about twenty-five settlements with an estimated population of around 9,000. Since the 1950s the figures have risen to about thirty-nine settlements and a population of about 16,500. The total population of settlements recorded in trade histories as ever providing trading partners prior to contact was around 12,000 in thirty-nine settlements. Since contact trade has been expanded to tap a population of about 25,000 in at least sixty-four settlements (excluding distant places in the Wahgi and coast).

There has been little growth of trade between Tsuwenkai and the Simbai. Contacts with new settlements have been mainly with those lying toward the center. Most of these contacts have been initiated by people of these areas pushing ever further afield. The Kundagai only infrequently have extended their travels far up and across the Jimi, although they do now occasionally journey to distant Down-Jimi and Trans-Simbai places.

Ultimate plume consumers can increase their supply of plumes by seeking out new supply areas. A consequence may be that primary and intermediate suppliers of plumes are not impelled to increase hunting, so that local bird populations may be cushioned from possible overexploitation. Although the upper and middle Jimi was no doubt a major source for plumes used by the center, the extension of trading relations does not constitute the addition of new supply areas as such. These areas were already integrated into the trade networks. But by increasing the distances traveled traders obtain plumes from closer to primary suppliers or send them further toward the center. Although traders therefore now reduce the number of links in chains leading to each settlement, they also maintain relations with more nearby settlements that traditionally provided or imported plumes. Thus, the Kundagai now deal directly with visiting Simbu plume consumers and middle-Wahgi pig traders but still maintain strong links with the Kauwatyi. Just as Up- and Cross-Jimi people living closer to the center have extended their trading relations to Tsuwenkai and more distant areas, so the Kundagai have extended their relations toward the periphery. Kundagai now visit settlements in the Kaironk and Asai Valleys formerly beyond their range. These contacts have usually been initiated by the Kundagai themselves.

It would appear, therefore, that the initiative to open up new trading networks with more distant communities has come from the direction of the center. As their demand for plumes has increased, or, at the least, their ability to satisfy more easily an already high demand has increased, the initiative to extend trading relations spread to nearby intermediate suppliers and consumers of plumes, in this case, in the upper Jimi. They in turn passed on the initiative to more peripheral suppliers and consumers such as the Kundagai. But as the distance from ultimate consumers increases the motivation or ability to initiate new trading relations diminishes, so that the Kundagai have added few new source areas for their own plume imports. The Kundagai have extended their trade chains toward the periphery over shorter distances than have more centrally located communities in the upper Jimi. For instance, the Kundagai would be capable of journeying to Aiome in the Ramu lowlands within about two days to seek plumes, but to my knowledge they have not done so.

In twelve months during 1973–1974, eleven trading expeditions visited Tsuwenkai. Each party had two or more members, but the two largest only had five. Most expeditions were from eastern-Jimi Maring groups, but there were also two from Simbu and one from Karap. Some parties traveled extensively in the Jimi and Simbai. One group of Simbu flew into Aiome in the Ramu Valley by light aircraft and worked their way through the upper Simbai and Kinenj before reaching Tsuwenkai. They went on to Koinambe where they planned to charter a plane back to Kerowagi. Nearly all traders sought plumes or cassowaries, bringing pigs and money to give in return. Only six of the parties had any trading success in Tsuwenkai. The Kundagai declined to offer any plumes to several of the earlier visitors because they were accumulating them for a dance in Kwima later in the year. Many plumes were offered to the two Karap traders who refused them, saying that they were of inferior quality.

During the same period the Kundagai mounted only two major expeditions. In one, four men took plumes and furs to Koriom. They were absent for six days and returned with pigs, shells, and money. The second expedition, of two men, visited the Kaironk Valley in search of plumes. Many more men visited kinsmen and affines alone in the upper Simbai and lower Jimi to acquire plumes by trade or loan for use in a ceremony in Kwima (which was later indefinitely postponed). Besides these travels primarily organized with trade in mind, a great deal of trade occurred in the context of visits to or from Tsuwenkai focused on other events: ceremonial exchanges, dances, visits to sick kinsmen, and so forth.

In the late 1970s a bridge was completed below Kwima linking the north bank of the Jimi to a dry-weather road through Tabibuga government station to the Wahgi Valley. Middle-Wahgi pig traders were quick to avail themselves of the opportunities to truck large animals into the Maring area. Generally, these traders demand money rather than plumes in exchange for their pigs.

Kundagai trade with regions closer to the periphery has increased in

The Development of Trade

intensity since the mid-1950s, and greater numbers of plumes have been exported Up- and Cross-Jimi. The effect has been to increase the number of plumes exported toward the center. There appears to have been no appreciable attendant increase in hunting in Kundagai land to supply the increasing flow of plumes (see chap. 3), which has therefore been funded mainly by increasing import from more peripheral communities. Table 34 shows the increased importance of imports of locally procurable species in funding the volume of plumes exported by the Kundagai. Only locally occurring species are listed, since it is only for these that increased imports in addition to local hunting can increase exports. To increase exports of nonlocal species, imports must be increased correspondingly, for growth of stocks by other means, such as gifts, is of only minor importance, although some species are hunted in coastal areas by contract laborers.

Tsuwenkai occupies a favored place in the plume trade in that several highly valued species are abundant in local forests, so that the Kundagai were a significant source of new plumes added to the trade flow, at least until the later 1970s, when hunting declined. This is demonstrated by excess of exports over imports of plumes (i.e., excluding figures for cassowaries): a ratio of 5.1 exports to 1 imported set prior to the mid-1950s, dropping to between 1.5 and 1.6 to 1 after contact. Although of greater incidence from the 1970s, prestations have never been a significant means for the transfer of plumes. Hunting was formerly the major means of sustaining exports of plumes from Tsuwenkai. With an initially steady, then declining, hunting rate since contact, the capacity of the Kundagai to increase the flow of plumes sent toward the central highlands derives largely from expanded imports. In other words, there is a greater flow in trade *through* rather than *from* Tsuwenkai (cf. also table 30).

As table 34 shows, in all but two species, imports prior to contact contributed less significantly to the number of exports than since then. Because hunting rates of all species have remained relatively constant till at least 1974, exports per unit of time must have increased in volume and therefore in rate since contact. (The figures in the table suggest this, but export totals for pre- and postcontact are based on different sample sizes of traders, must represent different proportions of unknown total numbers of plumes traded, and refer to different time intervals. Hence, one cannot argue directly from the export figures for an increase in the volume or rate of export since 1956.)

Not only has the volume of imports increased, but the number of

TABLE 34. IMPORTANCE OF PLUME IMPORTS IN FUNDING EXPORTS FROM TSUWENKAI

Species	Pre-1956			1956-1974			1974-1978			1979-1985		
	Import	Export	% of export funded by import	Import	Export	% of export funded by import	Import	Export	% of export funded by import	Import	Export	% of export funded by import
Cassowaries		13	0.0	4	31	12.9	3	2	150.0			
Long-tailed Buzzard	6	9	66.7	10	7	142.9	4	3	133.3			
Papuan Lory		42	0.0	84	101	88.3	21	19	110.5			
Fairy Lory		152	0.0	16	34	47.1	5	21	23.8	5	25	20.0
Black Sicklebill	10	9	111.1	20	22	90.9	5		83.3	6	7	85.7
Stephanie's Astrapia	12	27	44.4	38	64	59.4	10	11	90.1	13	17	76.5
Superb B. of P.		17	0.0	13	54	24.1	1	4	25.0	1	6	16.7
Saxony B. of P.	30	40	75.0	64	118	54.2	12	12	100.0	19	26	73.1
TOTALS	58	309	18.8	249	431	57.8	33	54	61.1	72	105	68.6

The Development of Trade 245

links through which plumes travel is often reduced. For instance, a Lesser Bird of Paradise plume from Waim in the lower Jimi may be transferred to Tsuwenkai and then Kol in only two transactions, whereas in the past four or more exchanges were usually necessary to move the same distance. By reducing the number of transactions to cover a certain distance, the time of the movement is usually reduced also. Fewer men are liable to retain an item for personal use before sending it on. By extending trade chains from each settlement, so reducing the number of links, plumes can be transferred more rapidly along trade chains. Loss through damage or age can therefore be reduced, permitting an increased supply of plumes reaching ultimate consumers.

I have indicated important changes in the catalogue of goods passed over time, with some items, such as greensnail shells and money being added to the trade flow, with others, such as stone axes, abandoned. But even for goods such as pigs and most plumes that have been traded for extended periods of time, their numerical importance as trade items may have varied. Table 35 shows the incidence of trade in particular items for different time periods, expressed as a proportion of all transactions conducted in each period. The table aggregates figures for imports and exports; if these were listed separately the proportions of transactions involving particular items would frequently show considerable variation between imports and exports. For example, pigs were involved in 24.5 percent of all transactions affecting the import of goods before 1956 and 12.3 percent of transactions by which goods were exported. The magnitude of variation between imports and exports of particular goods has been indicated in the previous chapter.

Nearly all of the goods mentioned in trade histories fall into one of the eighteen separate items specified in the table; very few fall into the more general "Other" categories listed.

The incidence of trade involving money must actually have been somewhat higher since postcontact up to 1974, as it was only used in the latter half of this period. The declining incidence of money in trade in the late 1970s was probably more marked than indicated. The reasons for this will be discussed later. What is noteworthy is that money is the most commonly used trade item and is used in just over one-third of all transactions.

Pigs have clearly become more important objects of trade over time, with the late 1970s being a time of particularly heavy pig trade. Shells and steel tools, however, showed a considerable decline in the incidence

TABLE 35. INCIDENCE OF TRADE BY ITEM AND PERIOD

Columns list proportion of all transactions (as percentages) involving listed items.

Item	Pre-1956	1956-1974	1974-1978	1979-1985
Money	-	22.2	19.1	36.6
Pigs	18.5	20.8	28.0	24.5
Shells (combined)	19.7	13.4	8.1	3.3
Kina	6.2	5.3	0.3	0.5
Greensnail	9.3	7.5	7.8	2.5
Other	4.2	0.6	-	0.3
Steel tools	13.6	4.5	1.9	1.0
Plumes (combined)	46.2	37.8	37.7	31.1
Long-tailed Buzzard	2.2	0.7	-	1.8
Papuan Lory	1.0	1.6	1.4	1.5
Fairy Lory	2.5	0.3	0.6	0.8
Vulturine Parrot	11.4	11.4	14.7	8.6
Hornbill	2.5	-	-	-
Black Sicklebill	2.8	1.6	3.0	3.3
Astrapia	5.8	4.0	5.8	6.6
Superb B. of P.	2.5	2.5	1.1	1.8
Lesser B. of P.	12.2	12.8	6.6	2.8
Saxony B. of P.	3.3	2.6	3.0	3.5
Other plumes	-ᵃ	-ᵃ	1.4	0.5
Marsupial Furs	-ᵃ	-ᵃ	5.0	1.0
Cassowaries	1.9	1.4	-	1.3
Other	-ᵃ	-ᵃ	0.3	1.3

ᵃ No transactions positively identified for this period. Totals for all trade up to 1974 suggest minor incidence of less than 0.5%.

of trade, although it is noteworthy that levels of trade in greensnail shell did not slacken appreciably until the 1980s.

The incidence of forest products in trade has diminished, but not dramatically. Assessment of change in the incidence of trade in marsupial skins and fur is hampered by the lack of clearly dated transactions before 1974. Cassowaries have long been traded in small numbers and, discounting the lack of records for 1974–1978, seem to have remained of comparable importance in the overall flow of goods. Plumes have diminished in importance from being involved in almost half of all transactions before contact to just under one-third in the 1980s. The long period of stability from 1956 to the late 1970s is noteworthy, however. The decline in the incidence of plumes in trade was not general. A number of species are of marginally greater significance as trade objects now than they were in the past, notably the highly valued Astrapia and Black Sicklebill. Indeed, the overall decline in the incidence of plumes in trade is attributable to the markedly diminished trade in the two most valuable nonlocal species, the Vulturine Parrot and the Lesser Bird of Paradise. Informants in 1985 remarked that it was becoming increasingly difficult to find traders Up- and Cross-Jimi prepared to accept plumes in trade. This applied particularly to the feathers of the Vulturine Parrot.

The data provided here suggest that changes in the incidence of trade, in particular goods as a proportion of the total flow, have not been particularly sudden or dramatic over the last five or six decades. This, however, gives no indication of changes in the volume or rates or velocities of trade in different goods and periods.

INTENSIFICATION OF TRADE

I have indicated that trade intensified around the date of first contact in the Jimi. This intensification took the form of increased rates of trade, both in terms of the average frequency of transactions an individual may conduct and in the volumes of goods transferred. Intensification of trade can therefore be assessed in two ways: by looking at how trading rates of individuals have changed since contact and by looking at changing rates of transfer of particular items of trade. Ideally, analysis should compare rates of trade over a series of equal time periods. Although many of the transactions recorded in Kundagai trade histories could be assigned to five-year intervals, others before 1974 could only be ascribed to the broad categories of before and after effective contact with the colonial government. Approximately 20 percent of all transactions up to 1973 could not even be assigned to these two periods with certainty. Despite these difficulties, a comparison of trading rates by age of traders does suggest an intensification of personal trading rates since the mid-1950s.

Table 36 gives some indication of how annual trading rates vary with age. It is based on the total of trade transactions conducted by the fifty-six men whose trade histories were collected in 1973–1974. The table aggregates traders by five-year age groups into three categories. Few males engage in trade until about fifteen years old, or did so in the past. Some men continue to trade well into old age; the oldest Tsuwenkai male, a frail man of over seventy, was still trading with visitors to the settlement in 1974. Others withdraw from trade as age and ill health sap their energies or as trade partners elsewhere die. Because a man trades less often as he ages, average rates for older age groups will

TABLE 36. RATES OF TRADE BY AGE GROUP, TO 1974

Age group	No.	Man-years of Trade[a]	Transactions No.	Range	No./Man /Year
A. ALL TRADE SINCE 1956					
15-20	4	10	4	0-3	0.4
20-25	6	45	80	2-19	1.8
25-30	9	112.5	267	6-47	2.4
30-35	14	245	682	2-126	2.8
Subtotal	33	412.5	1,033	0-126	2.5
B. MORE THAN 50 PERCENT OF TRADING TIME SINCE 1956					
35-40	5	112.5	397	26-211	3.5
40-45	5	137.5	397	2-180	2.9
45-50	1	32.5	105	-	3.2
Subtotal	11	282.5	899	2-211	3.2
C. MORE THAN 50 PERCENT OF TRADING TIME BEFORE 1956					
50-55	3	112.5	132	38-47	1.2
55-60	4	170	124	12-48	0.7
60-65	3	142.5	151	38-67	1.1
65-70	1	52.5	31	-	0.6
70-75	1	57.5	48	-	0.8
Subtotal	12	535.0	486	12-67	0.9
TOTAL	56	1,230.0	2,418	0-211	2.0

[a] Calculated from midpoint of age range; that is, 2.5 years per man in the 15–20 age group, through to 57.5 years in the 70–75 age group.

be biased toward lower overall rates. The figures must therefore be interpreted in the light of differential influences on age groups. Notwithstanding the difficulty of dating many transactions to pre- and post-1956, in general, the older a man is the more opportunity he has had to trade prior to contact and, bearing in mind the effects of age, the less opportunity since then. Men aged under thirty-five (category A in the table) had conducted all their trade since contact, whereas men aged thirty-five to fifty (category B) spent no more than half their trading lives before 1956—the younger men progressively less than this proportion. Only men aged over fifty (category C) spent more than half their trading lives before 1956.

Men who were aged in their early twenties at the time of contact (in the thirty-five to forty age group in table 36) show the highest average annual trading rates. These men, in their prime at the time of data collection, maintained a high involvement in trade since contact. The most vigorous Tsuwenkai trader, with over 200 transactions to his credit, at an annual rate of 9.4, falls into this group.

Two clear inferences can be drawn from this table. First, the longer a man's trading career extends before contact the lower his overall rate of trade. This indicates that rates of trade have increased since around the date of first contact, a conclusion supported by the opinions of older men who noted that their own trading activities intensified after contact. They explained this by saying that it was only since then that desirable items became available, making trade worthwhile. Prior to contact all that could be obtained in exchange for local products were "worthless" cowries, stone axes, and tasteless native salt. Undoubtedly they are evaluating older trade goods in the light of present views of the superiority of steel, kina, and greensnail. Younger men point out that their fathers obviously did value older goods just as highly as they do contemporary goods now, but that their opportunities for trade were fewer partly because many exotic goods were scarcer, and also because endemic warfare restricted movements.

The second inference is that rates of trade increase up to the age of about forty. Young men are yet to establish relationships with potential partners through their own and their siblings' marriages and through demonstrated competence as traders and producers of trade goods by pig breeding and hunting. There is a sharp disjunction between trading rates up to age fifty and after them. Lower rates in older age groups (category C) are a combination of increasing age (a postcontact effect) and precontact circumstances that inhibited more vigorous trade.

Warfare clearly had a depressant effect on both hunting and travel for trade and other reasons. The occurrence of war among the Maring was regulated to roughly eight- to twelve-year intervals by the ritual cycle that imposed inhibitions on warfare until spirits and allies had been rewarded in *konj kaiko* ceremonies for their assistance. Even when ritually promulgated truces were in place, major enemies occasionally mounted small raids into one anothers' territories. The risk of such attacks inhibited hunting in more remote stretches of forest, thus depressing the production of valuables for trade. Perhaps more significantly, a traveler was in danger of attack, either from major enemies or from allies of his enemies. Men visiting allies on the same valley flank had to pass surreptitiously through the forested upper or lower regions of enemy territory or make safer but long detours through more neutral territory. Even if they avoided physical attack they were in danger of mystical harm from spirits inhabiting enemy territory.

The government-imposed peace in the mid-1950s was very quickly accepted throughout the Jimi, with only a few minor exceptions. From the establishment of the permanent government presence in the Jimi with the formation of Tabibuga Patrol Post in 1956, the Maring and others, including upper-Jimi Kuma-speakers, began traveling openly and more widely. Although fear of physical attack seems to have lifted almost immediately, there is still seen to be a lingering if diminished risk of attack from enemy spirits and witches. This, coupled with continuing taboos on eating food grown in enemy territory or cooked over enemy fires, continues to inhibit direct trade with men of enemy populations.

With the data on hand, however, it is not possible to suggest the relative weight of the effects of postcontact aging and precontact hostilities in accounting for lower rates of trade among older men. The figures in table 36, nonetheless, lend broad support to the hypothesis that the government presence stimulated increasing rates of trade in the Jimi–Simbai region.

Rates of trade since 1974 have not intensified further and, indeed, seem to have declined somewhat. In the four years 1974 to 1978 a sample of twenty-four men conducted 223 transactions, or 2.3 per man per year. For the six-and-a-half years between early 1979 and mid-1985, a sample of fifteen men conducted 209 transactions, or 2.1 per man per year. The range of variation in rates by age group is moderate but shows no clear pattern, other than lower rates for older age groups. These post-1974 rates are only marginally higher than the aggregate rate to 1974, but less than rates for traders who in 1974 had spent more than half their trading lives since contact. Since the rates for the period to 1974 are depressed by lower precontact trade, the post-1974 rates may actually reflect a diminishing rate of trade in more recent years. What is noteworthy, however, is that representatives of the middle-age group in 1974 (category B in table 36), who had the highest rates of trade, continued to maintain the highest rates in succeeding periods.

Increasing trade rates and the extension of links to new communities is the work of individuals. It is therefore appropriate to discuss here factors contributing to individuals' variations from the average trading rates maintained by their age groups as a whole.[4] I confine my discussion to the early 1970s for which my trade data are richest.

The Kundagai refer to a particularly vigorous trader as *munggoi rigima yu pok wok lendo yu,* "valuables exchange man he-goes he-comes makes-thus man," or more briefly as *munggoi rigima lendo yu* or *munggoi rigima yu.* In other contexts the last term can mean a formal trade partner or friend, or simply a trader whether or not he has a formalized relationship with another. Informants identified five or six vigorous traders in Tsuwenkai, though they omitted another man aged about thirty who has conducted many more transactions than the average for his age group. Since no one keeps records of their transactions, there is no easy way of comparing performance in trade. Nonetheless, some men make proud public statements about their long trading experience and are accordingly labeled as "vigorous traders" by others, but there is no particular status attached to trading ability itself.

A man who seldom trades may be labeled *rukunemp yu munggoi namp lendo yu,* "nothing/rubbish man valuables he-does-not makes-thus man," or more simply as *munggoi namp lendo yu* or *rukunemp yu.* Informants declined to identify such persons in Tsuwenkai, even though one or two men are outstanding in their almost total lack of involvement in trade.

Both the most active and least active traders in all age groups over twenty years are in some ways atypical of their peers. The twelve Tsuwenkai big-men fall into all age groups from thirty-five to seventy-five. The two *tep yu* ("Talk men") are the sole representatives of the forty-five to fifty and seventy to seventy-five year age groups, and both are considered to be vigorous traders by themselves and others (see table 36).

Mengr yu ("Shell Men") fall into age groups between fifty and sixty-five years. Of the five *mengr yu* who are not also other types of big-men four have conducted more transactions than the average for their age groups. This is consistent with such big-men achieving their status through energy and strength. Similar qualities are required by the trader if he is to hunt to fund his trading activities and journey to other settlements in search of trade.

The last category of big-men, *bamp kunda yu* ("Fight Magic Men"), fall into the thirty-five to forty, forty to forty-five, sixty to sixty-five, and sixty-five to seventy year age groups. Only two men in the last two groups have participated significantly in ritual and sorcery associated with warfare. The oldest *bamp kunda yu* is the only member of his age group and has an annual trading rate below the average of all age groups combined. The remaining three men have conducted fewer transactions than the average for their age group. One, aged forty to forty-five, accounts for his own lack of trade by frequent illness and the fact that one of his most valuable trading partners in Nembenakump died many years ago so that he has lost contact with plume providers Up-Simbai.

There appears, then, to be a tendency for big-men who achieve status by virtue of physical strength and political acumen to engage in more trade than fellow age-group members. There is no such tendency for big-men accorded status because of ritual and magical knowledge. Indeed, it seems that they may be less likely to engage in trade. I am not aware of any personal taboos assumed by *bamp kunda yu* that might inhibit them from trading. Perhaps such men are more otherworldly than most.

All those considered to be big-men before the cessation of warfare were classed as *mengr yu* and were especially marked by the enemy for killing. Several big-men explained that this added threat to their lives inhibited them from traveling widely prior to contact and consequently that they had less opportunity to trade.

The most active traders in their age groups are all men renowned for their physical energy. Those who remain bachelors longer than their age mates seem to be particularly vigorous traders (though in all but one case, they are yet too young to have earned themselves the description of *munggoi rigima lendo yu*). The most active of all Tsuwenkai traders, with 211 remembered transactions to his credit (aged thirty-five to forty) remained a bachelor well into his thirties.

In age groups below about thirty years the least-active traders tend to be those who have spent long periods away from home: at school, or working for the mission, or on repeated periods of contract labor on coastal plantations. Such absences are both a product and consequence of acculturation and disenchantment with traditional life, a point that some made themselves.

Over the age of about thirty, less-active traders attributed the brevity of their trade histories to recurrent ill health or the pressure of local government duties for office-bearers. In addition, one man aged about thirty to thirty-five is considered to be a *yu plim*, "madman," and is not trusted to conduct trade competently. Another middle-aged man is widely feared as a witch, and it is probably for this reason that few people wish to trade with him.

Trading rates vary not only according to a man's health and energy but also in relation to social activities. In times of hostilities trading was less frequent, as the Kundagai themselves state, because of fear of ambush by enemy raiders. As ceremonies approach, trade increases as dancers acquire decorations that they can later dispose of in trade. Much of the trade that occurred during fieldwork was undoubtedly stimulated by my presence as a source of cash, but also by a desire to acquire plumes for ceremonies. A major ritual and dance in connection with preparations for the Tugumenga *konj kaiko* was planned for 1974. Before the occasion was postponed many Kundagai acquired plumes by gift, loan, and trade.

Ceremonies now occur more frequently than in the recent past. Although what will probably be the last of the Maring *konj kaiko* is in preparation in the 1980s, these prolonged ritual cycles and attendant dances are being replaced by *pati* (TP and Maring for "party") organized by several men, where people gather to dance and buy cooked pork specially prepared by sponsors. Dances at Christmas hosted by the mission and government, and to celebrate the opening of community buildings or roads, add to the occasions for which plumes are required. Immediately preceding and following a major dance, trade increases as men acquire and dispose of plumes. The added number of occasions for dances has therefore increased the rate of flow of plumes directed toward ultimate plume consumers, and of exchange goods toward primary plume suppliers.

Increasing rates of trade by age groups, together with greater contact with more distant people, should have resulted in the more rapid movement of forest products toward central-highlands consumers, and a more rapid movement of steel tools, shells, and pigs in the reverse direction.

Intensification of trade is more clearly evident if the focus of analysis is on objects, rather than the agents of trade; that is, where one considers the velocity of goods in passage or the number of times they move in a unit of time. Table 37 compares the velocity of trade for different periods expressed as the mean number of transactions per year in which selected major goods were traded. The table shows a weighted index of trading velocities for different periods in an attempt to provide a standardized measurement. This is necessary since the time periods compared are of unequal duration (see the note to the table), as are the number of active traders in each period.

The number of transactions listed in the table involving exotic and forest goods should be equal. They are not for two reasons. First, a very few transactions involve reciprocal movements of exotic goods or for-

TABLE 37. WEIGHTED ANNUAL TRADING VELOCITIES[a]

	A Pigs	Exotic Goods			D Total A, B, C	E Plumes	Forest Goods		H Total E, F, G
		B Shells	C Steel tools				F Furs.	G Casso- waries	

A. IMPORTS

Pre-1956									
Number trans.	84	95	54		233	124	9	-	133
Velocity/year	4.8	5.4	3.1		13.3	7.1	0.5	-	7.6
1956-1974									
Number trans.	363	250	65		678	457	43	4	488
Velocity/year	24.5	16.9	4.5		45.8	30.9	2.9	0.3	33.0
Change factor(%)	510	312	145		344	435	580	-	434
1974-1978									
Number trans.	75	8	3		86	60	5	-	65
Velocity/year	18.8	2.0	0.8		21.5	15.0	1.3	-	16.3
Change factor(%)	392	-270	-387		161	211	260	-	214
1979-1985									
Number trans.	84	4	1		89	56	2	3	61
Velocity/year	12.9	0.6	0.2		13.7	8.6	0.3	0.5	9.4
Change factor(%)	268	-900	-1,550		-103	121	-166	-	123

B. EXPORTS

Pre-1956									
Number trans.	41	57	38		136	190	22	13	214
Velocity/year	2.3	3.3	2.2		7.8	10.9	1.3	0.7	12.2
1956-1974									
Number trans.	172	94	51		317	532	129	31	647
Velocity/year	11.6	6.4	3.4		21.4	35.8	8.7	2.1	43.7
Change factor(%)	504	194	154		274	328	669	300	358

	1	2	3	4	5	6	7	8
1974-1978								
Number trans.	26	21	4	51	69	5	-	74
Velocity/year	6.5	5.3	1.0	12.8	17.3	1.3	-	18.5
Change factor(%)	282	160	-220	164	158	100	-	151
1979-1985								
Number trans.	13	9	3	25	66	2	2	70
Velocity/year	2.0	1.4	0.5	3.8	10.2	0.3	0.3	10.8
Change factor(%)	-115	-235	-440	-205	-106	-433	-233	-113

C. IMPORTS/EXPORTS

	1	2	3	4	5	6	7	8
Pre-1956								
Number trans.	125	92	152	369	312	22	13	347
Velocity/year	7.1	5.3	8.7	21.1	17.8	1.3	0.7	19.8
1956-1974								
Number trans.	535	116	344	995	971	129	35	1,135
Velocity/year	36.1	7.8	23.2	67.2	65.6	8.7	2.3	76.7
Change factor(%)	508	147	266	318	368	669	328	387
1974-1978								
Number trans.	101	29	7	137	129	10	-	139
Velocity/year	25.3	7.3	1.8	34.3	32.3	2.5	-	34.8
Change factor(%)	356	137	-483	162	181	192	-	175
1979-1985								
Number trans.	97	13	4	114	122	4	5	131
Velocity/year	14.9	2.0	0.6	17.5	18.8	0.6	0.8	20.2
Change factor(%)	210	-265	-1,450	-120	105	-216	114	102

[a] Represents number of transactions involving listed items, taken from tables in chapter 5. Velocity, that is, rates of transactions per annum, are calculated from average number of man-years of trade per trader operating in each period (see table 36). These averages are as follows: for pre–1956: 17.5 years per trader; for 1956–1974: 14.8 years per trader; for 1974–1978: 4 years per trader; for 1979–1985: 6.5 years per trader. Factors of change are calculated for each period using pre-1956 rates as a baseline. These are represented in percentages; a factor of 100 indicating no change, factors over 100 indicating increased rates of trade, a negative factor indicating decreased rates of trade.

est products. For example, I have a few records of pigs exchanged for shells, or axes for shells. Second, and more importantly, a variety of less commonly traded objects, and all transactions involving money, have been excluded.

The table confirms the inference drawn from table 36: that the colonial period saw an intensification of trading activities but that this increase in rates of trade was not sustained into recent times in all categories of goods. Furthermore, increases in the velocity of turnover of items has not been uniform across the range of goods, nor have factors of change in velocities of imports and exports been equal for the same item. These variations require some explanation.

Bird plumes are the most important trade good over time, in terms of the number of transactions in which they are involved and therefore in terms of annual trading rates. Pigs, moving almost exclusively in the reverse direction, are next in importance. These are the only two goods that have been imported into the 1980s at annual velocities in excess of precontact rates and that show only a marginally lower rate of export.

Imports of plumes have increased by larger factors than exports, confirming the conclusion that increasing rates of export of plumes since contact were achieved by greater imports rather than local hunting (chaps. 3 and 5).

Factors of increase in the rates of import and export of pigs were about equal in the period 1956–1974 at about five times the precontact rates. Since then, rates of export have fallen below rates of import. In the 1980s the rate of pig exports fell marginally below precontact rates, indicating greater accumulation of pigs within Tsuwenkai in this period.

The most dramatic variations in rates of trade are found in respect to shells and steel tools. The passage of steel tools through Tsuwenkai shows only a small factor of increase in annual rates of trade to 1974 but a considerable decline below precontact levels thereafter, especially for imports.

Imports of shells increased threefold and exports by almost twofold to 1974. Up to this date less shells were exported from Tsuwenkai, at diminished annual rates, than were imported. This indicates local accumulation or redistribution by means other than trade, as has been argued in preceding chapters. Although this was clearly the case for steel tools in the same period, differences between annual rates of import and export to 1974 are greater for shells, suggesting that they were involved in a much greater diversion from passage in trade. Since 1974 annual rates of import and export of shells have fallen below pre-1956 rates. But the greater rates of export indicate dispersion of shell stocks accumulated in trade in previous years.

Changing rates of trade involving money must now be considered. Although money has recently emerged as the item most commonly involved in trade (table 35), the actual annual rate of transactions involving money has declined appreciably. In the period from 1966 (when money was first used in trade) to 1974, money passed in trade at the rate of 76.1 transactions per annum. In 1974–1978 the rate dropped to 17.3, and rose slightly to 22.3 transactions per year in 1979–1985. Annual rates of export of money have always exceeded rates of import, but by a greater margin in recent times: in 1966–1974 imports of money ran at 30.5 transactions per annum against export rates of 45.6 transactions. In 1979–1985 the annual rates of trade had declined to 6.6 imports to 15.7 exports. Although the rate of trade involving money has declined considerably, I have already shown in chapter 5 that the patterns of cash flow changed markedly, while the average amount passed in each transaction also increased considerably, especially where money was exported from Tsuwenkai. Notwithstanding the decreasing rate of trade in money, the actual amounts of cash being drained out of village stocks had actually risen very considerably.

The overall picture of changes in trading rates is one of a roughly threefold increase since contact up to the mid-1970s across the range of items traded (sec. C of table 37). Thereafter there has been a general decline in annual trading rates to levels marginally below precontact levels. The continuing levels of intensified rates of trade in pigs and most forest products offset considerable declines in trade in shells and steel tools. Nonetheless, a return to a regime of annual trading rates on balance not much different from precontact rates should not be taken to mean that in the longer timeframe little has changed. In fact, there have been profound alterations in the place of the Kundagai in the wider complex of trading relations that connect them to the central highlands. These have involved increasingly dependent relations on the central highlands compounded by a massive drain of cash reserves in trade.

THE PERIPHERALIZATION OF THE KUNDAGAI

The patterns of trade that emerged in the 1930s and persist to the present were founded upon the complementarity and mutual dependence of centrally located plume consumers and peripherally dispersed plume suppliers. In the Jimi–Simbai region these peripheral communities were also consumers of shells, steel tools, and pigs which were withdrawn from the trade flow for redeployment in prestations. At the other end of trade webs, plumes and other forest products were similarly withdrawn from trade for use in decorations on ceremonial occasions and as objects of various prestations, notably bridewealth.

From the time of the first exploratory patrols into the central highlands in 1933, Europeans introduced ever-increasing volumes of shells into local economies, in exchange for produce, labor, and land (Hughes 1978; Leahy, in press). These shells included small cowries, dogwhelks, cut and uncut pearlshells (kina), besides lesser quantities of others, such as bailer shells and greensnail—the latter seemingly never greatly favored by central highlanders. In the first two decades after contact the Sinasina Simbu accumulated large stocks of shells, especially kina. As elsewhere in the highlands, abundant supplies of shells led to inflation in prestations (Hide 1981: 115 ff.; cf. Strathern 1971). From the early 1960s, however, the use of shells in Sinasina prestations diminished, and by the early 1970s Hide found shells largely absent from prestations and valuables stores (Hide 1981). Further westward, shells persisted in Simbu transactions, with the Naregu Simbu including up to thirty in kina in bridewealth into the late 1960s (Brown 1972: 91). Westward again, Heaney's (1982) data on Kuma bridewealth indicate the continuing use of kina until the late 1960s with a sharp decline thereafter. These Simbu and Kuma data suggest that large supplies of shells were available in the central highlands until at least the late 1960s. The rapid decline in the inclusion of shells in prestations indicates that large quantities of shells were available for deployment beyond the more limited geographic range of affinal and matrilateral ties. The use of steel tools in Sinasina and Kuma bridewealth payments follows a similar though less dramatic pattern to shells (Hide 1981: 131 ff.; Heaney 1982: 228).

The Jimi and other peripheral regions, already connected to the central highlands by trading networks, became the destination of excess stocks of shells and steel. Central highlanders offloaded devalued shells in exchange for forest products.

Bird plumes have long been important components of Simbu and Kuma prestations, especially bridewealth (Brown 1972; Hide 1981; Heaney 1982; Reay 1959). Significant changes in the kinds and quantities of plumes occurred in the first decades after contact. In both the

Simbu and middle-Wahgi area the Raggiana Bird of Paradise had initially been favored. This species was locally available in fallow growth, including casuarina thickets about homesteads. It was also traded in from more heavily forested areas to the south (Healey 1980). Subsequently, the long, black tailfeathers of Princess Stephanie's Astrapia and of the Black and Brown Sicklebills became most favored. These are birds of the mid- to high-altitude forest. The small patches of relict forest in the Simbu and Kuma heartland were unable to satisfy the increasing demand for plumes. Consequently trading for plumes with more heavily forested peripheral areas, including the Jimi and Simbai, intensified. The change from locally available red plumes to exotic black plumes occurred in the 1950s among the Kuma (Heaney 1982) and the mid-1960s among the Sinasina (Hide 1981). The accumulation of black plumes occurred in a context of the increasing cash wealth of the Wahgi relative to more peripheral areas. Up to the mid-1970s the number of Astrapia skins increased at almost the same rate as increases in the cash component of Kuma bridewealth (Heaney 1982: 230). The display and exchange of Astrapia plumes thus signaled superior access to and control of cash that central-Wahgi people enjoyed.

Importantly, the growing stress on exotic plumes in the central highlands overlaps the period of accumulation of shells in the Jimi. Furthermore, the replacement of red by black plumes progressed from west to east, whereas the earlier growth of shells and steel stocks and their subsequent decline progressed from east to west. The Jimi emerged as a significant source of black plumes, besides others, and a destination of shells and steel.

Needless to say, not all black plumes were necessarily acquired in exchange for shells and steel; indeed many were exchanged for pigs and more recently money, with shells and steel being given for less valuable plumes. The great variety of plumes and other valuables of comparable exchange values allowed considerable scope for substitution of other goods in different sectors of the trade network and at different times.

The importance of black plumes in the central highlands, however, has its limits. Heaney (1982: 230) remarks that from about 1975 Astrapia plumes were no longer demanded in bridewealth by Wahgi people. Marie Reay (pers. comm.) has kindly provided the following information on Kuma plume use that augments Heaney's material. The change from red to black plumes was sudden and almost complete, although Vulturine Parrot feathers remained important. (Parenthetically, I would suggest that the continuing popularity of this bird lies in its combining both favored colors. Further, as a lowland and hill-forest bird it is entirely an exotic import, unlike long black-tailed birds of paradise, which could be hunted by at least some Kuma. More than any other favored species, then, Vulturine Parrot feathers were a signal of command over wealth in trade goods, including cash, necessary for their acquisition.) By the mid-1980s Kuma plume use had fallen off considerably. Reay attributes this to a number of factors. First, everyone now has suitcases in which plumes are carefully stored. This has reduced wastage. Second, the number of plumes used in bridewealth has been much reduced. Previously, bridewealth presentations included large plaques mounted on poles, covered with money and other valuables. Numerous plumes were attached around the edges of the plaques. Recently, the Kuma have adopted the Simbu practice of "money trees"—tall bamboo poles to which money is attached. These leave no space for plumes. The only feathers included in bridewealth are the dozen or so black-tailed plumes used to decorate the bride. Finally, fundamentalist missions have had a wide influence in suppressing pig festivals. They have done this by branding them as satanic and also by persuading people to keep fewer pigs so that they do not have the capacity to hold a festival. Consequently festivals and accompanying performances by massed decorated dancers are much less frequent. The impact of these three factors has been to greatly reduce the occasions on which plumes are required and thus the number of fresh plumes needed. These changes in central-highlands circumstances help account for the greatly diminished interest in plumes by central-highlands traders visiting the Jimi in the 1980s.

As the number of plumes included in Simbu and Kuma prestations increased, so did quantities of shells and steel in Maring prestations. Inflation and changes in the composition of prestations among the Simbu, Kuma, and Maring were complementary. Around the time that shells and steel were dropping out of favor in the central highlands, they became increasingly important in Maring prestations. There have, however, been limits to the supply of these goods, beyond the control of the Maring, for as plumes became finally eclipsed by cash as bridewealth components among the Kuma, so use of shells and steel declined in Maring prestations.

When European explorers first penetrated the central highlands in 1933 they found shells to be scarce and of poor quality. They immediately saw the possibility of gaining allies and purchasing labor, food, and other services cheaply in exchange for shells. One of the recurrent problems of Jim Leahy's first exploratory patrol through the Simbu Valley to Mount Hagen was maintaining adequate supplies of shells from the coast (Leahy, in press). The practice of using shells rather than money was continued by the growing European population of colonial officials, missionaries, planters, and adventurers. As local economies were flooded with shells, the Simbu, Kuma, Melpa, and others were able to convert them, via trade, into valuable plumes that replaced devalued shells in prestations. Central highlanders were thus able to take advantage of the locally falling value of shells as objects of prestation by passing them on in trade to such areas as the Jimi, where they retained high local value. The history of early contact in the highlands consolidated the Jimi–central highlands trade networks to the perceived advantage of transactors in both areas. The Jimi and Simbai remained unvisited by Europeans, beyond a few brief forays, and totally uncontrolled for two decades after the rapid penetration of the Simbu and Wahgi Valleys. By the time colonial authority was extended to the Jimi the practice of distributing shells had been largely discontinued. This was primarily because of difficulties in maintaining high levels of supply after changes in the pearling industry, the main source of shells for distribution in the highlands (Hughes 1978). From the 1950s the supply of shells reaching the highlands was thus reduced to a trickle. Instead of paying for labor and produce in shells, Europeans working in the Jimi in the 1950s and early 1960s used salt as well as minor valuables such as beads. European contact did very little to alter the relative impoverishment of the Jimi in shells. Jimi people thus became structurally dependent upon their wealthier, centrally located neighbors for goods that had already become critical components of prestations.

With devaluation of shells in central-highlands exchange there was little incentive to retain large numbers, which were increasingly passed north to the Jimi in return for plumes. It would seem that by the late 1970s supplies of shells in the Jimi were no longer being augmented sufficiently by imports from the central highlands. This was reflected in the rather rapidly declining numbers passed in prestations. By the late 1970s shells and steel were being replaced by money in eastern-Jimi Maring prestations (Neil Maclean, pers. comm.), and by the early 1980s among the western Maring. According to my Kundagai informants, shells simply became hard to acquire in either trade or prestations.

By virtue of its earlier colonization, its large populations, benign climate, and extensive areas of relatively gentle terrain, the central highlands experienced economic development programs at an earlier stage than peripheral regions such as the Jimi. In particular, the introduction of the Highland Labour Scheme and of smallholder coffee growing led to the accumulation of new forms of wealth and increasing differentials in access to valuable resources between the central and fringing highlands. Some of this wealth was used in trade with the Jimi, especially as money from the mid-1960s. This signaled yet greater demand for forest products. As we have seen, however, the flow of money was by no means one way, and as the cash supply in the Jimi improved the amount of money channeled toward the central highlands in trade grew considerably.

The principle sources of cash for Jimi people have long been labor migration and coffee production. Recently, alluvial gold works have shown some promising returns. Both coffee production and labor migration began in the mid-1960s. Wage labor is the major source of cash inflow to Tsuwenkai. There are relatively few opportunities for employment within the valley, although by 1985 a few young men with secondary school or vocational education held clerical and service jobs with the mission. Most younger men have spent at least one two-year work contract on a coastal plantation. This work remains highly desirable among most Kundagai, even after the abolition (in the early 1970s) of the Highland Labour Scheme, which ensured basic subsistence, a savings plan, and repatriation at the expiration of the contract. Besides the increased basic rural wage a big attraction of such work, especially for young unmarried men, is the opportunity to savor new experiences and escape the dull round of village life. Older men often seek to accumulate money for a bridewealth payment or to establish a trade store. The amount of cash brought home has always been variable. To 1974 the average amount brought home at the termination of eleven contracts was K93 (range: K44 to K196). In 1978 men were bringing home K300 to K800, and in 1985 up to K3,000, but it was also not uncommon for men to return with nothing at all. These savings are usually quickly redistributed in Tsuwenkai and beyond in small gifts to kinsmen, in major prestations, the purchase of trade and luxury goods, and in gambling.

Coffee is the only source of outside cash available to most residents. Nearly all men have at least one small coffee grove planted in an abandoned garden or homestead site. Coffee was first planted in the early 1960s from seedlings obtained by trade and gift from Up-Jimi kinsmen.

Planting was not widespread until a decade later, but most plots suffer from inadequate care. Some indication of minor involvement in cash cropping is suggested by the annual income from sale of parchment coffee. Up to 1974 annual income averaged from K6 to K7 per grower. In 1978 the average income had risen to K30 per annum as later plantings came into production and the crisis in the Brazilian coffee industry pushed up prices. By 1985 the mean income per grower had slumped to K12 per annum.[5] This fall in earnings was largely due to most men's disenchantment with the productivity of coffee. Many men complained of fluctuating but generally low prices given by dealers in Tabibuga and itinerant coffee buyers at the roadhead near Kwima. They remarked that the tedium of hand processing small batches of coffee berries and carrying heavy bags over arduous footrails were considerable disincentives to production. Nonetheless, men generally allowed their wives to pick and dry coffee and sell the beans. Any earnings were regarded as the property of the women, who generally spent it on clothing or luxury foods, such as rice and tinned meat or fish.

The only other local venture of any significance for the inflow of cash from beyond the community is alluvial gold works. A single team of goldworkers operated in Tsuwenkai for most of the 1970s, but with very little success. In 1981, with assistance from the mission, several other teams were formed, under the direction of a registered *bosboi* who purchased a prospector's license and insurance coverage for his workers. Teams vary in size from two to six men. Goldworking is an intermittent enterprise, partly because of the difficulties of organizing cooperative labor on an extended basis. By 1985 few teams had earned more than about K2,000, and much of that had been redistributed in gifts and major prestations. When I enquired why teams did not devote more time to goldworking or why more teams were not formed, men stressed the backbreaking labor involved in heaving heavy boulders and shoveling gravel. The technology of goldworking is simple: a few shovels, pans, homemade sluice boxes, poles for levers, and swimming goggles to aid searching streambeds. A saleable quantity of small grains of gold is won at an enormous cost of time and labor. The perceived sheer intensity of labor involved dissuades many men from serious involvement in gold works.

The occasional sale of butchered and cooked pig to fellow residents in *konj maket* (pig markets) is an important means of redistributing money, mainly within the settlement. No one breeds pigs with the express aim of butchering them for sale, but of the sixty-six pigs killed in

Tsuwenkai in 1973–1974 part or all of twenty were cooked and sold by fourteen men. Only eleven of these pigs had been killed specially for sale, most of the rest had been killed for raiding gardens. Each pig brought an average of K18 (range K6 for only a portion of the carcass to K32 for a whole medium-sized pig). Undoubtedly such pork markets were encouraged by my own presence as purchaser and source of money for other buyers. The potential for *konj maket* to be exploited systematically by individuals as a source of cash is severely limited by the relatively low fertility of local pigs and the need to reserve stock for prestations.

When I entered the field in 1973 there were no trade stores in Tsuwenkai, although two were established within a few months. A year later five stores had been built and another was being planned. Four of these stores were in operation periodically, though their stocks usually ran out within a few days. Supplies of tinned meat and fish, rice, soap, biscuits, tobacco, and paper were bought from the Koinambe mission store and others in Tabibuga and Simbai Patrol Post. Stocks were carried by shareholders in the stores and their female kin, and sometimes by male relatives. Carriers who were not also shareholders were repaid with a small feast given by two of the store-holding groups. Each store was established by cash contributions of from three to six men, either close affines or cognates sharing a man's house. Only one store purchased a license to operate, shareholders for other stores preferring to have a trial period of operation before investing in a license. No storeholders kept written records. Only one store, established early in 1974, made a profit in the first months of operation: its major organizer claimed a profit of only K15.70 in five months. Partners in this store had already bought the roofing iron required under Council by-law, and their only outstanding expense was K6 for a license. Other stores were working at a loss or their operators' mental accounting was confused.

Four of the original five stores survived through to late 1978 and two until 1985, mainly by going into long periods of inactivity. They all had checkered fortunes, as shareholders withdrew their contributions in the course of personal disputes or when in need of money, or when principal shareholders and custodians of the till lost store money in gambling games. Customers chose which store to patronize in terms of convenient location and the range and price of the merchandise. One of the reasons several stores can survive in a small community is that they are actually in operation for only brief periods, which seldom coincide with cycles of other stores, and hence are not in direct competition for customers.

In the late 1970s many Tsuwenkai residents contributed to the establishment of a joint coffee-buying and trade-store enterprise run by a Kinimbong Kundagai big-man. The store provided the largest selection of wares in the vicinity, trucking supplies in from Simbai Patrol Post. Tsuwenkai Kundagai were proud of their association with this store, which was more a symbol of Tsuwenkai and Kinimbong solidarity than a source of income; no one received any return for their initial contribution to the establishment of the store. Within a few years the venture failed, allegedly with outstanding debts to contributors of tens of thousands of Kina.

It is hard to assess levels of income and expenditure in the present context. Although it is fairly easy to collect data on wages and income from the sale of cash crops and other commodities, there are also large and significant flows of cash in prestations and gambling. The first redistributes cash in a structured form within and beyond the settlement, the latter in an essentially erratic if, in the long run, balanced manner. The card game *laki* has gained a growing following, especially among younger men who are the principal medium for the introduction of wealth into the Jimi from wage labor. Since most serious gambling for high stakes is confined to sessions between members of different settlements, gambling is an important means of effecting a nondirectional or random redistribution of money between local groups.[6] Although large sums of money may be transferred in prestations or gambling, the amounts received by individuals tend to be relatively small.

The data on sources of cash indicate that individual cash incomes are generally low and erratic. Expenditure, however, is also low. For a modest outlay the Kundagai man is able to clothe himself and his family, provide them with occasional treats of tinned meat, fish, and rice, and purchase basic kitchen utensils. Even in 1985, nonetheless, the Kundagai had not become structurally dependent on manufactured items for survival, beyond axes and knives. Self-sufficiency was still the hallmark of the subsistence economy. Such things as kerosene lamps, blankets, and radios, considered essential basic equipment in many other parts of Papua New Guinea, were highly desirable but not owned by every household. By 1985 clothing was about the only commodity that was deemed essential and had to be purchased, although small children still went naked and some older people still dressed entirely in traditional styles. In terms of everyday survival, then, there was limited demand for money. Nonetheless, store-bought food became increasingly appropriate for certain ceremonial feasts, such as funeral celebrations. More significantly, money has become a mandatory component of most prestations and is needed to pay Council head-tax.

Although individuals may gain periodic large sums of money through wage labor, prestations, or other sources, there are, as yet, no permanently wealthy individuals in Tsuwenkai. The inevitability of economic inequality in rural communities of the Third World which Polly Hill (1986) claims as virtually a universal phenomenon has not emerged as a principle dividing Tsuwenkai into rich and poor sectors. Obligations to redistribute prestations received, to contribute to others, as well as purchases at local trade stores and gambling losses all serve to reduce an individual's savings and ensure a constant circulation of cash.

Since 1974 trade has increasingly become a context in which Kundagai cash earnings by other means are continually dissipated, so preventing the accumulation of money. The growing use of money in trade has contributed to the maintenance of the Jimi as a relatively peripheral, underdeveloped region compared to the central highlands. Until the early 1970s money flowed in roughly equal amounts in either direction. Since then most money has passed toward the central highlands, often directly to Kuma visitors, with cash inflow via trade falling far short of outflow. Inflation in the number of pigs in Maring prestations, coupled with a rise in their rates of exchange in trade (see chap. 7) has transformed central highlands–Jimi trade relations from an earlier complementarity to the dependence of the periphery on the center for access to critical resources necessary for the maintenance of social relations locally. Jimi people depended upon central highlanders for exotic valuables and more recently for supplies of pigs above the capacity of local levels of production. Although central highlanders acquired forest products from the Jimi, they were not reciprocally dependent on the Jimi for such goods since they could seek them out elsewhere on the highland fringe.

In the 1980s this growing dependence of the Jimi on a local center has become further consolidated with the decline of the trade in bird plumes. In 1985 the Kundagai remarked that it was increasingly difficult to find exchange partners Up- or Cross-Jimi who were prepared to accept plumes in trade. It was becoming common for traders from the upper Jimi and the Wahgi to demand only money in exchange for the pigs they brought. Given their continuing high demand for pigs to fund inflated prestations, the Kundagai express little option but to acquiesce to these demands for cash. The effect, however, is to drain the Jimi of its slender cash reserves, foster the accumulation of greater wealth in the central highlands, and thus contribute to the widening gap in the command of strategic resources between the central highlands and an underdeveloped periphery.

As a consequence of historical circumstances, compounded by geographic isolation that hampers local development projects, the Jimi has emerged as a region that central highlanders can exploit as a source of cash. This exploitation has occurred in the context of long-established traditional exchange systems. Relative to the Jimi the central highlands have enjoyed a long period of economic development of cash cropping and various entrepreneurial ventures, serviced by a more highly developed administrative and commercial infrastructure. Despite limitations on further development and the peasantization of the central highlands (cf. Howlett 1973), the region nonetheless appropriates surplus product, in the form of money, from the Jimi. The decline of trade in forest products and exotic shells and steel has resulted in a much simplified flow of goods. At the time of the greatest development of trade, a considerable variety of goods passed in both dominant directions. This allowed traders the opportunity to substitute a range of different goods of equivalent value. Further, given that forest goods gave a dominant structure to the trade networks and that production by hunting was under the ultimate control of individuals, Jimi traders were cushioned against exploitative extraction of surplus production.[7] By the mid-1980s, the contraction of trade to focus on the exchange of pigs for inflated sums of money meant that Kundagai traders, needing pigs to use in prestations to maintain or extend social relations, were forced to engage in cash-earning activities. They were already engaged in such activities to fund prestations and purchase desirable manufactured items, but this added burden on cash reserves involved increasing engagement in production geared to the national and international capitalist economy. The Kundagai secured their precarious position in an expanded political–economic universe primarily as petty producers of low-grade coffee and as unskilled plantation labor. Engagement in the "modern" cash sector of the national capitalist economy became a necessary precondition for maintenance of traditionally oriented trading networks, and those networks themselves a precondition for the maintenance of the traditional social order through the practice of prestations.

CONCLUSION

The trading network within which the Kundagai are enmeshed has become significantly transformed with the intrusion of the cash economy. Signs of collapse in the traditional organization of trade have, nonetheless, taken several decades to appear. Against the present decline, therefore, must be set a period of the vigorous persistence of a precapitalist trading network, and it is to this period that I turn my attention now.

The resilience, even expansion, of much New Guinea inland trade, as exemplified by the area under discussion, is in marked contrast to the fate of indigenous, precolonial trade in many parts of the world. In much of Africa, for example, a money economy weakened traditional, nonmonetized systems of exchange to the point of their collapse (see e.g., Bohannan 1959 on the Tiv; cf. Godelier 1972: 45). In providing a general medium of exchange, money brings distinct modes of exchange into connection: sumptuary or gift objects become commodities, available for purchase by those who have money, instead of for acquisition by those holding the appropriate social status. Money, therefore, may do more than threaten traditional trading systems; it may subvert the whole social and political organization, as many ethnographies have attested.

I would suggest that the trade networks dealt with here, and others in New Guinea, resisted such degenerative processes because money, like other exotic goods (mainly shells and steel), was incorporated into exchange catalogues not as a currency but as a valuable. Thus money maintains the same essential characteristics as any other valuable and may be passed along with other objects, or against them, without revealing a "price," or universal expression of value, an issue dealt with in the next chapter. As will become evident in the next two chapters, trade is not a means of generating and accumulating profit. It is, on the one hand, a means of acquiring goods for redeployment in prestations of social reproduction and, on the other hand, a powerful force in the integration of the individual into an expanded social order. Further, as I have argued elsewhere (Healey 1985*a*), prestations themselves are patterned on equivalence rather than competitive or incremental principles. There is therefore an absence of expansionary pressure on prestations which might be sustained by the proliferation of "financial" strategies (Strathern 1969) of diversifying and expanding prestations. To the extent that wealth passed in prestations tends to become dispersed generally rather than concentrated in the hands of wealthy bigmen, the development of competitive exchange is further inhibited. In turn, given the functional connection between the passage of goods in prestations and trade, there is also limited effective strain toward the intensification of production and trade.

In this context the currency potential of money is not realized in trade because there is no tendency in this direction. Trade did not become monetized because it was not a means of accumulating profit, so that the special capacity of money-as-currency to act as a store of value was denied. As a consequence, the essentially traditional organization of trade as a means of social integration and the acquisition of valuables to sustain prestations remained intact. This organization was, in fact, consolidated by the transformation of earlier patterns of trade following the introduction of new forms and sources of wealth, assimilated into existing schemes of valuables, and by the extension of colonial authority into the highlands. Notably in this regard, wage labor and other forms of outside income became incorporated into local processes of social reproduction. The cash accumulated by these pursuits is ultimately the basis of the major inflow of pigs to Tsuwenkai. Aside from the dissipation of cash in the purchase of petty consumer goods at stores, the great bulk of cash income is rapidly transformed in Maring praxis from a currency into a valuable through deployment in prestations, or by conversions in trade into pigs which in turn are passed in prestations. In this scheme, local markets and gambling serve a redistributive function (among others) rather than being symptomatic of a supposed increasing commercialization of social relations.[8] In the process of turning money directly or indirectly to account in prestations as a valuable, Maring cultural classifications of money dominate over those prevailing in the wider monetary economy, thereby inhibiting the disintegrative, transformative impact of the encapsulating political–economic order.

A further conclusion follows from this argument: that it would be wrong to regard hunting for trade as "petty commodity production" and to analyze the peripheral place of Kundagai trade in a capitalist mode of production. Certainly the Kundagai are petty producers of low-grade coffee and constitute a pool of cheap unskilled labor peripherally connected to the national and world economy. However, although I have argued that production of forest goods for trade has implications for the flow of cash by means other than trade (by cushioning the Kundagai against added pressure on their limited cash reserves), the point is that even though trade and prestations use money, these two modes of exchange are separate or disconnected from the externally oriented commercial transactions in which the Kundagai are caught up. Trade may therefore proceed independently of the penetration of modern capitalism, as long as money is not used as a currency in that sphere (cf. Healey 1985*a*).

As the preceding pages have indicated, however, there are limits to the resilience of trade to transformative pressures. Through the decline in acceptability of plumes in exchange for pigs, the Kundagai have had to employ money in a greater proportion of all transactions. In many instances their trading partners have ceased using money in indivisible quantities and have bargained vigorously over the exchange value of goods. The trade in pigs has thus become monetized. Nonetheless, to the extent that the Kundagai still produce plumes for trade and endeavor to exchange forest products for pigs, there is evidence for continuing resistance to the further monetization of trade and the threats it poses to the viability of exchange relations.

7
Exchange Rates

A consideration of rates of exchange is critical to any discussion of exchange, if only because it is through the mutual acceptance of such rates that transactions may proceed. Anthropologists have long recorded the nature and quantities of goods passed in ceremonial exchange and trade. Much of this work has resulted in the documentation of "spheres of exchange": hierarchically arranged categories within which there is relatively free convertibility of goods, but between which exchange (that is, conversions) are normatively circumscribed and institutionalized. Beyond the recognition, often repeated in ethnographies, that the goods in any one sphere are somehow of equivalent moral value, there has been little adequate attempt to discover how rates of exchange are set (cf. Sahlins 1972: 277). There are certainly a number of exceptions to this generalization, notably in the work of Strathern (1971), Salisbury (1962), and Godelier (1977) on highland ceremonial exchange and trade. The analyses of Chambri fish–sago barter by Gewertz (1983) and of Tolai market trading by Epstein (1968) and Salisbury (1970) are also important, if of less direct applicability to the Maring data, being concerned primarily with marketplace exchange and staple foodstuffs.

Although the recognition of spheres of exchange—or nexuses of activities, each associated with particular categories of goods (Salisbury 1962)—alerts one to differences in the cultural value of goods, it does not necessarily entail any understanding of the exchange values of goods (cf. Modjeska 1985: 148). Arguably, the economic and political consequences of the operation of spheres of exchange observed in Melanesia and elsewhere could only occur precisely if the institutionalized barriers between spheres are transcended. In short, there is a recurrent greater or lesser, overt or covert, subversion of the morally instituted disjunctions in the free interconvertibility of goods. I do not wish to elaborate on this argument here, which is only tangential to the present work. I merely refer to the circulation of *kula* valuables in and beyond the Trobriands: here it is possible for the individual, through a series of strategic transactions, to convert yams in one sphere of exchange to any other prize, including *kula* valuables in the theoretically insulated and highest sphere of exchange (Weiner 1976).[1]

More to the point, if one accepts the notion of generalized reciprocity in its various conceptual forms (Sahlins 1972: 194), then unrestricted conversions across categories are not only theoretically to be expected but ethnographically demonstrable. Hospitality received from a kinsman or friend may be reciprocated by bestowing the same favors. But in a generalized way—that is, not in return for any specific act of hospitality—it may be reciprocated by the presentation of a valuable, as with the gift of pigs, shells, feathers, money, and so forth among the Maring. Thus, Kundagai explain the minor prestation of a pig to a distant kinsman by saying that it is in appreciation for food and shelter received when traveling, even though in other contexts the exchange of food for valuables is inconceivable.[2]

What this example shows is that attention to spheres of exchange may tempt us to gloss over the sociological context of exchange, except at a rather general level where, for example, certain categories of goods are passed in only limited kinds of ceremonial exchange. But then, they may also be passed in mundane trade, as the Maring case illustrates. A focus on the kinds of exchange, or modes of conveyance, rather than on the goods themselves is more appropriate because it "frames" the exchange of goods and defines which confrontations of objects and transactors come within the orbit of our interest. Thus, seeking to discover what structures rates of exchange of pigs, canoes, sinnet rope, or whatever, relative to other valuables in one sphere of exchange, by examining all material transactions in which they are involved, requires the lumping together of various social acts that are not strictly comparable in important respects. Rather, one should examine the exchange of, say, pigs in specific social contexts: trade, or minor and major prestations of various kinds. This method of analysis is necessary because,

I suggest, rates of exchange in trade and prestation are not reducible to a common calculus. This is because the social and material interests in each mode of exchange differ, from an overt focus on material things in trade to one on social relationships in prestations.[3] Therefore, even if the same goods are involved (that is, exchange occurs within one sphere of exchange), the mechanisms of rate determination will not be identical, even if related. Put another way, the meanings attached to different modes of exchange by participants may be quite different.

Consonant with the ethnographic and substantive focus of this book I am not concerned with the critique or development of a general theory of exchange value. My aim is to document changes in rates over time and to discover how—if at all—rates of exchange are determined in relation to levels of supply and demand in Maring trade.

In the last chapter I showed that trade links were established from the 1950s between individuals scattered among communities already in the wider trade orbit but not in direct contact. Together with increasing rates of trade these new connections increased the rate of flow of all goods, with an attendant reduction in loss rates through age of plumes. Consequently, the number of plumes delivered to ultimate consumers must have risen, along with an accumulation of return goods among their suppliers.

There must have been some impetus to generate this increase in trading rates. The establishment of contact by upper-Jimi, Wahgi Valley, and Simbu people with the Kundagai following pacification constituted a dramatic expression on their part of greater desire for plumes and ability to acquire them. Changes in demand for plumes used in bridewealth payments among the Kuma and Sinasina Simbu have already been noted. In both cases there was a shift in emphasis from Red Bird of Paradise plumes to the long-tailed black plumes of Sicklebills and Princess Stephanie's Astrapia. The quantities of plumes included in bridewealth also increased dramatically, to decline again in the 1970s. Red plumes were primarily obtained locally, though increasingly by migrant laborers working in the Port Moresby region in the 1950s. Many of the black plumes, however, must have come from the Jimi. These changes in demand for plumes seem to have reflected inflation of bridewealth payments, at least among the Kuma, and an increased capacity to buy plumes with the proceeds of coffee sales and wage labor (cf. Heaney 1982).

As intermediate suppliers of plumes, the Kundagai maintained a high demand for plumes as items to exchange for other goods, for which they appear to have an unlimited desire. By increasing their plume exports they increased their supply of exchange items. Since these exchange goods are mostly of high durability one might suppose that their desire could eventually be satisfied and the economy saturated. I will suggest later how the Kundagai prevented this situation and maintained demand. The declining use of shells and steel in the 1980s reflects more changes in levels of supply than of desirability.

The demand—by which I mean here the capacity to acquire—of ultimate consumers for plumes, together with the demand of their suppliers for exchange items, are two necessary preconditions stimulating the increase in the volume of plumes traded. Ultimate consumers could signify their demand for plumes by increasing their supply of shells, axes, pigs, and other exchange items. To increase their exports of goods in return for plumes, consumers need an increased supply of these goods themselves. With the arrival of Europeans in the central highlands in the 1930s the highlanders could obtain shells, steel tools, and later money, directly in exchange for their land, labor, and garden produce (Hughes 1978; Salisbury 1962; Strathern 1971), "commodities" that formerly had no material valuations.[4] The influx of shells and steel was therefore sustained without a corresponding drain of valuable material resources to Europeans which in indigenous exchange systems were considered to be appropriate returns.[5] As Strathern (1971: 109) notes, the massive influx of shells among the Melpa led to inflation, although "this was delayed by the strength and elasticity of the demand for shells." Kina replaced other shells in Melpa transactions, but by the late 1960s kina themselves were being replaced by money in transactions. Stocks of kina were dispersed in redistributions between Melpa groups in moka ceremonial exchange and in trade, mainly north to the Jimi (Strathern 1971: 111 ff.). With the inflation in the numbers of kina, exchange rates for the shells dropped in the Melpa area. Apparently the Melpa offloaded shells on neighboring communities that still regarded them highly (cf. Strathern 1976: 279). By offering kina in trade at exchange rates current among their neighbors the Melpa were able to acquire return goods at a rate acceptable to their neighbors but greatly advantageous to themselves. That is, they could capitalize on the existence of two different exchange rates for the same item.

Devaluation of shells seems to have been general in the highlands, with wealthy, centrally placed groups offloading stocks on poorer neighbors.[6] In the previous chapter I noted the initial accumulation of shells after contact with Europeans in Simbu and Kuma areas, and their subsequent virtual abandonment as items of bridewealth. Among the Sinasina Simbu this decline in shell use appears to have coincided with the first major returns of cash from coffee and a major switch to using Sicklebill and Astrapia Bird of Paradise skins in prestations. Evidently most shells had passed out of the system that circulates valuables within Sinasina. Just where these shells went, however, remains unclear, although shells continued to be used in bridewealth westward among the Kuma until the late 1960s. This suggests that until at least this time considerable stocks of shells were available in the Wahgi–Simbu region for dispersion toward more distant regions. Since the western Wahgi was already saturated with shells, the Jimi, with a continuing high demand, must have been a major destination for kina.

At first sight such devaluations and consequent attempts to dump stocks elsewhere seem unremarkable. Yet, as Sahlins points out, changes in value of this order are not to be expected in tribal economies apparently not organized to respond to changes in supply and demand. In his review of "primitive trade" Sahlins (1972: 301) notes that in the universal absence of competitive, price-fixing markets, "buyers" and "sellers" are connected by their social relations, not by prices. The "diplomacy of primitive trade" makes it improper or even dangerous to demand higher exchange rates from a trading partner, or to offer lower rates than a fellow villager. Such diplomacy will tend to hold exchange rates constant; yet, in the Melanesian trade systems he examines, Sahlins finds that rates do vary in relation to both the unequal areal distribution of goods and temporal changes in supply and demand. He concludes, however, that rates tend to remain stable over short periods, adjusting only in the long term. It must be added that, as in the case of kina just cited, temporal rate changes Sahlins considers have all followed increased supply of goods effected by Europeans. Nonetheless, "if the trade is not classically constituted to absorb supply–demand pressure by price changes, the sensitivity we have observed in Melanesian exchange values remains an intriguing mystery" (Sahlins 1972: 301).

Spanning a sixty-year period, and three generations of traders, the Kundagai material provides detailed quantitative data to assess the question of changes in exchange rates over time and distance.

EXCHANGEABILITY OF ITEMS

In chapter 4 I noted that valuables of one order of use value are exchangeable for those of another. I also remarked that the hierarchy of valuables does not correspond to a ranking of the exchange values of goods. Despite the relatively free convertibility of goods, certain items would seldom if ever be exchanged by trade. The reason for this is that trade is structured to acquire goods that the trader has no or only limited ability to produce locally. Thus, for instance, kina and greensnail shells reach the Kundagai from the same directions, and I recorded no instance of their having been traded for each other.

Exchanges of shells for steel tools, pigs for shells or steel tools, or axes for bushknives have been uncommon. Where they have occurred they have frequently involved the transfer of goods in directions other than the dominant flows discussed in chapter 5—for example, exchanging shells for pigs from Up-Simbai. Such transfers were more common prior to contact than since. In part this was probably because of the scarcity of shells and steel tools in the Jimi and Simbai, so that men were prepared to seek out goods in settlements that were not the normal providers. Source areas of shells have not remained constant so that areas now importing shells from the Kundagai formerly supplied shells to them. There was therefore a period when more complex patterns of trade in shells existed.

Notwithstanding these rather few exceptions, and aside from variations in the exchange values of items which hinders their exchangeability, some other items of roughly equal value are not exchanged in trade because they are acquired from similar directions in the trade network. This situation further supports the conclusion that trade is based on ecologically and culturally specialized resource differences. The transfer of goods by ceremonial exchange and gift is not constrained by ecological or cultural differences in resources to the same degree. Although the "items" of ceremonial exchange—material goods, women, aid in warfare, and so on—are deemed to be roughly equivalent in value,[7] the same is not necessarily the same for minor prestations. As elements of generalized exchange a strict account of the value of the latter is not necessarily kept.

In trade, however, each item has a generally accepted value in relation to others, and this holds throughout most of the area through which the Kundagai trade.

All goods may be exchanged for a variety of others but, as indicated in the last chapter, there has been a decline in the number of items traded in the last two decades. Table 38 shows a matrix of the exchangeability of different items. This table, of course, does not reflect rates of exchange, merely the number of different items for which a

TABLE 38. EXCHANGEABILITY OF ITEMS

Items		1	2	3	4	5	6	7	8	9	10	11	12	13	14	15	16	17	18	19	20	21	22	23	24	25	26	27	28	29
Pig	1		x	x	x	x	x	x	x	x	x	x		x			x		x	x		x	x		x			x	x	x
Cassowary	2	x			x	x	x		x																		x		x	
Dog	3	x																											x	
Cowry/dogwhelk	4	x	x			x		x																		x	x	x	x	x
Kina	5	x	x		x				x	x	x	x	x	x	x	x	x	x	x			x	x		x	x	x	x	x	
Greensnail	6	x	x						x	x	x	x	x	x	x	x	x	x	x	x		x	x		x	x	x		x	
Stone axe	7	x			x																									
Steel tool	8	x	x			x	x			x	x	x		x	x	x	x	x	x	x	x	x	x		x		x	x	x	x
Salt	9	x				x	x		x		x			x	x	x	x		x				x							
Plumes of:																														
Buzzard[a]	10	x				x	x	x	x	x																			x	
Eagle[a]	11	x				x	x	x	x	x																				
Goura[a]	12					x	x	x	x																				x	
Papuan Lory[b]	13	x				x	x	x	x	x																				
Fairy Lory[b]	14	x				x	x	x	x																x					
Cockatoo[a]	15					x	x		x																					
Vulturine Parrot[a]	16	x				x	x	x	x	x																				
Kingfisher[b]	17					x		x	x	x																				
Hornbill[a]	18	x				x	x	x	x	x																				
Black Sicklebill	19	x				x	x		x																					
Brown Sicklebill	20								x																					
Astrapia	21	x				x	x		x																				x	x
Superb B. of P.[b]	22	x				x	x		x																x				x	
Raggiana B. of P.	23								x																				x	x
Lesser B. of P.	24	x			x	x	x		x	x																			x	x
Saxony B. of P.[b]	25	x			x	x	x		x	x																			x	x
Marsupial fur	26		x								x		x	x	x	x	x	x				x		x	x	x				
Marsupial skins	27	x			x						x		x	x	x	x	x	x				x		x	x	x				
Money	28	x	x	x	x	x	x		x											x	x	x	x	x	x	x	x	x		x
Other[c]	29	x			x				x																				x	

[a] Feathers from these birds may be divided into smaller bundles of less unit value than all feathers of single birds.
[b] Skins (or parts) of these birds may be passed in multiples of higher unit value than skin of single bird.
[c] Includes the following exchanges: pig for iron cooking pot; buzzard for store paint; Astrapia for beads; Superb Bird of Paradise for conus shell disks, live hen; Raggiana Bird of Paradise for tobacco; Lesser Bird of Paradise for drum, shovel; marsupial fur for three sets beads, two sets coffee seeds; marsupial skin for bar of soap; greensnail for orchid fiber belt, live hen; cowry/dogwhelk for drum.

good may be exchanged. It also does not indicate time periods in which exchanges were acceptable Thus, although twenty-three items are recorded as exchangeable for pigs, the actual number in any one period has varied. Figure 3 compares the exchangeability of items traded in selected periods since the introduction of money. The number of goods traded fell from twenty-one in 1965–1974 to sixteen in 1979–1985. Money was exchangeable for the greatest range of goods in both periods (all other items). Pigs are next in generality of exchange, but the range of goods for which they were exchangeable fell sharply in the later period.

In general, forest products have been exchangeable for a more limited range of other goods, and their declining exchangeability has been much less than that experienced by goods acquired from the direction of the central highlands. In the earlier period, the latter goods were exchangeable for a wider range of others (from eight to fifteen) and had greater exchangeability than forest products. These exotic goods still cluster toward the upper range of exchangeability in 1979–1985, with the exception of the disfavored kina shells, although several important trade plumes are of comparable exchangeability.

Given the strong directional flow of goods documented in chapter 5, with numerous forest products exchanged for a more limited number of exotic items from the central highlands, the pattern of restricted exchangeability of forest products relative to exotic goods is understandable. The significance of figure 3 is that it indicates that the range of acceptable exchange items for a particular good depends on its provenance in terms of a center-periphery dichotomy, not on its exchange rate. This should become clear in the following pages.

EXCHANGE RATES, PAST AND PRESENT

Quantitative analysis of detailed case material is the most satisfactory way for the ethnographer to discover exchange rates, although this will not exhaust the possibilities for understanding. Contemporary exchange rates can ideally be examined through the observation of transactions, but past rates can only be reconstructed from informants' testimony. There have been few attempts to investigate changes in exchange rates over time in Melanesia (see e.g., Harding 1967; Salisbury 1962; 1970; Strathern 1971; 106 ff.). Harding determined former exchange rates from interviews and early published reports, but he remarks that his informants could seldom remember the details of spe-

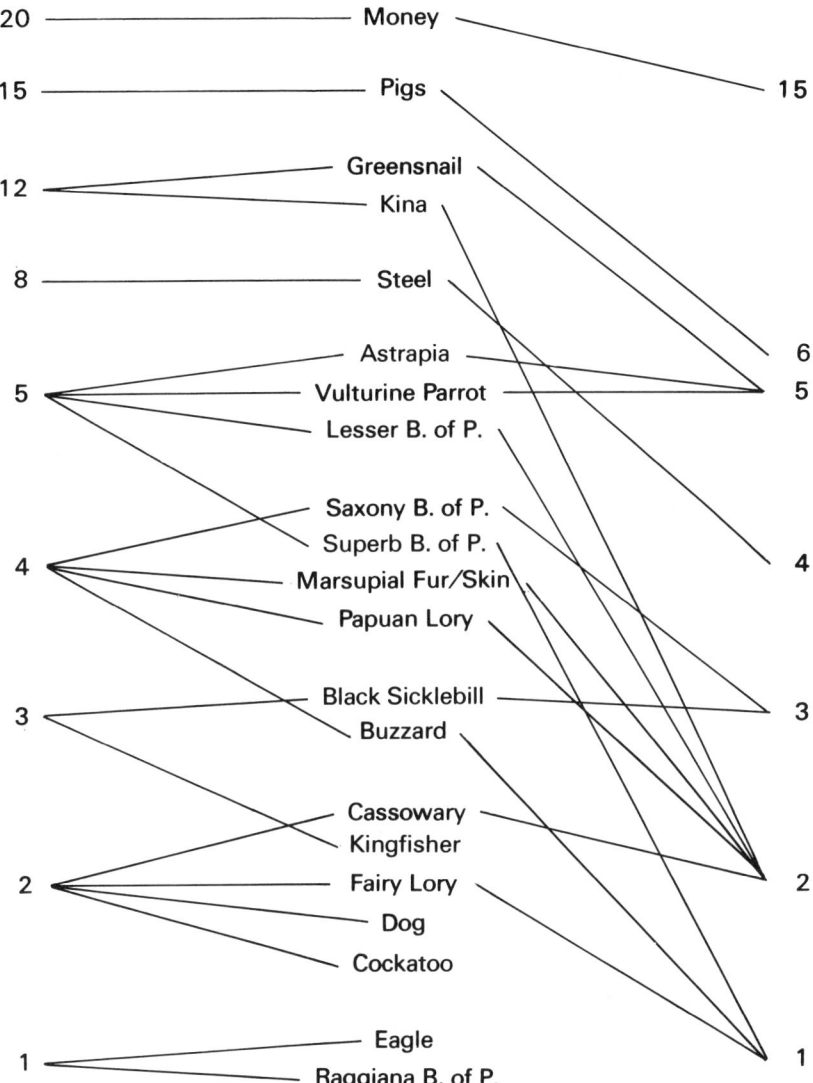

Figure 3. Exchangeability of Trade Goods, 1965–1974, 1979–1985

cific transactions undertaken years earlier. Salisbury's (1970) analysis of long- and short-term changes in Tolai market trade has a more substantial data base, drawing on published accounts of earlier times spanning almost a century and on exhaustive surveys of markets during his own fieldwork. My own data indicate that informants' generalized statements of earlier exchange rates are often at variance with actual rates determined from case material. I therefore base my discussion on actual cases of individual transactions. Supporting data for selected items are given in table 41.

Having referred several times to existing analyses of exchange rates in marketplace trade I should clarify why I consider this literature of limited direct applicability to the present case. This is the more necessary, given Modjeska's (1985) recent argument, contra Sahlins (1972), that "primitive" marketplace and nonmarketplace trade are directly comparable in their essentially confrontational, bargaining character. Modjeska argues against Sahlins's notion of the fair-dealing "diplomacy of primitive trade" in Melanesia. His evidence for explicit bargaining in nonmarket trade is limited, however, and is certainly not supported by the Maring data, as should become clear in the course of this chapter and the next.

A precise statement of the exchange rates of different goods is complicated by the fact that most items may be valued differentially according to their size or quality, whereas others can be divided or multiplied. For instance, most pigs are traded as piglets. On occasion adult pigs are traded and formerly, though rarely, even pregnant sows. In the 1980s Minj–Wahgi traders began bringing well-grown animals into the Jimi by truck. The exchange rate for larger pigs is now greater than for small pigs, though this was not always the case. The size and quality of shells, stone, and steel tools does not appear to be considered often in determining exchange rates, although small greensnail and kina shells or broken fragments command lesser rates. Cowries and dogwhelks, by contrast, allowed for multiplication and division. Ropes of these small shells of different lengths enjoyed different exchange rates. Ropes were measured roughly in units of arm-lengths and had the advantage of being easily divisible or multipliable depending on the appropriate exchange rate of a desired item. I recorded very few cases where other shells or steel tools were exchanged in multiple numbers; the great bulk of goods coming from the direction of the central highlands have always been transacted as single items.

Many plumes are transferred as single skins. Some, however, consist of bundles of loose feathers of certain species, such as Eagle, Hornbill, Cockatoo, and so forth. More highly valued bundles usually contain all flight feathers (the longer, stiffer feathers of wings and tail) from a single specimen, but smaller bundles of lesser value can be made up easily. Other plumes, notably whole skins of certain parrots, the Kingfisher, and the Superb and Saxony Birds of Paradise, may be traded singly as items of rather low value, or in multiples at exchange rates usually proportional to the number of skins making up a unit. Plumes subject to exchange rate variation in these ways are indicated in table 38. Marsupial skins may be similarly divided, by cutting into strips, and loose fur made into bundles of varying size.

The quality of feathers can vary widely. Lesser Bird of Paradise plumes fade rapidly, others retain the intensity of their colors for longer, but all become bedraggled with age. Ornamental plumes are sometimes damaged when a bird is shot. These may be in poor condition on the living bird also—for instance, shortly before the annual molt. Such defects may prompt a trader to lower the exchange rate he is prepared to receive for plumes. The Kundagai say that traders from the upper Jimi are more demanding of high quality than they were formerly. In view of the increasing difficulty of exporting plumes of lower quality to these traders it is probable that such plumes seldom reach areas of ultimate consumption. However, since they are generally accepted in nearby settlements by related and unrelated partners, of both long-term and transitory standing, lower-quality feathers may be important in replacing lost and damaged stocks in the middle Jimi, thus releasing high-quality ones for export to the upper Jimi and the Simbu and Wahgi areas.

Bearing in mind the size, quality, or quantity of items, each good has a commonly recognized range of exchange rates. All the more commonly traded goods have been exchanged for cash since 1966. Table 39 compares cash values of such goods for three time periods since the introduction of money. In most cases, modal values approximate means, suggesting considerable stability in rates of exchange in the short term, even given money's capacity to express subtle differences in evaluation. In part this is further indication of money's place in trade as a valuable rather than as currency. Extreme variations in value range for marsupial skins and some feathers relate to transactions involving small amounts of feathers and skins to the remains of whole animals. Notwithstanding the generally isostatic relation between mean and modal values there has been a general trend of rising cash values. Specification

TABLE 39. MONETARY VALUES OF TRADE GOODS, 1965–1985, IN KINA

Item	1965-1974 Mean	Mode	Range	No. cases[a]	1974-1978 Mean	Mode	Range	No. cases[a]	1979-1985 Mean	Mode	Range	No. cases[a]
Kina	1.39	1.00	1-3	35								
Greensnail	1.71	2.00	1-5	48	2.00	2.00		1	4.00	4.00		1
Steel tools	3.38	2.00	2-10	8					10.00	10.00		2
Pigs	10.30	10.00	2-20	119	39.81	20.00	10-110	31	59.06	50.00	10-120	64
Dogs	9.29	10.00	8-10	7								
Cassowaries	32.50	20.00	20-50	8					100.00	100.00		2
Buzzard	3.82	3.50	.90-8	5					10.67	10.00	10-14	6
Papuan Lory[b]	1.67	2.00	.40-2	30					2.60	2.00	2-5	5
Fairy Lory[b]	0.44	0.40	.40-.50	9	1.43	1.43		7	1.8	1.66	1.66-2.40	17
Cockatoo	1.00	1.00	-	4								
Vulturine Parrot	10.00	10.00	4-20	17	10.22	10.00	4-14	9	10.36	10.00	10-12	11
Kingfisher[b]	1.70	2.00	.40-3.50	101								
Brown Sicklebill	2.00	2.00	-	1	10.00	10.00		1				
Black Sicklebill	25.00	20.00	10-60	6	10.00	10.00		1	72.22	100.00	20-100	9
Astrapia	11.25	10.00	2-20	16	10.67	10.00	4-22	6	12.73	10.00	10-20	11
Superb B. of P.	2.07	2.00	1-10	27	2.00	2.00		4	4.00	4.00	2-6	6
Raggiana B. of P.	2.25	2.00	2-3	8								
Lesser B. of P.	2.42	2.00	1-10	139	5.13	4.00	.50-10	12	8.40	10.00	2-20	10
Saxony B. of P.[b]	3.00	2.00	.50-10	29	6.00		2-10	2	7.75	10.00	3-10	8
Marsupial fur	1.35	1.00	.40-2	40	2.00	2.00	1-3	6				
Marsupial skin	2.20	2.00	.10-10	23	5.71		1-12	7	35.00		10-60	2

[a] See text for discussion of what constitutes an instance of rate determination.
[b] Pro-rata rate where multiple skins exchanged for sum of money.

of change is difficult for many items because of the small number of records for the post-1974 periods. For goods with larger numbers of records the magnitude of changing values is highly variable, being greatest for pigs and least for plumes of the Astrapia and Vulturine Parrot. The minimal rising value of the latter is notable. These three goods are among the most frequently traded objects throughout the periods being considered here, though most exchanges until the 1980s did not involve cash.

This list is of limited utility in further discussion on rates of exchange since, as argued earlier, it is quite misleading to translate non-monetary values of exchanges into cash equivalents in order to arrive at a standard for comparison. As will become clear, rates of exchange of different items do not form a consistent system with complete transitivity of rates. This table, then, cannot be used to construct a scale of absolute value. Exchange value is obviously relational, and also contextual, so that the production of a single scale of value becomes an exercise in reification. Money is exchangeable for all trade goods but does not represent a unitary scale of relative value. It is not possible, for example, to express the value in 1974 of, say, the Saxony Bird of Paradise as equivalent to one-fifth of a pig because the modal value of the plume was K2 against the modal value of K10 for a pig. This is because three Saxony skins were commonly accepted as fair exchange for a pig, despite the descrepant values of the two goods when expressed in monetary terms. Money, then, does not constitute a general medium of exchange in the sense of representing an absolute measure of value. This lack of transitivity of values across a range of acceptable exchanges means that relative values of goods, and changes in values, cannot be assessed in simple monetary terms but must be subject to less precise evaluations. Given these reservations, some notion of broad categories of goods, hierarchically arranged and enjoying more or less equivalent rates of exchange, can be discerned, as should already be evident from chapter 5. Table 40 shows such arrangements for periods prior to and after contact.

It is most convenient to discuss exchange rates in relation to major imports obtained from regions closer to ultimate plume consumers, since these are exchangeable for the greatest variety of goods produced locally and imported from the periphery. Supporting data for the following analysis are presented in table 41, which shows the frequency of exchanges involving reciprocal movements of selected items, expressed as a proportion of all exchanges involving a particular good.

TABLE 40. HIERARCHIES OF EXCHANGE VALUE, 1940 AND POST-1970

Note: Each level embraces a range of values, and firm boundaries cannot be defined. The hierarchies are based upon informants' opinions and case material of rough equivalence of exchange items.

A. ABOUT 1940

Level 1: Pigs; dogs; cassowaries; kina; greensnail; long cowry/dogwhelk ropes and headbands; steel tools; large stone axes; salt packs; plumes/skins of Black Sicklebill, Astrapia, Vulturine Parrot, 3-4 Saxony Bird of Paradise, 4-5 Papuan Lory, 5-10 Fairy Lory; whole marsupial skins.
2: Short cowry/dogwhelk ropes and headbands; small stone axes; plumes/ skins of Long-tailed Buzzard, Harpy Eagle, Hornbill, Papuan Lory, Cockatoo, Goura Pigeon, Lesser Bird of Paradise, Superb Bird of Paradise, Saxony Bird of Paradise.
3: Other decorative items.

B. POST-1970

Level 1: K10+; pigs; dogs; cassowaries; plumes/skins of Black Sicklebill, Astrapia, Vulturine Parrot, 3-4 Saxony Bird of Paradise, 3-5 Superb Bird of Paradise, 4-5 Papuan Lory, 6 Kingfisher; whole marsupial skins; *glong* dancing wig with *mimola* beetles.
2: K3-8; greensnail shell; plumes/skins of Buzzard, Eagle, part Vulturine Parrot, 2-3 Saxony Bird of Paradise, 4 Kingfisher, Hornbill, much Cockatoo, Brown Sicklebill.
3: K1-2; kina shells; steel tools; single skins of Lesser Bird of Paradise, Raggiana Bird of Paradise, Papuan Lory, Fairy Lory, Kingfisher, Superb Bird of Paradise, Saxony Bird of Paradise, smaller collections of Buzzard, Eagle, Cockatoo, Vulturine Parrot feathers; marsupial fur and small strips of skin.
4: K0-1; other minor decorative plumes, shells, orchid fiber belts, tobacco, etc.

The data are arranged in the four time periods employed in other tables, although data relating to pre-1974 were initially arranged in five-year periods where dates could be estimated. It is important to stress that the table is not based on numbers of objects in transactions but on instances of rate determination. These instances are considerably fewer than the number of transactions, for where an object is passed in more than one transaction at the same rate of exchange, as is common when the Kundagai act as intermediaries between other trade partners (see chap. 8), I have treated this as a single instance of rate determination.

An examination of rates of exchange through time is made difficult by the fact that the number and identity of trade goods has changed. In particular, money has emerged as the single-most commonly employed exchange item for most recently traded goods. The number of goods traded from the mid-1950s to the mid-1970s exceeded that

TABLE 41. FREQUENCY OF EXCHANGE, BY ITEM

Exchange item given for:	Pre-1956 X̄*	%	1956-1974 X̄*	%	1974-1979 X̄*	%	1979-1985 X̄*	%
A. PIGS								
Money (K)			10.30	27.0	39.31	36.9	59.06	69.1
Cassowary		2.1		4.5				1.1
Dog				0.7				
Cowry/dogwhelk		5.3						
Kina	4.3			0.5				
Greensnail		4.3		0.9		1.2		
Stone axe		3.2						
Steel tool		2.1		0.2				
Salt		7.4		0.2				
Plumes: Total		65.9		63.1		59.5		21.3
Buzzard		2.1		0.2				
Eagle				0.5				
Papuan Lory	7.5	2.1	5.4	1.8	5.5	2.4		
Fairy Lory	6.0	1.1			10.0	1.2		
Vulturine Parrot		23.4		32.0		29.8		8.5
Kingfisher			6.6	1.6	10.0	1.2		
Hornbill		3.2		0.5				
Black Sicklebill		5.3		3.0		8.3		2.1
Astrapia		11.7		10.5		9.5	1.6	6.4
Superb B. of P.			3.5	0.9				
Lesser B. of P.		9.6		5.5		1.2		
Saxony B. of P.	3.4	7.4	3.7	6.6	2.8	5.9	3.8	4.3
Marsupial skin		5.3		2.7		1.2		
Mimola						1.2		
Other				0.2[a]				8.5[b]
Total number of rate determinations:		94		440		84		94

[a] One saucepan.
[b] One exchange each for 2 Saxony plumes + 4 Kingfisher skins; 1 Vulturine Parrot + 1 Superb B. of P.; 1 Vulturine Parrot + K60; 1 dancing wig + 6 packs beetle shards + K20; 3 exchanges for 1 Astrapia + K10; 2 exchanges for 1 Vulturine Parrot + K10.

Exchange item given for:	Pre-1956 X̄	%	1956-1974 X̄	%	1974-1979 X̄	%	1979-1985 X̄	%
B. COWRY/DOGWHELK								
Pig		10.2						
Cassowary		6.1						
Greensnail		2.0						
Stone axe		8.2						
Salt		4.1		8.3				
Plumes: Total		63.0		58.3				
Buzzard		2.0						
Eagle		2.0						
Goura								100.0
Papuan Lory	5.5	8.2	2.5	16.7				
Fairy Lory	5.0	6.1						
Cockatoo		2.0						
Vulturine Parrot		4.1						

TABLE 41. FREQUENCY OF EXCHANGE, BY ITEM (continued)

Exchange item given for:	Pre-1956 X̄	Pre-1956 %	1956-1974 X̄	1956-1974 %	1975-1978 X̄	1975-1978 %	1979-1985 X̄	1979-1985 %
Kingfisher			5.0	8.3				
Hornbill		2.0						
Astrapia		6.1						
Superb B. of P.		16.3		25.0				
Lesser B. of P.		10.2		8.3				
Blue B. of P.		2.0						
Saxony B. of P.		2.0						
Marsupial fur/skin		4.1		33.4				
Other (drum)		2.0						
Total number of rate determinations:		46		12				1
C. KINA								
Money (K)			1.39	27.6				
Pig		9.8		1.6				
Cassowary		4.9						
Steel tool				0.8				
Salt		2.4						
Plumes: Total		73.0		51.2				
Buzzard		2.4		2.4				
Eagle				0.8				
Goura				0.8				
Papuan Lory	3.0	2.4	3.4	3.9				
Fairy Lory	5.0	2.4	5.0	0.8				
Cockatoo				0.8				
Vulturine Parrot		22.0		4.7		100.0		
Hornbill		2.4		0.8				
Black Sicklebill		12.2		1.6				
Astrapia		7.3		5.5				50.0
Superb B. of P.	2.0	4.9		7.1				
Lesser B. of P.		14.6		11.8				
Saxony B. of P.		2.4	2.5	10.2			3.0	50.0
Marsupial fur/skin		9.8		18.9				
Total number of rate determinations:		41		127		1		2
D. GREENSNAIL								
Money (K)			1.71	27.6	2.00	3.4	4.0	10.0
Pig		8.2		2.3		3.4		
Cassowary		4.1						
Cowry/dogwhelk		2.0						
Steel tool		2.0						
Salt		8.2						
Plumes: Total		69.3		58.1		86.2		90.0
Buzzard		4.1		0.6				
Eagle				0.6				
Goura		4.1						
Papuan Lory	5.0	2.0	5.7	4.0				
Fairy Lory			5.0	0.6				
Cockatoo				0.6				
Vulturine Parrot		14.3		20.1		34.5		20.0
Kingfisher			2.6	2.3				
Hornbill		2.0						
Black Sicklebill		8.2						10.0

TABLE 41. FREQUENCY OF EXCHANGE, BY ITEM (continued)

Exchange item given for:	Pre-1956 X̄	Pre-1956 %	1956-1974 X̄	1956-1974 %	1974-1978 X̄	1974-1978 %	1979-1985 X̄	1979-1985 %
Astrapia		12.2		5.2		6.9		20.0
Superb B. of P.				5.2		6.9		
Lesser B. of P.		16.3		14.9		27.6		
Saxony B. of P.	3.0	6.1	2.3	4.0		10.3	3.0	40.0
Marsupial fur/skin		6.1		10.9		3.4		
Mimola						3.4		
Other				1.1[a]				
Total number of rate determinations:		49		174		29		10

[a] One for hen; one for orchid-fiber belt.

Exchange item given for:	Pre-1956 X̄	Pre-1956 %	1956-1974 X̄	1956-1974 %	1975-1978 X̄	1975-1978 %	1979-1985 X̄	1979-1985 %
E. STEEL TOOLS								
Money (K)			3.38	9.0			10.00	28.6
Cassowary		4.5						
Kina				1.1				
Greensnail		1.1						
Steel (knife for axe)		1.1						
Salt		1.1		2.3				
Plumes: Total		84.1		86.4		100.0		71.4
Buzzard		3.4		2.3				
Goura		2.3		1.1				
Papuan Lory			5.0	1.1				
Fairy Lory	7.9	10.2	8.2	5.6				
Cockatoo		1.1		1.1		12.5		
Vulturine Parrot		12.5		7.9				42.9
Kingfisher						12.5		
Hornbill		3.4		1.1				
Black Sicklebill		2.3		4.5				
Brown Sicklebill				1.1				
Astrapia		10.2		5.6				14.3
Superb B. of P.		6.8		21.3		25.0		
Lesser B. of P.		18.2		27.0		37.5		14.3
Saxony B. of P.	1.8	13.6		6.7		12.5		
Marsupial fur/skin		4.5						
Total number of rate determinations:		88		89		8		7
F. VULTURINE PARROT								
Money (K)			10.00	8.3	10.22	20.0	10.36	45.8
Pig		43.1		68.4		55.6		29.2
Cowry/dogwhelk		3.9						
Kina		17.6		2.9		2.2		
Greensnail		13.7		17.0		22.2		8.3
Steel tool		21.6		3.4				8.3
Papuan Lory							8.5	8.3

TABLE 41. FREQUENCY OF EXCHANGE, BY ITEM (continued)

Exchange item given for:	Pre-1956 $\bar{X}$	%	1956-1974 $\bar{X}$	%	1974-1978 $\bar{X}$	%	1979-1985 $\bar{X}$	%
G. PRINCESS STEPHANIE'S ASTRAPIA								
Money (K)			11.25	18.8	10.67	33.3	12.73	55.0
Pig		34.4		54.1		44.4	(1.6)	25.0
Cowry/dogwhelk		9.4						
Kina		9.4		8.2				5.0
Greensnail		18.8		10.6		11.1		10.0
Steel tool		28.1		5.9				5.0
Papuan Lory					5.0	11.1		
Lesser B. of P.				2.4				
Total number of rate determinations:		32		85		18		20
H. SUPERB BIRD OF PARADISE								
Money (K)			2.07	37.5	2.00	40.0	4.00	100.0
Pig			(3.5)	5.6				
Cowry/dogwhelk		44.4		4.2				
Kina	(2.0)	11.1		12.5				
Greensnail				12.5		20.0		
Stone axe		5.6						
Steel tool		33.3		26.4		20.0		
Marsupial skin						10.0		
Other		5.6[a]		1.4[b]		10.0[c]		
Total number of rate determinations:		18		72		10		6

[a] One for conus shell.
[b] One for hen.
[c] One for axe + K2.

Exchange item given for:	Pre-1956 $\bar{X}$	%	1956-1974 $\bar{X}$	%	1975-1978 $\bar{X}$	%	1979-1985 $\bar{X}$	%
I. LESSER BIRD OF PARADISE								
Money (K)			2.42	60.2	5.13	50.0	8.40	90.9
Pig		16.7		10.4		4.2		
Cowry/dogwhelk		9.3		0.4				
Kina		11.1		6.5				
Greensnail		14.8		11.2		33.3		
Steel tool		29.6				12.5		9.1
Salt		16.7						
Astrapia				0.4				
Other		1.8[a]		0.4[b]				
Total number of rate determinations:		54		231		24		11

[a] One for drum.
[b] One for shovel.

TABLE 41. FREQUENCY OF EXCHANGE, BY ITEM (continued)

Exchange item given for:	Pre-1956 X̄	Pre-1956 %	1956-1974 X̄	1956-1974 %	1975-1978 X̄	1975-1978 %	1979-1985 X̄	1979-1985 %
J. KING OF SAXONY BIRD OF PARADISE								
Money (K)			3.00	27.6	6.00	18.2	13.50	47.1
Pig	(3.4)	25.0	(3.7)	38.1	(2.8)	45.5	(3.8)	23.5
Cowry/dogwhelk		3.6						
Kina		3.6	(2.5)	17.1			(3.0)	5.9
Greensnail	(3.0)	10.7	(2.3)	9.2		27.3	(3.0)	23.5
Stone axe	(1.5)	7.1						
Steel tool	(1.7)	46.4		7.9		9.1		
Salt		3.6						
Total number of rate determinations:		28		76		11		17

*X̄ = mean number of items given in exchange for a single item in each section listed. No entry indicates exchange at one-for-one ratio. Figures in parentheses indicate the number of bird skins etc. given in exchange for single items listed in left-hand column.

traded prior to contact but declined thereafter. Comparison of pre- and postcontact exchange rates is difficult because neither investigator nor informant can assess the comparative quality of particular plumes, nor the quantities or sizes of feather collections, skins, fur bundles, salt packs, stone blades, or live cassowaries.

Items seem to have dropped out of trade usage not so much because their exchange rates depreciated or became prohibitively inflated, but because fashions changed and they became no longer desirable objects. Cowries and dogwhelks are a good example, having been widely used in the past. I can find no clear indication that rates of exchange for these goods altered over time. Rather, kina and greensnail came to be deemed more attractive. People ceased to desire the smaller shells, rather than seeking them but at lower exchange rates. By the 1960s cowries and dogwhelks were very seldom traded, although a single transaction in dogwhelks, conducted by a traditionalist, occurred in the 1980s.

The notion of fashion change, of course, is no final answer, for one must account for fashion itself. This surely cannot be explained in economic terms alone. Nonetheless, considerations of utility may have had some bearing on the growing disfavor of cowries and dogwhelks. Older men pointed out that through the disintegration of bark-cloth and string bindings of headbands and ropes the small shells were often lost. Although larger kina and greensnail are sometimes broken, they are seldom lost. Such greater durability has more than simply utilitarian benefits, however. The appearance of permanence has, I believe, an aesthetic appeal also, in a world where other of man's things are given to decay. Kina and greensnail combine this characteristic with another, hitherto confined to the most impermanent of all valuables—plumes—and that is irridescence and brightness.[8] The new shells, then, presented a merging of aesthetic qualities that were formerly manifested in quite different objects: durable but dull, bright but ephemeral. Further, large shells had the appeal of novelty. The same argument may apply to the replacement of stone tools by steel. After all, there is no necessary reason why the undoubted utility of steel work tools should lead to the eclipse of stone in prestations.

Although there was no apparent devaluation of cowries and dogwhelks before their abandonment, exchange rates of kina, greensnail, steel tools, and pigs have altered over time. Formerly, these goods were traded at a wider range of exchange rates than at present. For instance, single shells or steel tools were obtainable in exchange for cassowaries and pigs, but rarely so since contact. The exchange of pigs for shells or steel was rather uncommon, largely because they were usually obtained from the same direction. Pigs, however, have always been an acceptable exchange item for cassowaries. Since contact, money has also become an important return for cassowaries, and up to 1974 their average monetary value rose by about K6. The corresponding rise in the value of pigs was only about K2, with a subsequent sharp increase. Since pigs and cassowaries have always been acceptable in exchange for each other, but shells and steel tools are no longer given for these animals, it follows that the exchange rates of shells and steel have depreciated in relation to pigs and cassowaries but that there has been no corresponding change in the exchange rates of pigs or cassowaries in relation to each other.

The value of shells and steel expressed in yet other goods has also dropped. In the early 1970s they tended to be exchanged more often for plumes of lower value, such as single skins of the Superb Bird of Paradise, than in the past, and were less frequently given for more valuable plumes, such as Astrapia. From the mid-1970s trade in kina became negligible. Greensnail, however, remained an important trade item through the 1970s, though of declining significance thereafter (see e.g., tables 35 and 37). In these later periods greensnail was traded at higher cash values, and also in exchange for more valuable plumes, such as of the Vulturine Parrot. Since, as I shall argue below, the value of such plumes has not dropped relative to other goods, this represents a rising value of greensnail in terms of traditional trade goods over the last decade. There was, then, a decline in the value of shells from the 1950s into the mid-1970s, with a subsequent rise in value. The same analysis may apply to changing values of steel tools since the mid-1970s, although small numbers traded preclude any confident conclusions.

Against a fall in the value of shells and steel tools in terms of traditional trade goods into the 1970s is to be set a slight increase in their monetary values. Between about 1965 and 1974 the average cash value of kina rose by eighty-three Toea (cents) and of greensnail by seventeen Toea. Steel tools also rose a few Toea in value, but the small number of cases makes estimation difficult. Since 1974, cash values of greensnail and steel tools rose further but, again, small numbers of cases do not support more detailed analysis. Pigs and cassowaries are the only other goods that experienced similar increases in monetary value prior to the mid- to late 1970s. The mean and modal cash values of shells in 1974 remained, nonetheless, below costs at original wholesale sources. Since the mid-1960s contract laborers have purchased small numbers of shells from stores, and steel tools are also bought from trade stores in the Jimi and Simbai. Traders only rarely demand a higher exchange rate than that applied when they first acquired a particular item, since trade is not engaged in for the purpose of making a material profit. Taking into consideration any reduction in value of a good caused by wear and tear, a man expects to break even in a series of exchanges involving a particular item, receiving something of the same value as that he originally gave.

In the light of these expectations we may explain the rise in the average monetary value of shells and steel as follows. Where a man buys a shell for, say K1 from an Up-Jimi man, he will set its minimum resale price at the same amount.[9] Where he has paid more for a shell or steel tool from a store he will also try to resell it for the higher amount. With the more frequent purchase of shells and steel from stores charging higher prices, the range of cash values remains much the same, but the modal value tends to cluster in the upper part of the range of values, giving an increased mean cash value. Rising average cash values of shells and steel, therefore, do not reflect changes in supply and demand but are the result of the realized expectations of individuals to receive at least the same cash return for goods as they originally paid out for them.

Between 1965 and 1974 the minimum recorded cash value of pigs rose from K2 (two cases) to K4 (one case), and the maximum from K16 (one case) to K20 (six cases). Since 1974 the minimum values and range of cash values of pigs rose considerably, as did average cash values. Figure 4 provides a representation of these rising values. Although it appears that the range of values has expanded considerably, it must be remembered that since the late 1970s larger pigs, brought into the Jimi by truck, have become available, and that bigger beasts command higher cash values. Thus, although a rise in pig values is clearly evident, this is, perhaps, better represented by the minimum values of very small piglets, and by modal values that cluster in the lower half of the range of values with the exception of 1978–1985, when a bimodal distribution in values is evident. There is also evidence for a slight increase in values in terms of traditional exchange goods. If transactions involving money are omitted from the figures for exchange rates of pigs (table 41), then the frequency of exchanges for the eight goods most commonly given in exchange for pigs over time (out of twenty-three items ever given) is as follows (table 42).

These data indicate a clear decline in the exchange of pigs for Lesser Bird of Paradise plumes and marsupial furs. These, together with skins of the Papuan Lory, were no longer being traded for pigs by 1985. The frequency of other exchanges has fluctuated widely. Exchanges of pigs for Astrapia and Saxony plumes have shown a generally rising frequency. The Vulturine Parrot has been the single most frequently accepted exchange item for pigs (other than money since the mid-1970s), although the amplitude of variation in its frequency in exchange has also been greatest. Interestingly, however, changing frequency in exchange of pigs for Vulturine Parrot feathers is closely mirrored by changes in the frequency of exchange for "Other" goods—mainly various other plumes, as well as shells, steel or stone tools, and salt. This suggests that the desire of pig traders for Vulturine plumes is independent of their willingness to accept other major plumes. Both the Lesser Bird of Paradise and marsupial skins were commonly exchanged for shells and steel into the 1970s. Plumes of the higher-value Vulturine Parrot and Astrapia were, in the 1970s, more commonly given for pigs than in the past but, in general, less commonly exchanged for shells and steel than formerly. Although of relatively low value, Saxony plumes

Exchange Rates 293

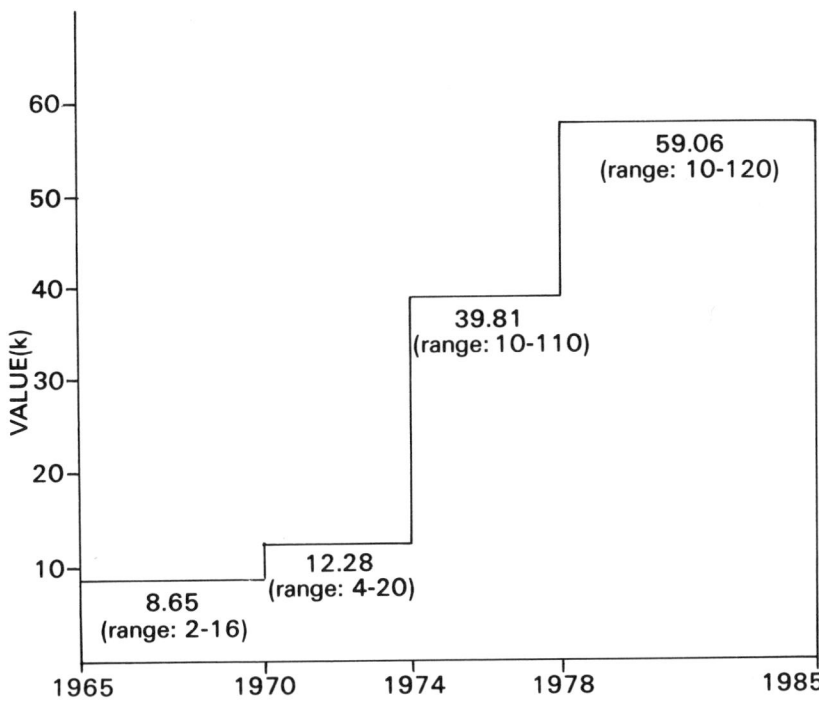

Figure 4. Changing Cash Values of Pigs, 1965–1985

are more often exchanged for pigs than before, but the average number of skins given for each pig has risen only marginally from 3.4 before contact to 3.8 by 1985. The most dramatic increases in the frequency of exchanges to the mid-1970s occurred with live cassowaries and the feathers and skins of the Vulturine Parrot and the Astrapia. These are among the most valuable forest products.

If goods that are no longer traded (salt, stone, cowries, and dog-whelks) are excluded from the "Other" category in the table, then the frequency of exchanges prior to 1956 involving the goods listed would be slightly higher. This would reduce the apparently increased frequency of exchanges of pigs for cassowaries and Vulturine Parrot, Astrapia, and Saxony plumes, but would increase the apparent reduction in the frequency of exchanges of pigs for Lesser Bird of Paradise and marsupial skins.

Up until the mid-1970s the values of most forest products remained stable. Since then, only cassowaries and the Lesser and Saxony Birds of Paradise have increased appreciably in value. Changes in exchange

TABLE 42. CHANGES IN FREQUENCY OF EXCHANGEABILITY OF SELECTED GOODS FOR PIGS[a]

Item	Pre 1956 No. cases	%	1956-74 No. cases	%	1974-78 No. cases	%	1979-85 No. cases	%
Cassowary	2	2.1	20	6.2			1	3.4
Plumes of:								
Papuan Lory	2	2.1	8	2.5	2	3.8		
Vulturine Parrot	22	23.4	141	43.9	25	47.2	8	27.6
Black Sicklebill	5	5.3	13	4.0	7	13.2	2	6.9
Astrapia	11	11.7	46	14.3	8	15.1	6	20.7
Lesser B. of P.	9	9.6	24	7.5	1	1.9		
Saxony B. of P.	7	7.4	29	9.0	5	9.4	4	13.8
Marsupial skins	5	5.3	12	3.7	1	1.9		
Other[b]	31	33.0	28	8.7	4	7.5	8	27.6
TOTALS	94		321		53		29	

[a] Entries indicate frequency of exchange of listed items for pigs adjusted to exclude cash transactions.
[b] Includes small numbers of exchanges for shells, stone and steel tools, salt, less commonly traded plumes, etc., and, for the last period, collections of several dissimilar goods.

rates of forest products are mainly confined to the most recent period of little over a decade. Data collected in 1973–1974 indicate a remarkable constancy of rates for the previous four or five decades.

By the 1970s cassowaries and the more valuable plumes were no longer exchanged as frequently for shells and steel as in the past. Conversely, less valuable plumes and marsupial skins were more often exchanged for shells and steel than previously. Although values of shells and steel fell up to the 1970s, alterations in the frequency of exchanges do not indicate absolute changes in the exchange rates of forest products but only in relation to shells and steel. The average cash values and ranges of cash values of plumes and marsupial skins showed no change until the mid- to late 1970s. Thus, although the value of pigs and cassowaries increased up to 1974 and that of shells and steel depreciated, values of plumes and skins remained unaltered.

An apparent exception to this generalization are feathers of the Vulturine Parrot. Even though the value in relation to shells and steel necessarily increased with devaluation of the latter goods, the particularly marked increase in the incidence of exchanges for pigs suggests that real values of the parrot also rose. This change is probably illusory, however, for it is only since contact that bicolored down feathers have been included in trade packages. Informants say that before contact most Vulturine Parrot collections were smaller, consisting only of larger body and flight feathers, and were exchanged at lower rates. Continuing transactions into the 1970s involving shells (notably greensnail) and steel tools mostly involve small collections of feathers, with only larger collections given for pigs.

By the 1970s live cassowaries were exchanged only for pigs and money. Since cash values of cassowaries rose over time, and the value of pigs also rose, it follows that the absolute value of cassowaries also increased. The minimum cash value of cassowaries (K20 in the early 1960s) was almost double the 1970–1974 mean value of pigs (K12.28). Although the range of cash values of pigs increased greatly after 1974, in 1985 the mean value of cassowaries remained considerably higher than that of pigs. Pigs and cassowaries, nonetheless, share a preeminent position in the ideological and symbolic significance of goods, and it is perhaps for this reason that they are frequently exchanged for each other despite their different material values (Healey 1985*b*).

At this point one might summarize changes in exchange rates as follows. The period from the mid- to late-1970s appears to mark a critical shift in rates of exchange. Until the mid-1970s, the values of most forest products show little appreciable change in monetary terms or in relation to other goods. By contrast, goods imported from the direction of the central highlands experienced greater fluctuations in exchange rates: shells and steel were traded at reduced rates, pigs at moderately increased rates. Through the latter part of the 1970s and into the 1980s, most goods show at least slightly increased monetary value. For more commonly traded items in recent times, higher values are most dramatic for pigs and plumes of the Black Sicklebill and the Lesser and Saxony Birds of Paradise, but the data are suggestive of rising values of at least greensnail shells and steel tools also. Bearing in mind the small number of cases of rate determination for most goods since 1974, it is noteworthy that the amplitude of increasing monetary value of most goods, excluding pigs, cassowaries, and the Black Sicklebill, is very similar. That is, the shift in monetary value of goods has been comparable, indicating that relative value in nonmonetary terms remained little changed across a range of goods. However, since the incidence of transactions involving cash has increased since 1974, and the incidence of transactions involving most forest products, shells, and steel has decreased in the same period, it becomes difficult to sustain further analysis of stability or change in relative values expressed as nonmonetary equivalences. Only pigs and the plumes of the Vulturine Parrot, Papuan Lory, Astrapia, and Saxony Bird of Paradise have been traded at roughly stable or moderately greater incidence over the whole timeframe for which records are available (see table 35). The notable decline in the frequency of pig exchanges for Vulturine Parrot and Astrapia plumes, the value of which in cash and other goods has remained more or less stable, and the considerable increase in the cash value of pigs, indicates a distinct rise in the absolute value of pigs which is unmatched by any other commonly traded item in recent decades.

Changes in exchange rates have occurred in the context of changes in the availability of goods, expressed as percentage incidence of the total flow of goods (table 35) or annual velocities of flow (table 37). These changes can be summarized as greater volumes of money and pigs being traded and diminished volumes of shells and forest products. Movements in exchange rates bear some relation to alterations in the quantitative availability of goods and the pressure of desire to acquire them. Thus, I turn now to a consideration of how values may be altered in response to levels of supply and demand.

When kina, greensnail, and steel tools first arrived in the Maring area they were adopted into the hierarchy of values at the same level as the items they were regarded as replacing—dogwhelks, cowries, and stone axes (see table 40). This would have been a logical course for the Maring to take. But it is also likely that such substitutions were influenced by suppliers of these goods dictating exchange rates corresponding to those of the superceded shells. These suppliers, who had already obtained large quantities of shells and steel from Europeans in the Wahgi, may have seen the relative deprivation of Jimi people as an opportunity to demand high exchange rates for the goods. I do not mean to suggest that there was necessarily anything deliberately exploitative in this strategy, since there is no evidence to suggest central highlanders inflated the value of shells and steel beyond rates acceptable locally. By about 1950, however, exchange rates for shells and steel tools had dropped to around a level sustained for more than twenty years. Two factors may have led to this devaluation. First, by this date, suppliers of shells and steel had amassed large stocks that were falling in value. Their principal imports from the Jimi were plumes, the exchange rates of which had not changed in relation to ancestrally present trade goods. By reducing the exchange rate of shells and steel in dealings with Jimi traders, a wider range of less valuable plumes would have come within the exchange value of shells and steel. Their supplies of plumes would thereby have increased to help meet their high demand for these goods, while at the same time they were, perhaps, able to limit the inflation of shell and steel stocks by releasing more of these goods into the trade system. By maintaining their export of pigs, and later adding money, they retained an ability to acquire plumes of higher value.

Second, the Maring themselves came to suffer from the inflation of shell and steel stocks, and began offering goods of lower value in exchange. To maintain their supplies of plumes, ultimate consumers would have had to comply with the change in exchange rates and, in view of their own high stocks of shells suffering devaluation locally, they may have been willing to do so in order to offload stocks.

The reasons for rising values of some forest products from the late 1970s are harder to determine. These rises are most dramatic for cassowaries, Black Sicklebill, and Lesser and Saxony Bird of Paradise plumes. The incidence of trade in these goods diminished, but their availability in the wild is unlikely to have altered appreciably. Reduced volume of trade is ascribed by informants to a lack of demand on the part of upper-Jimi and Wahgi traders. There is no evidence from either trade histories or general statements of informants that the Kundagai have put any significant pressure on upper-Jimi or Wahgi traders to increase the exchange rates of these plumes. Rather, rising values seem more the result of central-highlands traders offering higher rates of exchange. The reasons for these changes would therefore seem to lie beyond the immediate trading sphere of the Kundagai, and very probably in the Wahgi and Simbu Valleys themselves, as major destinations of Jimi plumes. Similarly, the reasons for the stability of rates for the Vulturine Parrot and Astrapia also reflect circumstances beyond the Jimi.

An analysis of exchange rates of plumes in the central highlands is clearly beyond the limits of this ethnography. I have noted in the previous chapter how occasions of plume use in the Wahgi and the volume of plumes required for decorations and ceremonial exchange have diminished. Rising values do not reflect the difficulty of acquiring plumes from the Jimi at lesser rates. Arguably, the unit value of plumes rose as their level of supply within the Wahgi fell, thereby raising their significance as markers of status (as decorations) and tokens of social relationships (as objects of prestation). Relative scarcity was generated by the decline in ceremonies requiring decorations and changes in the composition of bridewealth. Nonetheless, in a cultural context of intense competition among men for prestige involving an incremental tendency over a series of transactions, demonstrated control over access to plumes remained an important marker of status, inflecting the value of certain plumes upward. This interpretation must remain speculative in the absence of any specific data on the matter from the Simbu and Wahgi.

Although noting the correlation between exchange rates and supply and demand, the problem remains of accounting for the mechanisms that achieve rate changes (cf. Sahlins 1972: 297, 301). Critical in this regard is how information spreads through the trade networks. It might be argued, for example, that demand is erratic or "lumpy," as when members of a community preparing for a ceremony travel in search of plumes, signaling a heightened capacity to satisfy desire. In such circumstances, plume providers may be tempted to withhold plumes until more generous exchanges are offered. The argument is inapplicable to the Jimi–Simbai trade networks on two counts. First, there is no indication that Kundagai traders and their partners traditionally and consciously sought to maximize gains or generate profit over a series of transactions. In other words, there seems to have been no deliberate extraction of higher exchange rates from those deemed capable of complying. This is in accord with the convention in trade that the "seller" sets the "price." I believe that statement generally applies to the most recent period also. It is worth noting, however, that when recounting transactions occurring since 1979 a number of informants described vigorous bargaining with strangers over exchange rates—predominantly of pigs. This is a new phenomenon, as acknowledged by informants. In most instances of bargaining, what Kundagai traders were seeking was minimizing their loss of cash in trade rather than maximizing gains, and in only one instance was the good bargained over—a plume—resold at a profit, at a price deliberately negotiated by the Kundagai trader.

Second, the very structure of trade networks tends to iron out any lumpiness rapidly in time and space. Most especially in precontact times, when travel was highly restricted and trade in plumes less developed, any heightened demand attending ceremonies was highly localized. But even after contact, when parties of traders traveled widely and the velocity of plume trade increased, lumps in demand would have been dissipated quickly.

Plumes flow through the trade network more or less continually, through multifarious channels. Any sudden increased demand for plumes by central highlanders would thereby quickly become diluted, the more so with increasing distance and time from its point of origin. The postcontact development of long-range expeditions by parties of Simbu and Wahgi plume traders might be argued to circumvent the effect of complex and dense networks in evening out lumps in demand. I doubt, however, that this has had any significant impact in creating local pockets of greater demand and manipulation of the supply of plumes by Jimi traders. The penetration of such parties as far as the Kundagai remains limited. For example, although Hageners frequently mount trade (and hunting) expeditions into the Jimi they seem to confine their dealings to fellow Melpa-speakers south of the river (A. Strathern 1979; Strathern and Strathern 1971). As far as I am aware, they have never visited Tsuwenkai, although some Kundagai have traded with Melpa south of the Jimi. Although visits by Simbu and Wahgi traders are perhaps more common in the drier season, their timing and frequency are quite unpredictable, and traders appear with at best only a day or two's notice. In the 1970s the Kundagai welcomed visits from traders they identified as Simbu because they offered higher cash values for certain plumes, notably of the Lesser Bird of Paradise. But because of the erratic, infrequent, and unexpected appearance of such travelers there was no attempt to retain stocks of plumes for trade with distant strangers. By the 1980s, visits from Wahgi Valley traders had become much more frequent, but their interest in plumes had largely evaporated: they came as sellers of pigs, not buyers of forest products.

Essentially, then, knowledge of conditions of supply and demand is highly localized. The "market" is an indeterminate collection of individual transactors conducting exchanges in relative privacy. Thus, there is little opportunity for evaluating relative values of different goods on offer at any particular time and adjusting one's own asking rate accordingly as, for example, Salisbury (1970) argues for Tolai sellers in the Rabaul market. Certainly in conversation the Kundagai share their experiences in trade. But the dissemination of information in this context in no way corresponds to the presentation that a market provides of a range of goods of readily assessed quantity and quality, and the balancing of exchange rates offered by sellers and accepted by buyers. In short, the mechanisms of rate determination cannot be sought solely in the context of the cumulative experience of individuals and the dissemination of information in trading relations themselves.

In the similar absence of any form of organization reminiscent of a marketplace, Sahlins attempts an explanation of how acceptable exchange rates may be arrived at in relation to conditions of supply and demand. His theory of value is developed from an examination of a special kind of organization: partnership trade. Trade beyond the confines of the community or tribe, he suggests, takes the form of a confrontation that can easily escalate into hostility.

> In trade . . . the context of the confrontation is the acquisition of utilities; and the goods . . . may very well be urgent. When people meet who owe each other nothing yet presume to gain from each other something, peace of trade is the great uncertainty. In the absence of external guarantees, as of a Sovereign Power, peace must be otherwise secured: by extension of sociable relations to foreigners—thus, the trade-friendship or trade-kinship—and, most significantly, *by the terms of the exchange* itself. (Sahlins 1972: 302. Emphasis in original)

Sahlins suggests that where the ideal of alternate overreciprocation holds in exchanges between formal trade-partners, "a series of transactions . . . must stipulate by inference a ratio of equivalence between the goods exchanged. One arrives in due course at a fairly precise agreement on exchange values" (1972: 304). Since partners are generally aware of the balance of credit and indebtedness at any one time, the exchange rate around which their generous transactions cluster is mutually agreed upon without open negotiation. The question remains as to how this rate represents the current state of supply and demand. Sahlins argues that the answer hinges on the performance and meaning of the principle of generosity, by which a balance of exchanges is achieved over a series of transactions. He notes that his theory of exchange value is weakened by the ethnographically uncertain meaning of "generosity." From an examination of Huon Gulf and Vitiaz Strait trade, however, he draws the generalization that those who introduce a good into exchange "are related to it primarily in terms of labor value, the real effort required to produce it, while those to whom the good is tendered appreciate it primarily as a use value" (1972: 307). From this proposition a meaning of generosity can be deduced.

> Supposing the necessity of reciprocal good measure, it would follow that each party has to consider, in addition to the virtues of the goods he receives, the relative utility to the other party of the goods he gives, and in addition to the labour he has expended himself, the work also of the other. "Generosity" has to bring use value into relation with use value, and labor with labor. (Sahlins 1972: 307)

This being the case, generosity will apply on the exchange rate some of the forces that affect prices in competitive markets. Thus, in principle, goods of higher real (i.e., labor) cost will bring higher returns. Also in principle,

> ... if goods of greater utility oblige the recipient to greater generosity, it is as much as saying that price is disposed to increase with demand. Thus compensating efforts to the producer and utilities to the receiver, the rates set by tactful diplomacy will express many of the elemental conditions that are resumed otherwise in the economist's supply curves and demand curves. (Sahlins 1972: 307–308)

Hence, if levels of supply and demand should vary we might expect exchange rates to adjust accordingly.

In his analysis of exchange value, then, Sahlins adds a materialist theory of value to a rather vague understanding of generosity. Essentially, goods for Sahlins represent so much of Marx's (1976: 128 ff.) "congealed labour-time," as objective properties evaluated by traders themselves. Ethnographically and theoretically this is an unwarranted assumption. In his analysis of Siane exchange value, for example, Salisbury (1962: 186) applies a related concept of time, but recognizes that it in no way corresponds to Siane categories of evaluation. Rather, time is a purely analytic device for representing some common measure of value in the absence of an indigenous general medium of exchange. Even where such a general medium is available—as in the example of salt currency among the Baruya—the classic labor theory of value is inapplicable (Godelier 1977).

Labor is, perhaps, an even more elusive concept than generosity, and its application to cultural contexts where concepts of effort, work, labor and their products are not precisely delineated in a western scientific framework (cf. Schwimmer 1980; Damon 1983: 317, 341; Firth 1979) is at best questionable on a priori grounds.

Certainly the Kundagai do not determine the value of goods in terms of the time or labor costs of production, nor do they speak in comparative terms of such aspects of production of different trade goods. In time, effort, and material resources an Astrapia skin "costs" about as much as a parrot. Their use value in decorations is similar, yet the former is equivalent to a pig, whereas four or five of the latter are acceptable for a pig. The costs of producing a pig are much greater. A skin may be obtained in a few hours of hunting, whereas a pig takes months to produce, aside from additional costs such as the production of vegetables to feed it and the sow that farrowed it, and so forth. Indeed, one could argue that as culturally defined the respective labor tasks and the acquired skills and knowledge involved are essentially noncomparable. Again, further costs in time and effort are incurred in transporting trade goods, yet the Kundagai exchange, say, feathers at the same rate within Tsuwenkai as they do in Koriom or Bubgile, two and more days' walk away.

Certainly time is not a scarce resource to the Kundagai, and so it is not subject to means–ends decisions of choice in its allocation. (This is not to say that people are not faced with choices between activities, some of which may be more urgent or attractive than others.) As in many other tribal societies, the Maring concept *konggiang,* which might loosely be translated as "work," is somewhat diffuse in its meaning and is not confined to social labor resulting in the production or distribution of concrete utilities. Granted that everywhere there may be objective costs of labor, as in energy consumption, it remains the case that labor is not always culturally understood as something common to all products. To reduce the value of trade goods to such a common factor is to regard value as lying in some objectified property of the commodity itself. But that objectification must be culturally constructed. Where labor itself is not a commodity subject to a common scale of value there are conceptual difficulties in its measurement.

If the labor theory of value is not everywhere valid, the analytic distinction between use value and exchange value is also called into question. This is so because exchange value is allied to relative labor costs, as in Sahlins's model. The movement of certain objects in Maring trade is a case in point. Some feathers, notably of the Vulturine Parrot, have negligible use value as decorations or valuables to pass in prestations. Their most significant use is for exchange in trade. That is, their use value is realized in their circulation: use value lies in the fact that they have exchange value. Insofar as use and exchange values are merged in this instance, the distinction between kinds of value loses some analytic power. This is not to say that the use value/exchange value dichotomy is everywhere invalid, but rather that as an a priori construct it may lead to an insufficiently flexible approach to ethnographic data. It should therefore be understood that my reference to "use value" in what follows does not involve a rigid separation from "exchange value" but, rather, that the use value of any particular item is variable and contextually defined, such that it may have utility primarily as an object in exchange, when its "exchange value" is manifest. Godelier's notion of "social utility" (1977: 150), though unelaborated, seems to parallel my meaning of "use value."

Despite these reservations about Sahlins's treatment of rates of exchange in Melanesian trade, suitably adapted, his model retains some utility for the present analysis. Formal partnership trade of the sort Sahlins discusses is not highly developed in the Kundagai trading sphere. Furthermore, generosity of the type Sahlins discusses, which the Maring term *ko auwuk,* "over I-give," or *piak rima yem,* "above there place," is not normally practiced in Kundagai partnership trade. A willingness to permit delayed exchanges, however, mainly between kinsmen (but not necessarily trade partners of long standing), might be interpreted as a form of generosity. (See chap. 8 for a fuller discussion of generosity.) Delayed exchanges are a common phenomenon in trade between kinsmen, the debt thereby incurred being known as *menga.*

Sahlins's scheme is thus inapplicable to the analysis of determination of supply and demand of goods circulating exclusively in trade. It provides the basis, nonetheless, for a model of mechanisms for the assessment of levels of supply and demand in the medium of ceremonial exchange which is then translated into adjusted rates of exchange in trade. Critical in this analysis is the observation that up until the later 1970s, when most goods show rising cash values, it was only those goods employed in major prestations which experienced clear changes in their exchange rates in trade. The principle of generosity is central to the conduct of prestations, or rather, one might say the appearance of generosity, as there are a variety of accepted ways for recipients to negotiate the size of prestations without making any outright demands. In that sense, it is still up to the donors to determine the final size of any offering. Generosity is most evident in bridewealth, which establishes a sequence of intermittent reciprocal gifts of shells, steel, pigs, money, and occasionally cassowaries, besides various nonvaluable items such as minor decorations and food.

Well into the 1970s shells and steel were accumulated by trade and prestations. As stocks increased, so did the numbers transferred in prestations. This inflation was explained to me as follows: the size of ceremonial exchanges increased so that it remained just as difficult to amass payments as it had been in the past when valuables were scarcer. That is, it was considered to be as hard for a man to collect thirty kina in 1974 as it was to collect five kina some three decades before. In 1985 a similar argument was presented by informants to account for the dramatic decline in the number of shells and steel included in bridewealth. Their increasing rarity, at any cost, meant that it was simply impossible to amass as many items as in the mid-1970s. Greensnail shell in particular was still highly desirable, but its level of availability had shrunk to that characteristic of much earlier times. Filer (1985) and Newton (1989) have noted the similar and widespread escalation of the monetary value of bridewealth in contemporary Papua New Guinea, attributing this to the increasing supply of wealth, rather than demand for cash or the scarcity of brides.

Major prestations therefore constitute a public arena in which assessments of states of supply and demand of goods are made. Groups of men must cooperate in amassing a ceremonial exchange. A major donor must reciprocate help he receives in collecting goods, and so personal performances necessarily are compared, both in relation to a particular exchange and over a series through time. In such contexts men gain some measure of awareness of levels of available supply, however vague, through the ease or difficulty they experience collectively in meeting the size of a prestation deemed by innuendo to be acceptable to recipients. Similarly, the recipients of a major prestation gain some general appreciation of levels of supply to the extent that their covert demands are met or exceeded, and to the degree they find it easy or difficult to collect valuables for a return gift.

Prestations are therefore geared toward maintaining relative material deprivation on the part of donors against the ideally unchanged "value" or significance of the social relationship expressed in the exchange. With increasing ease of acquiring shells and steel in prestations the use value of these goods as symbolic markers of relationships dropped. Only by inflating the numbers transferred could their utility as symbols to those receiving them be balanced with that of the "goods" sent in exchange: women, children, military aid, homicides, and so on. Thus the value of shells and steel in prestations dropped as their supply and demand altered in relation to things received in exchange. I suggest that this drop in value was carried over into the trading sphere of exchanges. At the same time, by withdrawing shells and steel from circulation in trade to fund prestations a relative scarcity of these goods was maintained in the trading sphere, thus insulating them from further devaluation in trade. Subsequently, this scarcity became absolute as stocks of shells passed in trade were no longer augmented by fresh imports from the Wahgi. Prestations thus act as transducers, transferring information on reduced social utility of individual shells and steel to the trade sphere, in return for increased supplies of these goods.

A related argument can be applied to account for increased exchange rates of pigs. The argument may also apply to cassowaries, though insufficiency of data on the use of these birds in prestations hampers comparison.

With the imminent abandonment of *konj kaiko* ceremonies, the Maring will have no religiously sanctioned imperatives to build up large pig herds for sacrifice and prestation to allies. The last such Kundagai ceremony occurred in 1960, yet the pig herd is maintained at about the level necessary to hold a *kaiko*. Formerly most pigs were set aside for the *kaiko*, but with this major drain on the herd removed there is now an effective increase in the number of pigs available for other prestations. I suggest this is the reason the number of pigs killed for prestations, especially bridewealth, has increased: to keep pace with effective greater supply. Pigs are still killed as sacrifices in sickness, however, and the growing practice of slaughter for cash sale and to celebrate the return of migrant laborers further drains off the surplus in local herds. Moreover, since pigs are destroyed in prestations rather than accumulated and redeployed like other valuables, there is a continual demand for more pigs.

The requirement of a large herd to stage a *kaiko* somewhat inhibited pig kills for other purposes (Rappaport 1968). With this constraint removed, and new occasions for feasts and sacrifices added, the frequency of kills has undoubtedly increased (cf. table 19). This leads to a more rapid turnover of the pig population. Since this is occurring within a roughly stable herd size, severe strain is placed upon the capacity of the herd to maintain itself by local breeding. This difficulty is compounded by the fact that the total pig population is actually composed of the small herds of individual men, each of whom is pursuing personal strategies of management related to the age and sex structure of his herd and his assessments of his requirements in relation to outstanding or projected debts and credits in trade and prestation. These strategies often include preventing his sows from breeding, as this can result in rapid loss of condition, making them unsuitable for prestations. The preference for gelding most males to make them more tractable and promote growth of fat, coupled with an absence of feral boars, further limits breeding. The interests of individual pig owners are thus not necessarily coincident with those of the collectivity of owners.

This argument must remain speculative in the absence of adequate data on the demography of Kundagai pigs. However, material from trade histories provide some support. Since the mid-1950s the Kundagai have increased their rate of import of pigs nearly fivefold (table 37). The Kundagai are now more reliant upon imports to maintain their herds than they were in the past, a conclusion supported by the opinion of some men who suggest that local breeding is unable to meet demands for pigs. Their arguments parallel my suggestion of the incompatibility of individual and collective interests, as they reason that local breeding rates would increase if men could agree to fence in their pigs together instead of ensuring that their herds are kept separate.[10]

In short, the increasing number of live pigs relative to traditionally normative occasions for their slaughter has been reflected in larger prestations, which results in a reduced capacity for local breeding and a relative decline in local availability. The consequence is an increasing dependence on imports and a rise in the value of pigs which is carried over into the trading sphere of exchange. This trend was clearly still operating in the period 1974–1978, with the numbers of pigs passed in prestations increasing and the cash value of pigs in trade greatly inflated: a pig worth about K10 to K12 in 1974 cost up to K60 in 1978. It should be noted, however, that the qualities of many pigs were also rising somewhat. Increasingly in the late 1970s the Kundagai were obtaining *pig susu* (TP), beasts improved by crossing with introduced stock. Such pigs came mainly from the Wahgi and were highly sought after to form a nucleus of a new generation of local breeding stock producing larger litters without the attendant risk of gross loss of condition.

The absence until recently of temporal changes in exchange rates of goods that are not used in prestations can be accounted for by the fact that they are not subject to the public and collective assessment of alterations in supply and demand in the matching of social utilities through generosity in prestations.

This leaves the problem of just how the use value of one good is assessed in terms of another. The exchange value of each good can be expressed in terms of several others, but until the use of money there was no common unit of value. No single item other than money can be traded against all, even, most others. Pigs and plumes as categories come closest to fulfilling this function, since they are acceptable in return for the widest range of goods. Yet they do not constitute a currency as such, with standard denominations. The category *kabang an*, plumes, is composed of different kinds of feathers and skins, each with a slightly different use value or esteem, so that different plumes when combined do not add up to a single unit of higher value.[11]

All currently traded goods have an accepted and limited range of cash values (table 39). But even in these terms, money does not constitute a consistent common measure of value. That is, there is no transitivity in cash value across a series of transactions. For example, a Lesser Bird of Paradise skin was deemed an appropriate exchange for a kina or a pig in the mid-1970s, but their average cash values were unequal (K2.42, K1.40, and K10.69 respectively). Further, although pig-for-kina exchanges have occurred, they were generally regarded as grossly unequal in that kina was viewed as of much lesser value.[12]

Having shown there is no material logic to exchange value in terms of labor or other common units of measurement we are left reliant upon informants' assessments of relative use value. This, indeed, is the proper course, in that it must be in the context of the culturally articulated ideological, symbolic, social, and utilitarian significance of objects that traders offer their goods. These properties are expressed and negotiated in transactions. Thus, the relative values of some goods are, in part, related to their prestige value, as objects used in prestations (cf. Salisbury 1962). Hence, pigs and cassowaries, as the preeminent mediators of ceremonial exchange, are also among trade items commanding the highest exchange rates. Other goods, such as plumes and marsupial skins, are valued primarily according to their size and appropriateness as decorations. But values have not been determined by the Kundagai alone, for exchange rates of most goods are constant throughout their traditional trading range.

Exchange rates of some plumes in the upper Jimi and Wahgi, however, are higher than among people with whom the Kundagai traditionally traded. With the development of direct if infrequent trade relations between Tsuwenkai and these areas, the Kundagai have occasionally received higher than usual cash returns for skins sold to visiting traders. Since it is a convention in trade that the visitor displays his trade goods—that is, he initiates the exchange by setting the exchange rate— these exchanges may be taken to reflect values deemed appropriate by the visitors, and not as attempts by the Kundagai to capitalize on their visitors' ignorance of local conventions by demanding an exorbitant exchange rate.[13] In the 1970s the Narak and Kandawo generally paid K5 to K10 for Lesser Bird of Paradise skins and commonly exchanged them for pigs. These higher exchange rates suggest that certain species enjoy a higher use value. It is to be noted that the Narak, Kandawo,

Kuma, and Simbu employ plumes in bridewealth payments. Other plumes in the upper Jimi command roughly the same exchange rates as in the traditional Kundagai trading range, probably because it is these people who have sought plumes, such as of the Vulturine Parrot, from the Kundagai and have thus introduced their own exchange rates. Most Kundagai are aware of the higher exchange rates for some plumes in the upper Jimi, but are not often able to conduct transactions at these higher rates without traveling afar, for their nearer trading partners also know that the Kundagai rates are lower and apply these to transactions with lower-Jimi traders.

As noted earlier, Sahlins finds that, contrary to expectations, exchange rates show some responsiveness to areal variations in supply and demand. There are undoubted variations in exchange rates in the Jimi–Simbai trade area, as the above examples indicate, but there is no clear evidence to identify these changes with variations in conditions of supply and demand. From an examination of the stone axe and spear trade of the Australian Yir–Yoront, Sahlins infers that

> ... if, in an areal network, the exchange rate of a good (A) in terms of another (B) rises in proportion to distance from the source of A, it is reasonable to suppose that the relative value of A is increasing pari passu with "real" costs and scarcities, that is, with declining supply, and probably also with increasing demand. (Sahlins 1972: 282)[14]

Applying the same proposition to Maring stone axe trade one finds that a stone obtained directly from the manufacturers near Wum had the same exchange value as in the Asai over forty kilometers distant from the center of supply. With less certainty, it appears that blades possibly orginating in the Wahgi Valley Abiamp quarries about fifty kilometers away were obtained by the Kundagai at the same exchange rate as blades from the Wum area about twenty kilometers away. One reason for the constancy of rates may have been because throughout this region axes had the same use value as items of trade and prestation.

Among items given in exchange for plumes are shells, steel, and money, many coming from ultimate plume consumers. Plume supply is not restricted to limited areas as are the goods in Sahlins's model. Their exchange items, however, are somewhat restricted. Half of the conditions implicit in Sahlins's formula are therefore met, so that in principle one might expect shells and steel tools to command higher exchange rates with increasing distance from their source areas in the Wahgi and Simbu Valleys, as they become scarcer. I have noted that when these goods first entered the Jimi they were transferred at higher exchange rates. This was not necessarily because demand was high and supply low, but more likely because the goods were adopted at the exchange rates of other items they replaced. Exchange rates have thus remained relatively constant spatially with the exception of items just discussed. It is surely noteworthy that this constancy is preserved.

Within the Jimi–Simbai sector of the highlands plume trade at the peak of its development up to the 1970s, we find that, in the main, exchange rates remained constant with both distance from source areas of goods and with time. Exceptions were the areal change in Lesser Bird of Paradise plumes (increasing in value in the upper Jimi) and temporal changes in the value of shells, steel, pigs, and cassowaries.

From the different quantities of goods in circulation in different parts of a trade system Sahlins (1972: 295) infers that exchange rates are responsive to different conditions of supply and demand; where goods are few—that is, supply is low but demand is high—then exchange rates tend to be high. Yet this does not apply to all trade systems.

The volume of plumes in circulation in the lower Jimi and upper Simbai is lower than the volume in the upper Jimi (see chap. 2). Yet there is no attendant increase in exchange rates with distance from the upper Jimi. In the case of Lesser Bird of Paradise plumes, exchange rates increase in the upper Jimi with the increasing size of stocks. This would seem to indicate that demand and desire for these plumes are higher in the upper Jimi. Greater wealth, especially in cash terms, may account for the ability of upper-Jimi people to acquire many plumes. Different decoration styles and the use of feathers in prestations may also stimulate a higher desire. Yet the same arguments also apply to other plumes, the exchange rates of which do not vary from the upper Jimi to the Up-Simbai and Down-Jimi area. The higher value of the Lesser Bird of Paradise may reflect, rather, a higher use value placed upon plumes of this species.

In the situations that Sahlins is concerned with, desire for all trade goods is relatively uniform throughout a trade area, but demand—the willingness to meet stipulated exchange rates—is variable. In the Jimi–Simbai trade area, both desire and demand vary. The Kundagai have a relatively low desire for plumes as decorations but have access to supplies through hunting and trade in excess of this desire. Plume consumers have a higher desire for plumes and an even higher supply than the Kundagai by virtue of the structure of trade networks and their relatively greater wealth. Because of their supply of plumes, the Kundagai have a high demand for shells, steel tools, and pigs, and an almost unlimited desire for these goods, which can be absorbed by inflating the value of ceremonial prestations. The structure of the trade system as a web of trade links converging on a central point ensures that supply of goods to that point increases with diminishing distance from the center and decreases in the reverse direction. The supply and demand of goods is thus roughly proportional to distance from the central point of the trade networks. Where demand is high, supply is also high. Hence, upper-Jimi communities, obtaining plumes from numerous areas, are able to exercise a high demand for shells, steel, pigs, and money. In turn, supplies of the latter goods are also high. Further away from the center of the trade system, the Kundagai have a relatively lower supply of plumes and hence a lower capacity to acquire exchange goods.

CONCLUSION

Following Sahlins's model I have suggested that exchange rates for shells, steel, and pigs have been adjusted in relation to supply and demand. Similar mechanisms for the adjustment of exchange rates of plumes and skins do not operate as effectively in the Maring area. This is because these items are not involved in the same kinds of public and collective efforts in the preparation and redistribution of major prestations. I conclude, therefore, that exchange rates of plumes have not been fixed by forces of supply and demand in the Jimi–Simbai area, as the absence of rate variations over time and distance until recent times suggests.

There is also a virtual absence of bargaining for a "price" and of cheating. This is suggestive of two things: first, that everyone is aware of the "fair price" of any good, and in general this is clearly the case. Most lists of exchange rates for various goods collected from informants were similar, and these rates are generally adhered to in practice. I recorded few cases where goods were exchanged for others of much higher or lower value. Where unfair exchanges are made the victim is usually old or young. Such people, men explain, are thought to be both ignorant of current exchange rates and too timid to demand a more equitable return once an exchange has been made. Second, the absence of bargaining suggests that there is no need to make the history of an item known in order to fix its exchange rate—that it is valued for what it is, not what it cost to produce (since these costs may differ with circumstances). In the absence of a standard measure of value these costs cannot be expressed in material terms. It would seem, then, that exchange rates have been arrived at by convention and have therefore generally not been responsive to factors of changed supply and demand or to costs of production.

Godelier (1977) reaches much the same conclusion in his examination of rates of exchange in Baruya trade. The task of economic anthropology is therefore to discover the basis for such conventions. That can only be attempted if one sets aside the notion implicit in much of the ethnography on "value," and that is, that the fundamentals of value are to be found somewhere in the material, objective properties of things. This ignores another dimension of goods—that they are not only concrete utilities, or objects *of* exchange, but also objects *in* exchange and hence mediators of social relations. The search for exchange value must therefore have some connection with social relationships. In that sense, goods passed in transactions have a communicative or signal aspect, in addition to any more objective use value (cf. Ernst 1978; Sansom 1976). The mode of exchange may constitute one means of framing or defining which of the varied properties of an object are contextually relevant or dominant.

Exchange activities have long been subjected to analyses in the structuralist, "cultural," or symbolic modes, in the search for underlying forces giving shape to the diversity of observed forms. So far "mundane trade" has escaped such attention. Yet especially where objects passed in trade also figure in more ceremonialized transactions one might argue that the exchange value of goods in trade bears a relationship to their cultural meaning in other social contexts. I have already alluded to this issue in the conclusion to chapter 5.

A detailed analysis along these lines is beyond me at present, due to lack of adequate data on the meaningful dimensions of objects in exchange. Some indication, however, of how such an analysis might proceed is appropriate, both to justify my above remarks and to lead into the next chapter on the more sociological aspects of trade relationships.

Goods traded can be grouped into three major categories: ephemeral products of nature, extracted by humans—plumes and skins; living creatures nurtured by humans—pigs, cassowaries, and perhaps dogs; and durable, hard, exotic never-living things—shells, stone, steel, money. (It is true that the Maring now know that shells are from marine animals.) Each category of goods carries a different swag of meanings derived from the multivocal, contextually variable symbolic properties of goods. Plumes and furs are major objects of decoration that enhance, accentuate, and alter the self and the collectivity of dancers in ceremonies of social reproduction. Different kinds of decorations have a different relationship in this overall scheme. Shells, steel tools, and money are manipulated in prestations as tokens of social relationships, and at more general levels as signals of human worth or being.

As I indicated in chapter 2, plumes and furs as decorations mask the exterior self but reveal the inner soul, temporarily transforming young men into objects of lustrous beauty, like birds themselves. Decorations attract women: men are explicit about the way that a bedazzlingly decorated dancer "pulls" women into romantic marriage. But just as beauty and sexual attraction are fragile and fleeting, so are the means of achieving attractiveness: plumes quickly fade and break. Marriage, however, is paradigmatically a lasting relationship. Once attached to a man in marriage a woman's agnates must be compensated for her loss. In contrast to the objects that attract, objects that tie women permanently to men in marriage through compensation payments—shells and steel tools—are hard, strong, bright, and durable, both physically and metaphorically. Indeed, in bridewealth presentations there is often an explicit association between the shell and steel valuables and the bride's body. An orator may hold aloft a series of valuables calling out the name of the bride and adding in respect of each item, "this is her hand, her foot, her leg . . . ," and so on. This is indicative of durable shells and steel constituting compensation for the woman's body and her potentialities of a lasting productive and reproductive nature.

In similar vein, I have argued elsewhere (Healey 1985*b*) that pigs and cassowaries "stand for" categories of people, representing in exchange and sacrifice respectively the cultured and wild aspects of humanity. Pigs and cassowaries stand for humans both in a more or less literal sense of substitution and in a metaphorical sense, in dealings with the spirit world and affines.

Ultimately, value in use and exchange relates not to obvious and observable material and social ways in which trade goods may be manipulated but to these highly abstract and elusive symbolic and aesthetic "values" of things, which derive a potency precisely because their manipulators cannot articulate or consciously reflect upon them.

The meaning of exchange to actors, as opposed to the consequences of the act, has received increasing attention in recent years (e.g. Ernst 1978; Schwimmer 1979; Wagner 1967; Weiner 1976; and for the

Maring, LiPuma 1981).[15] Adequate attention is yet to be paid to the meaning of the objects of exchange, as they emerge in relation to the totality of objects and acts involved.

8
Utilitarianism, Sociability, and the Organization of Trade

The last three chapters have focused largely on the ecological structure of trade networks and the confrontation of goods: their patterns of movement and the assessment of value. I have indicated that trade is an important means of acquiring exotic goods that are then redeployed in prestations. This mode of "consuming" goods, of course, stimulates the production of other things to be used in transactions to sustain such transfers from one mode of exchange to another. Put simply, the demand for exotic goods to use in prestations constitutes an impetus to trade, and hunting provides the capacity to trade. I have shown the functional and ecological relationship between the exploitation of forest products—especially bird plumes—and trade, and between trade and prestation. I have also sought to indicate how these relationships are mediated by the cultural order.

By way of concluding the ethnography of trade I now shift attention from material goods to the persons involved in trade: to an examination of the social relationships by which the movement and evaluation of goods occurs and of the changes that have eventuated in the social organization of trade. The sociological dimensions of trading relationships seem to me of as much, if not more, importance in a consideration of why trade occurs as wider ecological forces. Although the discussion is centered on Maring ethnography, the material points to the need to refine present anthropological approaches to trade in Melanesia and elsewhere, and this chapter is constructed as a critique of certain anthropological approaches to trade. As such, it serves as both a substantive and theoretical conclusion to this study.[1]

Prevailing understandings of trade are that the activity is mundane and essentially sustained by resource differences and reciprocal understandings of "need" or "deprivation" on the part of transactors. The argument is thus basically materialist and utilitarian (and poorly developed). Certainly ecological forces and culturally defined notions of "need" or utility of objects set up conditions for trade: they generate differentials in supply and demand in an ecological sense and provide a context for the operation of cultural forces of desire. But these forces operate at gross regional or collective levels. In the absence of specialized institutions for its conduct, such as a marketplace, professional traders, guilds, and so forth, the kind of trade I am concerned with is a personal, individual affair. Something must therefore connect the regionally and collectively defined forces to the individual.

I contend that the forces that set the conditions for production and trade are not in themselves sufficient to impel trade on the part of individuals, even if that activity is ecologically or sociologically necessary for the adequate provisioning of society. Clearly individuals will try to overcome perceived deprivations by trading. But this understanding of trade, focusing on the utilities of goods, can only account for situations where each partner is deprived of what the other offers and possesses surplus to immediate requirements to match what the other seeks. Such an object-focused argument is insufficient to explain the more or less continuous movement of large quantities of goods in New Guinea, especially in the highlands, where individual social networks beyond the local community are typically restricted, and where opportunities for a particular trader finding a reciprocally deprived partner are therefore limited.[2] Although the importance of social relations, such as formal partnerships, in facilitating trade has been acknowledged (e.g., Harding 1967; Hughes 1977; Sahlins 1972), I suggest that social factors have been given insufficient systematic attention. In what follows I concentrate on the sociological dimensions of exchange, arguing that trade is not simply a utilitarian pursuit but one that allows individuals to make qualitative statements about social relationships. In short, I suggest that the nature of the social relationships involved in trade are critical in the maintenance of this form of exchange. These relationships bind the individual into an expanded social network. They may be established through the extension of trust and construction of kinship ties between parties and sustained by the appearance of generosity in otherwise balanced transactions.

OVERT REASONS FOR TRADE

When asked why they trade, men say they want to acquire goods for their own use: plumes for decorations; axes for garden work; money to pay Council head-tax; pigs, shells, or steel tools to use in prestations. Trade is the predominant mode by which many things change hands, and this is especially so for forest products. If one considers those decorative plumes and shells actually retained by their owners for personal use, however, less than one-third are acquired by trade (tables 14 and 16, chap. 4). In other words, informants' explanations, delivered with patience for the slow-witted ethnographer, do not seem to reflect accurately the true situation.

Some indication of the importance of trade in obtaining goods for personal use can be gained from table 43 based on data from trade histories collected in 1973–1974. Transactions are listed in two categories, depending on whether or not the Kundagai trader's own property was involved. Where this was not the case the Kundagai has acted as an intermediary on behalf of others who supply the goods involved.

All men have used their own goods in trade, but the relative amounts of transactions using personal items and those belonging exclusively to trading partners varies widely. This variation occurs across age groups, as the table indicates, with younger men tending to deal more in their own goods and less as an intermediary on behalf of others. But there is wide variation within age groups. For example, in the largest age group in 1973–1974 (aged thirty to thirty-five) the proportion of transactions involving the Kundagai trader's own stocks ranged from a low of 35.2 percent to 100 percent of all transactions. Ten men (17.5 percent of all traders) had not conducted any transactions using only goods belonging to other men, though most of them had acted as intermediaries, substituting their own goods for those received from trading partners. The relative importance of trade exclusively using one's own stocks has also varied over time. There has been a general trend toward greater emphasis on transactions using the trader's own stocks at the expense of acting as an intermediary for others. Up to 1974 just under 60 percent of all transactions involved the trader's own goods

TABLE 43. PROPORTION OF TRANSACTIONS USING TRADER'S OWN STOCKS, TO 1974

Age group	No. traders	Transactions using own goods		Transactions not using own goods		Total
		No.	% of total	No.	% of total	
15-20	2	2	50.0	2	50.0	4
20-25	6	69	85.2	12	14.8	81
25-30	9	193	72.3	74	27.7	267
30-35	14	437	64.2	244	35.8	681
35-40	5	155	39.0	242	61.0	397
40-45	6	207	47.9	225	52.1	432
45-50	2	95	78.5	26	21.5	121
50-55	3	52	39.4	80	60.6	132
55-60	4	85	68.0	40	32.0	125
60-65	3	82	53.9	70	46.1	152
65-70	2	20	58.8	14	41.2	34
70-75	1	23	46.0	27	54.0	50
TOTALS	57	1,420	57.4	1,056	42.6	2,476

(table 43). Between 1974 and 1978 the twenty-three traders whose trade histories for that period were collected had used their own goods in 66.8 percent of all transactions. By 1985 the proportion had risen to 76.1 percent of all transactions of the fifteen traders surveyed.

There has, then, been a general shift toward dealing for oneself in trade. This is not unexpected, given the decline of trade in forest products, the rise in pigs-for-cash trade, and the recent emergence of bargaining in some transactions. Nonetheless, the persistence of a significant proportion of transactions on behalf of others, with no immediate material advantage to the Kundagai trader, is a noteworthy feature of contemporary trade, in the face of increasing penetration of impersonal, monetized dealings with strangers, and the growing structural dependence on central-highlands pig traders.

The small numbers of traders in each age group—especially after 1974—makes any comparison of changes in the prevalence of dealing with traders' own goods by age group hazardous. I therefore confine further discussion of variations to data gathered in 1973–1974 and summarized in table 43.

In general, more active traders tend to be involved in a higher proportion of transactions using only goods provided by partners. For instance the most active Kundagai trader, aged thirty-five to forty, with

211 transactions to his credit, used his own goods in only 12 percent of these, the lowest proportion of all traders. Although no longer a particularly vigorous trader in the 1979–1985 period, he was still the least devoted to trade on his own account, though such transactions had risen to 28 percent of his total.

The proportion of transactions using the trader's own stocks declines from ages twenty to forty (I exclude from consideration the youngest age group listed, since the only two traders have conducted so few transactions). In older age groups the proportion varies, but the average is about that for all age groups combined (57.4 percent). In other words, once a man has established himself as a trader with increasing age he is much less likely to engage in trade solely in order to obtain goods for his own use and is more likely to act as an intermediary for others, passing goods over which he has only temporary stewardship. Overall, just under 43 percent of all transactions were of this kind. Some exceptions to this general proposition are instructive. Only in the age groups forty-five to fifty and fifty-five to sixty are the proportions of transactions using the traders' own stocks markedly higher than the mean. The first group consists of a Tuguma refugee who has been resident in Tsuwenkai since 1956 and another man who is one of the more successful hunters and traders. The refugee established few trading partners since moving to Tsuwenkai and therefore had to rely upon his own resources, while many of the successful trader's transactions involved the large number of birds he has shot. The fifty-five to sixty age group includes two men who traded only infrequently and another successful hunter. Success in hunting is of great benefit to the trader since any goods acquired in exchange for the fruits of hunting may be retained, thereby augmenting stocks of valuables without any reciprocal drain on resources. By contrast, goods acquired by other means involve the trader in material costs. If the good came by trade a man must return another item: he is also expected to reciprocate if the good is obtained by gift.

This is not to say that things obtained at material cost do not benefit the trader. One reason for exchanging items in trade is simply because the trader considers that the transaction will be to his immediate advantage. Such a view does not involve the notion of profit, for most transactions occur at standard exchange rates constituting conventional scales of equivalent value. If a Kundagai exchanges one of his own axes for a plume, however, he may see the transaction as being to his benefit. He can use the plume in decorations, hopefully attracting women and kudos, and later exchange it for another axe or some other item. That is, the "benefits" that are assessed may relate to the social utility of differing objects in particular circumstances. When a dance is approaching the use of plumes is at a premium for decorations, whereas axes in excess of subsistence requirements have negligible use value as long as dancing occupies the attention. In short, use values are never absolute but are ever contextually emergent and socially constructed.

Thus, on the surface, there appears to be no material advantage in acting as an intermediary for others. Why, then, are the Kundagai prepared to accept such transactions? When posed with this question the Kundagai give several reasons, couched in pragmatic terms.

Contrary to appearances, there is some material utility to be gained in acting as an intermediary. Frequently, a trader makes temporary use of plumes or marsupial skins he exchanges on behalf of others. Indeed, the Kundagai often seek out such transactionl sequences specifically to obtain plumes for temporary use in decorations as ceremonies approach. The difficulty of subsequently finding a trader willing to accept plumes has, perhaps, contributed to the declining incidence of trade as an intermediary since the mid-1970s.

Even when they make no use of trade goods temporarily in their possession the Kundagai nonetheless see some personal advantage in effecting these exchanges to the satisfaction of their trading partners. Men give two basic reasons for accepting such transactions: fear of gaining a reputation as a bad risk in trade and fear of witchcraft. Transactions in which a Kundagai acts solely as an intermediary are usually initiated by a trading partner, whom it is often difficult to refuse, even if one cannot give an immediate return. The Kundagai trader, feeling obliged to obtain an exchange item for that given him may in turn give it to someone else, who himself is obligated to return a suitable item. Often the initiator of such a sequence of transactions himself specifies what he wants in exchange: in return for a plume he may ask for a kina shell, or a pig, a female pig, a female white pig, and so on.

A trader rarely accepts an item without giving a return eventually. Sometimes a man dies before completing a delayed exchange, and his kinsmen may refuse to honor the trade claiming to know nothing of the arrangements. Deliberate cheating in the form of refusing to reciprocate or giving a return of lesser value is rare and mainly confined to transactions between distant kinsmen or strangers where the victim is very young or old. Several men recounted instances when trade partners had failed to honor arrangements; because they were boys at the time, they said, they felt unable to press their claims. Some old men similarly lack the temerity to demand fair treatment and cannot persuade others to act on their behalf. Such cases underscore the scrupulous fair-dealing that characterizes the great bulk of transactions.

Failure to satisfy requests to act as an intermediary may earn a man the reputation of unreliable trader. Both established and potential partners may therefore be disinclined to deal with him, so that his supply of goods is cut off. The most active Kundagai trader told me in 1974 that he accepted all trade goods given to him because if he satisfies his trading partners they will, from time to time, give him valuables as gifts, simply to maintain good relations with him, thus ensuring his continued cooperation in future transactions. Most of the transactions he has engaged in using his own goods involve gifts from appreciative trading partners in other settlements. He has done little hunting to provide himself with trade goods.

Failure to comply with a trading partner's requests, then, leads to bad feelings and the severing of further relations. Although no one admitted to being treated in this way, many did remark that they had ceased trading with certain men who had proved themselves unsatisfactory partners. I did not hear of any aggrieved trader taking recourse to violence, although a man will complain to his friends and associates who may also hesitate to deal with an unreliable trader.

Since the establishment of the Local Government Council in 1966, men who renege on a trade transaction may be called before a *kot*. I learned of only one case where a dispute over failure to complete a trade transaction was referred to a kiap. Since much trade is between kinsmen (see below) some Kundagai who have debts owed to them have done no more than make demands on their trading partners. It is improper, they say, to take a kinsman to *kot*. This inhibition on involving kin in public disputes seems to extend to close real collateral and affinal kin.

Disputes commonly arise over the trade of pigs, even when a transaction is completed in accordance with requests. The great majority of pigs are traded as small, recently weaned piglets, which suffer high mortality. If a man finds that an animal is sickly he may return it and ask for a replacement. The request is usually honored. If a pig dies of sickness within a period of up to about a month after being traded the pig's owner holds his trading partner responsible for the initial poor condition of the beast. His response varies, partly depending on his relationship with his trading partner. If the latter is a close kinsman or a particularly valuable partner, a man may accept the situation or ask for a few Kina or a small shell in compensation. Where the relationship is less close a replacement pig or its full value in money or other goods is usually demanded. The trading partner generally asserts that the pig was in good condition when he handed it over and that he is therefore not liable to pay compensation, though in the face of insistent demands he may give in. There is no recourse to compensation when the trader is a stranger from a distant place, as is increasingly the case in recent times.

Besides practical reasons of making temporary use of goods and maintaining a satisfactory reputation, some men gave another pressing reason for complying with partner's requests: fear of witchcraft. Witches are quick to anger, and failure to satisfy their expectations in trade may be sufficient to induce a mystical attack. My Kundagai friends were frequently concerned about witches and suspected that many went undetected. Witches are generally secretive about their powers and, although there are many suspicions and imputations spread in gossip, there are few divinations, open accusations, or confessions. Only the most notorious witches become at all known beyond their own settlements. Under these circumstances almost anyone might be a witch, and so it is thought wise to do one's best to comply with a partner's request to supply a particular item in case he is a witch.

There are, however, other powerful though unarticulated reasons for engaging in trade, whether transactions involve personal property or only other men's things. All goods traded are desired at a conscious, articulated level by the Maring because they are critical for the proper conduct of celebration, as decorations, or for use in prestations. But I would further argue that to engage in trade is to handle metaphorically or contact the symbolic properties of the goods also, as these are made manifest and meaningful in other contexts. To trade is to contact and reflect on what these goods mean in the contexts wherein they are engaged as signals of social reproduction. There is, for example, a sensuous quality to the way a man may examine a trade plume—running its filaments softly through his hand, waving it gently in the sunlight to catch the gleam of iridescence. Again, shells, axes, knives and, above all, piglets are delicately touched, stroked, held, and fondled in a dreamy way as a trader ponders whether to accept them. Trading is thus more than merely provisioning oneself with the means to participate in ceremony or prestation, or the conversion of use values of one kind into use values of another. This conclusion must be so, in that so much trade involves only a transient hold on goods and depends on continuing the flow, and so denying oneself the opportunity to fund prestations in particular. But even in such ephemeral contact with objects of value the trader may be brought into contact with their nonmaterial essence and significance. In that sense, trade may be an end in itself beside the contingent and pragmatic reasons discussed above. In similar vein, although an active trading career may gain a man some notoriety, there is no particular status as such attached to the big trader. Trade is, however, one indication to the self and others of the span and effectiveness of one's relationships.

OCCASIONS FOR TRADE AND THE CONDUCT OF TRANSACTIONS

Almost any public gathering is a suitable occasion for trade, as large numbers of people are present who may be approached in order to find a trading partner. Men therefore take plumes, pigs, or other items when accompanying a bridewealth payment to another settlement, or offer goods to such visitors. When visiting relatives in other settlements for one reason or another a man often takes items to exchange with his host or other men, and he can expect to be offered goods by men of his host's settlement. People also make journeys alone or in small parties to other settlements solely or principally to trade. The most fruitful occasions for trade are gatherings where men decorate themselves and dance. In the past dances were all associated with ceremonies in the Maring *konj kaiko* ritual cycle or the Kalam *semi* initiation ceremonies. Now, dances celebrating Christmas or the opening of new public amenities provide further occasions for gatherings and trade. Since the Kundagai and many other Maring groups retain small stocks of plumes suitable for major decorations, shortly before participating in a dance they visit other settlements to obtain plumes and marsupial skins to wear. Some decorations are later returned to their owners, but many are exchanged after the dancing. Dancers may carry extra plumes that they do not use in decorations but which they trade. Thus at the close of ceremonies the danceground becomes like a temporary market, where men exchange their decorations for pigs, shells, steel tools, and money brought by other visitors intending to trade. Goods also change hands when no immediate return can be made, and the partners pledge to supply requested exchange items later.

Dances are favored occasions for trade not only because they are the largest gatherings of people carrying many valuables, but because they attract visitors from many settlements, thus affording the prospective trader with a large number of potential exchange partners and exchange goods from a variety of resource zones. Table 44 shows the proportion of transactions conducted on different types of occasions. The table includes both occasions when the Kundagai made visits to other settlements and when traders from other places came to Tsuwenkai. The category "Dances" includes transactions conducted immediately after dances, most of which were *konj kaiko* or *semi* festivals. "Special trade visits" refers to journeys made by the Kundagai and other traders with the primary aim of trading. "Other visits" includes journeys made to or by relatives of other settlements, attending community activities, such as roadworking, and to various other visits, such as accompanying a government patrol.

Trade arising from "other visits" is probably considerably more important than the table suggests. However, a trader may serve many purposes in visiting other settlements—visiting matrikin or sisters and their husbands, renewing old acquaintances, attending ceremonies as a participant or spectator, as well as trading. Data for the table span a wide time spectrum. Although special trade visits were the predominant occasion for trade by 1974, and undoubtedly continue to be so, trade following dances and at specially prearranged trade gatherings was formerly more important. A great number of transactions conducted on special trade visits are with men from settlements beyond normal trading ranges in precontact times. Specially arranged trade gatherings[3] are seldom if ever organized nowadays. Before contact, however, they were occasionally held with the Manamban, Kauwatyi, and Cenda. Having fixed a date the Kundagai carried plumes, marsupial skins, and cassowaries to the appointed places—long grassy ridges near clan cluster boundaries affording safety from surprise attack—while men of the neighboring groups and their friends from elsewhere brought pigs, shells, or steel tools. Participants would then seek out individuals to trade with, and transactions were invariably completed immediately and usually with unrelated men. These occasions therefore were not unlike trade at dances, when many people who would not have contact otherwise were present. Kundagai also visited, but did not organize, similar gatherings in the Simbai.

A man wishing to trade either waits for visitors or takes his wares elsewhere. When visiting other settlements he may receive food and shelter from kin or affines, who often undertake to trade with him also.

TABLE 44. OCCASIONS FOR TRADE TO 1974

Occasion	No. of transactions	% of Total
Dances	123	21.1
Special trade visits	327	56.1
Other visits	124	21.3
Special trade gatherings	9	1.5
TOTAL	583	100.0

If he has no relatives in a settlement, another man, often a big-man, usually offers him hospitality. If a trader's host is not prepared to trade with him he displays his wares to others, stating what he wants in return. Potential partners may make counteroffers, often of goods not requested by the trader. Either he accepts such proposals immediately or, more often, he continues to search for someone willing to transact on his stipulated terms. This may involve moving to other settlements. This raises the question of whether such strategies are a masked form of haggling or bargaining. I argue that they are not, for two reasons. First, a refusal to accept terms different from those already stipulated is hardly a bargaining tactic if one has moved on. A trader does not threaten to pack up and leave if his terms are not met; he simply refuses any counteroffers and departs, thereby denying the possibility of further negotiation. Of course, others may well acquiesce to the trader's terms on seeing him prepare to depart. The point is that such confrontations are not structured by an orientation toward a negotiable outcome in which both parties may give ground on initial demands, privately determined in the expectation from the outset of haggling. In recounting trade histories during 1973–1974 and 1978 it was rare for informants to describe instances of bargaining. But in 1985 I gathered a number of explicit accounts of bargaining, mainly where a Kundagai attempted to beat down the amount of cash demanded by Minj–Wahgi traders in exchange for pigs. Informants agreed that bargaining was generally absent from trade before the 1980s, and the appearance of accounts of the practice in trade histories collected in 1985 certainly supports their opinion.

Second, I argue that continuing to search for someone willing to trade on particular terms and moving to other settlements are not bargaining tactics as such, since it is not the exchange value of what is offered that is being negotiated but the relative social utilities or use values involved. These utilities may shift in response to the trader's involvement in ceremonies, prestations, and the like, which render certain plumes desirable at one time but not another, or his present pig stocks surplus to his short-term requirements, and so on. The case of two Kuma men who visited Tsuwenkai in 1974 illustrates such negotiations. These traders arrived in the midafternoon and displayed their money to a few Kundagai who greeted them at the meeting ground. They said they wanted Vulturine Parrot and Lesser Bird of Paradise feathers. Several men produced Lesser Bird of Paradise skins and a set of eagle feathers, but no parrot feathers. The visitors pronounced disinterest in the eagle feathers and dismissed the Lesser Bird of Paradise as of inferior quality. A Kundagai then suggested exchanging his Lesser Bird of Paradise plume for an axe the visitors carried, but they declined; they wanted the axe for protection and announced their intention to move on to the next village. Loath to allow the men to carry their money elsewhere some Kundagai proposed a gambling session of *laki*—an aptly named card game of chance, in which the luck was with the visitors.

Trade is always a private matter between individuals. It is not, however, conducted in a secretive manner, especially during visits by trading expeditions, which sometimes generate small excited crowds of onlookers. Other than dealings with such expeditions, where the visitors are often cautious in strange surroundings, most transactions have a casual air about them. Even at dances when many men come to seek out partners, actual transactions remain unobtrusive.

The purpose of a visitor's journey is usually quickly learned in polite conversation with those met along the way. Unless the visitor intends to trade with a particular individual, such chance meetings may lead to a successful transaction.

Even today a man seldom travels alone to settlements where he has no relatives or friends to shelter him but brings another, if only a boy, for companionship and to help look out for witches and other hazards. In the past, the dangers of a journey were compounded by the fear of physical attack, and men rarely went to strange places unless accompanying others who had relatives or friends there. Trade with strangers in precontact times was often of a formal nature. An old man described dealings with axe-makers of Wum–Tsenga in these terms:

Men of Bokapai, Kompiai, and Koinambe had trade partners in Wum–Tsenga. They took plumes and salt there and slept in their friends' houses. Wum–Tsenga men especially desired *bunk* salt, as this was superior to the *aka* salt they obtained from elsewhere. Visiting traders went straight to their friends' houses, where they rested, ate, and talked first. Later the host would ask, "What have you brought—salt or plumes? I have stone axes and cowries here."

Stranger Wum–Tsenga men would gather, bringing axes or shells to trade with the visitors. They would ask, "Did you bring things to trade with us or to give only to your friend?" If trade was intended, the visitor and local men displayed their goods. If an exchange was agreed on, the visitor handed plumes or salt to his friend, who handed it to the local man. Exchange items were handed back to the visitor by way of his friend. The exchange was done through the host so that he would not be offended by thinking his guest had ignored him. A guest may also trade directly with his host or exchange gifts. A man who has no local friends trades directly with strangers.

Kundagai of Tsuwenkai and Kinimbong infrequently accompanied Bokapai kin to Wum–Tsenga, though they had no established friends there and never went alone. A similar formal approach is still occasionally followed when trading with the partner of a kinsman. For instance, Giewai's trade partner of Koriom brought a pig to Tsuwenkai in search of feathers. Giewai's sister's husband of Tsuwenkai, Pinai, wanted the pig and gave parrot skins to Giewai, asking him to exchange them for the animal. Soon after the Koriom man returned home the pig died, and Pinai asked Giewai to get another. The two men went to Koriom where Giewai gave K1 to his partner to solicit another pig. Both men then returned to Tsuwenkai, and Giewai later went back to Koriom to collect the pig. Several other Kundagai have traded with the same Koriom man but have dealt directly with him rather than using Giewai as an intermediary. Trade with this man is sought because of his reputation as a reliable trader.

If an exchange cannot be completed immediately the partners may set a date to finalize the transaction. Occasionally prearranged signals are displayed in an agreed place to show that a trader may come to collect a trade good. These consist of smoky fires or the glossy white bases of certain cultivated, broad-leaved ornamental plants, hung up in prominent places such as landslide scars.

In his exhaustive survey of precontact highlands trade Hughes (1977) observed that the initiative in trade was generally taken by those located at lower altitudes than their trade partners. In other words, traders tended to move uphill in search of partners. I gathered no ordered data on which party to a transaction initiated the exchange, but from informants' accounts the initiator is clearly stated or can be deduced in over 1,000 cases collected in the three periods of fieldwork. Table 45 indicates that up to the mid-1970s the initiative in proposing transactions tended to be taken by those more distant from centers of plume consumption. Almost two-thirds of transactions were initiated by men located in more peripheral areas relative to ultimate plume consumers. In other words, plume suppliers more generally suggested trade than did plume consumers. This means that in trade between Tsuwenkai and Down-Jimi, Up-Simbai, and Trans-Simbai the Kundagai were, relatively speaking, plume consumers and were less liable to initiate trade, whereas in dealings with Up- and Cross-Jimi and Down-Simbai they tended to initiate the majority of transactions.

In the above calculations I have taken transactions conducted with trade parties of strangers as being initiated by the visitors; their very presence is an indication of their wish to trade. Such visits have increased greatly since pacification in the late 1950s, and parties from the upper-Jimi, Wahgi, and Simbu areas now visit Tsuwenkai quite often.

The table indicates that the initiative in trade has progressively been taken by more centrally located traders from the mid-1970s. Increasingly, however, these traders have entered the Jimi as sellers of pigs rather than searchers for plumes and other forest products. Their growing domination of the trade links with the northern-highland periphery is signaled by the growing frequency of their visits, the resources they can marshal for expeditions—notably in the form of trucks or chartered aircraft—and their capacity to drain the slender cash reserves of Jimi people in return for high-quality pigs so desirable for deployment in prestations.

TRADE AND SOCIABILITY

Two characteristics commonly given in distinguishing trade or barter from gift or ceremonial exchange are that trade transactions are usually completed immediately and involve unrelated persons (e.g., Harding 1981; Hughes 1977; Tueting 1935; van Baal 1975). The same features are among those distinguishing Sahlins's paradigmatic forms of balanced and negative reciprocity—within which trade as understood here falls—from generalized reciprocity (Sahlins 1972). That

TABLE 45. DIRECTIONS IN INITIATIVE
IN PROPOSING TRADE

NOTE: Directions are relative to Tsuwenkai. Thus, transactions "from periphery toward center" include those initiated with Tsuwenkai men by partners Down-Jimi, Up- and Trans-Simbai, as well as by Tsuwenkai men with partners Up- and Cross-Jimi, and Down-Simbai. Similarly, transactions "from center toward periphery" include those initiated with Tsuwenkai traders by partners located closer to the central highlands as well as by Tsuwenkai traders with partners located toward the periphery.

	No.	%
A. Data to 1974		
From periphery toward center	524	61.4
From center toward periphery	329	38.6
Total	853	
B. 1974-1978		
From periphery toward center	50	47.2
From center toward periphery	56	52.8
Total	106	
C. 1979-1985		
From periphery toward center	53	40.2
From center toward periphery	79	59.8
Total	132	

Maring trade shows the reverse characteristics in itself is insufficient to invalidate such generalizations. I believe, however, an analysis of the Kundagai material does show such typifications of the trading relationship to be too rigidly drawn and sociologically naive.

In table 46 I present data showing the relative prevalence of delayed and immediate transactions in different periods. Just what amounts to a delay is, of course, problematic. Many transactions can be completed at once because the traders are carrying their wares at the moment of negotiation. This is a common pattern after dances. Often, however, one party to a transaction has to go to his house to collect an agreed exchange object, and the attendant delay may be a few minutes to several hours. Sometimes, as when visiting kinsmen, the delay between handing over a good and receiving a return may run into days, as the trader enjoys the hospitality of his partner.[4] I treat all such transactions as immediately completed, in the sense that neither party is inconvenienced by the waiting period and when they part both can carry away an exchange item. A delayed exchange, by contrast, is one in which one

TABLE 46. DELAYED AND IMMEDIATE EXCHANGE[a]

Period and relationship	Delayed No.	%	Immediate No.	%
A. Up to 1974:				
Kin	697	90.8	71	9.2
Nonkin	35	6.8	483	93.2
TOTAL	732	56.9	554	43.1
B. 1974-1978:				
Kin	74	91.4	7	8.6
Nonkin	5	11.4	39	88.6
TOTAL	79	63.2	46	36.8
C. 1979-1985:				
Kin	47	87.0	7	13.0
Nonkin	6	8.3	66	91.7
TOTAL	53	42.1	73	57.9

[a] This table reflects relative importance of kin ties in delayed/immediate exchange in terms of a restricted sample of cases. Relative importance of relationships between traders which can be calculated from these figures are not representative of a larger sample of transactions, for which see table 47.

party receives a good but the other still awaits a return when they part company. The length of such delays varies greatly from a few days to as long as two or three years. At the extreme the transaction shades off into the realization by the patient waiter that he is the victim of a failed exchange. When initiating trade a man may be setting in train a sequence of delayed exchanges along an extensive chain of partnerships, so that it is not at all uncommon for the sequence to take many months to complete. The extent of delays is largely dependent on the number of links in a transactional sequence and the distance between the consecutive links. Thus a Kundagai thinks little of taking a pig to Bokapai to complete a transaction: he can make the round trip easily in one day, but a journey to more distant places may be put off until he has some additional cause to travel.

Where a man acts as an intermediary in trade for someone else at least one delayed transaction necessarily is involved, since he is unable to give a return until he has made at least one other exchange. In most informants' case histories it is seldom clear whether this second transaction is delayed or immediate. It is therefore probable that delayed exchange is a good deal more prevalent than the table suggests. Most transactions with distant strangers on trading expeditions are completed immediately. Since the incidence of such trade has increased since about the mid-1950s it follows that trade with nonkin has also increased in importance. But table 46 gives a somewhat distorted view of the relative importance of trade with related and unrelated partners, since in most accounts the immediacy of completing transactions with kin is less readily determined when not specified by an informant.

Despite these cautions the patterns of immediacy of exchange are striking. The overwhelming proportion of dealings with kin in all periods involve delayed transactions, whereas the great majority of transactions with nonkin have been immediately concluded. Here I use the term kin somewhat loosely to refer to affines also. The magnitude of fluctuations in these proportions has been small, compared to shifts in the relative importance of delayed and immediate transactions regardless of relationship. Up to 1974 most transactions (57 percent) were delayed. In the six years to 1985 the pattern had almost exactly reversed, with 58 percent of transactions completed immediately. But unlike most other changes in the practice of trade so far discussed, there was no general trend in the reversal of patterns, for in the period 1974–1978 delayed exchanges were even more prevalent than in earlier times (63 percent of all transactions), a matter to which I shall return shortly.

Most of the delayed exchanges with nonkin have been with well-known individuals. These include formal trade partners, relatives of other Kundagai or with friends, such as men met on coastal plantations, or fellow office holders: councillors, committeemen, or luluais.

Delayed trading occurs mainly with those who may also exchange minor prestations as expressions of mutual regard and solidarity. The problem then arises of distinguishing delayed trade from reciprocal gift giving. This is especially so given the common observation that much "trade" actually takes the form of mutual gift giving between formal, unrelated trade friends (van Baal 1975; Harding 1967; Sahlins 1972). Employing the Maring concepts of transaction helps overcome the problem. In most cases informants described the conduct of exchange spontaneously in such a way that it was evident they regarded the transaction as trade. In the event of ambiguity I asked men to apply the appropriate term to describe a transaction—trade, *munggoi rigima*, or gift/minor prestation, *munggoi aure awom*. In only a small number of cases were my informants themselves unsure of the appropriate classification, and such exchanges are not included in the quantitative analysis of trade here.

An inference of the above figures is that the Kundagai and those with whom they trade have shown until recent times a marked preference for dealing with kinsmen and a readiness to accept delays. A consequence of extending trading relations to kinsmen is that the pool of potential partners is greatly expanded, and a willingness to allow delays in concluding a transaction facilitates the flow of goods that might otherwise not take place.[5] As I indicated above, not all nonkin with whom a man may trade are strangers. But it is also important to note that not all kin are nonstrangers, a point to which I return later.

A willingness to allow delay in trade involves an element of trust in one's partner. Kinsmen are more worthy of trust because they are also subject to moral ties. Indeed, trust is as much an aspect of kinship morality as is a commitment to reciprocate. But aside from these rather elusive dimensions of morality that I discuss further below there are more pragmatic considerations. Moral pressure to complete a transaction is more effective on a kinsman partly because it is with such people that the most enduring social relations are maintained. A kinsman who fails to complete a transaction may be confronted repeatedly with the fact by his aggrieved trading partner. Such pressure perhaps weakens as geographic and genealogical distances increase, at which stage the threat of severing further relationships or fear of a witchcraft attack by a disappointed partner provide added sanctions.

Having noted that kinsmen are favored trading partners it is now necessary to qualify the generalization in respect of the time periods and general directions involved. Data presented in table 47 show that there has been a general increase in dealings with nonkin since contact but that this trend has not been uniform in either space or time. The relative importance of trade with kin and nonkin by the Kundagai with more peripherally located partners (Down-Jimi, Up- and Trans-Simbai) has shown the least variation, ranging from 85 percent of all transactions in that direction to a low of 74 percent. Trade with nonkin has always been of considerably greater significance in dealings between Tsuwenkai men and partners in settlements located closer to the central highlands, ranging from almost 45 percent of all transactions in that direction before contact to 72 percent in the succeeding two decades. Interestingly, the importance of trade with nonkin in more recent times has been less than the immediate postcontact period. Bearing in mind the development of trade, this difference in the importance of trade with nonkin according to direction is not unexpected. Greater emphasis on trade with nonkin located toward the central highlands is under-

TABLE 47. RELATIONSHIP OF TRADERS BY
DIRECTION AND PERIOD[a]

Direction relative to Tsuwenkai	Relationship			
	Relatives		Nonrelatives[b]	
	No.	%	No.	%
A. Pre-1956				
Toward center	138	55.4	111	44.6
Toward periphery	124	84.4	23	15.6
Combined	262	66.2	134	33.8
B. 1956-1974:				
Toward center	245	28.0	630	72.0
Toward periphery	410	78.2	114	21.8
Combined	655	46.8	744	53.2
C. 1974-1978:				
Toward center	54	51.9	50	48.1
Toward periphery	59	85.5	10	14.5
Combined	113	65.3	60	34.7
D. 1979-1985:				
Toward center	44	32.6	91	67.4
Toward periphery	39	73.6	14	26.4
Combined	83	44.1	105	55.9

[a] This table is based on all records of transactions datable to the periods listed and for which adequate data are available on origins of traders and their relationships. The table thus draws on a considerably larger sample than table 46, and more accurately reflects the relative weight of dealings with kin/nonkin than that table.
[b] Includes formal trade-partners and friends.

standable given that Kundagai trade links have extended furthest up and across the Jimi, that is, toward ultimate plume consumers. At the same time, ties of marriage have not yet been extended to these more populous areas, so that necessarily most traders remain unrelated.

What is particularly striking about the distribution of transactions according to the relationships of partners is the period 1974 to 1978. The relevant figures are more characteristic of the precontact era. Thus, although trade in this period was becoming significantly transformed, with an impoverished inventory of acceptable trade goods and growing structural dependence on the central highlands, the social organization of trade more closely typified aboriginal practice. Although it is easy enough to demonstrate this changing organization of trade, it is less easy to account for it except in essentially subjective terms.

The decade from about the mid-1960s was a period of considerable confidence in the Jimi. The new colonial order had been well established by that time, with relatively little violence and disruption to modes of existence. Villagers had accommodated to the new order and were gaining access to the new wealth in traditional goods and cash that followed pacification. Central highlanders still maintained a high demand for forest products, which stimulated both short- and long-distance trade in and beyond the Jimi. If I were to characterize the prevailing moods of Tsuwenkai men in 1974 and 1978 I would contrast them as ones of confidence followed by a sense of profound uncertainty.

In 1978 Kundagai men remarked on the replacement of virtually all Australian Administration field staff by nationals. The latter seldom went on patrols to outlying settlements like Tsuwenkai, contributing to a general feeling of having been abandoned by the government. Compounding this sense of isolation local development projects—notably the road link to the Simbai and Tabibuga government center in the Jimi—were falling into disrepair. Kundagai pointed to the section of the road cut through their territory, now overgrown with weeds or swept away in landslides. This sorry state of government-sponsored development was paralleled by a perceived decline in the quality of services offered by the mission based in Koinambe. Inflation in the national economy had led to sharply rising prices of most store-bought commodities. Visitors to my house frequently remarked on the contrast between the period prior to Independence in 1975, when Australian patrol officers and Australian currency had been "strong," and the post-Independence period, when national patrol officers and currency had become "soft" and ineffective. On a number of occasions men expressed a concern that after the heady days of Australian administration, the country would revert to precolonial conditions. I suggest, then, that the reemergence of an essentially precolonial pattern of trading relations in the late 1970s was a reflection of a more general sense of disquiet among Jimi people about the stability of the new social order. Here it is relevant to note also that whereas money became more widely used in trade as other items dropped out of use, the actual incidence of transactions involving money fell in this period (see table 35, chap. 6). This occurred despite the growing availability of cash through wage labor, sales of coffee, and circulation in prestations. There was, in short, a retreat to long-established, traditionally based social relationships at a local level in the sphere of trading relations, in a context where the prospects for continuing enjoyment of the expanded social horizons and opportunities offered by the colonial regime were perceived as now doubtful. The postcolonial order had taken on an uncertain, potentially dangerous character, much as the precolonial social order had, and the Kundagai trader responded by concentrating his dealings with known partners.

Significantly, some of the increasing dealings with kinsmen were with well-known coresidents. The 1974–1978 period saw a rise in the importance of trade within the settlement from just under 10 percent up to 1974 to just over 14 percent. Since the late 1970s internal trade has returned to pre-1974 levels.

By 1985 a new sense of confidence in prospects for development projects had reemerged, with the establishment of several alluvial gold-finding ventures in Tsuwenkai and elsewhere. Men still expressed considerable frustration about what they viewed as profound disinterest in their aspirations on the part of the government. There was, however, a growing awareness that they shared the capacity of their fellow countrymen to manage their own affairs. This found some expression in a considerable hostility toward mining-company exploration teams and European gold buyers that would have been unthinkable in the 1970s. This hostility took the form of petty vandalism, verbal clashes, and threats of physical violence.

The conduct of trade, then, in terms of the willingness to deal with strangers or travel more widely, has been influenced by the perceived stability and predictability of the wider regional and national social order.

In reviewing maritime regional trade systems Harding (1967) for the Vitiaz Strait and Schwartz (1963) for the Manus Islands have suggested that trade provides a mechanism for ensuring a degree of areal "organic integration," binding together through economic interdependence otherwise politically and geographically autonomous communities. In the Kundagai trade sphere the preponderance of transactions with relatives, especially prior to contact, and most especially with communities lying closer to primary plume suppliers, might at first sight be taken as an indication that trade is significantly patterned on kinship relations; in short, that contrary to Harding and Schwartz's argument, areal integration is achieved primarily through kinship and resulting political alliances. But an examination of Kundagai trade in greater depth shows that this conclusion is not supported. On the contrary, I suggest that wider kinship relations are patterned on exchange relations, including trade. A discussion of this issue must await a more detailed analysis of relationships between traders.

The Kundagai recognize four broad categories in speaking of relationships between traders. These are kinsmen, unrelated formal trade partners, unrelated friends, and strangers with whom contacts are ephemeral. Any trader, whatever his relationship, may be called *munggoi rigima yu,* "valuables exchange man." The term also applies to those with whom one habitually trades and more specifically to formal trade partners. By the latter I mean unrelated men with whom more or less permanent relations have been established for the express purpose of facilitating trade. Such partners are always of different, usually distant settlements. When a man dies his son may continue the partner relationship. Formal partnerships were probably of more significance in the past when they ensured hospitality and protection in potentially hostile situations where men of the partner's group may be allies of the visitor's major enemies, and so tempted to kill the stranger. Nonetheless, only eleven out of fifty-seven men claimed in 1973–1974 to have had formal partnerships. One man had three partners, another two, the rest one each, most of whom were distributed Up- and Cross-Jimi. Only 2.4 percent of all transactions to that time had been between formal trade partners, while those men maintaining partnerships conducted an average of 6.2 percent of all their transactions with partners (range: 1.1 to 18.8 percent). Formal partnerships of this kind are therefore not very important in facilitating trade. Indeed, I recorded no cases of trade with trade partners since 1974.

Unrelated friends are now usually referred to by the Melanesian Pidgin *pren,* "friend," but may also be termed *yemp nunt yu,* "he-gives I-can-eat man," which reveals the basis of the friendship: such friends are those who provide food and shelter in distant settlements. Before contact friends were often big-men, as it was they who were, and are, quick to offer hospitality to visitors. Nowadays, holding of common offices, such as luluai or Local Government councillor, forms a basis for a friendship. Many friends who occasionally trade with one another first met as fellow laborers on coastal plantations. Migrant labor has thus not only expanded the horizons of Kundagai men but also their interpersonal networks of social relations within the Jimi–Simbai area. In 1973–1974 eighteen Kundagai claimed to have special friends in other settlements with whom they traded. Friends were distributed in fourteen settlements, mainly toward the center, and in settlements with which the Kundagai do not intermarry. As partners to trade they were of negligible importance, being involved in only 1.2 percent of all transactions. Since then their significance as partners has increased slightly: 3.4 percent of all transactions in 1974–1978, and 2.7 percent in 1979–1985.

By contrast, unrelated men, *yu aure*, "man nothing," with whom ties of friendship or continuing trade are not maintained, account for a considerable proportion of all transactions: 32.5 percent up to 1956, 49 percent in 1956–1974, 31.2 percent in 1974–1978, and 53.2 percent in 1979–1985. The decline in trade with unrelated strangers in the late 1970s, alluded to above, is again clearly evident in these figures.

Any consanguine or affine is regarded as a potential trading partner, but certain categories of kin predominate as trade partners. This is partly a function of generation, partly of the nature of classificatory kin terminology, which renders certain kin terms more widely applicable than others.

In the following analysis I confine my discussion to data gathered in 1973–1974. This material represents a near-total record of the trading activities of all Kundagai men up to that period. It thus embraces the experiences of several men who had all but completed their trading careers, as well as others just embarking on theirs. As such, it represents a very substantial sample of the total set of relationships activated in trade by a given population of men up to a point in time. Data gathered in subsequent fieldwork is not in general conflict with material gathered in 1973–1974. Trade histories since 1974, however, have been collected from smaller, uncontrolled samples of men. These samples were not representative of the total trading population as the earlier one was. Most informants in later fieldwork were men who had been in their twenties and thirties in 1973–1974. As they aged, so had their personal kindreds changed in composition, with the death of older trading partners and the emergence of new, younger ones, and so on. Thus, for example, to observe that trade with brothers-in-law increased sharply between 1974 and 1978 tells us something about the activation of relationships among the sample of men interviewed in 1978, and possibly something about their shifting webs of kin ties, but does not necessarily represent a more general shift of emphasis in the kinds of relationships involved in partnerships in the population at large. In short, changes in the distribution of partnerships by kin category more likely reflect the particular age structure of the sample interviewed. Nonetheless, the distribution of frequencies of dealings with categories of kin remained fairly stable across the three samples with the exception of increased incidence of trade with brothers-in-law in 1974–1978 and fathers-/sons-in-law in 1979–1985.

Most trade between relatives involves same-generation men (65 percent of such trade), a feature that has remained little changed over time (table 48). Although many men favor trade with particular relatives (in the same or ascending or descending generations) on the basis of such partners' demonstrated reliability, there seems to be no actual preference for dealing with men of the same generation. The statistical preponderance of such relationships is explained by the simple fact that most men have more kinsmen of same-generation categories to choose as trading partners, especially in their active middle age when senior kinsmen (such as mother's brothers or wife's fathers) are dead or inactive, and younger men (e.g., sister's sons) are not yet engaged in trade.

Since the terms listed in table 48 may be widely extended to classificatory kin, it is not possible to determine the relative proportions of dealings with kin and affines who can be placed precisely in a genealogical framework as compared with those who cannot. As elsewhere in Melanesia, however, Maring kinship does not adhere to genealogical models, so that the determination of "real" and "classificatory" is problematic. As I indicate below, trade may be a significant mode of constructing relationships between men, which are articulated in kinship idioms.

In addition to the kinship categories listed in the tables, men occasionally trade with *koka,* grandfather/grandson. Disparities in age explain the rarity of such exchanges. A little more commonly, men deal with women—mainly sisters, daughters, and mother's or father's sisters. Usually women only act as intermediaries, passing on goods to other men. Women, however, occasionally trade with men on their own behalf in minor goods, such as marsupial fur used to decorate string aprons. Trade with women accounts for 0.7 percent of all transactions. The incidence rose from 0.2 percent of all transactions before contact, to 0.8 percent up to 1974, 1.7 percent in 1974–1978, and down to 0.5 percent in 1979–1985. Trade is therefore very much a male activity; women do not trade among themselves outside of recent and infrequent minor transactions of loose fur, string bags, or vegetables for small sums of cash.

The majority of close collateral kin generally live in settlements with which the Kundagai have intermarried at some time. By the extension of kinship terms to classificatory kin the Kundagai can claim relation-

TABLE 48. KUNDAGAI TRADE WITH RELATIVES

Maring category	Relationships
1. *anya, wowa*	F and those real F called *gwite*
2. *gwite*	B, MZS, WZH, SWF, DHF and *wai nako* of *anya*
3. *wai nako*	S, and S of *gwite*
4. *latse*	WB, ZH, of self and *gwite*, H of anyone called "sister" (*atsa*)
5. *imatse*	WF, WM, DH, WMB, BWF of self and *gwite*
6. *alianggai*	FZH and H of women real F called "sister"
7. *bapa*	MB, MMBS, FBWB and men real M called "brother"
8. *wai wump*	ZS and sons of women *gwite* calls sister
9. *wambe*	Sons of *alianggai* and *bapa*
10. *mamia*	FFZS, FMBS (those whom *anya* called *wambe*)

Trade relationships by category:

	1	2	3	4	5	6	7	8	9	10
No. cases	76	258	50	300	87	27	62	57	158	22
% of total	6.9	23.5	4.6	27.3	7.9	2.5	5.7	5.2	14.4	2.0
(n=1,097)										

ships to a great number of kinsmen in many other settlements as well. Many kin are encountered, nonetheless, even "created," solely in the context of trade.

Maring notions of relatedness, as elsewhere in New Guinea, are only loosely grounded in a genealogical framework. At collateral peripheries a geneological idiom is substituted by a more general one: that of residence. This idiom itself is based on ideas of commonality contingent on coresidence. It is through common residence that people share, first, a common substance derived from the contributions of blood, semen, and mother's milk to the development of body and mind, and from consuming products of the land. The fertility of crops, pigs, and people, and hence continuity of groups, is ensured by ritual supplication of ancestral spirits. Rituals of this kind engage collectivities at various structural levels from family to clan cluster depending on context (cf. Rappaport 1968). Second, groups of greater or lesser inclusiveness participate in giving or receiving group-defining exchanges such as bridewealth (at subclan and clan level) or salt-pork prestations to military allies (at local-group level). This diffuse notion of common identity is represented in another idiom, that of agnation. Agnation is therefore not the principle underlying relatedness, nor is coresidence itself the principle underlying idioms of agnation. Rather, coresidence itself is a metaphor for an underlying commonality derived from common participation in exchange and ingestion of common substance through the sharing of food produced on a particular territory. According to the Kundagai, these entailments of coresidence lie behind the assimilation of nonagnates who demonstrate a commitment to the affairs of their hosts, regardless of the nature of prior kin ties (see Healey 1979 for a fuller treatment). The Maring, however, do not appear to have an explicitly elaborated or coherent ideology of what constitutes substance and how it is transmitted. Although recognizing this, LiPuma (1988) nonetheless proceeds to identify an implicit model of substance for the Maring that leads to a view of social organization contrary to my own. Some brief comment on his treatment of Maring kinship is therefore appropriate here.

LiPuma considers that his systematic model of the principles of Maring substance generates the observed regularities of cultural practice (1988). In this model, agnatic substance ("grease") is transmitted through a line of males, maternal substance (blood) through a line of females; the intersection of these substances, effected through marriage exchange and reciprocal compensatory payments, defines a person's identity and the boundaries of clans. Agnatic substance is further incorporated by sharing food grown on clan land, which embodies the agnatic substance of those whose bodies have decayed and been buried on that land.

To this point LiPuma's interpretation clearly parallels my own and enriches the ethnographic record. His model is arguably overdetermined, however, in the sense that it becomes the organizing principle for the presentation of ethnographic data, while at the same time being acknowledged as a highly systematic explication of an implicit, unarticulated native model in the first place. That is, the model is essentially a distillation of ethnographic data but in turn becomes a mechanism by which other data become ordered. As such, the model of substance and its role in the organization of social reproduction is given an unwarranted degree of consistency, facticity, and generality. Thus, for example, although LiPuma's research was conducted primarily among the Kauwatyi—which in terms of size, unity, political and military power, and ecology is atypical of Maring communities—his analysis is cast in terms of an idealized, undifferentiated construct: "the Maring." Furthermore, his approach gives insufficient weight to a recurrent feature of Melanesian cosmologies: their tendency toward contradictory, even inchoate, formulations (cf. Brunton 1980; Healey 1988), as well as individual, historical, and regional variations. There are, for example, significant differences between aspects of Kundagai and Kauwatyi social and political organization, ecology, and cosmology which cannot simply be ascribed to the distorting tendencies of different analytic approaches, or even, I think, of favored expert informants.

LiPuma's model of Maring social organization gives categorical significance to cultural conceptions of substance. He sees exchange as flowing from the conceptions of substance and its transmission. Gift exchange for him compensates agnatic lines for their loss of substance in the marriage of female members. That is, exchange is contingent on the operation of the model of substance transmission: it is an aspect of social practice which expresses relationships already logically prefigured in ideology.

Kundagai praxis leads me to ascribe to exchange a more prominent, dialectical significance in social organization. It expresses given relationships, but it may also be a constitutive and creative act that pushes the idioms of relatedness beyond notions of both genealogy and substance. Thus, those who contribute to one another's prestations and who share wealth received may seize on this as indicative of a relationship, marked by the use of agnatic kin terms. Common identity as expressed through the use of agnatic kin terms (and their matrilateral and affinal permutations) is the basis of the common extension of "brother" (*gwite*) relationships to men of distant places, whose mothers are regarded as sisters (*atsa*) because they were residents of the same settlement prior to their marriages (regardless of any known clan affiliations). The preponderance of trade with "brothers" and "brothers-in-law" stems in large part from the extension of kin terms to classificatory MZS, MZDH, and MZSWB. Quite often, none of these links can be specified genealogically at any point.

Several Kundagai made it clear that they sought out such kin—whom I shall refer to as "constructed kin"[6]—solely as trading partners; in other words, trade is the overt reason for contacts, not kinship, and the relationship is generally confined to the context of trade. By invoking kinship relations a man is making a moral claim to hospitality and compliance in exchange.

Generally, these constructed kin are sought in more distant settlements, mainly in the Simbai and beyond and in the lower Jimi, and may be as far afield as the middle Kaironk Valley and the Asai. A man has kin in such places because he trades there; he does not trade in regions because he knows he has kin there, as is borne out by the fact that much trade also occurs between unrelated people. Thus, although I have shown that a large proportion of trading partners, at least toward primary plume suppliers, are kinsmen, it is clear that their interactions are confined solely to trading with and sheltering their visitors. The relationship is not necessarily an enduring one, since the partners are separated by gulfs of geographic and genealogical distance, so that the maintenance of mutual assistance and affectivity is difficult. Indeed, they often do not even know one another's names. Trade, nonetheless, provides the opportunity for the establishment of wide-ranging personal networks, expressed in the idiom of kinship, which serve to bind the Kundagai into an extensive region. This is important in the postcontact era with its greatly expanded horizons encompassing a larger and mainly unknown world. The creation of kinship ties, however tenuously, extending into that expanded world where relationships are otherwise dominated by new and foreign idioms, gives individuals a degree of familiarity and control over the erstwhile strange and potentially hostile.

The material here is at odds with prevailing notions of trade which typify it as an impersonal, self-interested act, wherein the necessity for ongoing social relations are denied precisely because the terms of exchange are stipulated, balanced, and concluded immediately, occasioning no basis for further meetings. At the same time, that very state of requital allows (but does not impel) traders to come together in peace again as if there had never been anything between them (cf. van Baal 1975; Sahlins 1972). It also confounds the simplistic analytic distinction between commodity and gift exchange, as developed in Marxist theory, which holds that commodity exchange (conforming to my use of the notion trade) mainly occurs across societal boundaries, whereas gift exchange is confined mainly within social groups (e.g., Godelier 1977: 128–129).

On the one hand, much trade occurs between close kinsmen, and so in the models developed by Sahlins, van Baal, and others could be interpreted as a denial of social relationships normatively characterized by generalized reciprocity. On the other hand, much trade occurs between comparative strangers, who nonetheless construct kinship relations between them to sustain a mutual interest that might otherwise not develop.

Clearly, more is involved in trade than the equivalence of goods and the satisfaction of material wants. There is also a heavy sociable dimension that goes beyond a preference for dealing with kin out of reasons of pragmatic self-interest and is masked to the participants themselves by the general and more or less automatic adoption of customary rates of exchange. All trade transactions have the appearance of sameness in their capacity to move objects and satisfy wants, which are the overt objectives of trade in Maring exegesis and the major focus of most studies of trade. Thus, related and unrelated partners of long-standing or ephemeral relationships will trade the same goods at the same rates of exchange. But if one shifts focus from the act itself to the embeddedness of the transaction in its wider social milieu, one realizes that though the material consequences of Maring transactions are always much the same, there is the capacity for the sociable dimensions of the transaction to be contextually and meaningfully variable (cf. Bourdieu 1977). More specifically, what is associated with trade transactions, and can make subtle statements about different events, is the sociability of the exchange as implicated in such features as the kind of hospitality given to a visiting trader, the acceptance of goods one has no personal desire for, and the demonstration of trust in allowing a delay in completing a transaction. This occurs in a context where much trade is clearly self-interested and where relationships are completely unmarked. The common experience of such trade itself heightens awareness of the meaningful, qualitative differences in overtly similar transactions between friends and kinsmen.

Trade always results in the movement of goods, subject to ecological constraints discussed in earlier chapters, but the sociable dimensions framing the outcome may vary. At one extreme is the polite impersonality of unrelated strangers who each desire the goods offered by the other and make an immediate exchange.[7] At the other is the acceptance from an esteemed kinsman of something the trader does not personally want, with a pledge to make a return in the future, the whole negotiations occurring while the visitor enjoys the food and shelter of his host, perhaps for days.

Hospitality ranges from the exchange of pleasantries and perhaps tobacco with strangers to the offering of prestige foods, shelter, entertainment, companionship, and protection. More substantial hospitality of the latter kind is morally due to close matrikin and affines, in accordance with notions of generalized reciprocity proper between such persons. Yet the Kundagai are reluctant to presume on the hospitality of all kinsmen on the basis of putative kinship alone. Claiming kinship does not itself give one the right to expect hospitality. Many men are careful to avoid arriving uninvited on others' doorsteps hoping for hospitality unless they have particular business with them, such as completing or initiating a trade transaction. Such punctiliousness is thought unnecessary when visiting a close consanguine, such as a sister and her husband, or a mother's brother, among whom a welcome should be assured. Thus, when a trader seeks out a constructed kinsman he is not simply making a moral claim to receive hospitality. Rather, he is making a qualitative statement about the nature of the relationship, or what it could be, in the sense that to seek hospitality (if only implicitly) is to convey a message that the relationship is regarded as sufficiently close in the particular context for the visitor to feel free to presume upon the generosity of the other. This is because, as I argue below, the offer of trade is itself a reciprocal act of generosity. The search for kinship ties between erstwhile strangers introduces moral principles that should obtain between the parties. Such appeals are therefore liable to introduce a strained formality between constructed kin that may be tested over a series of reciprocal visits for the purpose of trade. Kinship here is clearly a processual rather than categorical relationship. In such contexts, the morality of kinship has the appearance of generalized, disinterested reciprocity expressed in generous hospitality and is spoken of as such by the Kundagai, but it may actually constitute a form of exploitation. Certainly, some men complain of those who, invoking ties of kinship, presume upon their hospitality without recompense. If the relationship can weather such strains, however, what began as conformity to moral principles may end as hospitality freely given on the basis of mutual respect and affection for the other, not as a category of kinsman but as an individual. To the observer the outward form of the transactions is the same, but to the participants there is a wealth of difference in their experience of the events.

Besides reciprocal hospitality what tests a trading relationship is the performance of the parties as traders. I have already noted that one is more likely to accept goods one has no desire for from a kinsman because, as the Kundagai say, of the obligation to satisfy a kinsman's demands. If pressed, some men couch acceptance in the more pragmatic terms of maintaining trading relationships or avoiding exposing themselves to possible attacks by aggrieved witches. In addition, I also suggested that the mere handling of objects, which have powerful if unarticulated symbolic meanings in other contexts of use, may be an end in itself to some degree. Whatever a recipient's justifications, to the donor acceptance has something of the quality of generosity. Indeed, as some men indicated, the recipient himself may see his acceptance of trade as an act of generosity, in recognition of the hospitality received from his partner or a past exemplary trading record. Men said such things as, "I did not want what my partner offered; I was tired of traveling to find suitable return objects. I accepted it because he had been good to me in the past, and always honored our trade transactions."

A long delay in completing a transaction is more likely to be tolerated where a partner has otherwise shown good faith. A nonkin relationship is less likely to support delayed exchange because of the lesser sociable content that provides both extenuating circumstances and some moral obligation to conclude an exchange. I have noted that accepting delays implies trust in one's partner and that kinsmen are more worthy of trust because they are the subject of moral ties. These moral ties, nonetheless, find relatively frequent expression in a wide range of contexts between close collaterals and affines. The social identities of such kin tend to be complex, and they are bound together by many-stranded ties. Thus, matrikin not only favor one another with trade but contribute to one another's major prestations, share in those received, exchange gifts, render aid in gardening work and formerly in war, and so on. The relationship between affines tends to be rather more strained and formal, and involves the transfer of major prestations. But it also encompasses gifts and mutual assistance and has the potential to become consolidated with the growth of friendship. In short, in dealings with close kin and affines, people can rely on past experience and the complexity of their ties which render the other's responses in any particular transaction relatively predictable.

Relations between constructed kin of distant settlements, in contrast, tend to be confined to the context of trading. Trusting such a kinsman is, by and large, a more risky undertaking than trusting a well-known kinsman. To trust a distant kinsman is to put greater faith in him, since actual ties of other kinds are minimal if not absent. Initially there is no social predictability on the basis of past behavior or adherence to moral principles. Certainly, there are sanctions, already discussed, which may induce compliance in trade. But men mentioned these sanctions to explain why they themselves tried to honor transactions that they did not initiate; they say there is no guarantee that others will be constrained by the possibility of severing further trade relations or the risk of a witchcraft attack. Besides, very few men believe themselves to be witches, leaving cessation of further trading ties as the effective sanction, and that can only be invoked in the event of the failure of a transaction. In other words, sanctions are only effective in the breach of a relationship, when there is no recourse to redress. Trust in such a relationship is therefore a more potent means of constructing and expressing the relationship than it is between close and frequently interacting kin.

Men assess the reliability of their trading partners by considering their diligence in returning a requested item and the speed with which they complete a transaction. A man who long delays and then returns a different good from that asked for does not inspire confidence and is less likely to be entrusted with further trade. In general, it is the man who travels a lot, for whatever reason, who is given trade goods by distant kinsmen. His mobility fosters confidence in his wide-ranging social relationships and hence his capacity to find other partners to complete a transaction. Thus, although travel is a consequence of heavy involvement in trade, it also generates yet greater trade, since it is the "big walker" in particular who receives unsolicited overtures to trade as expressions of confidence in his abilities. Several particularly diligent traders remarked how they were continually given new items to trade by distant kinsmen whenever they completed a delayed transaction, and how they eventually refused to accept the proffered goods, complaining that they were worn out by incessant travel.

Reliability, however, is not a mechanical or absolute thing, rather, it is relative to the degree of sociability involved in any particular relationship. On the one hand, one accepts long delays in trade with close or well-known kin and is less put out if they fail to return what one asked for, because it is regarded as churlish to hold such a man too closely to the stipulations of the exchange, provided he has made a "reasonable" effort to comply. On the other hand, distant kin whose dealings are largely or wholly confined to trade expect more careful compliance with requests for specific exchange goods, and a speedy completion to a transaction. In the last analysis reliability is a matter of personal expectations and evaluations. Although it does not involve kinsmen the formal trade partnership between Giewai and a Koriom man is a case in point. Several men told me that they had also traded with this man, or hoped to, because he had a reputation as an exemplary trader—he always returns exactly what one requests and with goods of fine quality.[8] Giewai, however, complained that his partner was often tardy in completing a transaction and said he was considering terminating the partnership on this account.

What this discussion of sociability so far indicates is that there is an element of generosity associated with the trading transaction. This is not unexpected, since it is obvious that men do not simply engage in trade but establish trading relationships. If the terms of the actual exchange—the rates applied—are not varied to create or sustain such a relationship, then the social context within which it occurs must be subject to manipulation. What is less obvious, and is not given credence in most discussions of trade, barter, or commodity exchange, is that the act itself can be a form of generosity. On the contrary, trade is paradigmatically seen as a denial of generosity.

Trade as generosity is evident, if in a rather weak form, in the fairly common practice between kin, where one initiates an exchange by offering, usually, a plume without specifying what he wants in return. Sometimes the man will say, "Get what you like at your leisure, but pass it on to me." (It is noteworthy that it is transactions of this kind that were liable to be ambiguously classified by informants as either trade or a minor prestation.) Such an arrangement not only implies trust in one's partner, and preparedness to accept a return of disparate value, but also expresses a desire not to encumber one's partner with precise demands for objects and timetables that are sometimes difficult to fulfill.

More explicitly generous is the practice of offering an established trading partner, or a close kinsman, a plume for use in decorations when he wishes to dance at a ceremony. Quite often, such transactions are not solicited by the man needing the plumes. The following case illustrates such generosity.

> In 1974 Munggoma learned that his sister's son of Kompiai was preparing for a dance, and he felt obliged to help by providing decorations. He therefore gave one of his own pigs to his classificatory brother, Menek, of Tsuwenkai, asking for a set of Vulturine Parrot feathers in return. Menek sent the pig on to his Timbeganji sister's husband with a request for the feathers. He passed these on to Munggoma in due course. Munggoma then gave the Vulturine feathers to his sister's son, saying why he was offering it, that the transaction was a trading one, and that he wanted a pig in return. After the dancing, the Kompiai man exchanged the feathers for a pig, which he sent to Munggoma.

When men visit kinsmen or attend ceremonies in other settlements, they are often given objects to trade by their hosts, or other men seeking to construct ties of kinship. Although such offers may involve a man in subsequent efforts to reciprocate that may be inconvenient, they do nonetheless express something about the quality of the social relationship, as I have argued above. In this regard, the offer of trade constitutes an additional aspect of the generosity of hospitality, even though the host will receive a specific return: it is an expression of faith in the guest's ability and reliability.

More generally, the offer of goods in trade calls for complete requital, so that there is no lingering indebtedness or imbalance in the relationship between the parties. By contrast, a gift is only a moment in an unending sequence of reciprocities: every gift requires a return, no two form a discrete sequence. Trade, therefore, may imply or construct equality and balance between transactors, which is a necessary condition for their willingness to maintain a relationship.

This interpretation is, of course, contrary to orthodox exchange theory and its application to Melanesian material (cf. Gouldner 1960; Harding 1967: 243; Sahlins 1972). Certainly, a range of social relations are maintained, at least in part, because of relationships of lingering debt and credit between the parties. Those clustered around the exchange of women are a case in point. It is just such exchange relations that tend to be mediated by ceremonialized exchange, in which elements of competition emerge. Exchange relations involving transfers of women between clans are fundamental to the constitution and continuity of the social order. Major prestations patterned by ties of marriage are mandatory and overtly generous, a point played upon in accompanying speeches that stress the size of a prestation in aggressive hyperbole or by ironic self-deprecation for the inadequate offering. Yet although the amounts given may be varied within customary limits, the size of prestations actually may be negotiated, if only covertly. This establishes a cultural ambience where there is a recurrent and normative establishment and expression of relationships through the manipulation of imbalances in material flows in major prestations. Public, corporate, ceremonial exchanges, such as bridewealth, always contain an element of confrontation and competition, sometimes overt, sometimes all but suppressed. What appears as generosity in ceremonial exchange is actually a challenge to the equality of transactors, a challenge that is ultimately averted by the suppression of memory of the transactional details of major prestations.

Trade transactions, by comparison, though sometimes guarded and cautious, as between strangers, lack the theatrical sense of tension and suppressed antagonism characteristic of ceremonialized encounters between transactors. In the praxis of exchange, the appearance of generosity in prestations is negated via covert negotiation of the value of transactions and elements of confrontation. But in trade there is no negotiation of "generosity": a transaction proceeds according to accepted scales of value or not at all. Generosity in trade, appearing as unnegotiated offers or acceptance of transactions, is unsolicited and not normatively constrained, and in that sense generosity appears in its purer form in trade.

The more recent practice of trade constitutes a threat to the equalitarian order of Maring social relations with trading partners. The emergence of bargaining over the exchange value of goods amounts to open confrontation between traders and has occurred as the incidence or frequency of trade and the volume of goods passed has declined. It is important to note, however, that this aggressively self-interested style of trade is largely confined to dealings with strangers who, moreover, are from distant places far beyond the traditional sphere of direct Kundagai trading links. In other words, much trade maintains the more equalitarian character that I have been discussing. As such, haggling trade may be interpreted as an expression of essentially political relations between a self-consciously underdeveloped lower Jimi and a relatively sophisticated core area—the Wahgi—increasingly perceived as exploitative of lower-Jimi cash-generating enterprises.

The Kundagai recognize their increasing dependence on Wahgi pig traders for the reproduction of local social relations, and the privileged capacity of central highlanders to extract wealth from them in return. In that respect the emergence of bargaining in such trade is an expression of the fundamental inequality that divides Wahgi and lower-Jimi transactors in their access to political–economic resources and highlights the continuing moral dimensions of dealings with friends and kinsmen.

If trading relations between kinsmen take on a moral character, as revealed in the operation of generosity in varied forms, the question arises whether it is possible to refuse trade. Strangers will turn down offers to trade if they consider the terms unacceptable. Many trading parties visiting Tsuwenkai in 1974 moved on empty-handed, as no Kundagai wished to part with plumes. Similarly, some other traders refused plumes offered by Kundagai men as substandard. Kinsmen may also refuse to trade with one another. One man no longer trades with his mother's brother who, he felt, made unreasonable demands for compensation for pigs given him in trade that later sickened. He reasons that their relationship can better withstand this limitation on their activities than the likelihood of further acrimonious disputes in what ought to be a close and affectionate, mutually supportive association.

Offers of trade from kinsmen are, it seems, quite readily refused if those offers are made in a social context mutually understood as confined to trade, but are more likely to be accepted if the transaction is incidental to a meeting focused on other aspects of the relationship. Thus, when kinsmen visit one another for the express purpose of trade, whatever their relationship, they are more likely to refuse transactions. If, however, offers of trade have the appearance of generosity associated with contacts for other purposes, the offer is less likely to be refused because it then becomes a statement of relationship as much as a self-interested desire for goods. Since visits to constructed kin primarily occur in the context of trading expeditions, trade with such categories of persons is more likely to be refused than with closer matrilateral and affinal kin. It is the possibility of refusing invitations to trade that prevents the construction of kinship ties from becoming a strategy of self-interested attempts to impose more pressure on others to one's material advantage. In other words, and somewhat paradoxically, it is the appearance of self-interest in avoiding a proffered exchange that underlines and sustains the sociable character of trade between constructed kin. It does this by demonstrating that the particular interests of individual transactors override any sense of obligation to comply with a kinsman's request. As such, occasional refusals to transact indicate the sincerity of constructed kinsmen to maintain their relationship for the mutual interest of further trade at some unspecified point in the future. In that sense, the assertion of self-interest is a denial of the possibility of exploitation and therefore itself communicates sociability in an equalitarian frame (cf. Widegren 1983: 323–324 for a theoretical discussion of sincerity and sociability in exchange).

Trade, then, is neither always impersonal nor strictly self-interested. Through trade, individuals extend their social horizons, linking themselves into a wider network than the limits of genealogical and coresidential reckoning encompass. Trade can mediate relationships between distant people by more than the equitable transfer of material goods. It does this by providing a context for other expressions of social solidarity, such as hospitality, trust, and generosity. These are articulated in the idiom of kinship and serve to bind the individual into an open-ended moral universe far exceeding the limitations of the everyday exigencies of group definition and political process.

Unlike prestations, trade *in itself* is not represented by the Maring as establishing or expressing long-term social relationships. Although the Maring made a rigid conceptual distinction between trade and prestation, in the praxis of trade, at least in those contexts where it gains a dimension of generosity, these forms of exchange are merged to some extent. In that sense, trade may become a valence of long-term relationships, which, in the world of material goods, are otherwise paradigmatically signaled in Maring understandings by prestations. Thus, in particular contexts trade may take on some of the social attributes of prestation. Since Maring notions of trade themselves explicitly focus on material aspects of the transaction, this merging of modes of exchange is masked. Yet, although I have followed the Maring in representing trade and prestation as distinct modes, trade can assume certain communicative or signal properties concerning social relationships normally associated with prestations, insofar as these two kinds of transaction are also *aspects* of exchange as a general category of activity.

CONCLUSION

This analysis of Kundagai trade progresses from a concern for the material bases of exchange through to its embeddedness in wider social and cultural contexts. Initial attention is on the articulation of local ecological processes—by which valuables are produced—with regional economic and ecological processes—by which valuables are redistributed and consumed. The focus is thus on the confrontation of objects and a numerically based description of patterns and volumes of flow. I have also sought, however, to show how these ecological dimensions of production and exchange are articulated with the social and cultural organization of trade. This analysis has been guided by the conviction—itself hardly radical—that although there is a definite ecological structure to production, distribution, and consumption of goods, these activities occur in and are mediated by the cultural order, which transcends pragmatic considerations.

The data have demonstrated the material importance to the Kundagai of trade as distinct from prestations, as a stimulus to the production of valuables and as a means of effecting the distribution of goods. The treatment therefore relates to an aspect of the integration of individuals and groups as producers, transactors, and consumers into a larger sphere. This has been a theme pursued in many analyses of ceremonial exchange also. My attention to trade as a means of distribution and as a kind of social relationship has pointed to the significance of a particular mode of exchange that has often been passed over in ethnographies as of largely utilitarian but limited and subsidiary importance.

Trade as I have defined it theoretically and ethnographically emerges as an important category of activity among the Maring and their neighbors. It moves large volumes of goods along very distinct and limited paths, generates the production of others, and absorbs the attentions and energies of many people. It is significant as an aspect of the material provisioning of society but, beyond this, it is also important in the construction, interpretation, and experience of social relations. Despite this heavy involvement of the Kundagai in trade the activity is actually rather low-key, pursued by individuals in much the same matter-of-fact way as gardening or hunting. In this respect it differs dramatically from some forms of prestation that are the focus of intense collective efforts of coordination and dramatization. As a consequence trade is not readily observable, and I suspect that this circumstance has led many ethnographers elsewhere in the interior of New Guinea to give less attention to the activity than it deserves.[9]

By contrast ceremonial exchange in the New Guinea highlands and elsewhere has attracted a great deal of attention. It is highly visible, is of consuming interest to participants in many societies, and has far-reaching economic, political, and ecological consequences (e.g., Bulmer 1960; Meggitt 1974; Strathern 1969, 1971).

Given the cultural, ultimately semiotic and arbitrary, definition of the objects, relationships, and values involved in trade, an ecological framework provides some insights into the levels of trade that particular societies may achieve. It is clear that different groups in New Guinea, as elsewhere, have a variable involvement in trade. Nowhere in the preindustrial world were there totally isolated communities. But the permeability of their boundaries and the manner of interchange varied. There are, as yet, no good comparative data for a detailed comparison of relative involvement in trade in different New Guinea societies. Detailed numerical material is virtually lacking for the whole of Melanesia. This means that I cannot compare rates or volumes of production of valuables and trade between the Maring and other groups and attempt to account for any differences by examining variations in ecological and social–structural conditions.

I suggest on necessarily impressionistic grounds, however, that the Kundagai and nearby groups are more heavily involved in trade than many highlanders. This high level of trade is partially accounted for by the fact that the great bulk of locally produced goods are, or at least were until recently, in high demand among the Simbu, Kuma, and Melpa of the central highlands for ceremonial exchanges and decorations used in major celebrations. In short, that the prevalence and heavy involvement in ceremonial exchange in the central highlands sets up economic and ecological conditions within which Kundagai trade may then develop. This interpretation is lent support by the discussion of historical development of trade in chapter 6: levels of involvement in trade appear to have been much lower in the distant past before major trade routes were oriented toward the central highlands with their more elaborate and integrated systems of ceremonial exchange. This interpretation has a more general significance: that exchange networks, both trade and ceremonial, and their evolution can only be understood in a larger, regional context (cf. Feil 1987; Healey 1985*a*). This requires attention to variable social–structural dimensions of exchange, different cultural codes for exchange, and the economic and ecological interlocking of relations of production, transfer, and consumption of goods over a wide area transcending ethnic units or their subdivisions which are the usual focus of analyses of exchange. Even so, the reason Maring trade became more closely connected to the central highlands does not lie within material or ecological factors alone. The particular social and cultural meanings of the activity to the participants involved also has a strong bearing.

Because trade involves material goods it is liable to be analyzed from various materialistic and utilitarian perspectives. Hence the maintenance of trading relations is treated in terms of "needs" on the part of consumers to be disposed of in material fashions. The social relations of trade then become merely instrumental, or derivative of the material forces underlying exchange.[10] Prevailing views present the social relations involved as achieving a minimum of mutual interest to establish peace. The closest many analyses get to probing beyond material bases of trading is when they introduce such notions as generosity, overriding principles of kinship, fear of retaliation by witches or sorcerers, and the like. Not denying the effectiveness of these factors, such explanations seem to be saying that nonmaterial conditions concerning the quality and nature of social relations intervene in the trading transaction and so impel exchange that might otherwise not take place at all, or not on those terms, to the material deprivation of society. This kind of perspective cannot account for variations in the intensity or volume of trade which may be independent of ecological factors. Rather, I argue that it is the capacity of a trade transaction to be expressive, creative, and innovative that partly sustains high levels of trade.

This bears on the question of motives. Certainly individuals may be induced to trade because the goods are culturally defined as necessary: for their practical utility or for use in prestations as tokens of "symbolic labor." Some goods passed in trade are diverted into prestations, thus drawing trade peripherally into the orbit of corporate intergroup relations and political influences, so that political motives become implicated in trade (see e.g., Malinowski 1922; Harding 1967). Indeed, since Maring trade and prestation are clearly linked because they deal (partly) in the same goods but have somewhat different patterns of distribution, they are mutually sustaining. But this does not exhaust motivations to trade. A further stimulus lies in the fact that although Kundagai trade is culturally typified as self-interested, object-centered, but nonexploitative of others, it has the capacity to express a range of social relationships and sentiments.

The sociable dimensions of trade, such as generosity and demonstrations of trust, are not simply secondary or facilitating aspects of trade. They are central to the organization of trade and its meaning to participants as a category of social activity. What I have argued is that a primary objective and consequence of trade as practiced by the Maring is the activation or construction of relationships—the creation of an expanded social universe—rather than the movement of goods as such. It is, then, a cultural form capable of making statements about social relations beyond the pragmatics of satisfying material wants in the context of ecological diversity.

A trade system is therefore not driven by its ecological structure. This is ultimately constraining but not determinative. I have shown that the social and cultural organization introduces important constraints on the productive and trading activity of individuals. Trade and hunting are therefore not produced by the local or regional ecosystem but by the Maring cultural order. Ecological forces are material, but constraints on hunting and trade are not exclusively so. This work, then, has proceeded from the view that ecological, social, and cultural parameters are only partially integrated. This means that in ecological terms the unit of analysis is but poorly defined and internally not fully integrated.

One consequence of this line of argument is that it becomes problematic to speak of local ecosystems, or of trade systems that connect local ecosystems into larger regional units. Thus, although the model of trade sketched in the introduction and elaborated on in the body of this book may have the appearance of an integrated system, I must stress that what I have actually produced is a systematic analysis of part of a larger network of trade that encompasses a substantial part of the highlands but certainly does not constitute a well-bounded, totally integrated system.

The Kundagai ethnography provides an insight into the articulation of production and consumption of valuables with diverse forms of exchange in diachronic perspective. It also points to how prevailing anthropological approaches to trade and its relation to other forms of exchange may be refined and made more productive analytically.

Trade is a form of exchange that has been a neglected field of study in recent decades. This neglect is itself sufficient reason to warrant further study. But beyond this, our understanding of Melanesian exchange will be deficient if the totality of the phenomenon is not considered and, if nothing else, I hope that this book has demonstrated that trade, and its relation to production, consumption, and other forms of exchange, is a rich field for research.

In this book I have stressed that although trade is responsive to ecological and economic constraints, it is also meaningful to actors as a set of equalitarian social relationships. As such, it is a critical element in the wider social order. It has become conventional to examine the role of exchange in the constitution of the social order, including gender identity and relations (see e.g., Feil 1984; Josephides 1985; Lederman 1986; LiPuma 1988 for recent treatments). Most analyses, however, focus on ceremonial exchange and the relations among men mediated by women, and between men and women, in the context of such exchange.

Among the Maring the exchange of valuables is almost exclusively an activity of males. I have noted the general absence of highly competitive and incremental ceremonial exchange, which has come to be treated, erroneously, as characteristic of most Melanesian societies. Rather, there is a strain toward equality in Maring exchanges. Writing of "equal exchange," Forge (1972: 535) remarks on "the virtual impossibility of achieving perfect balance; the equality that is achieved is never perfect." He goes on to note that what makes men unequal are women, who as wives and sisters mediate between men and structure their exchange relations. It is clear that Forge is dealing with a particular subset of exchanges: gifts or prestations, and not trade. I would argue that the significance of trade for such societies as the Maring is precisely the fact that it does enable the attainment of "perfect balance" in exchange relations.

Men establish trading relations without reference to women. Trade is purely a male affair that men enter into freely, on equal terms, without women providing mediating links. It is true that marriage ties create affinal and matrilateral links that may become activated as trading ties. But the important point is that such marriage ties only establish *potential* trade relations; they do not determine them as such. By contrast, marriage ties normatively establish gift exchange relations between men. These relations are unequal in terms of material flows of valuables. Further, although men control the goods used in prestations, unlike their involvement in trade, they do not manage the social relations marked by the passage of goods. This is because though men attempt to control women as objects of exchange—just like the valuables sent in return—women themselves neither constitute nor act as objects. By their own humanity and assertions of freedom and autonomy in marriage, women continually subvert male control (Healey 1989), an enterprise in which they are from time to time assisted by sympathetic or antagonistic men as fathers, brothers, sons, husbands, or lovers. Men linked through women are thereby brought into conflict and inequalitarian relations.

Prestations patterned on marriage are socially "necessary" or unavoidable but divide men between donors and recipients, and between major donors and their helpers to whom they are beholden. To a degree, the unequal relations between men which emerge in the context of prestations are subverted by the suppression of recall of individual transactions. In this way, exact reciprocation of gifts is obviated and strict comparison of efforts forestalled.

In contrast to prestations, trade is neither "necessary" nor obligatory. There is neither compulsion to engage in trade, nor stigma attached to nonparticipation. Trade is a relation entered into or refused voluntarily, in which the fundamental and precise equality of all partners is taken for granted, not negotiated. Trade is ostensibly a means by which men provision themselves with desirable goods for consumption, display, or redeployment in prestations. But more than serving these utilitarian functions, trade as practiced by the Maring is a form of exchange expressing unambiguous relations of equality between all transactors.

Gift exchange and the sharing of wealth and substance are highly salient in differentiating between clans and clansmen. Trade as practiced by the Maring, being overtly focused on objects rather than persons, treats all individuals as equivalent and equal transactors and stewards of objects. The ultimate social meaning of trade is quite different from that of gift exchange and sharing: it does not define the limits of relatedness, the boundaries of social discontinuities. Rather, trade encompasses all its practitioners in a single social and moral universe.

Appendix 1
Marriage Patterns

The following table indicates the regional distribution of incoming and outgoing wives by five periods to 1985. (See map 4 for locations or regions.) Data are drawn from 263 records of marriages gained by census of the Tsuwenkai population and collection of genealogies. These records include 166 marriages (dating from the late 1920s) in which the wife survives and 97 marriages in which the woman is dead (the earliest of the latter records relates to the early 1870s).

There are no records of women sent out in marriage before about 1915, as genealogies for distant generations tend to include men only. Any women recorded are wives of these men. Despite this deficiency of data for early times, there is clearly a strong connection between the Kundagai and the Simbai. Most such marriages date from around the turn of the century.

In 1915–1934, Up-Jimi links gain greater importance, with a net outflow of women to this region (exclusively to Kompiai). Connections with the Simbai still predominate, however, with a net inflow of women from these areas.

In 1935–1954 ties with Jimi settlements predominate, and the number of settlements involved proliferate, although ties across the Jimi cease in this period (perhaps correlating with the collapse of trade in stone axes, which came from Cross-Jimi). Links with the Simbai decline in proportion to the increase in ties with Jimi settlements, despite the addition of marriages Cross-Simbai. Marriages within Kundagai–Aikupa increase considerably.

In 1955–1974 marriages with Up-Jimi settlements become yet more pronounced, with a marked excess of Kundagai women sent in marriage. Down-Jimi and Down-Simbai connections decline in importance, Up-Simbai links increasing marginally. High rates of marriage within Kundagai–Aikupa are maintained, with most links with Bokapai, which sends a slight excess of women to Tsuwenkai.

In 1974–1985 a net outflow of women in marriage to, and increasing concentration of marriages with, Up-Jimi settlements is consolidated. The proportion of marriages within the Kundagai–Aikupa population continues to increase. Marriage ties with the Simbai decline.

If pre-1915 figures are excluded, then the total excess of out-marriages to Up-Jimi (mainly Kompiai) becomes more marked, and the excess of in-marriages from Down-Jimi (mainly Kandambiamp), Up-Simbai (mainly Nembenakump), and Down-Simbai (mainly Mondo) become slightly less marked. The overall trend has been to increase intermarriage with the upper-Jimi and within the Kundagai–Aikupa, at the expense of the lower Jimi and the Simbai. But marriages have not been balanced, so that an excess of women has been sent out to the upper-Jimi and an excess received from the Simbai and from Bokapai.

MARRIAGE PATTERNS[a]

Region	Pre-1915 In	Out	Tot.	%	1915-1934 In	Out	Tot.	%	1935-1954 In	Out	Tot.	%	1955-1974 In	Out	Tot.	%	1974-1985 In	Out	Tot.	%
Up-Jimi	2	2		10.5	2	4	6	20.0	7	5	12	38.7	6	17	23	47.9	2	8	10	58.8
Down-Jimi	2	2		10.5	2	4	6	20.0	5	2	7	22.6	4	5	9	18.7	2	1	3	17.6
Cross-Jimi	3	3		15.8	1	3	4	13.4										1	1	5.9
Up-Simbai	5	5		26.3	5	3	8	26.7	5		5	16.1	3	6	9	18.7				
Down-Simbai	7	5		36.8	5	4	9	30.0	5	2	7	22.6	3	4	7	14.6	3		3	17.6
Sub-Total	19		19	73.1	15	15	30	65.2	22	9	31	52.5	16	32	48	51.6	7	10	17	43.6
Kundagai -Aikupa		7	7	26.9		16	16	38.4		28	28	47.5		45	45	48.4		22	22	56.4
TOTAL			26				46				59				93				39	

[a] Settlements in each region, and number of marriages are as follows:

Up-Jimi:	Kompiai	33	Down-Jimi:	Kandambiamp	16	Up-Simbai:	Nembenakump	19
	Koinambe	4		Ginjinji	6		Tekerau	2
	Yimpigema	1		Gondomben	1		Kumbruf	6
	Kupeng	8		Waim	1			
	Kwima	3				Kundagai-		
	Dega	1	Down-Simbai:	Konggerau	2	Aikupa:	Tsuwenkai	46
	Togban	1		Tsunggup	1		Bokapai	45
	Kwiop	1		Tsembaga	8		Kinimbong	27
	Koriom	1		Mondo	10			
				Gai	10			
Cross-Jimi:	Rinyimp	7		Nimbra	2			
	Timbunki	1						

Appendix 2
Birds Used in Decorations

Appendix 2 lists the 53 species of birds represented in collections of decorations examined during fieldwork. At least a further 10 species listed are probably used by some Maring including the Kundagai and were either not seen or not positively identified. About 180 or more species inhabit Maring lands (at least 150 in Tsuwenkai territory), and many more species inhabiting distant areas such as the coast are known to travelers and are occasionally brought home for decorations.

Scientific names and their arrangement follow Rand and Gilliard (1967). For further details of New Guinea ornithology the reader is also referred to Beehler, Pratt, and Zimmerman (1986), Coates (1985), and Diamond (1972). Maring vernaculars listed are only the most commonly used terms among the Kundagai; some species, especially important trade items, have several names, some of which are loan words from Kalam, Narak, or Kuma. Where similar species listed are usually referred to by "generic" terms, I have used Maring specific terms to differentiate them.

Symbols used in the columns are as follows:

Habitat:
- I zone of human habitation
- II montane zone
- III lower altitudes in Jimi or Simbai within about one day's walk of Tsuwenkai
- IV accessible lowlands beyond III
- V distant, mainly coastal regions

Appendix 2

Status: Not indicated for species outside zones I–III

    a   very common

    b   common

    c   uncommon

    d   rare or vagrant

    e   status unknown

Parts Used: B   body feathers (may include F)

    F   flight feathers (wing and/or tail)

    P   ornamental plumes (crests, flank plumes, occipitals, etc.)

    S   whole or part of skin, flat or stuffed

    W   wings fanned

SPECIES USED FOR DECORATIVE PLUMES

Species	Maring	Habitat, status	Parts used	No. birds[a]	No. men owning
CASUARIIDAE: Cassowaries					
Casuarius casuarius Double-wattled Cassowary	?kombli	V	B		
Casuarius unappendiculatus Single-wattled Cassowary	rankrank	IV	B		
Casuarius bennetti Dwarf Cassowary	kombli	IIb	B	4	4
ARDEIDAE: Herons & Bitterns					
Egretta sp(p).	nink pato	V	B,P	2	2
ANATIDAE: Ducks & Geese					
Sp. unident. Domestic Duck	pato	V	B	5	5
ACCIPITRIDAE: Hawks, Eagles Etc.					
Henicopernis longicauda Long-tailed Buzzard	rukump	IIb	F	14	13
Haliastur indus Brahminy Kite	kaneg	Ib	B	1	1
Accipiter novaehollandiae Grey Goshawk	apng titep	Ic	B		
Accipiter ?fasciatus Australian Goshawk	apng titep	Ic	B		
Accipiter melanochlamys Black-mantled Goshawk	nink titep	IIb	B	2	2
Harpyopsis novaeguineae Harpy Eagle	binam	IIc	F	6	6

SPECIES USED FOR DECORATIVE PLUMES (continued)

Species	Maring	Habitat, status	Parts used	No. birds[a]	No. men owning
FALCONIDAE: Falcons					
Falco berigora Brown Falcon	kiakia	Ia	B	2	2
MEGAPODIIDAE: Megapodes					
Aepypodius arfakianus Wattled Brush Turkey	komami	IIb	B	1	2
PHASIANIDAE: Quails, Pheasants etc.					
Gallus gallus Domestic Fowl	kloklo	Ia	B	15	11
COLUMBIDAE: Pigeons & Doves					
Ptilinopus superbus Superb Fruit Dove	piyaundekai	I,IIIe	F,W		
Ptilinopus rivoli White-breasted Fruit Dove	gondamamp	I,IIa	F,W	8	7
Ptilinopus ornatus Ornate Fruit Dove	park	IIe	F,W		
Ducula chalconota Rufous-breasted Pigeon	makama	IIb	F	6	6
Ducula ?zoeae Black-belted Pigeon	makama	IIe	F		
Macropygia nigrirostris Rusty Cuckoo-dove	kuwl	Ia	W	1	1
Reinwardtoena reinwardtsi Great Cuckoo-dove	jamba	Ia	F	6	5
Goura ?victoria Victoria Goura	komben	IV	P,F	1	1
PSITTACIDAE: Parrots, Lories etc.					
Pseudeos fuscata Dusky Lory	kiki	IIa	F,W	15	7
Trichoglossus haematodus Rainbow Lory	gir	IIIa	W	8	6
Lorius hypoinochrous Purple-bellied Lory	yindama	V	S,W	34[b]	12[b]
Lorius lory Black-capped Lory	yindama	IV	S,W		
Charmosyna papou Papuan Lory	goli	IIb,V	S,F,W	33	14
Charmosyna pulchella Fairy Lory	jimbonk	IIb	S,F	35	9
Charmosyna ?placentis Red-flaked Lory	jimbonk nambis	V	S	1	1
Oreopsittacus arfaki Whiskered Lorikeet	muramura	IIb	F,W	2	2
Neopsittacus muschenbroekii Muschenbroek's Lorikeet	ringgop pendent	Ia	S,W,F	25	15
Neopsittacus pullicauda Emerald Lorikeet	pendent cenda wunt	IIb	S,W,F		
Probosciger aterrimus	cendokoi	IV,V	P	1	1

Appendix 2

SPECIES USED FOR DECORATIVE PLUMES (continued)

Species	Maring	Habitat, status	Parts used	No. birds[a]	No. men owning
Palm Cockatoo *Cacatua galerita*	kiame	IId,IIIa,V	B,P	50	33
White Cockatoo *Psittrichas fulgidus*	kopel	IV	B	8	8
Vulturine Parrot *Larius roratus*	gimenda	IIIe	B,S,W	3	3
Eclectus Parrot *Alisterus chloropterus*	kambai	IIb	S,W	3	3
Papuan King Parrot *Psittacella brehmii*	menyang mopmai	IIb	W	1	1
Brehm's Parrot					
CUCULIDAE: Cuckoos *Centropus phasianinus* Pheasant Coucal	dui	Ic	F	1	1
TYTONIDAE: Barn Owls *Tyto ?alba* Barn Owl	rumunggup	Ie	B,W	3	3
PODARGIDAE: Frogmouths *Podargus papuensis* Giant Frogmouth	momung	Ie	B	3	3
ALCEDINIDAE: Kingfishers *Dacelo leachii* Blue-winged Kookaburra	(none)	V	W	1	1
Tanysiptera galatea Common Paradise Kingfisher	joli	IV,V	S,F	68	16
CORACIIDAE: Rollers *Eurystomus orientalis* Dollarbird	kombianggas	IIIe	W	1	1
BUCEROTIDAE: Hornbills *Aceros plicatus* Papuan Hornbill	kauwia	IV,V	F	16	13
PITTIDAE: Pittas *Pitta erythrogaster* Blue-breasted Pitta	golembeli	IIIe	S,W	3	3
MUSICAPIDAE: Flycatchers *Peltops montanus* Mountain Peltops	binjaga	Ia	S	1	1
STURNIDAE: Starlings *?Mino dumonti* Yellow-faced Grackle	?kombianggas piak	IIIe	W	1	1
GRALLINIDAE: Magpielarks *Grallina bruijni* Torrentlark	jenjenggaiyang	I,IIb	W,F	1	1

SPECIES USED FOR DECORATIVE PLUMES (continued)

Species	Maring	Habitat status	Parts used	No. birds[a]	No. men owning
CORVIDAE: Crows					
Gymnocorvus tristis Bare-eyed Crow	kangganeme	I,IIIb	F	1	1
PARADISAEIDAE: Birds of Paradise					
Epimachus fastosus Black Sicklebill	kalanc gi	IId	S,F		
Epimachus meyeri Brown Sicklebill	kalanc gurunt	IId	S,F	1	1
Astrapia stephaniae Stephanie's Astrapia	kombam	IIb	S,F	4	3
Parotia carolae Carola's Parotia	kiawoi	I,IIb	S,P	2	2
Parotia lawesii Lawes' Parotia	kiawoi	I,IIe	S,P		
Lophorina superba Superb Bird of Paradise	yenandiok	I,IIa	P	5	5
Diphyllodes magnificus Magnificent Bird of Paradise	pengaluo	Ib	S	1	1
Cicinnurus regius King Bird of Paradise	cendemai	IV,?III	S,P		
Paradisaea raggiana Red Bird of Paradise	parka	V	S	30	11
Paradisaea minor Lesser Bird of Paradise	yambai	IIIa	S	37	25
Paradisaea rudolphi Blue Bird of Paradise	aweng	Id	W	1	1
Pteridophora alberti King of Saxony Bird of Paradise	balpan	IIb	P,S	12	9
PTILONORHYNCHIDAE: Bowerbirds					
Amblyornis macgregoriae MacGregor's Bowerbird	mowai	IIb	P	2	2
UNIDENTIFIED					
?Hawk	rukump acokae	Ie	F	2	2

[a] In many cases only fragments of birds are represented. The figures represent estimated minimum numbers.

[b] Some of these records apply to the next species, precise numbers unknown. I was unable to make consistent distinctions between the remains of these very similar species.

Appendix 3
Valuables and Trade Goods

The following table lists goods recorded as ever traded and the period of such use. Also indicated are Maring names, whether the objects are classed as valuables (*munggoi*) and/or decorations (*mokiang*), whether they are used in major prestations, and whether they are products of specialized regions.

TRADE GOODS

Item	Maring Name	Valuable	Used in Decoration	Used in Prestation	Specialized product[a]	Approx. period of use
A. SHELLS	mengr					
Kina	anggani	+	+	+	+	1940+
Greensnail	jenja	+	+	+	+	1945+
Cowry	ambapo	+	+	+	+	1925-60
Dogwhelk	gram, yamapiak	+	+	+	+	1920-70
Bailer	mendema	(+)[b]	+	-	+	?1950+
Disk & anulus	wurawura	-	+	-	+	?1920+
B. CUTTING TOOLS	cenang					
Stone axe/adze	cenang	+	-	+	+	to 1950s
Steel-bladed adze	kopiama	-	-	-	-	1930-50s
Steel axe, bushknife	role, cenang dukump	+	-	+	-	1950s+
C. LIVE ANIMALS						
Pigs	konj	+	-	+	-	a[c]
Dogs	cena	+	-	-	-	a
Cassowaries	kombli	+	-	+	-	a
Domestic fowls	kloklo	-	-	-	-	?a

TRADE GOODS (continued)

Item	Maring Name	Valuable	Used in Decoration	Used in Prestation	Specialized product[a]	Approx. period of use
D. ANIMAL REMAINS						
1. Bird skins, plumes[d]:	kabang an					
Duck	pato	-	+	-	+	1960+
Buzzard	rukump	+	+	-	-	a
Eagle	binam	+	+	-	-	a
Goura	komben	+	+	-	+	a
Lory	kiki	-	+	-	-	a
Lory	gir	-	+	-	+	a
Lory	yindama	-	+	-	+	a
Papuan Lory	goli	+	+	-	-	a
Fairy Lory	jimbonk	+	+	-	-	a
Lorikeet	muramura	-	+	-	-	a
Lorikeet	pendent	-	+	-	-	a
Palm Cockatoo	cendokoi	-	+	-	+	a
White Cockatoo	kiame	+	+	-	+	a
Vulturine Parrot	kopel	+	+	-	+	a
Kingfisher	joli	+	+	(+)	+	?a
Hornbill	kauwia	+	+	(+)	+	a
Black Sicklebill	kalanc gi	+	+	-	-	a
Brown Sicklebill	kalanc gurunt	+	+	-	-	a
Astrapia	kombam	+	+	-	-	a
Parotia	kiawoi	(+)	+	-	-	a
Superb B. of P.	yenandiok	+	+	-	-	a
Magnificent B. of P.	pengaluo	(+)	+	-	-	a
Red B. of P.	parka	+	+	+	+	1955+
Lesser B. of P.	yambai	+	+	-	+	a
Blue B. of P.	aweng	(+)	+	-	?+	a
King of Saxony B. of P.	balpan	+	+	-	-	a
Bowerbird	kombek	(+)	+	-	-	a
2. Marsupial furs and skins:						
Phalanger ?orientalis (2 forms)	tinggenambang mul	(+)	+	-	+	a
Phalanger maculatus (2 forms)	aklang, tembobin	+	+	-	+	a
Phalanger gymnotis	yuwanoi	-	+	-	-	a
Phalanger vestitus (2 or 3 forms)	kanggem, wulami	-	+	-	-	a
Pseudocheirus forbesi	benyai	-	-	-	-	a
Dendrolagus ?goodfellowi	riawe	+	+	-	-	a
3. Animal tooth necklaces:	yakai	+	+	+	-	to 1940
4. Beetle shards: Scarabaeidae	mimola	+	+	-	+	a

Appendix 3   367

TRADE GOODS (continued)

Item	Maring Name	Valuable	Used in Decoration	Used in Prestation	Specialized product[a]	Approx. period of use
E. VEGETABLE PRODUCTS						
Seed beads	nonema	+	+	+	-	to 1940
Marita pandanus cosmetic oil	komba yinggamp	-	+	-	+	a
Orchid fibre products	(various)	-	+	-	-	a
Drums	muwa	-	-	-	-	a
Arrows	wula	-	-	-	-	a
String bags	kun	(+)	-	-	-	a
Tobacco	yur	-	-	-	-	?a
Luxury & exotic foods	(various)	-	-	-	+	1965+
Coffee seeds & seedlings	kopi	-	-	-	-	1965+
F. MINERAL PRODUCTS						
1. Pigments:	minyamo					
red	klumkoi	(+)	+	-	+	a
red	kalom	(+)	+	-	+	?a
blue	muk	(+)	+	-	+	?1940-50
2. Salt	kura					
	aka	+	-	-	+	to 1960
	bunk	+	-	-	+	to 1960
	wum	+	-	-	+	to 1960
	kanji	+	-	-	+	to 1960
	kiyop	+	-	-	?-	to 1960
G. EUROPEAN GOODS						
Beads	bis	(+)	+	-	-	1950+
Matches	masis	-	-	-	-	1956+
Soap	sop	-	-	-	-	1956+
Shovels, cooking pots	savel, sospan	-	-	-	-	1960+
H. MONEY	mani	+	-	+	-	1960+

[a] i.e. product of region of special ecological or manufacturing characteristics.
[b] Not all informants agree to classification shown thus.
[c] Indicates always present or used as far as informants are aware.
[d] See app. 2 for specific names.

Appendix 4
Trade Regions

The manner of demarcating these regions is discussed in chapter 5. These lists include only those settlements with which the Kundagai have at some time traded. Not all settlements in each region are therefore listed here, although in general it is only the most distant ones that were not mentioned in trade histories.

Maring, Narak, and Kandawo clan clusters are listed, where known, although the Kundagai are unaware of many of these names outside the Maring area. A few Kuma local group names are also given.

The following symbols are used: an asterisk (*) indicates frequent trade links throughout the period for which records are available; a plus sign (+) indicates frequent trade links only since the mid-1950s.

SETTLEMENTS THAT TRADE WITH KUNDAGAI

1. *Up-Jimi*
    Yimpigema   Ambrakwi
    * Koinambe   Cenda
    * Kompiai   Kauwatyi
    * Kupeng   Manamban
    * Kwima   Tugumenga
    Dega   Iremban
    + Togban   Yomban
    + Kwiop   Manga
    + Koriom   Ogona
    Mogine   Kaureka

Appendix 4

		Kulunga	Teregan
		Kosap	Owelga
		Bubgile	Kamam
		Magen	Nimbika
		Olna	Kubungga
		Manz	Wika
	+	Kol	Parau Agliyeka
	+	Karap	Nimbika
2.		*Down-Jimi*	
	*	Bokapai	Kundagai
	*	Kandambiamp	
	*	Tsembant	
	*	Ginjinji	
	+	Gondomben	
	*	Waim	
	+	Tsalip	
	+	Tsendiap	
3.		*Cross-Jimi*	
	*	Rinyimp	Went–Kai; Kolomp–Kambek
	+	Timbunki	
	*	Kwibun	Mima
		Tsinggoropa	Molima
		Waramis	Morkai
	+	Tabibuga	Morkai
		Wanku	Kolika
		Korendiu	
	+	Wum	Kumom
		Tsenga	
		Por	Kapukai
		Toli	Pelka Cagaika
		Maigmol	Bomamdu
		Kauwil	Mongelka
	+	Malamp	
		Menjim	
4.		*Up-Simbai*	
	*	Kinimbong	Kundagai–Aikupa
	*	Nembenakump	
	*	Tekerau	

	* Timbeganji	
	* Kumbruf	
	Koki	
	* Simbai	
	Miami	
5.	*Down-Simbai*	
	Kenmongga	Tsembaga
	* Mondo	Tuguma
	* Gai	Kanump–Kauwil
	* Nimbra	Kandambent–Namikai
	Ringginai	Ipai–Makap
	Gunts	Funggai–Korama
	Tebabe	Bomagai–Angoiang
	* Pogaikump	Kono
	* Bank	Aungdagai
	* Konggerau	Kekai
	Tsunggup	
6.	*Trans-Simbai*	
	+ Kaironk Valley	Various Kalam settlements, the names of which the Kundagai often do not know.
	* Kinenj Valley	
	* Asai Valley	
7.	*Other*	
	Mala	
	+ Banz	
	+ Port Moresby	
	+ Rabaul	
	Madang	
	+ Simbu Province	

Notes

INTRODUCTION

1. I substantiate these assertions elsewhere (Healey 1980).
2. See Healey (1977; 1980; 1986) for various such elaborations.
3. More importantly at this stage is that through analysis one can disattend to, or account for, apparent disconfirming evidence that is almost certain to be discovered in field research. By its very nature, anthropological fieldwork amounts to a constant challenge to theory.

1. THE KUNDAGAI: ENVIRONMENT AND SOCIETY

1. Some botanists and biogeographers would call it lower-montane forest (Paijmans 1976).
2. All identifications are tentative. Some are my own, but most were made by matching Maring terms I recorded with those listed by Clarke (1971) and Rappaport (1968).
3. A contraction of *rawa ku,* "spirit stone."
4. This estimate represents seventeen ha. per person, surely a gross exaggeration (cf. Rappaport 1968: 287 ff.) and is no doubt a consequence of crude survey methods. The area of gardens is not derived from measurements of individual plots but from the total area of gardens entered onto a master map, partly by reference to compass points and partly by dead reckoning. The use of this method is obviously prone to high degrees of error, especially when dealing with very small areas. Estimates for areas of other vegetation types are more accurate and are partly derived from aerial photographs.
5. Garden sites are occasionally cleared but not planted.

6. It appears from figures given here that there is insufficient secondary forest to sustain a sixteen-year fallow cycle. I am confident, however, that the Kundagai are correct when they say they have more than enough secondary growth in reserve. Extensive areas of forest I estimate at twenty-five years old support their judgment. The problem evidently lies in my own inadequate surveying rather than in actual agricultural practice (see n. 4).

7. There are two more Maring populations to the southwest of the Kundagai: the Went–Kai and Kolomp–Kambek at Rinyimp. I was unable to determine whether they are clans or clan clusters.

8. Rappaport (1968: 20 ff.) has used the term "cognatic cluster" to refer to similarly constituted associations of clans, where cognatic connections stem not from presumed common ancestry but from repeated intermarriage over time and the obliteration of territorial divisions following affinal transfers of land.

9. The occasional exception is classificatory affines (e.g., "Z"H, W"B"), which may use agnatic terms in preference to assuming an affinal relationship and its attendant avoidances regarded as a nuisance where close contact is maintained.

10. Such marriages are proscribed among the Tsembaga (Rappaport 1969).

11. Lowman-Vayda (1971) identifies six categories but notes that there are variable conceptions of big-man status in different Maring groups. Differences between my own and Lowman-Vayda's material are detailed elsewhere (Healey 1977: 115 ff.).

12. The kiap is nonetheless feared to some extent. To the Kundagai many of his directives bear the stamp of irrational anger. The replacement of Australian administrators by national staff has not made the kiap any more accessible to the Kundagai. Indeed, the kiap and the government he represents are now seen as even more distant. For a detailed analysis of the impact of the state on local and regional political organization, see Maclean (1984*b*).

13. Some kaunsils of other settlements have other views concerning their rights to demand labor of their constituents. I was told that some kaunsils threaten to bring before the kiap those who refuse to work in their coffee gardens.

14. The material here differs in some significant respects from that provided by Rappaport (1968; 1979) for the Tsembaga and Lowman-Vayda (1971) for several, mainly Simbai, Maring groups. My own brief inquiries among the Manamban yielded yet further differences. I am confident that divergences in Maring testimony reflect real variations in conceptions of the supernatural and further support the contention that the Maring are not a composite of structurally and culturally unitary groups, aside from the obvious broad similarities. This conclusion undoubtedly fits other "societies" in New Guinea. It must also be admitted that some of the differences may be a product of idiosyncracies in collecting or presenting information on the part of both ethnographers and informants.

15. Briefly, the Maring etiology of illness is as follows: spirits and witches are considered to be the most frequent causes of illness and injury. This is also true statistically. Many minor ailments are not ascribed to supernatural causes.

Illness caused by contagion following the transgression of taboos or from contamination with polluting agents occurs less often. See also Lowman (1980).

2. THE USES AND SIGNIFICANCE OF PLUMES

1. See Patterson (1974–1975) for a list of species available in the market.
2. Prior to contact skins of females of these species were also used.
3. Men and women have the nasal septum and alae and earlobes pierced, and may wear pegs and spikes in the holes. Noses and ears are no longer pierced.

3. HUNTING AND ITS REGULATION

1. Although this concentration on tree-dwelling game is partly determined by the fact that there are few large terrestrial animals available, I should stress that it is also bound up in the ideology of gender. Briefly stated, the forest, high altitudes, the space above the ground, and thus arboreal animals, are associated with maleness and vitality. This by no means exhausts the symbolic properties of the environment in relation to gender.

2. Surprisingly, all three New Guinea groups compare favorably with hunting yields of the Kalahari San (Bushmen), among whom, of course, hunting assumes far greater nutritional and ideological importance, although the environments and fauna are very different. The San favor large prey, such as antelopes, but more often rely on medium- to small-sized prey. On the one hand, Lee's (1979: 265 ff.) work diary of one camp shows that seven hunters spent 78 man days to kill 18 animals, or a mean of 4.3 man days per kill. This is a much slower rate than those shown in table 8. On the other hand, the weight yield was 2.6 kg. per man day, which is probably a higher rate than the Wopkaimin. Lee does not indicate the number of hours in a work day, so a more precise comparison cannot be made.

The productivity of New Guinea hunters also compares quite well with that of the Bisa of Zambia. Though horticulture provides the mainstay of Bisa subsistence, Marks (1976: 203) provides data on productivity of specialists armed with firearms, who select relatively abundant large game, such as buffalo and impala. Seven men spent 1,132 man hours to secure 61.5(?) prey, yielding 12,072 kg. This amounts to 0.1 hr. expended to secure 1 kg. of meat. Against this high yield must be set a low killing rate of 18.4 hr. per prey.

3. This and other cases are all brief summaries based on informants' recollections, since no public disputes over hunting rights occurred while I was in the field.

4. I recorded several conflicting accounts of the significance of these markers. In 1972 I was told that one set marked the site where a cassowary had been killed. Another suggestion was that the stakes had a commemorative or mystical significance, marking the place where a Kolomp man was killed by witches. This explanation can be discounted since the man died after 1972. On another occasion as I rested by the stakes, one man began to explain their significance but was silenced by a Kolomp clansman. In the light of this incident

I suspect that the stakes have some further supernatural significance beyond being territory markers.

5. This is an interesting contrast with foraging societies, where property rights to game are typically collective or absent, and a parallel with certain predatory herding societies, such as the Reindeer Lapps, where communally pastured wild beasts are owned individually (cf. Ingold 1980).

6. Irrespective of Yekwai's perhaps modest views, he is undoubtedly one of the keenest, most knowledgeable, and skillful natural historians and hunters in Tsuwenkai. A reputation as a prominent hunter derives as much from real success as from broadcasting that success. Yekwai represents himself as somewhat reticent in the face of others' braggadocio.

7. That is, female birds, and immature males whose plumage for the first few years resembles the females'.

8. Rappaport (pers. comm.) states that there was no such intensification during the Tsembaga *kaiko* he observed.

9. Many individuals recognize an unnamed taxonomic category that conforms to the scientific family of birds of paradise. Maring ethnozoological categories, however, lack the neat exclusivity normally associated with taxonomies in most studies in ethnoscience.

10. Indeed, many government officers share this view, which further confused the issue.

11. Early in 1979 such *kots* became legalized under the system of Village Courts managed by locally elected officers. These courts in theory are not under the control of councillors. See Maclean (1984*b*) for a detailed analysis of Maring *kots*.

12. Possibly the Kundagai spend less time on gardening tasks than the Kauwatyi and many others. Kundagai gardens are not as tidy or carefully weeded, nor the fences as tall or sturdy, as among the Kauwatyi, which all bespeaks less intensive garden work. Further, unlike other Maring, the Tsuwenkai Kundagai do not have to fence distant gardens against the depredations of feral pigs, which are generally absent. In short, the Kundagai may have more available hunting time than most other Maring groups.

13. Certainly men say that wives and children are often hungry for meat, but the principal focus of such desire is the domestic pig. Although women are responsible for the care of pigs, men represent themselves as bearing the prime responsibility for decisions concerning the slaughter and distribution of pork. Men do not vie for prestige in competitive gifts of pork or other valuables, but a man who does not live up to his obligations to make prestations of pork to his affines and matrikin, or to assist his agnates in their own like gifts, suffers a loss of prestige. By contrast, among Amazonian horticulturalists, who lack domesticated, meat-yielding animals, a man's prestige is dependent on his gifts of meat from wild animals (Siskind 1973; Turner 1979). Here, male gender identity is strongly linked to prowess as a hunter, in opposition to female gender identity, which is associated with horticultural activities—this notwithstanding the material importance of the male contribution to horticulture, a contribution which is ideologically suppressed (cf. Turner 1979). Among the Maring, however, male gender identity focuses more on domination and control of processes

of production and reproduction in general. Domestication of animals here arguably shifts the "token" of prestige from the *material object* of meat, made socially meaningful by the act of presentation (as in Amazonia), to the *act* of presentation itself, made socially meaningful by the symbolic properties of pork. On the cultural meaning of domestic pig flesh see Healey (1985*b*).

14. Another reason may be that there is a natural bias toward males—a common feature in many species—which is reduced to near equality by human agency.

15. The paper in question expands and corrects a similar argument in my Ph.D. dissertation (Healey 1977). Much of the limited biological data on which this argument is based is supported by Kwapena (1985).

16. None of the species listed in table 12 are regarded as more scarce now than in the past. Some informants, however, do consider that the two Sicklebill Bird of Paradise species were more numerous a few decades ago. They are now rarely killed in Tsuwenkai.

4. VALUABLES AND PRESTATIONS

1. Sahlins (1963) is one influential example, but there are numerous such statements, often as asides in the course of some other argument.

2. There are a number of examples of such a characterization in the literature. A similar distinction has been made recently specifically for the Maring by LiPuma (1988: 5), who distinguishes between what he calls "commerce" and "exchange." In his treatment, commerce is dominated by a desocialized, economic orientation involving those who do not otherwise engage in the sociability of sharing within a clan or in gift exchange between clans. My fundamental disagreement with this view on theoretical and ethnographic grounds should become evident in this and subsequent chapters.

3. Women are mostly married between the ages of twenty to twenty-five, men a few years later. Thus, a woman who is an eldest child will not be married until her father is at least forty-five to fifty.

4. Contributions from real fathers, brothers, or sons are seldom repaid.

5. Data were collected by two literate assistants who filled out cards for each pig owner. These assistants spent several days collecting information by asking men and women about their pigs and the pigs of absentees, on visits to homesteads, community work projects, and at a church service.

6. Recently the Kundagai have acquired by trade several crossbred pigs of part-European strains which are prized for their higher meat yields. They are reputed to have higher fertility rates than indigenous sows, which may be a further factor of increase in local herds. The Kundagai, however, may be faced with the problem of ensuring the survival of piglets, and, irrespective of litter size, it is possible that they are unable or unwilling to care for more than a certain number of piglets from a litter.

7. Although many pigs are later killed by recipients, e.g., among the Enga and Melpa.

8. Robin Hide (pers. comm.), who has studied pig husbandry among the Sinasina Simbu, suggests that in areas such as Maring lands with lower popu-

lation densities and less grassland, pigs may actually mature faster and have higher fertility than in the central highlands where forests have been virtually replaced by poor foraging grasslands. If this is the case then the cultural variation in the disposal of pigs assumes greater importance in regulating pig herds. Even if Kundagai pigs are more fertile than central-highlands pigs, I would suggest that imports are necessary to maintain the present herd size.

9. Ralph Bulmer (pers. comm.) informs me that although this is technically correct, the Kalam do in fact make payments to both categories of affines (ZH etc. and WB etc.) at *semi* initiation festivals. In contrast, death payments (see below) are specifically divided into portions for which a return gift is and is not expected.

10. For a discussion of anomolous circumstances see Healey (1979).

11. A man refers to his sister's daughter as *wamb wump nako*, "daughter planting-material mine." *Wump* also refers to seedling runners, corms, and cuttings of, mainly, domesticated plants.

12. A *bamp kunda yu* may perform protective ritual and magic for allies of other clan clusters. Although Atikai clan had its own *bamp kunda yu* during the last war with the Tsembaga, who performed magic against the enemy, a Kanump–Kauwil ally performed some of the necessary ritual for Atikai.

13. E.g., between FMBS and FZSS.

5. THE STRUCTURE OF TRADE

1. This material is a summary of more detailed tables in Healey (1977: app. 7).

2. This assertion can be verified with reference to more detailed quantitative data in Healey (1977: chap. 13, apps. 7 and 8).

3. Tables and subsequent text take the cutoff date as 1956, the year Tabibuga Patrol Post was established in the Jimi and Tsuwenkai was first officially visited by a patrol (see chap. 1).

4. Other valued species traded are excluded for insufficiency of cases, and the Common Paradise Kingfisher and Raggiana Bird of Paradise are omitted because of special patterns as indicated in the text.

5. The species are: three locally recognized forms of the silky cuscus, *Phalanger vestitus*; one of the terrestrial cuscus, *P. gymnotis*; and one of the ringtail possum, *Pseudocheirus cupreus*. Their loose fur and sometimes the pelts of *P. vestitus* are traded. Drumskins are made of painted ringtail, *Pseudocheirus forbesi* (other possum and reptile skins, even of the introduced Cane Toad, *Bufo marinus,* found in some coastal areas, are also used as drumskins but are not traded).

6. The main species used were *Phalanger gymnotis* and *P. vestitus,* and the giant rat, *Mallomys rothschildi.*

7. However, the Maring are (or were) subject to iodine deficiency, which may contribute to hyperthyroidism and cretinism (Buchbinder 1973; Pharoah 1971). Iodine salts may be important in lessening the incidence of these conditions. Sale of noniodized salt is now illegal.

8. Neil Maclean (pers. comm.) found in 1980 that kina was beginning to

be replaced in prestations by money, at least among the eastern Maring. By 1985 it had all but dropped out of Kundagai exchange also.

9. This is the Maring rendition of the more orthodox *talbum*.

10. See Healey (1978c) for a discussion of types of stone and steel cutting tools and their classification.

11. Hence the specific names for this blade, meaning "Goipai Creek stone" and "Kant River product." The second name was used to identify the stone when talking to those unfamiliar with Tsuwenkai geography, who would be more likely to know of the Kant River than its tributary, Goipai Creek.

12. The imprecise number results from my inability to determine if two axe names referred to different stones or were alternatives for one type.

13. Called *mani* or *ku mani*, "stone money." Coins are sometimes called *ku meng*, "stone fruit."

14. I am grateful to Neil Maclean (pers. comm.) for drawing my attention to such behavior.

15. In this last case, of course, the recipient of the desired item acts as a carrier on behalf of the initiator of the arrangement. But the Kundagai see this as a trade transaction, *munggoi rigima*.

16. See appendix 4 for a list of settlements and their locations.

17. Indeed, Ernst (1978) importantly questions this aspect of Etoro–Onabasulu trade, couched as it is in a normative framework.

18. I am aware of the commercial connotations of the term "fund." The term is used for convenience without any formalist intentions.

19. This is in marked contrast to Sillitoe's (1979) claims for the Wola. Although he provides the only other detailed numerically based study of exchange in Melanesia, regrettably Sillitoe's data are not amenable to a numerically comparative analysis, since they are presented in chart form and actual numbers are not always evident.

20. Since these figures include plumes acquired by gift that were not later traded, the numbers differ from those in table 31.

21. This is a greater percentage than indicated in table 26. The present figure includes undated transactions, which are not considered in the table.

22. For example, of the sixty-six pigs killed during 1973–1974, twenty-seven or 40.9 percent were distributed in major prestations. The discrepancy between these figures may be accounted for if the Kundagai tend to choose homebred rather than imported pigs for prestations. I do not have adequate data on life histories of pigs to evaluate this suggestion, although informants deny such preference.

6. THE DEVELOPMENT OF TRADE

1. See Heaney (1982) for similar changes in Kuma use of plumes, which began somewhat earlier and must also have had a more direct effect upon Kundagai trade.

2. Bear in mind that histories of only a few men aged in their seventies in 1974 stretch back to the 1920s.

3. All distances are in a straight line. Actual distances traveled would in many cases be considerably greater.

4. The Kundagai are not organized into formal age grades. Men of similar ages may be termed *komba rangwai*, "marita-pandanus one," a reference to having ritually assumed the *mamp ku gunc* (stained with marita oil) at the same time. The practice was discontinued in the late 1950s or early 1960s.

5. The figure for the first period is based on a small sample of growers: 10, of whom two had no trees bearing yet. The remaining growers had produced beans for 2 to 8 years, mean yearly income range K1.41 to K19.50. The sample for the period to 1978 includes 18 men, with a mean yearly income ranging from K2.25 to K78.50. The sample to 1985 includes 16 men, with a mean yearly income ranging from zero to K35.40.

6. Maclean (1984a) provides an excellent analysis of Maring gambling and its relation to group definition and modern politics.

7. I use the term "exploitative" here in the simple sense of impelling surplus production in order to engage in trade. At the height of its development, Kundagai participation in trade was self-sustaining without any necessity to *produce* in order to participate.

8. See Maclean (1984a; 1984b; 1989) who provides a detailed analysis of *bisnis* practice and ideology among the Tugumenga Maring. Importantly, markets, gambling, coffee production, and so forth are all conceived of as a *bisnis* and implicated in a commitment to "development." Maclean argues persuasively that these activities are preeminently political and ideological, rather than economic.

7. EXCHANGE RATES

1. See also Persson (1983) on the *kula* ring as a whole, where in different sectors valuables may be rediverted by their use in bridewealth and mortuary payments. Note also that the *kula* is not an insulated system but is connected to other exchange systems in the southern Massim and mainland. See also Bohannan (1955) on the legitimate process of conversion between spheres in Tiv economy.

2. With the recent exception of the purchase of rare or exotic foods for small sums of money, and recently established weekly markets in some settlements (but not Tsuwenkai) (Maclean 1989).

3. Sahlins (1972) recognizes much the same point in his chapter on "The Sociology of Primitive Exchange."

4. European presence and the imposed peace it brought may itself have been an agent for increasing desire for plumes. With peace some highlanders have sought other forms of intercommunity competition, such as intensifying ceremonial exchange (Strathern 1971) with its attendant competitive dances. Thus, occasions for increased plume use probably occurred. In areas where plumes are used in prestations there was also inflation in the numbers required (e.g., Heaney 1982; Hide 1981). In contrast, I have already noted the decline of ceremonial activity requiring plumes among the Kuma.

5. By the time Europeans entered the Jimi, policy had shifted away from

the large-scale use of traditional valuables in payments for goods and services. This meant that the Maring could not enter into direct relations with Europeans for access to traditional wealth but had to seek such goods in exchange for other valuables from trading partners. Shells were therefore acquired at a greater productive cost. In that sense colonial penetration further stimulated production and strengthened newly realigned trade networks, and reproduced the structural dependence of such peripheral communities as the Kundagai on the central highlands as a source of wealth (see Healey 1985*a*; 1989).

6. See Meggitt (1971: 202–203) for the Mae Enga, Hide (1981) for the Sinasina Simbu, Dubbeldam (1964) for the Kapauku, Ernst (1978) for the Huli–Onabasulu trade, and Kelly (1977: 15) for Mendi–Etoro trade. The Wola of the southern highlands, by contrast, have opted for accumulation of kina at the expense of other valuables (Sillitoe 1979: 153 ff.). See also Hughes (1978).

7. Or rather, the equivalence of these "items" is agreed to by custom. That a woman's agnates expect repeated prestations for her suggests that the Kundagai (as others) do not put a material value or price on their womenfolk and offspring, and acknowledge the necessity of counterprestations from wife-givers to wife-receivers.

8. Greensnail shells hold these qualities above all others, which may explain the higher esteem in which they continue to be held by the Kundagai, whereas kina is now regarded with disfavor.

9. I use the terms "buy" and "sell" here and elsewhere as shorthands for "exchange for money," on the understanding that money is used as a valuable, not a currency.

10. Men said that in some other settlements pigs and most gardens have been separated by a single, communally maintained fence running from valley bottom to above the range of foraging pigs in high-altitude forest. This obviates fencing individual gardens. The Kundagai say they tried this once, but the fence fell into disrepair because people could not agree to a program of maintenance. In fact, there is much mingling of herds in pig-foraging land, although any larger congregations of pigs tend to split up in the evening as beasts return to their accustomed places for receiving rations from their mistresses. New Guinea pig-raising strategies form an interesting contrast with pastoralists, especially those dependent on meat rather than milk, where there is an impetus toward unlimited accumulation of private herds that are nonetheless pastured on a collective basis (cf. Ingold 1980).

11. There have been a very few exceptions to this observation, involving only lower-value skins.

12. It is true that the range of cash values of Lesser Bird of Paradise, kina, and pigs overlapped marginally. Yet these extremes—especially minima of K2 for pigs—were seen by the Kundagai as exceptional.

13. See Godelier's (1977) discussion of similar variations in Baruya salt trade.

14. A similar effect is discernible in Vitiaz Strait trade but not in the Huon Gulf. Both systems have a different structure from the Yir–Yoront trade (Sahlins 1972).

15. My interpretation of Maring concepts of value, especially of pigs, differs

in some key respects from LiPuma's, though this is not the place to go into detail.

8. UTILITARIANISM, SOCIABILITY, AND THE ORGANIZATION OF TRADE

1. Much of this chapter is a revised and expanded version of my paper, "Trade and sociability: Balanced reciprocity as generosity in the New Guinea highlands," *American Ethnologist* 11 (1) 1984, 42–60.

2. Rappaport's (1968: 106 ff.) influential model of Tsembaga trade, which I have already discussed in chapter 5, is an example of such an approach. See also Hughes (1977) and Brookfield with Hart (1972).

3. I use the term "trade gathering" in preference to "market." Although these meetings brought together men whose primary goals were to trade with one another, I found no indication that traders competed for commerce. As such, they did not constitute markets properly so called (cf. Sahlins 1972: 297–301), which were generally absent in highlands New Guinea (cf. Keil 1977).

4. These delays are not enjoined by etiquette; it is not thought impolite for host and visitor to hand over their wares at the same time.

5. See Kelly (1977: 14) on the Etoro ban on trade with tribal kinsmen and Meggitt (1974: 169) on the Enga insistence on immediate exchange in trade.

6. There are difficulties in choosing a suitable label. "Fictive kin" has a special meaning in Latin American studies and, with Bloch's (1973) distinction between "real" and "artificial" kin, suggests that such people are somehow not kinsmen at all. This seems contrary to the Kundagai view that sees kinship as qualitative not absolute.

7. As already noted, deliberate attempts to cheat, by refusing to give a return or by giving an inferior or damaged return, are rare. In the past unknown strangers might be waylaid by armed parties and robbed of their trade goods. The Kundagai said the practice was very rare and is now unheard of. It is certainly liable to discourage further visits, to the detriment of the robbers. That weaker form of hostile relations—bargaining—is mainly practiced between strangers rather than previously known partners.

8. Some were introduced to the Koriom man by Giewai (as in the example of Pinai given earlier), others sought him out on their own account in their travels up-river.

9. This is notwithstanding Hughes's (1977) important contribution. Keil's (1974) unpublished ethnography of Benabena exchange is the only monographic work that gives substantial attention to trade. Even journal articles wholly or largely dealing with highlands trade are few. Trade in the lowlands and islands of New Guinea has attracted little more attention.

10. Even Sahlins's (1972) treatment of trade falls into this trap.

Bibliography

Baal, J. van
    1975   *Reciprocity and the position of women: Anthropological papers.* Assen: Van Gorcum.
Barlow, Kathleen
    1985   "The role of women in intertribal trade among the Murik of Papua New Guinea." *Research in Economic Anthropology* 7: 95–122.
Beehler, Bruce M., Thane K. Pratt, and Dale A. Zimmerman
    1986   *Birds of New Guinea.* Princeton: Princeton University Press.
Belshaw, Cyril S.
    1955   *In search of wealth: A study of the emergence of commercial operations in the Melanesian society of Southeastern Papua.* American Anthropological Association, vol. 57, no. 1, pt. 2, memoir no. 80.
Bloch, Maurice
    1973   "The long term and the short term: The economic and political significance of the morality of kinship." In J. Goody, ed., *The character of kinship.* Cambridge: Cambridge University Press, 75–87.
Bohannan, Paul
    1955   "Some principles of exchange and investment among the Tiv." *American Anthropologist* 57: 60–70.
    1959   "The impact of money on an African subsistence economy." *Journal of Economic History* 19: 491–503.
Bourdieu, Pierre
    1977   *Outline of a theory of practice.* Cambridge: Cambridge University Press.
Brookfield, H. C., with Doreen Hart
    1971   *Melanesia: A geographical interpretation of an island world.* London: Methuen.

Brown, Paula
  1972 *The Chimbu: A study of change in the New Guinea highlands.* Cambridge, Mass.: Schenkman.
Brown, Paula, and Aaron Podolefsky
  1976 "Population density, agricultural intensity, land tenure, and group size in the New Guinea highlands." *Ethnology* 15: 211–238.
Brunton, Ron
  1980 "Misconstrued order in Melanesian religion." *Man* 15: 112–128.
Buchbinder, Georgeda
  1973 *Maring microadaptation: A study of demographic, nutritional, genetic and phenotypic variation in a highland New Guinea population.* Ph.D. dissertation. New York: Columbia University.
Bulmer, R. N. H.
  1960 "Political aspects of the moka ceremonial exchange system among the Kyaka people of the Western Highlands of New Guinea." *Oceania* 31: 1–13.
  1968 "The strategies of hunting in New Guinea." *Oceania* 38: 302–318.
  1976 "Selectivity in hunting and in disposal of animal bone by the Kalam of the New Guinea highlands." In G. de G. Sieveking, I. H. Longworth, and K. E. Wilson, eds., *Problems in economic and social archaeology.* London: Duckworth, 169–186.
  1982 "Traditional conservation practices in Papua New Guinea." In L. Morauta, J. Pernetta, and W. Heaney, eds., *Traditional conservation in Papua New Guinea: Implications for today* (Monograph 16). Boroko: Papua New Guinea: Institute of Applied Social and Economic Research, 59–77.
Chappell, J.
  1966 "Stone axe factories in the highlands of east New Guinea." *Proceedings of the Prehistoric Society* 32: 96–121.
Clark, J.
  1989 "The incredible shrinking men: Male ideology and development in a Southern Highlands society." *Canberra Anthropology* 12: 120–143.
Clarke, William C.
  1971 *Place and people: An ecology of a New Guinea community.* Canberra: Australian National University Press.
  1973 "Temporary madness as theatre: Wild-man behaviour in New Guinea." *Oceania* 43: 198–214.
Coates, Brian J.
  1985 *The birds of Papua New Guinea:* vol. 1, *Non-passerines.* Alderley, Queensland: Dove Publications.
Damon, Frederick H.
  1983 "What moves the kula: Opening and closing gifts on Woodlark Island." In J. W. Leach and E. Leach, eds., *The Kula: New perspectives on Massim exchange.* Cambridge: Cambridge University Press, 309–342.

Diamond, Jared M.
 1972 *Avifauna of the eastern highlands of New Guinea* (Publications of the Nuttall Ornithological Club, no. 12). Cambridge, Mass.: The Nuttall Ornithological Club.

Dornstreich, Mark
 1973 *An ecological study of Gadio Enga (New Guinea) subsistence.* Ph.D. dissertation. New York: Columbia University.

Dubbeldam, L. F. B.
 1964 "The devaluation of the Kapauku-cowrie as a factor of social disintegration." *American Anthropologist* Special Publication 66 (4) pt. 2: 293–303.

Dutton, Tom (ed.)
 1982 *The "Hiri" in history: Further aspects of long-distance Motu trade in central Papua* (Pacific Research Monograph no. 8). Canberra: Australian National University Press.

Dwyer, Peter D.
 1974 "The price of protein: Five hundred hours of hunting in the New Guinean highlands." *Oceania* 44: 278–293.
 1982 "Wildlife conservation and tradition in the highlands of Papua New Guinea." In L. Morauta, J. Pernetta, and W. Heaney, eds., *Traditional conservation in Papua New Guinea: Implications for today* (Monograph 16). Boroko: Papua New Guinea: Institute of Applied Social and Economic Research, 173–188.
 1983 "Etolo hunting performance and energetics." *Human Ecology* 11: 145–174.

Epstein, T. Scarlett
 1968 *Capitalism, primitive and modern: Some aspects of Tolai economic growth.* Canberra: Australian National University Press.

Ernst, T. M.
 1978 "Aspects of meaning of exchanges and exchange items among the Onabasulu of the Great Papuan Plateau." *Mankind* 11: 187–197.

Feachem, Richard
 1973 "The Raiapu Enga pig herd." *Mankind* 9: 25–31.

Feil, Daryl
 1984 *Ways of exchange: The Enga "tee" of Papua New Guinea.* St. Lucia: University of Queensland Press.
 1987 *The evolution of highland Papua New Guinea societies.* Cambridge: Cambridge University Press.

Feld, Steven
 1982 *Sound and sentiment: Birds, weeping, politics, and song in Kaluli expression.* Philadelphia: University of Pennsylvania Press.

Filer, Colin
 1985 "What is this thing called 'brideprice'?" *Mankind* 15: 163–183.

Firth, Raymond
 1979 "Work and value: Reflections on ideas of Karl Marx." In S. Wallman, ed., *Social anthropology of work* (ASA Monograph 19). London: Academic Press, 177–206.

Forge, Anthony
1972 "The Golden Fleece." *Man* 7: 527–540.
Gewertz, Deborah B.
1983 *Sepik River societies: A historical ethnography of the Chambri and their neighbors.* New Haven: Yale University Press.
Godelier, Maurice
1972 *Rationality and irrationality in economics.* London: NLB.
1977 *Perspectives in Marxist anthropology.* Cambridge: Cambridge University Press.
1986 *The making of great men: Male domination and power among the New Guinea Baruya.* Cambridge: Cambridge University Press.
Goodale, Jane C.
1978 "Saying it with shells in Southwest New Britain." Unpublished paper, American Anthropological Association Annual Meeting, Los Angeles.
Gouldner, Alvin
1960 "The norm of reciprocity: A preliminary statement." *American Sociological Review* 25: 161–178.
Gregory, C. A.
1982 *Gifts and commodities.* London: Academic Press.
Harding, Thomas G.
1967 *Voyagers of the Vitiaz Strait: A study of a New Guinea trade system.* Seattle: University of Washington Press.
1981 "Material consequences of ceremonial exchange." In R. W. Force and B. Bishop, eds., *Persistence and exchange: Papers from a symposium on ecological problems of the traditional societies of the Pacific region.* Honolulu: Pacific Science Association, 141–143.
Healey, Christopher J.
1973 *Hunting of birds of paradise and trade in plumes in the Jimi Valley, Western Highlands District.* M.A. qualifying essay. Port Moresby: University of Papua New Guinea.
1977 *Maring hunters and traders: The ecology of an exploitative, nonsubsistence activity.* Ph.D. dissertation. Port Moresby: University of Papua New Guinea.
1978a "The adaptive significance of systems of ceremonial exchange and trade in the New Guinea highlands." *Mankind* 11: 198–207.
1978b "Effects of human activity on *Paradisaea minor* in the Jimi Valley, New Guinea." *The Emu* 78: 149–155.
1978c "Maring classification of cutting tools." *Journal of the Polynesian Society* 87: 215–229.
1979 "Assimilation of nonagnates among the Kundagai Maring of the Papua New Guinea highlands." *Oceania* 50: 103–117.
1980 "The trade in bird plumes in the New Guinea region." *Occasional Papers in Anthropology*, no. 10. Brisbane: Anthropology Museum, University of Queensland, 249–275.
1985a "New Guinea inland trade: Transformation and resilience in the context of capitalist penetration." *Mankind* 15: 127–144.

1985b "Pigs, cassowaries, and the gift of the flesh: A symbolic triad in Maring cosmology." *Ethnology* 24: 153–165.

1985c *Pioneers of the mountain forest: Settlement and land redistribution among the Kundagai Maring of the Papua New Guinea highlands* (Oceania Monograph 29). Sydney: University of Sydney.

1986 "Men and birds in the Jimi Valley: The impact of man on birds of paradise in the Papua New Guinea highlands." *The Muruk* 1 (2): 4–33.

1988 "Culture as transformed disorder: Cosmological evocations among the Maring." *Oceania* 59: 106–122.

1989 "Trade, marriage and unequal development in the Papua New Guinea highlands." *Canberra Anthropology* 12: 48–73.

Heaney, William
1982 "The changing role of Bird of Paradise plumes in bridewealth in the Wahgi Valley." In L. Morauta, J. Pernetta, and W. Heaney, eds., *Traditional conservation in Papua New Guinea: Implications for today* (Monograph 16). Boroko: Papua New Guinea: Institute of Applied Social and Economic Research, 227–231.

Heider, Karl G.
1970 *The Dugum Dani: A Papuan culture in the highlands of West New Guinea.* Chicago: Aldine.

Henty, E. E.
1969 *A manual of the grasses of New Guinea* (Botany Bulletin no. 1). Lae, Papua New Guinea: Department of Forests.

Hide, Robin Lamond
1981 *Aspects of pig production and use in colonial Sinasina, Papua New Guinea.* Ph.D. dissertation. New York: Columbia University.

Hill, Polly
1986 *Development economics on trial: The anthropological case for a prosecution.* Cambridge: Cambridge University Press.

Hogbin, H. Ian
1951 *Transformation scene: The changing culture of a New Guinea village.* London: Routledge & Kegan Paul.

Howlett, Diana
1973 "Terminal development: From tribalism to peasantry." In H. C. Brookfield, ed., *The Pacific in transition: Geographical perspectives on adaptation and change.* Canberra: Australian National University Press, 249–274.

Hughes, Ian
1973 "Stone-age trade in the New Guinea inland: Historical geography without history." In H. C. Brookfield, ed., *The Pacific in transition: Geographical perspectives on adaptation and change.* Canberra: Australian National University Press, 97–126.

1977 *New Guinea stone age trade: The geography and ecology of traffic in the interior* (Terra Australis no. 3). Canberra: Department of Prehistory, Research School of Pacific Studies, Australian National University.

1978 "Good money and bad: Inflation and devaluation in the colonial process." *Mankind* 11: 308–318.
Hyndman, David Charles
1979 *Wopkaimin subsistence: Cultural ecology in the New Guinea highland fringe*. Ph.D. dissertation. St. Lucia: University of Queensland.
Ingold, Tim
1980 *Hunters, pastoralists and ranchers: Reindeer economies and their transformations*. Cambridge: Cambridge University Press.
Josephides, Lisette
1985 *The production of inequality: Gender and exchange among the Kewa*. London: Tavistock.
Kapferer, Bruce
1976 "Introduction: Transactional models reconsidered." in B. Kapferer, ed., *Transaction and meaning: Directions in the anthropology of exchange and symbolic behavior*. Philadelphia: Institute for the Study of Human Issues, 1–22.
Keil, Dana Eddy
1974 *The inter-group economy of the Nekematigi, Eastern Highlands District*. Ph.D. dissertation. Evanston: Northwestern University.
1977 "Markets in Melanesia? A comparison of traditional economic transactions in New Guinea with African markets." *Journal of Anthropological Research* 33: 258–276.
Kelly, Raymond C.
1977 *Etoro social structure: A study in structural contradiction*. Ann Arbor: University of Michigan Press.
Kormondy, Edward J.
1969 *Concepts of ecology*. Englewood Cliffs, N. J.: Prentice-Hall.
Kwapena, Navu
1985 *The ecology and conservation of six species of birds of paradise in Papua New Guinea*. Port Moresby: PNG Government Printer.
Landtman, Gunnar
1927 *The Kiwai Papuans of British New Guinea*. London: Macmillan.
Leahy, Michael J.
in press *New Guinea probes into new areas, 1930–1934*. Birmingham: University of Alabama Press.
Lederman, Rena
1986 *What gifts engender: Social relations and politics in Mendi, highland Papua New Guinea*. Cambridge: Cambridge University Press.
Lee, Richard Borshay
1979 *The !Kung San: Men, women and work in a foraging society*. Cambridge: Cambridge University Press.
Lipset, David M.
1985 "Seafaring Sepiks: Ecology warfare, and prestige in Murik trade." *Research in Economic Anthropology* 7: 67–94.
LiPuma, Edward
1980 "Sexual symmetry and social reproduction among the Maring of Papua New Guinea." *Ethos* 1–2: 34–57.

1981 "Cosmology and economy among the Maring of highland New Guinea." *Oceania* 51: 266–285.
1983 "On the preference for marriage rules: A Melanesian example." *Man* 18: 766–785.
1988 *The gift of kinship: Structure and practice in Maring social organization*. Cambridge: Cambridge University Press.

Lowman, Cherry
1973 *Displays of power: Art and war among the Marings of New Guinea* (Studies no. 6). New York: The Museum of Primitive Arts.
1980 *Environment, society and health: Ecological bases of community growth and decline in the Maring region of Papua New Guinea.* Ph.D. dissertation. New York: Columbia University.

Lowman-Vayda, Cherry
1971 "Maring big men." In R. M. Berndt and P. Lawrence eds., *Politics in New Guinea*. Nedlands: University of Western Australia Press, 317–361.

McArthur, Margaret
1974 "Pigs for the ancestors: A review article." *Oceania* 45: 87–123.

MacIntyre, Martha, and Michael Young
1982 "The persistence of traditional trade and ceremonial exchange in the Massim." In R. J. May and H. Nelson, eds., *Melanesia: Beyond diversity*, vol. 1. Canberra: Research School of Pacific Studies, Australian National University, 207–222.

Maclean, Neil
1984a "Is gambling 'bisnis'?: The economic and political functions of gambling in the Jimi Valley." *Social Analysis* 16: 44–59.
1984b *"To develop our place": A political economy of the Maring*. Ph.D. dissertation. Adelaide: University of Adelaide.
1985 "Understanding Maring marriage: A question of the analytic utility of the domestic mode of production." *Mankind* 15: 110–126.
1989 "The commoditisation of food: An analysis of a Maring market." *Canberra Anthropology* 12: 74–98.

Majnep, Ian Saem, and Ralph Bulmer
1977 *Birds of my Kalam country*. New Zealand: Oxford/Auckland University Press.

Malinowski, Bronislaw
1915 "The natives of Mailu: Preliminary results of the Robert Mond research work in British New Guinea." *Transactions of the Royal Society of South Australia* 39: 494–706.
1922 *Argonauts of the Western Pacific*. London: Routledge & Kegan Paul.

Manner, Harley
1977 "Biomass: Its determination in tropical agro-ecosystems: An example from montane New Guinea." In T. P. Bayliss-Smith and R. G. Feachem, eds., *Subsistence and survival: Rural ecology in the Pacific*. London: Academic Press, 215–242.

Marks, Stuart A.
  1976   *Large mammals and a brave people: Subsistence hunters in Zambia.* Seattle: University of Washington Press.
Marx, Karl
  1976 [1867]   *Capital: A critique of political economy,* vol. 1. Harmondsworth: Penguin Books.
Mauss, Marcel
  1954   *The gift: Forms and functions of exchange in archaic societies,* trans. I. Cunnison. London: Cohen and West.
Meggitt, M. J.
  1964   "Male–female relationships in the highlands of Australian New Guinea." *American Anthropologist* Special Publication 66 (4) pt. 2: 204–224.
  1971   "From tribesmen to peasants: The case of the Mae Enga of New Guinea." In L. R. Hiatt and C. Jayawardena, eds., *Anthropology in Oceania: Essays presented to Ian Hogbin.* Sydney: Angus and Robertson, 191–209.
  1974   "'Pigs are our hearts!': The *te* exchange cycle among the Mae Enga of New Guinea." *Oceania* 44: 165–203.
Modjeska, Nicholas
  1985   "Exchange value and Melanesian trade reconsidered." *Mankind* 15: 145–162.
Morren, George Edward Bradshaw Jr.
  1986   *The Miyanmin: Human ecology of a Papua New Guinea society.* Ann Arbor: UMI Research Press.
Newton, Janice
  1989   "Women and modern marriage among the Orokaiva." *Canberra Anthropology* 12: 28–47.
Nihill, M.
  1989   "The new pearlshells: Aspects of money and meaning in Anganen exchange." *Canberra Anthropology* 12: 144–160.
O'Hanlon, Michael
  1983   "Handsome is as handsome does: Display and betrayal in the Wahgi." *Oceania* 53: 317–333.
Paijmans, K.
  1976   "Vegetation." In K. Paijmans, ed., *New Guinea vegetation.* Canberra: Australian National University Press, 23–105.
Paine, Brenda G.
  1971   "Growth and development." In B. S. Hetzel and P. O. D. Pharoah, eds., *Endemic cretinism.* Goroka: Institute of Human Biology, Papua–New Guinea, 94–103.
Patterson, Ted
  1974–   "Survey of birds traded at Koki Market." *New Guinea Bird Society*
  1975   *Newsletter* 104: 5–6; 105: 3; 106: 3; 107: 3.
Persson, Johnny
  1983   "Cyclical change and circular exchange: A re-examination of the Kula Ring." *Oceania* 54: 32–47.

Pharoah, P. O. D.
1971 "Epidemiological studies of endemic cretinism in the Jimi Valley in New Guinea." In B. S. Hetzel and P. O. D. Pharoah, eds., *Endemic cretinism*. Goroka: Institute of Human Biology, Papua–New Guinea, 109–116.

Podolefsky, Aaron
1984 "Contemporary warfare in the New Guinea highlands." *Ethnology* 23: 73–87.

Polanyi, Karl
1968 *Primitive, archaic and modern economies: Essays of Karl Polanyi*, ed. George Dalton. Boston: Beacon Press.

Pospisil, Leopold
1963 *Kapauku Papuan economy*. New Haven: Yale University Publications in Anthropology, no. 67.

Pryor, Frederic L.
1977 *The origins of the economy*. New York: Academic Press.

Rand, Austin L., and E. Thomas Gilliard
1967 *Handbook of New Guinea birds*. London: Weidenfeld and Nicolson.

Rappaport, Roy A.
1968 *Pigs for the ancestors: Ritual in the ecology of a New Guinea people*. New Haven: Yale University Press.
1969 "Marriage among the Maring." In R. M. Glasse and M. J. Meggitt, eds., *Pigs, pearlshells and women: Marriage in the New Guinea highlands*. Englewood Cliffs, N. J.: Prentice-Hall, 117–137.
1971 The Editors of *Scientific American*, "The flow of energy in an agricultural society." In *Energy and Power*. San Francisco: W. H. Freeman, 69–80.
1979 *Ecology, meaning and religion*. Richmond, Va.: North Atlantic Books.

Reay, Marie
1959 *The Kuma: Freedom and conformity in the New Guinea highlands*. Melbourne: Melbourne University Press.

Ryan, D'Arcy
1959 "Clan formation in the Mendi Valley." *Oceania* 29: 257–289.

Sahlins, Marshall D.
1963 "Poor man, rich man, big-man, chief: Political types in Melanesia and Polynesia." *Comparative Studies in Society and History* 5: 285–303.
1972 *Stone age economics*. Chicago: Aldine-Atherton.

Salisbury, R. F.
1962 *From stone to steel: Economic consequences of a technological change in New Guinea*. Melbourne: Melbourne University Press.
1970 *Vunamami: Economic transformation in a traditional society*. Melbourne: Melbourne University Press.

Sansom, Basil
1976 "A signal transaction and its currency." In B. Kapferer, ed., *Trans-*

action and meaning: Directions in the anthropology of exchange and symbolic behavior. Philadelphia: Institute for the Study of Human Issues, 143–161.

Schwartz, Theodore
- 1963 "Systems of areal integration: Some considerations based on the Admiralty Islands of northern Melanesia." *Anthropological Forum* 1: 56–97.

Schwimmer, Erik
- 1979 "Reciprocity and structure: A semiotic analysis of some Orokaiva exchange data." *Man* 14: 271–285.
- 1980 "The limits of economic ideology: A comparative anthropological study of work concepts." *International Social Science Journal* 32: 517–531.

Seligman, C. G.
- 1910 *The Melanesians of British New Guinea.* Cambridge: Cambridge University Press.

Sillitoe, Paul
- 1979 *Give and take: Exchange in Wola society.* Canberra: Australian National University Press.
- 1988 "From head-dresses to head-messages: The art of self-decoration in the highlands of Papua New Guinea." *Man* 23: 298–318.

Siskind, Janet
- 1973 *To hunt in the morning.* London: Oxford University Press.

Strathern, Andrew
- 1969 "Finance and production: Two strategies in New Guinea highlands exchange systems." *Oceania* 40: 42–67.
- 1971 *The rope of moka: Big-men and ceremonial exchange in Mount Hagen, New Guinea.* Cambridge: Cambridge University Press.
- 1976 "Transactional continuity in Mount Hagen." In B. Kapferer, ed., *Transactions and meaning: Directions in the anthropology of exchange and symbolic behavior.* Philadelphia: Institute for the Study of Human Issues, 277–287.
- 1979 *Ongka: A self-account by a New Guinea big-man.* London: Duckworth.
- 1985 "'A line of boys': Melpa dance as a symbol of maturation." In P. Spencer, ed., *Society and the dance: The social anthropology of process and performance.* Cambridge: Cambridge University Press, 119–139.

Strathern, Andrew, and Marilyn Strathern
- 1971 *Self-decoration in Mount Hagen.* London: Gerald Duckworth.

Strathern, Marilyn
- 1979 "The self in self-decoration." *Oceania* 49: 241–257.

Thurnwald, Richard
- 1932 *Economics in primitive communities.* London: Oxford University Press.

Tiesler, F.
- 1969 "Die intertribalen Beziehungen an der Nordkuste Neuguineas

Gebiet der Kleinen Schouten-Inseln." *Arbhandlungen und Berichte des Staatlichen Museums für Volkenkunde Dresden* 30–31: 1–122.

Tueting, Laura Thompson
    1935   *Native trade in southeast New Guinea* (Occasional Papers, vol. 11, no. 15). Honolulu: Bernice P. Bishop Museum.

Turner, Terence S.
    1979   "The Ge and Bororo as dialectical systems: A general model." In D. Maybury–Lewis, ed., *Dialectical societies: The Ge and Bororo of central Brazil*. Cambridge: Harvard University Press, 147–178.

Vayda, Andrew P.
    1971   "Phases of the process of war and peace among the Marings of New Guinea," *Oceania* 42: 1–24.

Vayda, A. P., and E. A. Cook
    1964   "Structural variability in the Bismarck Mountain cultures of New Guinea: A preliminary report." *Transactions of the New York Academy of Sciences,* series 2, 26: 798–803.

Vicedom, Georg F., and Herbert Tischner
    1983   *The Mbowamb: The culture of the Mount Hagen tribes in east central New Guinea,* vol. 1 (Oceania Monograph no. 25), trans. Helen M. Groger-Wurm. Sydney: University of Sydney.

VPR (Village Population Register)
    1973   VPR: Kunoga Census Division. Unpublished record, Tabibuga.

Wagner, Roy
    1967   *The curse of Souw: Principles of Daribi clan definition and alliance in New Guinea*. Chicago: University of Chicago Press.

Wallerstein, Immanuel
    1974   *The modern world-system.* Vol. 1, *Capitalist agriculture and the origins of the European world-economy in the sixteenth century.* New York: Academic Press.

Weiner, Annette B.
    1976   *Women of value, men of renown: New perspectives in Trobriand exchange*. St. Lucia: University of Queensland Press.

Widegren, Orjan
    1983   "The general principles of sociability: Developing Sahlins' theory of 'primitive exchange.'" *Sociology* 17: 319–338.

Wright, Henry, and Melinda Zeder
    1977   "The simulation of a linear exchange system under equilibrium conditions." In T. K. Earle and J. E. Ericson, eds., *Exchange systems in prehistory*. New York: Academic Press, 233–253.

Wurm, S. A.
    1964   "Australian New Guinea highlands languages and the distribution of their typological features." *American Anthropologist* Special Publication 66 (4) pt. 2: 77–97.

Index

Accumulation, 269, 273; of money, 262, 267; of pigs, 190, 229, 230–231; of plumes, 228–229; of shells, 141, 229, 230, 258, 303; of steel tools, 229, 230, 303; of valuables, 237
Aesthetics: of decorations, 76; and value, 194, 290, 312
Age groups: and pig ownership, 143–145; and shell ownership, 138–140; and trading, 247–253 passim, 316–318
Agnation, 32, 36, 338–339
Agriculture. *See* Coffee; Crops; Gardens
Allies, 32, 102, 158, 160, 163, 164
Am yundem (girl's puberty payments), 155–157, 163, 164
Arrows, 89, 121
Assassination, 41, 48, 112, 162
Astrapia, Princess Stephanie's. *See* Bird of Paradise, Princess Stephanie's
Axes, 89, 142, 215. *See also* Steel tools; Stone axes

Baal, J. van, 6, 327, 330, 341
Bailer shells, ownership of, 135
Bamp kunda yu. See Big-men
Bargaining, 280, 380 n. 8; absence of, 128, 209, 324–325; recent emergence of, 248, 270, 298, 317, 324
Barlow, K., 3
Barter. *See* Trade
Baruya, 301, 311
Beehler, B. M., 360

Belshaw, C. S., 3
Big-men, 40–41, 48, 108, 150, 162, 269, 372 n. 11, 376 n. 12; and dance magic, 74; and hunting, 110, 112; recruitment of allies by, 160; and shell ownership, 141–142; and trade, 251–252, 335
Bird of Paradise, xiv, 7, 87, 119, 122, 374 n. 9; Black Sicklebill, 67, 71, 80, 87, 122, 176, 246, 259, 273, 275, 295; breeding of, 94, 111, 121, 122; Brown Sicklebill, 87, 122, 259; display of, 80, 106; display sites of, 92, 100, 104–108 passim, 113, 121, 122; King of Saxony, 67, 71, 80, 83, 87, 103, 111, 229, 281, 283, 292, 293, 295; Lesser, 61, 67, 68, 70, 71, 73, 80, 83, 87, 90, 106, 115, 176, 182, 187, 209, 227, 245, 247, 292, 293, 295, 299, 307, 309, 325; molt of, 112; Parotia, 92; Princess Stephanie's, 67, 71, 80, 87, 90, 92, 103, 106, 107, 108, 111, 113, 122, 209, 246, 259, 273, 275, 283, 290, 293, 297, 301; Raggiana (Red), 63, 70, 131, 169, 176, 179, 186, 203, 226, 259, 273; sex ratios of, 123; Superb, 80, 87, 92, 104, 111, 229, 281, 290
Bird populations, 8, 58, 115, 116, 123–126, 241
Birds, 13; breeding, 9; as decorations, 60–65, 360–364; kinds of, 87, 360–364; plume-bearing, xiii, xiv, 87, 120,

393

121; as property, 104–105. *See also* Bird of Paradise; Buzzard; Cassowaries; Cockatoo; Eagle; Goura; Hornbill; Kingfisher; Lory; Parrot; Plumes
Bisa (Central African people), 11, 373 n. 2
Bisnis, 54, 122, 378 n. 8; plumes as, 115
Bohannan, P., 268
Bosboi, 42
Bourdieu, P., 127, 342
Bows, 89, 121
Bridewealth, 7, 129, 149, 152–153, 156, 157, 163, 164, 297, 305, 312, 322; negotiation of, 150, 347; return gift for, 138–141 passim, 152–153
Brookfield, H. C., 232
Brown, P., 27, 258
Brunton, R., 339
Buchbinder, G., 25, 34, 43, 118, 119, 146, 168
Bulmer, R., xv, xvii, xix, 3, 87, 92, 122, 351, 376 n. 9
Burial, changing practices, 43
Bush fallow, 20, 21
Bushknives, 89, 142. *See also* Steel tools
Buzzard, Long-tailed, 65, 71, 87, 93, 176

Carrying capacity, 27–28
Cassowaries, 2, 13, 60, 131, 175, 222–223, 290, 293, 307, 312; in decorations, 73; hunting of, 94, 98, 104; ownership of, 148; and spirits, 47; trapping of, 90
Cemeteries. *See Raku*
Center. *See* Central highlands; Ultimate plume consumers
Central highlands: accumulation of wealth in, 267; demand for forest products in, 333; demand for plumes in, 7, 60, 299; economic development in, 262, 266; European penetration of, 12, 234, 258; exchange rates in, 296, 297; pig kills in, 148; shells in, 194, 230, 232, 258–261, 296; as source of money, 202; trade goods from, 206, 278, 280, 295; trade links with, 174, 219, 236–238, 243, 253, 331; use of plumes in, 259–260
Ceremonial exchange, 3, 5, 127, 276, 303, 307, 327, 347, 351. *See also* Prestations
Chambri, 271
Chappell, J., 196
Child reclamation payments, 157–158
Chimbu. *See* Simbu
Christians, and food taboos, 45

Clan clusters, 29, 30
Clans, 29, 30–34 passim, 356; fission of, 30, 33; and land rights, 31, 56
Clan subclusters, 31–32; and land rights, 56
Clark, J., 200
Clarke, W. C., 17, 19, 20, 22, 36, 42, 195
Climate, 17–18
Clothing, 68, 265
Coates, B. J., 360
Cockatoo, White (Sulphur-crested), 61, 63, 65, 71, 83, 180, 209, 281
Coffee, 26, 54, 262, 267, 269; income from, 26, 262–263, 273, 275, 333, 378 n. 5; plantations and groves, 20–21
Cognatic clusters, 32–34, 36, 372 n. 8; and land rights, 56
Colonial authority, 234, 250, 269, 333
Committee member (L.G.C.). *See Komiti*
Commodity exchange. *See* Trade
Compensation payments, 103, 107, 162–163. *See also* Disputes
Conservation, of game, 115, 119, 120, 121–126
Conus shells, ownership of, 135
Cook, E. A., 30, 31
Councillor (L.G.C.). *See Kaunsil*
Cowrie shells, 190, 237, 258, 280, 289–290, 293, 296; ownership of, 135
Crops, 13, 21, 22; pandanus, 21; sweet potato, 22

Damon, F. H., 301
Dancegrounds, 64
Dancers, 41, 74
Dances, 67, 73, 74, 129, 134; and gender, 78, 80; and trade, 214, 253, 322–323, 325, 328
Death-payments, 129, 149, 153–155, 156, 157, 163, 164; return gift for, 138–141 passim
Decorations, ix, 7, 68–71, 134, 207, 309, 312, 316, 360–364, 365–367; attract women, 76, 312; changing styles of, 70, 180; meanings of, 78–80, 312; occasions for, 70; passed in trade, 132, 214, 319, 322; production of, 86 ff.; social significance of, 68–70, 71–80; and warfare, 73
Deforestation, xiv, 7
Delayed exchange. *See* Trade transactions
Dependence, on central highlands, 237, 261, 266–267, 317, 332, 348
Devaluation: of shells, 258, 261, 274–

275, 290, 296–297, 379 n. 6; of steel tools, 296. *See also* Exchange rates
Development, 262, 267, 334, 378 n. 8
Diamond, J. M., 360
Diet, 13, 119, 120; protein in, 88, 95; salt in, 186, 214
Disputes: over hunting rights, 102–103, 106–108, 115, 374 n. 11; over land, 56; over trade, 320–321
Divorce, 151
Dogs, 2, 13, 148, 184; used in hunting, 93
Dogwhelk shells, 184, 190, 197, 199, 237, 258, 280, 289–290, 293, 296; ownership of, 135
Dornstreich, M., 95
Downes, M., xv
Dutton, T., 3
Dwyer, P. D., 95, 96, 98, 99, 122

Eagle, Harpy, 71, 87, 93, 281, 325
Ecological specialization, 1, 10, 210, 216–217, 233, 276
Ecological zones, 18–23
Eels: and spirits, 47; trapping of, 90
Egality, 150, 347–349 passim
Enemies, 32, 102, 112, 239
Environment, 15 ff.
Epidemics. *See* Sickness
Epstein, T. S., 3, 271
Equilibrium. *See* Homeostasis
Ernst, T. M., 217, 311
Ethnic identity, 28
Etoro (Etolo), 95–99 passim, 217–218
Europeans, contact with, 48, 123, 240, 258, 260–262, 274, 378 n. 4, n. 5. *See also* Central highlands
Exchange, 1, 34, 127, 232, 269, 347, 354; and definition of groups, 149, 338–340 passim, 355–356; modes of, 128, 230, 268, 270, 272–273, 311, 314, 350, 351. *See also* Ceremonial exchange; Gifts; Prestations; Trade transactions
Exchange rates, 132, 172, 209, 271–313 passim, 318, 342; as cash equivalent, 281–283, 306–307; of cassowaries, 294–295, 297, 305–306, 307, 309; changing fashions, 289; constancy of, 275, 294–296 passim, 297, 308–309; of forest products, 293–295, 297; of marsupial skins, 307, 310; of pigs, 292–296 passim, 305–306, 307, 309, 310; of plumes, 281, 292–297 passim, 299, 307, 309, 310; and prestations, 303–306, 310; and quality of goods, 280–281, 306; and quantity of goods, 280–281; regional variations in, 307–310; of shells, 194, 274, 290–292, 294, 308–309, 310; of steel tools, 290–292, 294, 295, 308–309, 310; of stone axes, 308; temporal changes of, 273, 275, 278–310 passim; and trade partnerships, 300–301, 346
Exotic goods, 253, 254–255, 278, 314; in prestations, 169, 223–226, 227. *See also* Pigs; Shells; Steel tools

Feachem, R. G., 145
Feathers. *See* Plumes
Feil, D. K., 3, 235, 352, 354
Feld, S., 76, 80
Fight magic man. *See* Big-men
Filer, C., 304
Firth, R., 301
Forest: area of, 25; area of montane, 19; area of secondary, 21; exploitation of, 24; lower montane, 23; primary montane, 19, 87; secondary, 19–20; types of, 18–20
Forest products, 12, 299, 333; and *bisnis*, 122; dominate structure of trade networks, xiv, 207, 267; exchangeability of, 278; production of, 86 ff., 226; as trade goods, xiii, 8, 60, 175
Forge, A., 354
Fowls, 2, 13, 148
Furs: of marsupials, 2, 133, 175, 199, 292; in prestations, 226

Gadio Enga, 95
Gainj, 13, 28
Gambling, 262, 265, 266, 325, 378 n. 6
Game, 13, 87; abundance of, 119, 125; kinds of, 88–89; as property, 105; restricted, 100–101
Gardens, 22–23, 24, 35, 57, 58, 374 n. 12; altitudinal distribution of, 22; area of, 22, 371 n. 4; fallow, 22–23, 372 n. 6; and land tenure, 55; ownership, 55; and spirits, 52
Genealogies, 38, 357
Generosity: in prestations, 150, 303, 347; in trade, 300–301, 303, 343–349 passim, 361
Gewertz, D. B., 1, 3, 271
Gift exchange. *See* Prestations
Gifts, 128, 138, 303, 318, 327, 330, 344; of plumes, 63, 64, 135, 179. *See also* Prestations, minor
Gilliard, E. T., 360
Godelier, M., 2, 268, 271, 301, 302, 311, 341

Gold, 262, 263, 334
Goodale, J. C., 151
Gouldner, A., 347
Goura. See Pigeon, Goura
Government officer. See *Kiap*
Grassland, 23, 24–25; area of, 23, 25
Greensnail shell, 139, 245, 276, 280, 289, 290, 295, 296, 379 n. 8; declining supply of, 194, 304; origins of, 194; in prestations, 227
Gregory, C. A., 127
Guns, 89, 114–115, 121
Gunts, 17, 118, 119

Habitat destruction, 120
Harding, T. G., 1, 3, 200, 278, 315, 327, 330, 347, 353; on regional trade, 232, 334
Hart, D., 232
Headdress, 64, 70–71
Healey, C. J., 3, 9, 25, 32, 47, 51, 58, 83, 106, 116, 120, 122, 123, 149, 161, 211, 237, 259, 270, 295, 312, 339, 352
Heaney, W., 258–259, 273
Heider, K. G., 2, 95, 212
Henty, E. E., 23
Hide, R. L., 235, 258–259, 375–376 n. 8
Highlands Labour Scheme: and cash earnings, 262; and trade, 240
Hill, P., 266
Hogbin, H. I., 3
Homeostasis, 4, 8–9, 11, 58, 125–126
Homesteads, 20–21, 35–36
Homicide bribes, 161–162
Hornbill, 63, 65, 71, 131, 180, 281
Hospitality, 272, 324, 342–343. See also Trade partners, hospitality given to
Houses, 34–36
Howlett, D., 267
Hughes, I., 1, 6, 187, 193, 195, 196, 197, 212, 213, 235, 240, 258, 261, 274, 315, 327; on highlands trade, 2, 10, 216, 217, 229, 232; on sorcery fears and trade, 239
Huli, 217
Hunter-gatherers, 119–120, 374 n. 5
Hunters: abilities of, 94–95, 118, 120; density of, 116–120; prominent, 94–95, 96, 109, 374 n. 6; and yield, 95
Hunting, 58, 60, 86–126 passim, 269, 301, 353; of birds, 63, 86–126 passim, 309; by children, 88; declining yield of, 95, 121; definition of, 86–87; effects on prey populations of, 118–126 passim; equipment used in, 88, 89, 114, 121; and gender, 86, 88, 89, 120, 373 n. 1, 374–375 n. 13; influence of spirits on, 47, 52, 90–91, 102, 110; intensity of, 94, 110, 116–121, 122, 374 n. 8; magic used in, 88, 90, 91; of mammals, 92–93; methods of, 86–94; productivity of, 95–99, 116–118, 373 n. 2; rates of, 123–126, 243; and ritual cycle, 112; seasonality of, 93–94, 111, 121; selectivity of prey in, 98, 99, 110, 111, 116, 119, 120, 123; and subsistence, 119–120; supplies trade, 15, 176, 181, 203, 206, 207, 222, 228, 241, 243, 267, 314, 318; and taboos, 110, 112, 120; use of blinds in, 89, 90, 92, 103, 105, 121; use of lures in, 90, 103; voluntary restraints on, 110–111, 113, 122; and warfare, 110, 112, 121; by women, 88, 89
Hunting rights, 100–116 passim, 118, 122; of individuals, 103–109 passim, 113, 121; inheritance of, 106; and kinship, 101; purchase of, 106; and territories, 100–103, 121. See also Disputes
Hunting territories, 100, 103, 373–374 n. 4; personal, 108–109, 122
Hyndman, D. C., 95, 96

Income. See Coffee; Labor migration
Inflation. See Exchange rates; Prestations, inflation in
Intermediate plume suppliers, 8, 241, 273

Josephides, L., 3, 354

Kalahari San (Bushmen), 120, 373 n. 2
Kalam, 13, 28, 29, 48, 71, 87, 153, 161, 168, 180, 184, 195, 239, 322, 360; pigs among, 148, 207; plume use among, 179, 182. See also *Semi*
Kamungga (primary montane forest). See Forest
Kandawo, 13, 240, 368; plume use by, 67, 83, 131, 180; population, 29
Kapferer, B., 127
Kaunsil, 42, 102, 108, 115, 116, 330, 335, 372 n. 13
Kauwatyi clan cluster, 119; compared with Kundagai, 339–340; decoration styles of, 71; population density of, 27; and territorial expansion, 57; trade by, 238; and war, 38, 53
Keil, D. E., 1, 2, 232
Kelly, R. C., 2, 217

Index 397

Kiap (government officer), 42, 55, 100, 112, 115, 372 n. 12
Kina, 258, 276, 280, 289, 290, 296, 307; declining supply of, 194; origins of, 191–192; in prestations, 139, 191, 194, 215, 274, 376–377 n. 8
Kingfisher, Common Paradise, 61, 63, 65, 67, 71, 131, 176, 180, 281
Knowledge, and property rights, 105–106
Koinambe (mission station), 25, 48, 73, 142, 264, 333
Komiti, 42, 115, 330
Konj kaiko (pig-killing ceremony), 25, 29, 32, 40, 48, 49, 73, 110, 112, 129, 145, 146, 193, 238, 249, 253, 322, 323
Konj kura (salt pork prestations), 158–161, 163, 164, 214
Kopon, 13
Kormondy, E. J., 4
Kot. See Disputes
Kula ring, 378 n. 1
Kuma, 240, 360; decorations, 71; demand for plumes by, 259–260, 273; plume use by, 308, 352; shells in, 258–261, 274–275; trade with, 176, 181, 250, 266, 325
Kwapena, N., 85

Labor: and property rights, 105–106; and value, 300–302, 307
Labor migration, 200, 252, 267, 305, 335; as source of money, 201, 262; as source of plumes, 63–64, 273; as source of shells, 194
Land: deserted, 53; purchase of, 53–54, 57; rights to, 31, 33, 51, 54
Land redistribution, 51–53, 57
Landslides, 18
Land tenure, 49–57 passim, 109
Landtman, G., 3
Language, xxi, 28, 240
Leahy, M. J., 240, 258, 261
Lederman, R., 3, 354
Lee, R. B., 120, 373 n. 2
Lipset, D. M., 3
LiPuma, E., 30, 32, 36, 39, 51, 54, 150, 313, 354, 375 n. 2; on Maring social organization, 33–34, 38, 149, 339–340
Local Government Council, 24, 42, 56, 90, 113, 266, 316, 320; and hunting restrictions, 100, 112–114, 115. See also *Kaunsil; Komiti*
Lory, Fairy, 80, 87
Lory, Papuan, 64, 65, 67, 71, 80, 87, 104, 172, 179, 181–182, 292
Lowman, C., 30, 38, 40, 44, 54, 73, 372 n. 14
Lowman-Vayda, C. *See* Lowman, C.
Luluai, 42, 108, 330, 335

McArthur, M., 186
MacIntyre, M., 3
Maclean, N., xvii, 30, 36, 157, 261, 376–377 n. 8, 378 n. 8
Madmen, 42–43
Mae Enga, 37, 132, 133, 145
Magic, 41, 74, 90, 106
Majnep, I. S., 87
Malinowski, B., 3, 5, 353
Mammals, 13, 99, 110, 184; hunting of, 92–93, 98; kinds of, 87, 366. *See also* Marsupials
Manner, H., 22
Markets, 3, 9, 64, 183, 280, 299, 322, 378 n. 2, 380 n. 3
Marks, S. A., 11, 373 n. 2
Marriage, 355, 375 n. 3; with allies, 37–38; within clan cluster, 36; with enemies, 36–37; forms of, 38–40 passim; and land grants, 51–54 passim; patterns of, 36–40, 149, 163–164, 166–169, 237, 332, 357–359; reasons for, 38–39
Marsupials, 87, 120, 183, 376 n. 5; as decorations, 73–74, 366; hunting of, 93, 119. *See also* Skins
Marx, K., 301
Massim, 3
Mauss, M., 6, 129
Meggitt, M. J., 3, 37, 132, 133, 145, 351
Melpa, 151, 240, 274, 352; trade, 176, 187, 193, 195, 299
Mendi, 85
Mianmin, 95
Middlemen in trade, 3. *See also* Traders, act as intermediaries
Mimola beetle, 70, 135, 366
Minerals, 2, 175
Mining, xvii, 334
Missions, 49, 200, 253, 333
Modjeska, C. N., 272, 280
Money, xxii, 131, 133, 237, 245, 268, 274, 278, 283, 284, 290, 296, 333, 377 n. 13; facilitates trade, 132; lost in trade, 266–267, 269; in prestations, 153, 157, 158, 162–163, 200–201, 230, 261, 262, 266, 269, 274, 304, 312; sources of, 262–266 passim; as valuable, 200–201, 268–270, 281
Morren, G. E. B., 95

Narak, 13, 28, 240, 360, 368; decoration styles, 71, 83, 180; pig use, 148, 207; plume use, 67, 83, 131; population, 29; traders, 239
Necklaces: animal-tooth, 2, 132, 184, 190; vegetable-bead, 2, 190
Newton, J., 200, 304
Nihill, M., 200, 201

O'Hanlon, M., 76
Onabasulu, 217–218
Oral traditions, 19, 23, 47–49, 58, 235

Paine, B. G., 43
Parrot, Vulturine, 61, 83, 180–181, 208, 227–228, 247, 260, 283, 291, 292, 293, 297, 302, 308, 325
Pati, 73, 253
Patrol Officer. See *Kiap*
Pearlshells. See Kina
Periphery, highland. See Primary plume suppliers
Persson, J., 378 n. 1
Pharoah, P. O. D., 43
Pigeon, Goura, 180, 237
Pigments, 2, 132, 197–199
Pigs, 2, 3, 13, 106, 131, 133, 175, 183, 184, 187, 200, 207, 245, 276, 278, 290, 296, 299, 301, 307, 310, 312, 375 n. 6; census of herd, 142–143; disposal of, 231–232; effects on environment of, 24, 58; feral, 24, 45, 47, 48, 98, 99, 119, 374 n. 12; herd dynamics, 25, 145–148, 231, 305, 375–376 n. 8, 379 n. 10; housing of, 35; hunting of, 89; ownership of, 143–145; in prestations, 148, 190, 214–215, 231, 267, 305, 327; ratio to people, 145–146; sickness of, 145, 147; size of, 147–148, 190, 280, 292, 320; slaughter of, 145–147, 160, 305, 377 n. 22
Plantations. See Coffee
Plumes, 2, 7, 8, 60–85 passim, 131, 133, 175, 197, 199, 200, 245, 292, 298; acquisition of, 63–65, 125, 134–135, 226–228, 316; age of, 65–68; availability of, 63, 80–85, 175–176, 219, 243, 297; cultural meanings of, 76–80; damage of, 67; as decorations, 61, 64, 175, 297, 309, 312; ownership of, 61, 81, 361–364; in prestations, 7, 67, 131, 169, 226, 243, 258–260, 273, 297, 308, 309; social significance of, 71–80 passim, storage of, 65–68
Poachers, 104, 107

Podolefsky, A., 5, 27
Polanyi, K., 6
Population, 34–36; density, 26–28, 99, 119; distribution, 29; trends, 25, 26
Pork: and prestations, 145, 226, 374–375 n. 13; sale of, 146–147, 263–264, 305. See also Pigs; Prestations
Pospisil, L., 95
Pratt, T. K., 360
Prestations, xiv, 5, 127, 148–169 passim, 235, 266, 304, 307, 314, 350, 354; changing goods in, 133, 153, 236; character of, 128–129, 347, 351; defined, 127–130; flow of valuables in, 149, 163–169 passim, 226–227, 230, 237, 333; fund trade, 226–232 passim; goods used in, 131, 261; ideal of equivalence in, 149–150, 268–269; inflation of, 153, 155, 163, 230, 237, 258–261 passim, 266, 267, 273, 274, 303, 304–306 passim; major, 129, 131, 237, 304, 344; mandatory, 164–168 passim; minor, 63, 129, 163, 222, 226, 272, 276, 330; poor recall of, 149–151, 223, 227, 347, 355. See also Ceremonial exchange; Gifts
Primary plume suppliers, 8, 169, 174, 218, 227, 241, 327
Production, xv, 3, 34, 60, 125, 129, 172, 207; ecology of, 4, 86, 116, 126, 314, 350; for trade, 219–229 passim, 270. See also Hunting
Profit, absence of, 128, 298, 318
Protein. See Diet
Pryor, F. L., 210

Raku (cemeteries and pig-killing groves), 21, 32
Ramu Valley, 13, 119, 195
Rand, A. L., 360
Rappaport, R. A., xiii, xvii, 2, 4, 17, 19, 22, 24, 27, 29, 30, 36, 40, 44, 45, 46, 70, 73, 74, 95, 145, 147, 157, 160, 200, 305, 338, 372 n. 14; analysis of Maring trade, 211–216 passim, 380 n. 2; on dances, 76; on hunting pressure, 110, 122, 374 n. 8; on land grants, 51, 54; on Maring marriage, 37, 38; on utility of salt, 186
Reay, M., 2, 258, 259–260
Reciprocity, 5–6, 128, 130, 163, 214, 272, 327, 341
Refugee payments, 161
Roads, 15, 56, 190, 242, 253, 333
Rofaifo, 96–99 passim

Index

Rubbish-men, 41–42, 251
Ryan, D'A., 29

Sacrifice: and hunting success, 91; and land rights, 52, 55; of pigs, 305, 312
Sahlins, M. D., 120, 127, 271, 272, 298, 315, 327, 330, 341, 347; on exchange and reciprocity, 5–6, 128, 130, 163, 280, 380 n. 10; on exchange rates, 275, 300–303 passim
Salisbury, R. F., 3, 95, 200, 271, 274, 278, 307; on exchange rates, 280, 299, 301
Salt, 2, 132, 183, 186–187, 212–213, 214–215, 261, 292, 293, 301; and cretinism, 43, 376 n. 7
Sansom, B., 311
Schwartz, T., 1, 3, 334
Schwimmer, E., 301, 312
Self-interest, 128, 130, 349
Seligman, C. G., 3
Semi (Kalam initiations), 73, 182, 322, 323, 376 n. 9
Settlement: duration of, 25; history of, 47–49; patterns, 20
Shaman, 40, 45
Sharanahua, 120
Shells, 2, 131, 133, 175, 211, 226, 235, 276, 280, 292, 296, 310; acquisition of, 135–140, 224–225, 274, 316, 379 n. 5; declining supply of, 227, 261, 274, 303–304; disposal of, 140–141, 224–225; ownership of, 135–140; in prestations, 135–141 passim, 223, 228, 258, 260–262, 275, 303–304, 312
Siane, 301
Sickness, 25, 37, 45, 47, 49, 305, 372–373 n. 15
Sillitoe, P., 3, 76, 80, 151, 377 n. 19
Simbai Patrol Post, 17, 142, 264
Simbu: accumulation of plumes in, 85; exchange rates of plumes in, 297–298; pigs in, 207; shells in, 193, 194, 260–261, 274–275; trade with, 174, 176, 242, 273, 281, 299, 327; use of plumes, 7, 235, 258–259, 275, 297, 308, 352
Siskind, J., 120
Skins: acquisition of, 134–135; of marsupials, 2, 60, 131, 133, 175, 293. *See also* Furs
Sociability, in trade, 5, 128, 210, 341–356 passim
Social organization, 28–34, 338–340
Soil, 18; fertility, 22, 23
Songs, 73, 80

Sorcery, 49, 239, 251. *See also* Witches
Spears, 89
Spheres of exchange, 271–272
Spirits, 21, 44–47, 52, 239, 250, 372 n. 14; and fertility, 46; and game, 47, 90–91; and hunting success, 90–91; inhabit forest, 46
Steel tools, 131, 133, 175, 206, 211, 215, 226, 232, 274, 276, 280, 290, 292, 296, 310; acquisition of, 224–225; declining supply of, 274, 303–304; disposal of, 224–225; ownership of, 142; in prestations, 142, 223, 227, 228, 258, 260–261, 303–304, 312. *See also* Axes; Bushknives
Stone axes, 2, 131, 132, 175, 183, 184, 187, 196, 212–213, 215, 232, 245, 280, 290, 292, 293, 296, 308, 377 n. 11
Strathern, A. J., xvii, 2, 3, 7, 41, 73, 76, 78, 85, 151, 212, 269, 271, 274, 278, 299, 351
Strathern, M., 7, 73, 76, 85, 299
Subclans, 30, 33–34
Substance, and kinship, 34, 338–339, 355
Supply and demand, 4, 273, 296, 298, 300–301, 303, 304, 306, 308–309, 310–311, 315

Tabibuga Government Station, 17, 142, 197, 240, 242, 333
Taboos, 252; dietary, 40, 45, 98, 121; and hunting intensity, 110; on interdining, 37, 239, 250
Talk Man. *See* Big-men
Tep yu. See Big-men
Territory, divisions, 47, 49–57 passim, 102. *See also* Land tenure
Theft, 380 n. 8
Thurnwald, R., 128
Tiesler, F., 3
Time, and value, 301–302
Tischner, H., 195
Tobacco, 2, 20
Tolai, 271, 280, 299
Trade, xiv, xv, 1, 60, 63, 272; anomalous patterns explained, 178–179, 181–183, 197, 207–209, 216–218; in axes, 197, 199; in bailer shell, 195; in bushknives, 197, 199; case material, 171–172, 175, 213, 222, 223, 230, 238, 240, 247, 280, 317, 327, 336; in cassowaries, 185, 206, 219–222, 232, 246; in cats, 185; changing patterns of, 170–233 passim, 234–270 passim; in coffee seedlings, 186;

and colonial authority, 170, 234; and construction of kinship, 316, 338, 340–346 passim, 349, 353; in conus shells, 195–196; in cowrie shells, 193, 195, 236, 289, 326; decline of, 237, 268, 317, 319, 348; definition of, 5–7, 127–130, 327–328, 350, 375 n. 2; in dogs, 185, 219–222; in dogwhelk shells, 193, 195, 206, 236, 289; ecology of, 12, 170 ff., 210, 232, 314, 350, 351, 352, 353; and European contact, 186, 193, 197, 206, 232, 234–270 passim, 296; in European goods, 199–200; in exotic vegetables, 186; in forest products, xiv, 8, 122, 169, 224–225, 228, 232, 236, 246, 253, 254–255, 267, 296, 316, 317; in fowls, 185; funds prestations, 222, 226–227, 230, 268, 304, 314, 352, 353; geographic regions, 167, 172–175, 368–370; in greensnail shell, 193, 194–195, 206, 236, 246; in highlands, 2, 216, 315, 354, 380 n. 9; initiative taken in, 209, 241–242, 326–327, 328, 346; intensification of, 123, 237, 247 ff.; in iron, 197; in islands, 3; with kin, 209, 214, 323, 329, 330–334 passim, 336–349 passim; in kina, 191–194, 206, 236; in lowlands, 3; in marsupial furs and skins, 183–184, 206, 219–222, 232, 236, 246; in *mimola* beetles, 184; model of, 7–10, 174, 182, 206, 215, 232, 354, 380 n. 2; in money, 200–203, 204–205, 237, 245, 257, 262, 266, 333; moral pressure in, 212–214, 331; with non-kin, 329, 330–331, 332; occasions for, 242, 332–337 passim; phases of historical development of, 235–237, 352; in pigments, 197–199; in pigs, 146, 148, 184, 187–190, 191, 203, 206, 208, 229, 231, 236–237, 242, 245, 256, 270, 280, 306, 320; in plumes, 9, 63–64, 132, 175–183, 203, 206, 208–209, 211, 212, 219, 227–230, 232, 236–247 passim, 256, 309, 326; and prestations, 130–131, 151, 169, 236–237; in salt, 182, 186–187, 203, 212–215, 236, 326; in shells, 136, 139, 169, 190–196, 203–206, 212, 228–230, 232, 236–237, 245, 256, 267; and social integration, 269, 315, 334, 341, 349; and social relations, 314–356 passim; in steel tools, 169, 197, 198–199, 203, 228–230, 232, 236–237, 245, 256, 267; in stone axes, 176, 196–197, 203, 212–215, 230, 236, 308, 326; with strangers, 299, 317, 330, 334, 341, 348; in tobacco, 186; in tooth necklaces, 184, 206, 236; within Tsuwenkai, 171, 208, 334; in vegetable-beads, 186, 236; with women, 337

Trade expeditions, 242, 299, 322, 323, 325, 330, 348

Trade goods, 2, 130–131, 132, 206, 316, 365–367; changes in, 234–267 passim, 284–289, 296; cultural meanings of, 233, 307, 311–313, 321–322; exchangeability of, 275–278, 279, 306–307; production of, 86 ff., 172. *See also* Production; Valuables

Trade networks, 9, 126, 170 ff., 210 ff., 236–237, 258, 267–268, 309, 352, 354; expansion of, 238–243 passim, 307, 332; information flows in, 298–299

Trade partners, 5, 130, 175, 210, 240, 270, 326–327; formal, 300, 315, 330, 335, 345; friends as, 335–336; hospitality given to, 335, 342, 349; kin as, 303, 321, 336–349 passim; reputations of, 214, 319–320, 326, 343, 345; strangers as, 325–326, 327, 335, 336; trust in, 331, 342, 344–345, 346, 349; variation of exchange rates between 275; and witchcraft fears, 214, 240, 319, 321, 331, 343

Trade rates, 247–257 passim, 273, 296, 306; and age, 247–250, 252; and European contact, 249, 256, 298; of individuals, 247–253 passim; inhibited by war, 249, 252, 253; of objects, 253–257; and status, 251–252; stimulated by ceremonies, 253

Traders, 241; act as intermediaries, 316–321 passim, 329, 377 n. 15; goods sought by, 242; motives of, 129, 170, 209–210, 233, 315, 316–322 passim, 343, 352–353; vigorous, 251, 318, 345. *See also* Trade partners

Trade stores, 264–265, 266

Trade systems, xiv, 3, 4, 10, 210, 211, 232, 353–354

Trade transactions, 209 ff., 245, 342; character of, 128, 299, 307, 323–327 passim, 347–348, 351; cultural meanings of, 233, 342, 352–356 passim; defined, 172; delayed, 209, 303, 319, 326, 328–331, 344, 345; failed, 319–320; immediate, 328, 329, 330, 341; recall of, 150–151, 227

Traps, types of, 90. *See also* Hunting

Tree oil, 2, 217
Trobriand Islands, 5, 129, 272
Tsembaga clan cluster, 17, 38, 122; pig herd, 145; pig-kill by, 160; sorcery sent by, 49; spirits, 44–46 passim; trade, 212, 239; war with, 29, 48
Tueting, L. T., 1, 5, 327
Tultul, 42

Ultimate plume consumers, 234; demand for plumes, 274, 297, 309; location of, 8, 174, 219; supply of trade goods, 10, 227, 283; trade with, 169, 230, 241, 273, 327, 332
Use value, 300, 302, 306–309 passim, 319, 325
Utilitarianism, 5, 11, 233, 315, 352–353
Utility, of objects, 130, 212, 215–216, 300, 311, 315, 319

Valuables, 3, 215; acquisition of, 134–142 passim, 227; census of, 60–61, 133; as decorations, 131, 365–367; defined, 131; hierarchy of, 132, 134, 275–276, 283, 284, 296; ownership of, 133–145; production of, 1, 11, 301–302, 350, 354; storage of, 65–67. *See also* Prestations, goods used in; Trade goods
Value, 133, 194, 215, 271, 276, 283, 295, 311; of pigs, 131; theories of, 300–302
Vayda, A. P., 27, 30, 31, 73, 240
Vegetation, 18–26. *See also* Bush fallow; Forest; Grassland
Vengeance payments, 161–162
Vicedom, G. F., 195
Vitiaz Strait, 3

Wage labor, 266, 333. *See also* Highlands Labour Scheme; Labor migration
Wagner, R., 149, 312
Wahgi Valley: accumulation of plumes in, 85; communications with, 15, 242; exchange rates of plumes in, 297–298, exploits lower Jimi, 348; pigs from, 190, 306; pigs in, 207; shells in, 193, 275, 296; steel axes in, 197, 296; stone axes from, 196, 308; trade with, 83, 174–178 passim, 183, 189, 193, 196, 197, 280, 281, 299, 304, 327; use of plumes in, 7, 180, 259, 297
Wallerstein, E., 174
Warfare, 37, 45, 48, 49, 158, 160, 164, 249, 251; and display, 73
Warriors, 40, 41
Weiner, A. B., 272, 312
Widegren, O., 349
Wigs, 67, 70–71
Witches, 41–44 passim, 107, 162, 240, 250, 321, 344, 373 n. 4
Wola, 151, 377 n. 19
Women, 304, 312, 347, 354–355; and care of pigs, 142–145; and *konj kaiko*, 160; as traders, 3, 171, 337
Wopkaimin, 95–99 passim
Work. *See* Labor
Wright, H., 212
Wurm, S. A., 29

Young, M. W., 3

Zeder, M., 212
Zimmerman, D. A., 360

Designer:	U.C. Press Staff
Compositor:	Prestige Typography
Text:	10/13 Sabon
Display:	Sabon
Printer:	Braun-Brumfield, Inc.
Binder:	Braun-Brumfield, Inc.

LIBRARY OF DAVIDSON COLLEGE

Books on regular loan may be checked out for four weeks. Books must be presented at the Circulation Desk in order to be renewed.

A fine is charged after date due.

Special books are subject to special regulations at the discretion of the library staff.

NOV 1 8 1992 NOV 1 8 1992 FEB 2 4 1993			